DEPENDENCE, DEVELOPMENT, AND STATE REPRESSION

Recent Titles in
Contributions in Political Science

DEPENDENCE, DEVELOPMENT, AND STATE REPRESSION

Edited by GEORGE A. LOPEZ
and MICHAEL STOHL

CONTRIBUTIONS IN POLITICAL SCIENCE,
NUMBER 209

Bernard K. Johnpoll, Series Editor

GREENWOOD PRESS
New York
Westport, Connecticut
London

Library of Congress Cataloging-in-Publication Data

Dependence, development, and state repression / edited by George A.
   Lopez and Michael Stohl.
         p.   cm. — (Contributions in political science, ISSN 0147-1066
   ; no. 209)
     Bibliography: p.
     Includes index.
     ISBN 0-313-25298-X (lib. bdg. : alk. paper)
     1. Economic development. 2. Dependency. 3. Authoritarianism.
   I. Lopez, George A. II. Stohl, Michael, 1947-   . III. Series.
   HD75.D46   1989
   338.9—dc19   87-32258

British Library Cataloguing in Publication Data is available.

Library of Congress Catalog Card Number: 87-32258
ISBN: 0-313-25298-X
ISSN: 0147-1066

First published in 1989

Greenwood Press, Inc.
88 Post Road West, Westport, Connecticut 06881

Printed in the United States of America

The paper used in this book complies with the
Permanent Paper Standard issued by the National
Information Standards Organization (Z39.48-1984).

10 9 8 7 6 5 4 3 2 1

Contents

Figures and Tables

FIGURES

TABLES

Introduction: The Development and Dependence Factors of State Repression

George A. Lopez and Michael Stohl _____

During the past decade the repressive violence of government against its own citizens has been the subject of increased scholarly attention. As a result of this effort, scholars now discriminate conceptually and empirically among types of government violence (of which repression is but one variant) and posit the basic processes by which repressive violence unfolds.[1] Yet little progress in establishing the conditions associated with the onset of (not to mention those that "cause") government repression has been made.[2] This is especially worrisome because of the continued increase in the number of repressive regimes over the past two decades. Among the many critical queries that might be generated in an attempt to explain this phenomenon among Second and Third World states, a particularly pressing one guides this volume: To what extent is government repression a function of the political or economic development situation of that country? The contributors to this volume believe that examining this question may prove fruitful both to students of repression and to students of development processes.

In few other areas of social science has there been such systematic and concentrated debate about the adequacy of conceptualization and theory as in the area of political and economic development studies. Within our own discipline of political science, it is clear that analyses of political development have occupied center stage in the subfield of comparative politics for nearly three decades. As the widely read assessment of James Bill and Robert Hardgrave and the more recent essay by Joel S. Migdal both note, the earliest efforts of comparativists focused on patterns of modernity and of social and political change.[3] These factors were envisioned as critical to the emergence of the modern centralized state, while relatively little regarding the structure of the state itself or the violence of its ruling style came under scrutiny. Thus the earliest theories of political development paid scant attention to government violence in general and none to repressive acts of the state in particular.[4]

Heavily influenced by Samuel P. Huntington, scholars shifted their concerns to examinations of societal institutions that wielded the power and authority to effect the political and economic direction of the state. These analyses ranged from discussions of social mobilization to a focus on problems of political stability. With the investigation of the latter came the theoretical shift to a focus on corporatism and bureaucratic-authoritarian (B-A) modes of government.[5] This conceptualization of political development resulted in a diverse set of studies that varied according to the region under investigation.[6] But as a distinct framework the B-A and corporatist approaches were the first to include government coercive ability and repressive action as a meaningful variable.

With the emergence of a transnational economy and the demise of some of the colonial empires in Africa and Asia, economic development theory burst into prominence as well.[7] In a manner similar to the debates that surrounded political development, economic theorists proffered rather distinct development models. The first, represented by W. W. Rostow's stages-of-growth approach, considered economic improvement in basic factors a linear-oriented phenomenon.[8] The "bias" of the framework was toward steady, cyclical economic development over time. By the late 1960s the pervasiveness of continued underdevelopment and maldevelopment prompted other scholars to develop structural interpretations of internal economic performance. These researchers postulated that the relevant predictor factors of economic development were not indigenous to the state but were present in the external linkages of the nation. The extraction of natural resources by larger states, the prevalence of cash-crop over subsistence economies, and the penetration of the capital market by foreign investors who take advantage of cheap labor all were identified as factors that contributed to continuous cycles of poverty.[9]

As if controversy within each of the fields of politics and economics was not sufficient to occupy the energy of scholars and policymakers, the dual reality of increased poverty and increasing governmental repression challenged both conventional scholarly theory and propriety. It had become apparent that the emergence of economic growth, even when it did occur, could not ensure the development of a democratic way of political life. Further, the existence of participatory and responsive government, in its rare manifestations, did not, in and of itself, predict economic prosperity. The dilemma begged for at least a new political economy of development, if not also a new general theory of comparative and international affairs.

Sections of the bridge across these areas of inquiry were built by a number of international relations scholars, with those interested in theories of political economy most active in exploring the relative contributions of external factors to political and economic development.[10] Influential in this dialogue were "dependency" theorists, who in many ways were direct descendants of the various critics of economic growth theory. Some of the dependency scholars were forging new explanations of conditions of retarded development in Third World states, while others cast their challenge to the fields of comparative and international politics. The latter postulated that the essence of development, the ability of resident elites to make choices regarding the economic and political direction of the society, was delimited by the character of the economic linkages of the developing state to developed nations.[11]

Dependency analysts claimed that though the overt political institutions that sustained colonial and imperial rule had vanished, the stranglehold of the dominant state remained in the form of trade, technology, and capital dependence. At best, a dependent development resulted; at worst, economic prosperity accrued to the advanced country, with chronic maldevelopment and poverty the continued result in the new state.[12] The vicious economic cycle seemed, at times, paralleled only by the vicious actions of economic and political elites against those of their state who protested the decisions taken to cope with this development dilemma.

To some observers such harsh governmental action was an unfortunate, possibly temporary, but still somewhat automatic process in the development cycle of a state in the post-1945 era. In the drive toward modernity, the social mobilization of various groups would produce unprecedented demands on a government with limited capacity to respond effectively. Under such conditions, and until social institutions could arise and government capacity improve to meet such pressures, the theorists stipulated, governing elites would opt for order, lest whatever economic progress had been made would deteriorate in the ensuing political violence and instability.[13]

For others the management of a dependent developing economy created the pressing need for new coalitions of ruling elites who would increasingly resort to harsh treatment of their own citizens in order to sustain momentum on economic policies that were likely to attract dissent. Often this led to the creation of a garrison state in which local elites opted for their own gain in conjunction with external patrons, all at the economic and political expense of the bulk of the citizenry.[14] However, some analysts claimed that no observable association existed between economic dependence and the rise of political repression.[15]

As is the case with other researchers who are interested in these intriguing theoretical questions and who are also moved by the important human issue at hand, we hold our own assessment of the research and queries we have detailed here. We believe that the dependency literature has made significant contributions to understanding the reasons why elites would face dissent to their economic policies. But it has fallen short, except by correlational inference, in establishing why elites elect repression to cope with dissent.[16] We sense that portions of the "missing link" between development choices in dependent economies and the occurrence of repression may lie in the decisional settings faced by decisionmakers and how they perceive their options. We are especially persuaded by discussions of the role of ideological disposition, calculations by decisionmakers of the merit of repression, and the perceived gravity of the perceived challenge to the state leaders of their power.[17]

We are also persuaded that an insufficient amount of case-study material and quantitative analysis exists in which economic and political hypotheses from the development literature are tested with repression considered as a dependent variable. This epistemological concern, as well as our substantive curiosity about the central query posed earlier, prompted us to assemble the research contained in this volume. Each of the contributors examines a theoretically important proposition concerning the links among development, dependence, and state repression. In addition to being diverse in their methodological approach, the chapters represent countries of geographic and ideological diversity in their focus on the central question.

We commence our study with Robert Elias' chapter, which discusses various controversies in the development literature and policy. He then illustrates these in an examination of Central America and analyzes the potential of nongovernmental organizations, in this case Oxfam, for reversing the dependent development and state repressive cycle. In the second chapter, Paul Buchanan provides an exceptionally detailed analysis of the implementation of the Proceso of Argentina under the authoritarian military regime that fell in 1981. His study illustrates the power of microeconomic policy analysis and how, under given policy directions, the potential targets of repression become identified.

The examination of repression in Asian states provided by David Kowalewski in chapter three brings together a number of important aspects of the development-dependence and repression linkage. In testing whether macro or micro dependence linkages are better predictors of repression, Kowalewski focuses on strikes against transnational corporations as the units of analysis. In chapter four, Thomas Callaghy shifts the theoretical emphasis in his analysis of Zaire. Callaghy asserts that central to an understanding of repression in many African states, and in Zaire in particular, is the tradition of internal rivalries amidst a pattern of personalist, strongarm rule.

Whereas the explanation of repression in Africa may seem somewhat idiosyncratic and personalistic, Lester Ruiz indicates that in the case of the Philippines repression may not involve extralegal approaches or low levels of institutional capacity in government. In fact, as he documents in chapter five, the unique aspect of the Marcos regime was the painstaking manner in which political development and the legitimation of martial law intertwined.

In chapter six Adamantia Pollis mixes theory with a historical case study of Turkey. She demonstrates how the economic choices elected by state officials and the subsequent level of economic benefits and political repression within the society are very much a function of the military-security dependence of the state. The seventh chapter of the book examines Poland since the late 1970s. Here Robin Remington discusses how repression can clearly result from economic and political dependence, while also being sustained over time by the political decay of existing institutions and their consequent inability to meet increasing citizen demands.

The final two contributions to the volume provide methodological approaches to the study of repression distinct from those of other chapters in the volume. In chapter eight David Carleton derives alternative explanations of repression from the literature on the new international division of labor and tests them via path analysis. In the final chapter Micheal Schwartz and Harry Targ posit competing models of state violence in agriculturally modernizing nations. Using Central America as a test case, their findings indicate that agricultural change is not a sufficient explanation for increases in repressive violence.

The rich mix of essays in this volume cautions researchers that the context of repression resides very much in the local culture and decisional settings of elites within particular states. It also provides ample evidence of the linkage between repression and those larger economic and political factors that bind states together in international affairs. This combination of findings and insights should stimulate further systematic research in this controversial area.

NOTES

1. See especially Ernest A. Duff and John F. McCamant, *Violence and Repression in Latin America* (New York: Free Press, 1976); M. Hoefnagels, ed., *Repression and Repressive Violence* (Amsterdam: Swets and Zeitlinger, 1977); Michael Stohl and George A. Lopez, eds., *The State as Terrorist: The Dynamics of Governmental Violence and Repression* (Westport, Conn.: Greenwood Press, 1984); and idem, *Government Violence and Repression: An Agenda for Research* (Westport, Conn.: Greenwood Press, 1986).

2. Exceptions to this include George A. Lopez, "National Security Ideology as an Impetus to State Terror," pp. 73-96, and Ted Robert Gurr, "The Political Origins of State Violence and State Terror: A Theoretical Analysis," pp. 45-72, in Stohl and Lopez, *Government Violence and Repression;* and David Pion-Berlin, "Ideas as Predictors: A Comparative Study of Coercion in Peru and Argentina" (Ph.D. diss., University of Denver, 1984).

3. James A. Bill and Robert L. Hardgrave, *Comparative Politics: The Quest for Theory* (Columbus, Ohio: Bell and Howell, 1973), pp. 66-84; Joel S. Migdal, "Studying the Politics of Development and Change: The State of the Art," in Ada W. Finifter, ed., *Political Science: The State of the Discipline* (Washington, D.C.: American Political Science Association, 1983), pp. 309-338.

4. John F. McCamant, "Governance without Blood: Social Science's Antiseptic View of Rule; or, The Neglect of Political Repression," pp. 11-42, in Stohl and Lopez, *The State as Terrorist,* argues that a number of social science theories and models suffer from this nonrecognition of the violence of the state.

5. See Samuel P. Huntington, *Political Order in Changing Societies* (New

Haven: Yale University Press, 1968); Guillermo O'Donnell, *Modernization and Bureaucratic-Authoritarianism* (Berkeley and Los Angeles: University of California Press, 1973); James M. Malloy, ed., *Authoritarianism and Corporatism in Latin America* (Pittsburgh: University of Pittsburgh Press, 1977); and David Collier, ed., *The New Authoritarianism in Latin America* (Princeton: Princeton University Press, 1979).

6. For example, Alfred Stepan, ed., *Authoritarian Brazil: Origins, Policies, and Future* (New Haven: Yale University Press, 1973); Frederick B. Pike and Thomas Stritch, eds., *The New Corporatism: Socio-political Structures in the Iberian World* (Notre Dame, Ind.: University of Notre Dame Press, 1974); and Philippe C. Schmitter and Gerhard Lehmbruch, eds., *Trends toward Corporatist Intermediation* (Beverly Hills: Sage, 1979).

7. The best-known works are probably Charles P. Kindleberger, *Economic Development* (New York: McGraw-Hill, 1965); and Everett Hagen, *The Economics of Development* (Chicago: Irwin, 1968).

8. W. W. Rostow, *The Stages of Economic Growth: A Non-Communist Manifesto* (London: Cambridge University Press, 1960).

9. See Theotonio dos Santos, "The Structure of Dependence," *American Economic Review* 60 (May 1970): 231-236; Paul Baran, *The Political Economy of Growth* (New York: Monthly Review Press, 1958); Immanuel Wallerstein, *The Modern World-System* (New York: Academic Press, 1974); and Samir Amin, *Unequal Development* (New York: Monthly Review Press, 1976).

10. See Teresa Hayter, *Aid as Imperialism* (Baltimore: Penguin Books, 1971); Gabriel Kolko, *The Roots of American Foreign Policy* (Boston: Beacon Press, 1969); and Pierre Uri, *Development without Dependence* (New York: Praeger, 1976), for dependence political economy, and Robert O. Keohane and Joseph S. Nye, *Power and Interdependence* (Boston: Little, Brown, 1977) for interdependence.

11. See especially Ronald H. Chilcote, "Dependency: A Critical Synthesis of the Literature," *Latin American Perspectives* 1, no. 1 (Spring 1974): 4-29; Barbara Stallings, *Economic Dependency in Africa and Latin America* (Beverly Hills: Sage, 1972); Andre Gunder Frank, *Capitalism and Underdevelopment in Latin America* (New York: Monthly Review Press, 1967); and Wallerstein, *The Modern World-System*.

12. Amin, *Unequal Development*.

13. See Huntington, *Political Order In Changing Societies,* for a discussion of this as a "natural" process, and Alexander Dallin and George W. Breslauer, *Political Terror in Communist Systems* (Stanford University Press, 1970) for use of repression consciously in consolidation periods.

14. This is the essential argument of the corporatists and B-A model theorists, especially O'Donnell, *Modernization and Bureaucratic-Authoritarianism*.

15. Edward N. Muller, "Dependent Economic Development, Aid Dependence on the United States, and Democratic Breakdown in the Third World," *International Studies Quarterly* 29 (1985): 445-469.

16. This may best be illustrated by the work of Noam Chomsky and Edward S. Herman, *The Washington Connection and Third World Fascism* (Boston: South End Press, 1979). There are, of course, other critiques of dependence theory; see especially Tony Smith, "The Underdevelopment of Development Literature: The Case of Dependency Theory," *World Politics* 31 (January 1979): 247-288.

17. See Lopez, "National Security Ideology"; Raymond D. Duvall and Michael Stohl, "Governance by Terror," in Michael Stohl, ed., *The Politics of Terrorism,* 2d ed. (New York: Marcel Dekker, 1983), especially pp. 201-212; Gurr, "Political Origins of State Violence and State Terror"; and David Pion-Berlin, "Testing Hypotheses of the National Security Ideology" (forthcoming in *Comparative Political Studies*).

1

Alternative Development in Central America: A Role for Oxfam?

Robert Elias

For over three decades the industrialized nations have emphasized a development model that would reproduce the First World in Asia, Africa, and Latin America. The strategy has remained remarkably consistent: provide remedial aid through governments and private charity from the First to the Third World. We have practiced a kind of "international welfare,"[1] yet we have seen little improvement in economic development. In the last few years this approach has increasingly been challenged in favor of "alternative development": models that would break the paternalistic relationship between the developed and developing worlds.

Besides inappropriate methods of assistance, the developing world must overcome other barriers to development, especially from dependence and repression. Dependence represents both a symptom and a cause of underdevelopment, as poor nations remain unable to break their reliance on their richer neighbors. Repression interferes directly by denying basic human needs and indirectly by imposing political and security constraints on local and national development.

Repression, dependence, and underdevelopment typically coexist. We can expect little success in eliminating one if we ignore the other two. If we try to promote development, for example, but ignore how poor nations may depend structurally on rich nations, or how repression cripples, prevents, or co-opts development projects, we may never break the cycle of failure.

To examine this interrelationship, I consider the sources of repression, dependence, and underdevelopment, especially as they exist in Central America. I assess the needs emerging from repressive, dependent, and underdeveloped societies, and the methods used to address them. I examine why the conventional development model and standard approaches to repression have been so severely criticized and contrast them with "alternative development" models that may better overcome the obstacles to real development.

I examine private voluntary organizations that claim to promote alternative development. I will consider one private voluntary organization in particular, Oxfam America, by reviewing its recent work in three Central American nations: Guatemala, El Salvador, and Nicaragua. This permits an examination of the dynamics of repression, dependence, and underdevelopment and of the impact of Oxfam's alternative development strategies for breaking the cycle of poverty and oppression in the developing world.

DEPENDENCE, DEVELOPMENT, AND CONVENTIONAL AID

Despite decades of work, little Third World progress has been made, particularly outside the socialist world. Underdevelopment persists in continuing illiteracy, poverty, disease, labor and indigenous exploitation, sexual and racial discrimination, homelessness, inequality, passivity, unproductiveness, and insecurity. In particular, we face an increasing crisis of malnutrition and starvation.[2] Dependence feeds on underdevelopment as poor nations and peoples experience an ever-widening gap between themselves and the First World. Like its spiraling debt, the Third World's dependence multiplies steadily. In Central America recent civil wars only intensify the problems.

Some view these conditions as an unfortunate or inevitable reality. We must, proceeds the argument, either keep helping where we can, or forsake some of the destitute to save the vast majority. Yet many others challenge the "business as usual" or "lifeboat ethics" mentality, finding Third World poverty far from inevitable. Critics believe that dependence and underdevelopment arise mainly from political and economic policies that we could reverse.

Aid as Imperialism

Contrary to foreign aid's ostensible benevolence, it appears instead to help maintain dependence and underdevelopment. While the direct intervention relied on now by the USSR and previously emphasized by Western powers has an obvious impact, the Third World may be victimized more by indirect, economic imperialism.[3] Aid promotes primarily the Western development model, foreign objectives, or corporate interests.

The First World takes the Western development model for granted, despite its considerable ill effects. That model favors industrialization, high growth and investment, the free market, and urbanization. Any inequalities in access to productive resources, the model assumes, will be overcome when wealth "trickles down" to the less fortunate. The Third World will develop by adopting the Western model, stimulated by First World aid and investment. Yet in perhaps its purest form the model has completely failed in the "Chicago School" experiment in Pinochet's Chile.[4] Strongly embraced by Central American governments, except in Sandinist Nicaragua, it has produced no noticeable benefits there either.[5] Instead, this school of thought questions the North's benevolence toward the South in the first place.[6]

Foreign aid often supports donor foreign policy goals more than development. Rather than providing genuine assistance and new structures, not merely for survival, but for real independence and development, aid often emphasizes strategic objectives, such as fighting communism, thwarting the USSR and its surrogates, or promoting other national interests abroad.[7] With dependence firmly established, aid has been used to prop pliant allies such as Guatemala or El Salvador, or withheld to destabilize "enemy" nations such as Allende's Chile, Castro's Cuba, and Sandinist Nicaragua.[8] The United States has intervened financially and militarily in Central America repeatedly with little apparent benefit to the region.[9] The existing aid relationship may maintain dependence, which enhances First World control and wealth, especially as the Third World increasingly exports more resources than it receives.[10]

Aid may also help multinational banks and corporations develop new markets, investments, and profits. To receive bilateral aid, developing nations usually must accept heavy corporate involvement in their economies and buy their products or services. They must promote a "favorable business climate" even if it means lowering living standards and exploiting native workers and businesses.[11] Even where the specific financial yield may not be that high, maintaining the capitalist world system may be more important.[12]

Multinational banks share these benefits and those from the debt spiral the developing nations incur through the conventional aid model, providing banks with overwhelming profits, even with defaulted loans.[13] Some apparently benign initiatives for reordering the international economy may also serve to resist challenges to First World multinational dominance. The Trilateral Commission, for example, joins U.S., European, and Japanese financial and government leaders to plan the future world economy, with few concessions to the developing world.[14]

Some believe that international financial organizations can prevent the bilateral perversion of foreign aid. But can the World Bank, the International Monetary Fund, or regional institutions avoid using aid for foreign policy or corporate profits? The evidence indicates otherwise. Heavily dominated by the Western development model and functioning as a support for American, or at least Western, priorities, the World Bank for the most part promotes world capitalism, helping dominant Western nations overcome obstacles to giving aid directly, such as U.S. congressional bans on aid to repressive allies.[15] The IMF often seems most interested in helping banks grant Third World loans, protecting banks against debt crises, and imposing "austerity" programs on Third World defaulters, which may do much more to enhance First World control and profits and impoverish Third World peoples than to promote independence and development.[16]

Aid as Obstacle

Aid may actually be counterproductive to development.[17] First, it may perpetuate harmful assumptions that if we give aid, we have really done our part. It may help us ignore the political and economic sources of poverty, dependence, and underdevelopment, suggesting that we need only make First World peoples and governments more generous. It may mislead us to believe that innovations such as the "green revolution" or the new emphasis on "rural aid" have really occurred or have made a significant difference.[18] In Central America the Kissinger Commission report, while paying lip service to "historic" conditions, nevertheless promised us only more of the same old "solutions." These included a replay of failed Alliance for Progress programs, bolstered by a new dose of military support.[19]

Second, we often wrongly assume that aid reaches its intended target. Instead, most aid goes to administrative expenses, to the less needy, to those who use it to build fortunes or to tighten their grip on political and economic power. As in Central America, aid not closely monitored may preserve in power precisely those interests who care the least about national development.[20] Aid may be used to maintain public control or for counter-insurgency against interests who are promoting their schemes for the nation's genuine development.[21]

Third, aid may maintain relationships that perpetuate dependence, draining more resources than it produces. It may undermine local economies, as when unnecessary food aid to Guatemala after the 1976 earthquake undercut its local producers, resulting in disincentives and economic failure.[22] It may also perpetuate paternalism or cultural imperialism in the process, promoting a sense of inferiority and passivity.[23]

Aid and Repression

When imposed by either First or Third World governments and by other institutions, dependence and underdevelopment may be viewed, by defini-tion, as forms of repression. Here the repression violates basic economic rights and human needs. More overt political repression will only intensify the problem, impeding efforts for fundamental change.

Such political repression often aims to maintain the existing political inequities that cause economic inequality and deprivation. It opposes, often violently, those who challenge existing political and economic relations. These repressive governments usually view development work as subversive since at least implicitly it challenges the status quo.[24] In many nations repression will only intensify underdevelopment, producing increasing casualties, draining valuable resources from social services for military pur-poses, and disrupting, if not destroying, infrastructure for future develop-ment. Even when relatively inactive in civil wars or repression, military gov-ernments impose crippling costs on national development.[25]

Yet repression rarely springs solely from any single underdeveloped nation. While national characteristics, such as its military's historic role, might influence the precise circumstances, most repression comes from the developed world, despite its human rights rhetoric and legislation. It comes indirectly by generating the conditions conducive to repression, and directly by aiding repression through bilateral and multilateral policy.

A number of analysts have demonstrated that the United States, for example, exports repression extensively to its Third World allies, including military and police training, arms and hardware, and torture devices and techniques.[26] Arms transfers rarely satisfy legitimate Third World defense needs, but rather go mostly to counterinsurgency, repression, and police control.[27] We might even "aid" a nation by helping its military stage a coup, as in Guatemala in 1954 or Chile in 1973.[28] When we consider the "aid" we give to developing nations, we must remember the amount given directly for military or security purposes, not to mention the "economic" aid diverted to similar ends.[29] Evidence indicates that when legislation would appear to halt direct military aid, a substantial amount arrives at the nation under question through biased State Department reports on human rights "progress," loopholes allowing emergency aid (despite the repression), or aid channeled through intermediate nations (such as Brazil and Israel), international financial institutions (such as the World Bank), or U.S. multinational banks and corporations.[30]

Altogether, we might well view foreign aid, and North-South relations generally, as actually "underdeveloping" the Third World, not developing it.[31] In response, some have proposed alternatives to "development as usual."

ALTERNATIVE DEVELOPMENT

The need for development and independence grows steadily, not only as the Third World continues losing ground to the First World, but also as we increasingly recognize the relationship between development, human rights, and peace.[32] Yet existing structures and relationships and conventional aid policies seem unable to provide any effective relief; indeed, they may make things worse. We might be tempted to oppose foreign aid altogether until it can be used productively. Yet a middle course between conventional aid and no aid may also exist.

"Alternative development," originating largely from nongovernmental or private voluntary organizations, has even influenced mainstream aid institutions. While it may not yet have noticeably altered conventional aid policies,[33] it does provide a formidable counterstrategy for granting aid.

Authentic Development

Pursuing alternative development paths requires new objectives, not merely new strategies. Many reject conventional aid not merely as failed process, but because it seeks unacceptable ends: largely alien and counter-productive Western development objectives, from which we can expect only partial human development at best. Instead, we might well pursue "authentic" development, characterized by different values, objectives, and strategies.[34] Authentic development recognizes the interrelationship between personal and social development, or among individual, local, national, and international development. It emphasizes local self-reliance, popular empowerment and consciousness, and just work policies. It considers the relationship between development, peace, and justice and recognizes, for example, that development often depends much less on aid and much more on freedom and tranquility.[35]

Authentic development cannot occur without fundamental social change, both locally and internationally: change not likely from existing structures and institutions, no matter how well reformed. It treats development not merely as a technical or productive problem, but rather as a political, economic, and structural problem. It goes to the root causes of dependence and underdevelopment, confronting them at their source, or at least side-stepping conventional "solutions."

Self-Reliance

Alternative development devises concrete actions to help remove under-developed peoples from their cycles of dependence.[36] It relies on decentral-ized, self-sufficient, grass roots, bottom-up planning and organization,[37] using local skills and resources.[38] It promotes diverse, nonelitist, non-bureaucratic decision making and leadership. It stresses mass-based, participatory development and local control.[39] Self-reliance provides not merely an objective but a process of individual and community develop-ment.[40] It promotes political power and mobilization, and joint action, not accommodation or stagnation.[41] While "volunteerism" and "self-help" can often become a new way of "blaming victims" for not solving their own problems, self-reliance instead recognizes the broader political and economic failures that really underlie dependence and underdevelopment and offers practical countermeasures.[42]

Self-reliance, as embodied in Tanzania's Arusha Declaration or in the UN's Cocoyoc Declaration,[43] promotes local independence from outside forces, avoiding "welfare" development.[44] It emphasizes production for local use and consumption, not for export. It encourages diverse production and self-sufficiency in basic needs to avoid being held hostage to First World consumer preferences or corporate profits.[45] It has local people, not outside donors, judging their own needs, allowing them to develop the most appropriate projects. It promotes cooperative self-management, collective projects, and participatory evaluations.[46] It counters the Western, urban-industrial model with agrarian, steady-state economics and appropriate technology for even, equitable, and ecologically balanced development.[47] It deemphasizes urban development in favor of rural development based on genuine land reform.[48] It helps build natural, "horizontal" communities designed to withstand outside dominance and reliance.[49]

Alternative development strategists differ about whether to accept conventional aid. Some advocate a complete "dissociation" from external aid.[50] "Development without aid" emphasizes alternative institutions outside the conventional world economy and North-South relations.[51] Yet this may take self-reliance too far. Others favor a mid-range strategy stressing self-sufficiency where possible, but welcoming "appropriate" assistance. This requires aid that avoids supporting repressive governments and corporate dominance, that balances resources between the North and South (such as by cancelling Third World debts), and that allows indigenous peoples to shape their own development.[52]

Conscientization

Although spontaneous, indigenous organizing has increasingly characterized various depressed regions, few in the Third World have probably embraced alternative development consciously. Will people develop a consciousness for development alternatives as they begin to organize and govern themselves, or must their consciousness be "raised" beforehand?

Alternative development relies on people sensing their own capabilities and power and translating them into grass roots organizations for social change. Much of this occurs on its own; the rest may be stimulated by outsiders. Yet even culturally sensitive First World development workers, opposed to "top-down" aid and committed to popular self-reliance, usually do not influence directly from the "bottom up." Instead, they contribute "sideways-in" by helping communities better understand their role in North-South relations, by coaxing them toward self-controlled alternatives, and by materially aiding them on their own projects.[53]

Successful projects may have much more to do with personal development and awareness than with materially productive outcomes.[54] Alternative development involves a "revolution of being"[55] that helps people think differently about themselves. Living by "being," which measures humans by their contributions, relationships, and individual development, can help people avoid living by "having," which measures them only by their status, consumption, or acquisitions.[56] Whether it entails getting the poor to stop blaming themselves for their poverty, getting men to realize how they oppress women, or getting women and Indians to overcome their fears and realize their power and dignity, alternative development requires an altered consciousness.[57]

In some respects underdevelopment may be a state of mind as much as anything else. If we were honest in the First World, we might admit that as people who have been basically unwilling to share our surpluses with the poor or to alter structures that produce poverty, however indirectly, we may be the most "underdeveloped" people of all.[58] As for the poor, emerging from dependence and underdevelopment certainly requires material change, but self-awakening to their own capabilities and role in the world system might contribute even more.[59] Passivity and hopelessness, while perhaps natural reactions to repression and deprivation, only intensify the crisis.[60] Fragmentation and individualism will perpetually frustrate a collective response. The choice requires neither isolated individualism nor faceless collectivism, but rather actions that allow maximum individual development through collective strategies. Changing people's view about their relationship to their community and its potential for power and fulfillment underlie all strategies for alternative development.[61]

Thus the experience of development may be what Paulo Freire has called "conscientization," or the process of developing personal confidence and power by clarifying one's role and situation and by contemplating self-directed alternatives to the status quo.[62] This awareness might come spontaneously, or by organizing one's community, or from external development workers, or from indigenous institutions. In Latin America, in particular, we cannot underestimate the important contributions to alternative development and human rights made by "liberation theology." In this doctrine for the poor existed the seeds for building the development-oriented (both individually and commercially) Christian-based communities promoted by segments of the Catholic and other churches.[63] Whether religious or secular, alternative development helps change Third World consciousness, allowing it to contemplate and later to create a different future.

World Policy

Finally, alternative development fundamentally reassesses international policies. While much can be accomplished locally in the Third World, significantly alleviating dependence and underdevelopment requires restructured world policies.

In part, changing global structures requires considerable self-reliance and conscientization in the First World, not merely in the Third World. Changing lifestyles, personal awareness, and local practices in the North will help break the cycle of poverty in the South.[64] Recognizing the extensive poverty and its causes, which also exist in the First World, helps us to design strategies to alleviate poverty throughout the world. Admitting that First World policies perpetuate dependence and underdevelopment may help create a much more constructive relationship, perhaps a genuine New International Economic Order, rather than a restructured international welfare system.[65]

A world policy transformation requires a new sensitivity to how militarism and repression impede development.[66] It would preserve cultural diversity[67] and enhance transnational relations, while eroding destructive national structures and competitions. It would begin globalizing production to meet fundamental needs before satisfying consumption or luxury needs. It would help create ties of international solidarity between groups and peoples around the world for common objectives. It would share and distribute wealth and especially prevent a further drain of income and resources from the poor. It would develop real transition paths toward a just world, not merely idealize universal social and individual development.[68]

PROMOTING ALTERNATIVE DEVELOPMENT

Sensing the limitations, if not the failure, of conventional assistance, governmental aid agencies have worked increasingly with nongovernmental organizations to help better distribute assistance and have ostensibly reoriented their work toward rural development. Working with nongovernmental organizations does bring aid much closer to an alternative development model.[69] Why do these private voluntary organizations appear preferable, and can one expect these organizations to make any real difference in foreign aid?

Private Voluntary Organizations

American private philanthropy abroad dates well back into the last century and thus far surpasses, at least in longevity, official aid, which only began in earnest in the 1950s. The private voluntary organizations (PVOs) dispensing unofficial aid have much experience and a method that may contribute significantly to their success.[70]

Varieties

To understand their role, we must first recognize their significant differences in type, method, purpose, and ideology. They include foundations, corporations, churches, and independent nongovernmental organizations. Some are highly bureaucratic, resembling government agencies, while others, much more streamlined, minimize administrative cost. Some work directly in devising, implementing, and evaluating development projects, while others merely identify good candidates to assist. Some give relief exclusively; others treat the symptoms of underdevelopment; and some promote participatory development and social change. Some emphasize technical approaches, while others stress personal empowerment. PVOs vary from being subservient to their nations' aid programs and foreign policy interests to being partners, reformers, rebels, or even subversives.[71]

As such, some relate closely with their national governments (possibly using their funding) or recipient governments, while others specifically reject such ties. Still others interact selectively with governments.[72] They work with international governmental agencies (such as UNICEF, FAO, or WHO) or with indigenous groups.[73] Finally, PVOs differ considerably in how much they deviate from conventional aid policies to embrace alternative development strategies.

Disadvantages

PVO work provides various advantages and disadvantages that we should evaluate, not from the conventional aid perspective, but rather by their effect on alternative development. By that measure, PVOs have many disadvantages in practice; mostly, they do not provide as significant an alternative as some development strategists would seek.

Several PVO evaluations conclude that while they might potentially provide more effective aid, they often fall short for the same reasons that limit conventional governmental aid. PVOs often act paternalistically toward recipients, even when they believe that they have overcome the "mission" mentality of previous eras.[74] Moreover, their analysis of the source of Third World problems does not differ significantly from standard First World conceptions. PVOs routinely describe underdevelopment or poverty as being "out there," stemming from personal drawbacks or from social and national forces portrayed as quite separate form First World actions and policies. They portray the rich as blameworthy not for having caused underdevelopment, but for having given insufficiently to redress it. Wasteful First World lifestyles get treated more as the unfortunate effects of progress than as sources of underdevelopment elsewhere.[75]

PVO critics often come from opposing perspectives. Some believe that their work could be done much better by large governmental donors, that governmental aid does not necessarily fail, that donors must work with recipient governments, and that local organizations may not channel aid as effectively.[76] In the other direction, some argue that PVOs have not fulfilled their potential as effective alternatives to conventional aid. Replicating many characteristics of government aid, PVOs may perpetuate an "alms race" that produces much more material or psychological gain to donors than to recipients.[77] In addition, PVOs have been criticized for scarce resources, for poor management, and for failure to coordinate their work with governments or other PVOs.

More fundamentally, PVOs seem unable to directly combat the structures producing underdevelopment. They can rarely get to the poverty's roots, sometimes because they fail to recognize them, but often because their meager resources and power prevent them from doing so. Lobbying against the economic imperialism of their home state will cost most PVOs their tax-exempt status and thus close them as aid agencies. PVOs must constantly balance their values against those of their funding sources. PVOs might be wasting their time and assistance giving aid to repressive regimes, which may routinely undermine their work. Even worse, by funding indigenous organizations considered subversive by their governments, PVO aid might make local leaders targets of repression. Finally, private aid might provide just the bare assistance a repressive regime needs to remain in power; the aid may be counterproductive to creating a better development atmosphere.

Advantages

Despite these misgivings, some PVOs still contribute significantly to alternative development. A few PVOs take steps to specifically avoid their disadvantages. They also offer advantages that may, in many cases, give some substance to the quest for alternative development.[78]

PVOs generally seem more effective than governments in delivering aid quickly, cheaply, and nonbureaucratically to more people who need it the most. They can and will promote small projects that government aid programs usually exclude. They can avoid working directly with repressive or corrupt recipient governments and can perhaps help counter that repression. They need not promote their nation's foreign policy, especially when it is counterproductive to authentic development. They can work in underdeveloped nations where their government withholds aid and may, as in the case of Nicaragua, work directly with cooperative, nonrepressive governments that their home nations, like the United States, either shun or directly oppose.[79]

Aside from their direct project work, progressive PVOs can help promote the self-reliance, conscientization, and just world policies integral to alternative development. They promote development education in both the First and Third Worlds, emphasizing the value of and also the obstacles to authentic development. Within the limits of their tax-exempt status, they lobby for more enlightened First World and international policy. Even when their specific projects achieve less than dramatic tangible results, they often provide a powerful groundwork for broader movement and models for new community initiatives.[80] While their successes in repressive societies might seem to support brutal governments over the short term, the process and consciousness of alternative development serve far more to challenge, even subvert, those forces over the long term.

Officially, even the most active and progressive PVOs remain politically neutral for tax purposes, for fundraising, and for access to recipient nations. Not specifically taking sides creates many frustrations, since it often directly contradicts their values and even the alternative development they claim to promote. On the other hand, not officially taking sides overtly need not be entirely neutral, especially with development work that at least implicitly challenges the status quo. If successful, alternative development counters not merely dependence and underdevelopment, but the repressive and inequitable structures that produce them. It will rarely choose directly between competing sides, such as granting medical assistance to only one side in civil war; yet the kind of projects it requires does make some choices automatically. Its aid will never go to governments using assistance as counterinsurgency or imposing development without local control. Political choices, almost by definition, occur implicitly every time a project is chosen. And if alternative development succeeds, it may be revolutionary. Even so, when real national revolutions do occur, more than one progressive but officially neutral PVO has been asked where it was in those pre-revolutionary days when it was most needed.[81]

While many, perhaps most, PVOs deserve criticism for so closely replicating official aid policies, several stand apart, maintaining their values despite the obstacles. PVOs such as the American Friends Service Committee, the Unitarian Universalists Service Committee, the Economic Development Bureau, the World Neighbors, and the Mennonite Central Committee have remained true to their broader visions of social change, not merely to remedial aid and comfort. Examining one other PVO, Oxfam, will help us evaluate how well the few progressive PVOs have met the ideal of alternative development.

Oxfam

Oxfam, or Oxford Famine Relief, began in 1942 by aiding war refugees in southern Europe. It now includes offices in Belgium, Mexico, the United States (America), and two in Canada. While they have many common characteristics, here we will emphasize Oxfam America, which began in 1970. Oxfam America works either alone or with its sister offices in Asia, Africa, and Latin America. Although it accepts no governmental aid, it has an annual budget of over $5.5 million, only 6 percent of which goes to administration. Its financial independence has given it some considerable political independence as well, allowing it to evaluate and critique American foreign policy, particularly in regard to its effect on Oxfam's own projects.

Much administrative work is devoted to evaluating, and especially to selecting, appropriate projects. Oxfam administers no projects on its own. Instead, it identifies and funds indigenous projects that meet Oxfam's project criteria, sometimes discussing project ideas with Third World organizers beforehand. Oxfam stresses food self-sufficiency, living standards, social change, and rural, women's, and indigenous groups.[82] Although Oxfam cannot guarantee its objectives, it tries to promote "aid that works." According to Oxfam criteria, aid works if it improves the lives of the poorest, encourages community life, empowers individuals and groups, promotes self-reliance, multiplies into new projects, works efficiently and manageably at the local level, and develops real partnerships among local groups.[83] Besides satisfying particular food crises, Oxfam provides a laboratory for self-development; it believes its best investment is in people. Shunning a role merely limited to providing relief or to placing "band-aids" on the symptoms of underdevelopment, Oxfam mostly strives for popular empowerment, the foundation of alternative development.[84]

Does Oxfam achieve these goals? While it might be hard-pressed to show, as one of its reports claims, that it contributes "to significant change in structures,"[85] nevertheless it can probably claim some notable effectiveness. It can often ensure that the aid it sends reaches the intended recipients by the criteria it uses to select groups and projects in the first place. Its own project officers or other monitors frequently visit projects to evaluate their progress, often jointly with project holders. Occasionally, "impact audits" evaluate conditions in even greater detail.[86]

As the following Oxfam projects in El Salvador and Guatemala indicate, it faces many obstacles to effective development work, imposed not merely by inadequate resources and counterproductive international and national structures, but by government repression. This contrasts dramatically with Oxfam projects in Nicaragua, where, despite similar barriers, the government has substituted substantive policies to promote popular development without similar repression.

OXFAM IN GUATEMALA AND EL SALVADOR

Background

El Salvador and Guatemala share many conditions of repression, dependence, and underdevelopment. While El Salvador's civil war has received far more attention, similar circumstances have existed in Guatemala, especially prior to 1986. In both cases the wars mostly pit military governments against civilian populations loosely organized by opposition forces. Independent human rights organizations have characterized both nations as gross violators, engaging in massive killings, torture, disappearances, and detentions, not to mention deprivations of basic human needs. So-called democratization through elections (as with Duarte in El Salvador) or reforms (as with Mejia's overthrow of Rios Montt in Guatemala) produced few changes.[87] In Guatemala, for example, the military government committed at least 112 massacres in the first five years of the 1980s, and in El Salvador over 40,000 people have been killed by the military and death squads during the same time frame. Villages have been destroyed, millions have been displaced through "scorched-earth" policies, and most nongovernmental organizations suffer harassment, murders, or other repression. In Guatemala leafletting is punishable by automatic execution.[88]

Likewise, both nations suffer from considerable dependence and underdevelopment, including extensive poverty, malnutrition, sickness, illiteracy, and exploitation. Wealth is highly concentrated, with little "trickling down" to most people. With 2 percent owning half the land in El Salvador and 3 percent owning three-quarters in Guatemala, no real agrarian reform has occurred. Both nations have agrarian economies, highly oriented toward exports, with little industrial development. With foreign business dominance and external debts, both nations routinely lose income, wealth, and resources annually, in a trend that makes them progressively more dependent and underdeveloped.[89]

Little aid reaches most people in each nation, going instead to the military and the rich. Development aid might be better understood as reinforcing underdevelopment and repression, since it more often promotes "counterinsurgency" or "rural pacification" than anything else. In Guatemala the military government's "beans and bullets" program extorts civilian support, military service, and "ideological reversion" under threat of repression or starvation. Driven from their land, work, food, and crafts, thousands must labor as near slaves for the government's food-for-work program in order to survive. Over 1.2 million Guatemalan refugees (and 800,000 from El Salvador) search for new homes. Indians must flee government raids and massacres in their villages. Thousands have fled to cities, causing overcrowding and leaving destroyed or unworked farms behind.[90]

El Salvador and Guatemala show in classic form the interrelationship of repression, dependence, and underdevelopment, and how outside aid may not merely fail to help, but make conditions worse. Under these circumstances, PVOs such as Oxfam have promoted an alternative approach.

Oxfam Projects

Except for one project, Oxfam provides no direct development support for El Salvador and Guatemala. The civil wars and the governments' repression of independent community work force Oxfam to operate through intermediaries in Mexico and Costa Rica and with an American intermediary, the Program for Emergency Assistance, Cooperation, and Education (PEACE). The repression can be so severe as to affect the project, as in 1982 when Oxfam ceased its El Salvador projects for one year because its intermediary could not operate nor could any effective substitute be found.

Guatemala

Oxfam supports projects here primarily through two intermediary organizations: the Office of Solidarity Services (OSS) and the Emergency Organization of Laborers and Peasants (IOCE). In turn, they support several groups, mostly working within Guatemalan networks before international funding agencies, to consult in planning, organizing, implementing, and evaluating relief efforts and project proposals and to coordinate humanitarian aid programs.

The OSS was created in 1981 by 40 church, Indian, peasant, labor, cooperative, and development groups to provide emergency assistance to

Guatemalan refugees. It sponsors and coordinates several groups. The Committee for Justice and Peace (CJP) was created in 1978 to defend human rights through public demonstrations. Christian based, it promotes liberation theology, international relief and development aid, and grass roots organizing. It serves families in several Guatemalan regions with humanitarian assistance, including food, clothing, transportation, medicine, and tools.

The Emergency Relief Committee (EMR) was created in 1981 from work dating back to the 1976 earthquake. Its committees, mostly indigenous, work democratically and cooperatively on projects for emergency food, health care, housing, food production, community organizing and mobilization, security, and international representation. The Peasant Projects Committee (PPC) was formed in the central highlands and emerged in 1982 with public denunciations of massacres and refugee conditions. Comprised mainly of Indian peasants, it works closely with the National Center of Laborers (CNT) to promote communal projects, including programs for handicraft cooperatives and tortilla factories. The Emergency Action Plan (PACE) organizes action committees and coordinates the refugee work of several other groups, helping with shelter and resettlement.[91]

The Christian Grassroots Committee (CGC), which operates primarily in Quiche and the western highlands, began in 1980 as an organization of Christian grass roots communities, some of which have had to work underground or in exile. Tapping into community development work done sporadically over the past 30 years, CGC promotes development, education, leadership training, and health care. Mobile teams of CGC workers provide emergency humanitarian aid as well.

The Coordinator for Assistance to the Guatemalan Refugees (CARG) was formed in 1982 by the Mexican Catholic church and other religious groups to aid Guatemalan refugees. Comprised of regional committees organized by the refugees themselves, CARG provides basic necessities, such as food, medicine, clothing, housing, and work, for refugees who have fled to Mexico. It also provides training for self-sufficiency and security.

The Rural Cooperative Association (RCA), also formed in 1982, consists entirely of highland Indians and peasants and unites them with poor Latino farm workers. Responding to the government's "rural pacification" program, RCA has organized for better pay and working conditions, land tenure, self-sufficiency, food distribution, cultural survival, and self-defense, and against repression, displacement, and forced military service. It has provided emergency assistance, cottage industries, model agricultural plots, and literacy and training programs. It has organized refugee populations in the northwest around food production projects. It has developed an alternative development model based on leasing small family-sized farms, which are run collectively for subsistence and surplus production. It also promotes ecological balance between highland and lowland communities.

The RCA has been persistently impeded by adverse government actions. Security risks have forced it to remain very loosely organized, which hampers its effectiveness and communications.

The other major coordinating group, the IOCE, also runs its own programs. Begun in 1982 by labor, student, peasant, and church groups, it assists Guatemalan refugees in both Guatemala and Mexico. Often working covertly to avoid government repression, it promotes grass roots community activities, purposely decentralized and dispersed to help withstand military disruptions. It promotes development and training in agricultural production and a series of marketing, consumer, and farming cooperatives. It develops cooperatives, providing technical training and agricultural organization, and it promotes higher production yields, courses, tools and land development, experimentation, and distribution.

The Food Production and Emergency Assistance Program, run jointly by OSS and IOCE, stresses Guatemala's northern and central highlands. It provides food, handicraft, and emergency assistance to Guatemalans displaced by the civil war, responding particularly to malnutrition and unemployment crises. It maintains or rebuilds food production infrastructures, restoring rural community self-sufficiency and services. Rural defense programs include evacuation plans, dispersed fields, outdoor schools, mobile clinics, and communal work coordination.

The Christian Committee for Health (CCH) began in 1980 to provide training, health promoters, primary health care, regional health centers, medicines, emergency medical equipment, first-aid kits, and village health workers. Through its Emergency Medical Aid Program it has established 36 regional centers for emergency health care. It has been preoccupied increasingly with maladies (such as polio, malaria, nutritional deficiencies, and infant mortality) that have been newly reintroduced by civil war conditions. Responding to severe government health care cuts (in favor of military spending), CCH provides local, more efficient substitutes, organized to overcome public fears and withstand government repression.

Finally, Oxfam supports the IXQIUC Weaving Cooperative directly in Guatemala. It promotes self-reliance among indigenous women victimized by the civil war, offering them alternatives to fleeing the country.[92] Comprised of 30 women so far, it provides looms, training, food supplies, and marketing assistance for promoting weaving cooperatives as economically self-sufficient cottage industries. Reaching people generally ignored by government assistance, it also promotes community subsistence projects for various handicrafts and artisanry.

El Salvador

Oxfam supports projects in El Salvador primarily through the Mexican offices of the Coordinator of Churches and Christian Based Institutions United for Humanitarian Service (DIACONIA), the Salvadoran Health

Professionals Committee (COPROSAL), and CARITAS. DIACONIA, comprised of organizations sponsored by 37 Salvadoran churches, provides short-term and medium-term aid to Salvadoran civilians displaced, both internally and externally, by the civil war, including emergency aid, small community income-generating projects, health clinics, and agricultural production.

DIACONIA's Global Emergency Committee, for example, has provided five new clinics, several communal first-aid stations, and courses for health care providers. Its Production for Local Consumption Program promotes self-sufficiency, copes with problems of crime and war, helps construct living quarters, sponsors a sewing workshop, small-scale candy production, and orphan centers, promotes cooperatives, resettles refugees, and distributes small emergency grants for sudden crises. Impeded by the government, but supported by the opposition forces, DIACONIA also promotes experimental relocation communities, providing aid particularly in areas not held by the military. Its decentralized, grass roots organization helps protect its projects from government intimidation and helps them succeed as well.

COPROSAL responds to El Salvador's health care crisis. Since the country suffers from an increase in serious and contagious diseases, contaminated water, declining health resources, increasing malnutrition, insufficient health training, declining medical personnel, and dramatic increases in violence and repression, health needs have never been greater.[93] Through the Salvadoran Institute for Health Promotion, COPROSAL promotes decentralized regional health teams for direct primary health care services, including clinic rehabilitation, emergency handicapped care, preventive education and treatment, technical training, "barefoot doctors," and physical and mental health teams (for research, referrals, and child stimulation centers). COPROSAL provides an organic health care system linked to broader civilian political movements for health, education, economic development, and food production. It promotes mostly rural, nondiscriminatory health care in conjunction with labor unions and humanitarian organizations.

Beyond organization, COPROSAL also provides money for personnel, equipment, materials and supplies transportation, and sophisticated first-aid kits. Although it treats military personnel as well as civilians, COPROSAL also documents the military's harassment, repression, and murder of medical and health workers, which directly violate their neutrality under Geneva conventions. To help avoid government opposition, it coordinates some of its activities (such as its research)[94] externally, usually in its Costa Rican office. COPROSAL works mostly in rural areas outside government control, often replacing military health care programs lost when opposition forces gain new ground. The projects involve local populations extensively in running and designing appropriate programs.

CARITAS was supported by the government in the early 1980s but now receives UN High Commission on Refugees funding. It helps Salvadoran refugees in Honduras, providing educational programs for developing skills, literacy, community organizing, hygiene, and self-sufficiency. Now operating in at least 14 camps, mostly in southern Honduras, CARITAS also promotes food, nutrition, health care, and social work services. Since Salvadorans cannot use Honduran lands for cultivation, CARITAS has helped refugees develop various self-sufficient cottage industries, producing utensils, pottery, tinware, ovens, latrines, furniture, and shoes and other clothing.

OXFAM IN NICARAGUA

Background

Prior to the 1979 Sandinist revolution, Nicaragua shared with El Salvador and Guatemala similar conditions of repression, dependence, and underdevelopment. Since then some dramatic differences have emerged. In contrast to Nicaragua under Somoza, which was characterized by massive repression and deprivation, the nation's postrevolutionary human rights record has improved significantly.[95] Although critics cite violations of the press, the church, and the Miskito Indians, independent human rights evaluations from 1979 to 1985 (by groups such as Americas Watch and Amnesty International) characterize the violations as minor.[96] Haunted by U.S.-supported contras, by American economic strangulation (now a formal embargo),[97] and by an enormous debt inherited from Somoza, the government nevertheless seems willing to protect most rights and to provide real development for its people.[98] Ironically, the United States has reacted to Nicaragua's concern for genuine development not with assistance, but with extensive opposition. Unable to manipulate local Nicaraguan elites, the United States has imposed repression more directly. Nicaragua appears to be no exception in this respect; alternative development tried almost everywhere before has elicited strong intervention or repression.

Nicaragua faces a resource problem very similar to that of El Salvador and Guatemala. Significant wealth goes to military spending, making it difficult to satisfy basic needs, much less development. Here the similarity ends, however. While El Salvador and Guatemala divert their resources to repress and deprive their populations, often targeting groups seeking genuine national development, Nicaragua diverts its resources to protect not merely the government, but its people and their progressive organizations. Nevertheless, the resource drain persists, making even more difficult any serious headway against dependence and underdevelopment.[99]

Nicaragua has adopted structural changes that could dramatically enhance its people's development, especially if international and internal threats were ended. It already provides an exceptional model for testing the value of "alternative development."[100] The government has avoided diverting foreign aid away from intended recipients or using it for counter-insurgency and has also supported and helped create the decentralized, mass-based, self-sufficient organizations that "alternative development" calls for.[101] Given this atmosphere, Oxfam supports many Nicaraguan projects and, unlike in El Salvador and Guatemala, can directly visit them and count on the government's full cooperation, if not direct financial assistance.[102]

Oxfam Projects

Since the 1979 revolution Oxfam has supported numerous Nicaraguan projects, mostly to develop food security and primarily through three national, nongovernmental organizations. The National Union of Small Farmers (UNAG) represents most small and medium farmers who work their own land, either individually or cooperatively. Designed to increase farm production and raise living standards for peasants and their families, it promotes extensive farmer participation in storing, transporting, distributing, and pricing their produce. Peasants are organized by zones, with each area having its own group and leadership. UNAG-trained "promoters" work full-time serving local cooperatives and farmers' associations.[103] It also trains farm association leaders in technical and organizational skills. Through the associations, farmers share information and skills and plan Nicaragua's overall agricultural development.[104]

The Association of Rural Workers (ATC) represents over 120,000 rural and landless workers. It organizes unions on state and private farms, and production and service cooperatives. It negotiates wage increases and improved living and working conditions and health care, and monitors state policy for rural interests. ATC also runs agricultural and extension courses. Its adult education program has trained 15,000 workers, and its leadership training program prepares members to help manage farms and to influence public policy.

The Association of Nicaraguan Women (AMNLAE) is a broad-based, democratic national organization that integrates women into the nation's economic, social, and political life. Now numbering 50,000 members, AMNLAE promotes mother-child health programs to reduce infant mortality, vegetable production for nutrition, technical training workshops for family and collective gardens, and the national literacy campaign. AMNLAE works to influence public policy, producing laws against sex discrimination, female exploitation in advertising, and bias against widows and pregnant women.[105]

UNAG Projects

Oxfam has supported many UNAG projects. The Animal Health on Cooperative and Livestock Farms Project promotes higher cattle production by curbing illnesses, improving herds, and increasing milk yields. It provides veterinary services, mobile health and pharmaceutical units, and animal health training, emphasizing widespread farmer and public participation. The Project Team initiative has trained staff and promoters to develop, monitor, administer, and evaluate farming projects. By incorporating professional economists and business administrators, as well as training selected lay people, the Project Team improves the quality of agricultural projects.

The Project Counterparts (Homologos) initiative expanded the Project Team by providing nine regionally based "counterparts" to promote local projects full-time. Counterparts have worked to improve technical and practical skills, consolidate local programs nationally, and assist local promoters to implement projects. Shunning "top-down" organizations, the counterparts link local areas to UNAG's national assembly. Finally, the counterparts have helped UNAG to design projects that will attract greater international aid.

UNAG's Municipal Council Training Project provides technical and organizational training at the county level for over 1,100 cooperative and farm association leaders in farm management, planning, and decision making. It also promotes citizen participation and cooperative development strategies. To identify and solve local problems to improve long-term production, it trains leaders to participate before local municipal councils. Oxfam now funds the program's third stage, part of a five-year training project.

The UNAG Small Farmer Extension Program has used a village-level, democratic network to organize over 2,900 agricultural co-op members. It promotes financial and political independence, increased production levels, literacy training, increased participation of producers in storing, distributing, marketing, and pricing, co-op management, enhanced living standards, better-trained organizers, and improved social and economic development. It works closely with governmental or quasi-governmental organizations such as the National Development Bank (for credit), the Center for Investigation and Study of Agrarian Reform (CIEBA) (for technical, production, and credit information), PROCAMPO (on agricultural extension), and the Agrarian Reform Program of the Sandinistas' Government of National Reconstruction. The Basic Grains Priority Action Zones Project also works with the government's National Granaries Campaign to develop priority zones for increased grain production and to improve grain storage techniques.[106]

The final UNAG project, the Pedro Altamirano Cooperative Housing Program, was designed to improve living conditions for 17 peasant families. Although Oxfam generally avoids housing projects as costly and unproductive, at this unique agricultural cooperative housing can actually improve productivity. The cooperative received land from the Agrarian Reform, which it has been using for cattle and crops, but it has had a serious housing shortage (three houses for 90 people). The project allowed co-op members to build six new houses and three latrines.

ATC Projects

Oxfam has supported three ATC projects. The ATC Training Project helped create the Farm Worker Center for Research and Training. Partially supported by the Nicaraguan Ministry of Agriculture, the project and center provide rural training on Nicaraguan history, agriculture and livestock policies, labor patterns, unionization, and public speaking. They also promote research on worker participation and crop economics and generate awareness about the role of rural workers in Nicaraguan development.

The ATC Delegation to the U.S. Project allowed an ATC preparatory visit to the United States before the ATC hosted its International Convention on Trade Unions for World Peace. The support helped develop U.S. worker participation and communication between the ATC and U.S. trade unions. The twelve-day tour, stopping in five American cities, increased U.S. awareness of work and conditions in Nicaragua and generated U.S. union support for common goals within the North American and international union movements, including improved living and working conditions and global peace.

The ATC Women Farmworkers Participatory Research and Training Project emerged in cooperation with the Laura Amada Cuadra Study Center (CELAC). A five-year project, it evaluates and improves living and working conditions for women farmworkers. Collaborating with two other study teams at the government's Ministry of Labor (CETRA) and the Center for Investigation and Study of Agrarian Reform (CIERA), and coordinated by the government's Office of Women, it addresses women's various needs, including legal assistance, work organization, unemployment, seasonal employment, occupational health and safety, inadequate training, supply problems, union participation, and women's rights. Founded at the 1983 National Meeting of Rural Women Workers, where government ministers pledged to fight "machismo" and women's subordinate status, the project investigates women's functions in the economy, including not only their workplace roles, but also their "second shift" of unpaid labor in the home. Promoting policy, training, and research to implement the nation's many laws against sex discrimination, the project will eventually train women to increase awareness about their contribution to agricultural production, incorporate more women into production, and generally improve their work and social status.

Emergencies

Two Oxfam projects have focused specifically on national or regional emergencies. The 1982 Emergency Relief for Flood Disaster Project, coordinated by the National Disaster Committee, responded to the extensive flooding of the Pacific Coast region, which left 60,000 homeless and caused extensive crop loss and widespread damage to bridges, roads, warehouses, health facilities, electric lines, soil, and livestock. Forced to cope with a far more serious disaster than the 1976 earthquake, but far less relieved by outside, international aid, the project helped create a local-level, decentralized response system to channel outside support and domestic initiatives. Moving quickly beyond relief to providing intermediate, semi-development projects, Oxfam helped build the infrastructure and self-sufficiency so essential to its development model.

The other emergency came from unnatural causes. The Pantasma Emergency Support Project responded to the devastation left by a contra attack in Jinotega, in north central Nicaragua. The attack destroyed buildings, savings, lives, supplies, homes, warehouses, health posts, and the community's large sawmill. The support program provided clothing, shoes, tools, utensils, first-aid kits, and makeshift shelters. It also promoted integrated, community coordination for relocation, planting and harvesting, feeding children, and other reconstructive and development efforts. Receiving support from the National Food Program (PAN) and the National System of Professional Educators (SINARFOP), and working cooperatively with the government's National Emergency Committee, Civil Defense Program, Housing and Planning ministries, and its Institute for Social Services and Welfare (INSSBI), UNAG and AMNLAE were largely responsible for organizing and completing the reconstruction. Women, in particular, played a great role in the recovery.

Other Projects

The 1984 Tools for Peace Project was coordinated through UNAG, ATC, AMNLAE, and the Augusto Sandino Foundation (FACS). Responding to the over $600 million in losses due to contra attacks and to America's economic boycott (of aid, international assistance, and business contracts), Oxfam has helped these groups acquire agricultural tools and spare parts used mostly for food production by farmers, peasants, and rural women. With an unwieldy foreign debt, which has prevented Nicaragua from accumulating foreign exchange to purchase tools, seeds, machinery, equipment, and spare parts, the Tools for Peace program, which Oxfam renewed again for 1985, helps satisfy a crucial need. In typical fashion the project has not merely gathered and distributed tools, but rather has created a structure for longer-term development: a revolving tool bank where users cooperate to share and maintain tools and equipment.[107]

Finally, Oxfam also supports the Salvadoran Literacy Project in Nicaragua. Created by the now-exiled National Association of Salvadoran Educators (ANDES) as part of its Comprehensive Central American Literacy Project, it now operates mainly from Managua. Cooperating with Nicaragua's Literacy Campaign, it also works with exiled Salvadorans living in Nicaraguan refugee camps. It trains literacy workers to teach throughout Nicaragua, El Salvador, and eventually the rest of Central America. It helps repatriate Salvadorans and promotes citizen empowerment as well as practical skills.

CONCLUSION

Central America, like the Third World generally, faces many obstacles to development. They include not merely inadequate resources, but dependence and repression often imposed through prevailing political and economic structures and relationships. Since conventional aid models do not significantly alter these arrangements, they have failed to reverse underdevelopment, despite years of trying. In response, some private voluntary organizations have promoted an alternative development model, emphasizing self-sufficiency, popular empowerment, and new international economic relations.

One of these organizations, Oxfam, has, more than most groups, self-consciously promoted alternative development in its work, including its projects in Central America. By avoiding conventional aid given through governments, Oxfam has gone more directly to communities, emphasizing development by people.

While overcoming many of the structural obstacles to conventional aid, Oxfam encounters many other barriers. A review of its projects in Guatemala and El Salvador shows that repression, in particular, impedes its efforts for alternative development. It must face the extra burden on development imposed by routine repression and raging civil wars. Its projects have also become the particular targets of repression. Because community work has been identified as inherently subversive, projects suffer daily government threats of kidnapping, murder, torture, bombing, and evacuation. This violence prevents Oxfam from directly monitoring projects and forces project holders to constantly emphasize security, whether by developing "rural defense" systems, by operating phantom offices, or by drastically fragmenting their work.

Somewhat ironically, much of this repression results from the continued support provided by donor governments and most private organizations, which perpetuate the conventional aid model. In repressive regimes, measured only over the last few years, we cannot say whether Oxfam actually reduces repression overall or influences repressive cycles, although the violence of hunger and poverty undoubtedly decreases among those involved in its projects.

Despite the barriers of repression, and despite the difficulties in quantifying how well development projects work, Oxfam has made some important inroads. It clearly embraces the alternative development model, offering much more than rhetorical substitutes for conventional aid. Its projects have demonstrably provided local communities with some important measure of self-reliance, self-sufficiency, material improvement, and psychological empowerment. While much remains to be done, Oxfam has also contributed to altering international policy toward a more just world order.

In Nicaragua the successes have been much more profound. Although Oxfam contributes very little to the nation's overall national development, its projects show how much more can be achieved without government repression, and especially with a government that is itself substantively dedicated to the alternative development model. But in regimes like this one, an alternative development model may increase local violence when regional powers like the United States sponsor (or even directly impose) external opposition, such as that of the contras. Nevertheless, the gains from working with governments dedicated to alternative development seem real enough. Without the favorable conditions these governments help provide, or dramatic changes in world policy, Oxfam faces an uphill battle. Yet even in repressive societies such as Guatemala and El Salvador, Oxfam has helped plant the seeds not only for authentic development, but for fundamental social change.

NOTES

I owe many thanks to Jethro Pettit, Ann Seidman, Kathy Durham, and the rest of the Oxfam America staff for their help in analyzing Oxfam projects. To protect the names of some Oxfam project holders in El Salvador and Guatemala, I have used several pseudonyms. The need to operate indirectly and to protect the names of indigenous groups shows the repression against which these organizations and Oxfam must work.

1. Teresa Hayter, *Aid as Imperialism* (London: Penguin Books, 1971); Holly Sklar, *Trilateralism* (Boston: South End Press, 1980).

2. Roger Burbach and Patricia Flynn, *Agribusiness in the Americas* (New York: Monthly Review Press, 1980); Susan George, *Feeding the Few* (Washington, D.C.: Institute for Policy Studies, 1980); Frances Moore Lappé and Joseph Collins, *Food First* (New York: Ballantine Books, 1978); Jack Nelson, *Hunger for Justice* (Maryknoll, N.Y.: Orbis Books, 1980); Arthur Simon, *Bread for the World* (New York: Paulist Press, 1975).

3. Hayter, *Aid as Imperialism*.

4. Martin Honeywell, ed., *The Poverty Brokers: The IMF and Latin America* (London: Latin America Bureau, 1983).

5. Tom Barry, *Dollars and Dictators: A Guide to Central America* (New York: Grove Press, 1983); Richard Fagen and Olga Pellicer, eds., *The Future of Central America* (Stanford, Calif.: Stanford University Press, 1983).

6. Samir Amin, *Unequal Development* (New York: Monthly Review Press, 1976); Independent Commission on International Development Issues, *North-South* (Cambridge, Mass.: MIT Press, 1980); Andre Gunder Frank, *Capitalism and Under-*

development in Latin America (New York: Monthly Review Press, 1967); Michael Harrington, *The Vast Majority* (New York: Touchstone Books, 1977); Teresa Hayter, *The Creation of World Poverty: An Alternative View to the Brandt Report* (London: Pluto Press, 1981); Heraldo Munoz, ed., *From Dependency to Development* (Boulder, Colo.: Westview Press, 1981); Robert Wood, "Foreign Aid and the Capitalist State in Underdeveloped Countries," *Politics and Society* 10 (1980): 1.

7. Richard Fagen, ed., *Capitalism and the State in U.S.-Latin American Relations* (Stanford, Calif.: Stanford University Press, 1979).

8. Jim Morrill and William Jesse Biddle, "Central America: The Financial War," *International Policy Report,* March 1983; Honeywell, *Poverty Brokers.*

9. Martin Diskin, ed., *Trouble in Our Backyard: Central America and the United States in the Eighties* (New York: Pantheon Books, 1984); Eduardo Galeano, *Open Veins of Latin America* (New York: Monthly Review Press, 1973); James Cockcroft et al., eds., *Dependence and Underdevelopment: Latin America's Political Economy* (Garden City, N.Y.: Doubleday, 1972); Jenny Pearce, *Under the Eagle* (Boston: South End Press, 1982); "Dependency Theory and the Dimensions of Imperialism," *Latin American Perspectives* 3 (Spring 1976); Thomas Harding and Hobart Spalding, eds., "Imperialism and the Working Class in Latin America," *Latin American Perspectives* 3 (Winter 1976); Roger Burbach and Patricia Flynn, eds., *The Politics of Intervention: The United States in Central America* (New York: Monthly Review Press, 1984).

10. Denis Goulet and Michael Hudson, *The Myth of Aid* (Maryknoll, N.Y.: Orbis Books, 1971); Judith Hart, *Aid and Liberation* (London: Victor Golancz, 1973); Charlotte Waterlow, *Superpowers and Victims* (Englewood Cliffs, N.J.: Prentice-Hall, 1974); Hayter, *Aid as Imperialism;* Wood, "Foreign Aid and the Capitalist State in Underdeveloped Countries."

11. Richard Barnet and Ronald Müller, *Global Reach* (New York: Simon Schuster, 1974); Noam Chomsky and Edward Herman, *The Washington Connection and Third World Fascism* (Boston: South End Press, 1979); David Goodman and Michael Redclift, *From Peasant to Proletarian* (Oxford: Basil Blackwell, 1981); Peter Evans, *Dependent Development* (Princeton: Princeton University Press, 1979); Norman Girvan, *Corporate Imperialism* (New York: Monthly Review Press, 1976); James McGinnis, *Bread and Justice: Toward a New International Economic Order* (New York: Paulist Press, 1979).

12. Penny Lernoux, *Cry of the People* (Garden City, N.Y.: Doubleday, 1980); Burbach and Flynn, *Agribusiness in the Americas.*

13. Penny Lernoux, *In Banks We Trust* (Garden City, N.Y.: Doubleday, 1984); Michael Moffitt, *The World's Money* (New York: Touchstone Books, 1983); Maurice Odle, *Multinational Banks and Underdevelopment* (New York: Pergamon Press, 1981); Miguel Wionczek, ed., *Politics and Economics of External Debt Crisis: The Latin American Experience* (Boulder, Colo.: Westview Press, 1984); Honeywell, *Poverty Brokers.*

14. Sklar, *Trilaterialism.*

15. Cheryl Payer, *The World Bank: A Critical Analysis* (New York: Monthly Review Press, 1982); Hayter, *Creation of World Poverty.*

16. Margaret Crahan, ed., *Human Rights and Basic Needs in the Americas* (Washington, D.C.: Georgetown University Press, 1982); James Petras, *Critical*

Perspectives on Imperialism and Social Class in the Third World (New York: Monthly Review Press, 1978); Honeywell, *Poverty Brokers.*

17. Frances Moore Lappé et al., *Aid as Obstacle* (San Francisco: Institute for Food and Development Policy, 1980).

18. J. S. Brara, *The Political Economy of Rural Development: Strategies for Poverty Alleviation* (New Delhi: Allied Press, 1983); Lappé, *Aid as Obstacle.*

19. Norma Stolz Chinchilla, "Class Struggle in Central America," *Latin American Perspectives* 7 (1980): 2; Walter LeFeber, *Inevitable Revolutions: The United States in Central America* (New York: Norton, 1984); Robert Leiken, ed., *Central America: Anatomy of Conflict* (New York: Pergamon Press, 1984); Phillip Berryman, *What's Wrong in Central America?* (Philadelphia: American Friends Service Committee, 1983); William LeoGrande, "Through the Looking Glass: The Report of the National Bipartisan Commission on Central America," *World Policy Journal* 1 (1984): 251; Policy Alternatives for the Caribbean and Central America, *Changing Course: Blueprint for Peace in Central America and the Caribbean* (Washington, D.C.: Institute for Policy Studies, 1984); Trin Yarborough, "Central America in Crisis: Special Report," *Oxfam America News,* Summer 1983, 5.

20. Hayter, *Creation of World Poverty;* Lappé, *Aid as Obstacle;* "Dependency Theory and the Dimensions of Imperialism," *Latin American Perspectives* 3 (Fall 1976).

21. Robert Alan White, *The Morass: United States Intervention in Central America* (New York: Harper and Row, 1984).

22. Tony Jackson, *Against the Grain* (Oxford: Oxfam, 1982); John Sommer, *Beyond Charity: U.S. Voluntary Aid for a Changing Third World* (Washington, D.C.: Overseas Development Council, 1977).

23. James Midgley, *Professional Imperialism: Social Work in the Third World* (London: Heinemann, 1981).

24. Ben Whitaker, *A Bridge of People: A Personal View of Oxfam's First Forty Years* (London: Heimemann, 1983).

25. Henry Dietz, *Poverty and Problem-Solving under Military Rule* (Austin, Tex.: University of Texas Press, 1980); Miles Wolpin, *Militarism and Social Revolution in the Third World* (Totowa, N.J.: Allenheld, Osmun, 1981); Crahan, *Human Rights and Basic Needs in the Americas.*

26. Michael Klare and Cynthia Arnson, *Supplying Repression* (Washington, D.C.: Institute for Policy Studies, 1981).

27. Ruth Sivard, *World Military and Social Expenditures* (Leesburg, Va.: World Priorities, 1983); Chomsky and Herman, *Washington Connection and Third World Fascism.*

28. Stephen Schlesinger and Stephen Kinzer, *Bitter Fruit,* 2d ed. (Garden City, N.Y.: Doubleday, 1983).

29. Lars Schoultz, *Human Rights and United States Policy toward Latin America* (Princeton: Princeton University Press, 1981).

30. Isabel Letelier and Michael Moffitt, "How American Banks Keep the Chilean Junta Going," in Mark Green and Robert Massie, Jr., eds., *The Big Business Reader* (New York: Pilgrim Press, 1980), p. 399.

31. Frank, *Capitalism and Underdevelopment in Latin America.*

32. Stephen Marks, "The Peace–Human Rights–Development Dialectic," *Bulletin of Peace Proposals* 8 (1980): 339.

33. Elliott Morss and Victoria Morss, *U.S. Foreign Aid: An Assessment of New and Traditional Development Strategies* (Boulder, Colo.: Westview Press, 1982); Brara, *Political Economy of Rural Development.*

34. Denis Goulet, *The Cruel Choice: A New Concept in the Theory of Development* (New York: Atheneum, 1973).

35. Penny Lernoux, *Fear and Hope: Toward Political Democracy in Central America* (New York: Field Foundation, 1984).

36. Kim Hill, ed., *Toward a New Strategy for Development* (New York: Pergamon Press, 1979).

37. Leonore Ralston et al., *Voluntary Efforts in Decentralized Management* (Berkeley: Institute of International Studies, 1983).

38. D. L. Sheth, "Grass Roots Stirrings and the Future of Politics," *Alternatives* 9 (1983): 1.

39. Guy Gran, *Development by People* (New York: Praeger, 1983); Albert Hirschman, *Getting Ahead Collectively: Grassroots Experiences in Latin America* (New York: Pergamon Press, 1984).

40. Johan Galtung et al., *Self-Reliance: A Strategy for Development* (London: Bogle-L'Ouverture, 1980).

41. Peter Hakim, "Lessons from the Interamerican Foundation Experience" (Arlington, Va.: Interamerican Foundation, 1982).

42. Chadwick Alger, "Creating Participatory Global Cultures," *Alternatives* 6 (1981): 575; David Korten and Rudi Klauss, eds., *People-Centered Development* (West Hartford, Conn.: Kumarian Press, 1984); Leonard Berry and Robert Kates, *Making the Most of the Least: Alternative Ways to Development* (New York: Holmes and Meier, 1980); David Leonard and Dale Rogers Marshall, eds., *Institutions of Rural Development for the Poor* (Berkeley: Institute of International Studies, 1982).

43. Galtung et al., *Self-Reliance.*

44. Gilbert Rist, "Alternative Strategies to Development," *Development* 2 (1980): 102.

45. Lappé, *Aid as Obstacle.*

46. Gran, *Development by People;* Galtung et al., *Self-Reliance.*

47. Claes Brundenius and Mats Lundahl, *Development Strategies and Basic Needs in Latin America* (Boulder, Colo.: Westview Press, 1982); Johan Galtung, *The True Worlds* (New York: Free Press, 1980).

48. Claire Whittemore, *Land for People: Land Tenure and the Very Poor* (Oxford: Oxfam Public Affairs Unit, 1981).

49. Christian Bay, *Strategies of Political Emancipation* (Notre Dame, Ind.: University of Notre Dame Press, 1981).

50. Dieter Senghaas, "The Case for Autarchy," *Development* 1 (1980): 3.

51. Leopold Kohr, *Development without Aid* (New York: Schocken Books, 1973).

52. Glen Williams, ed., "Reaching the Poorest: Six Rules for Real Aid," *New Internationalist,* August 1983, 7.

53. Joe Short, "Development: A Process of Empowerment," *Oxfam America News,* Summer 1984, 2.

54. Korten and Klauss, *People-Centered Development.*

55. Gustavo Lagos and Horacio Godoy, *Revolution of Being: A Latin American View of the Future* (New York: Free Press, 1977).

56. Erich Fromm, *To Have or to Be?* (New York: Bantam Books, 1978).

57. Marc Nerfin, ed., *Another Development* (Uppsala: Dag Hammarskjold Foundation, 1977); Audrey Bronstein, *The Triple Struggle: Latin American Peasant Women* (Boston: South End Press, 1982); Oxfam America, "Facts for Action," nos. 2, 3, 4, 8, 10 (Boston: Oxfam America); Carol Wells, "Women's Participation in the Central American Revolutions," *Latin American Perspectives* 10 (1983): 109.

58. Whitaker, *Bridge of People.*

59. A. T. Ariyaratne, *A Struggle to Awaken* (Morutuwa, Sri Lanka: Sarvodaya Shramadana Movement, 1978).

60. Gene Sharp, *Social Power and Political Freedom* (Boston: Porter Sargent, 1980).

61. Galtung et al., *Self-Reliance.*

62. Paulo Freire, *Pedagogy of the Oppressed* (New York: Continuum, 1970).

63. Blase Bonpane, "The Church and Revolutionary Struggle in Central America," *Latin American Perspectives* 7 (1980): 178; Lernoux, *Cry of the People.*

64. Galtung et al., *Self-Reliance.*

65. Third World First, *Beyond Brandt* (London: Third World First, 1981).

66. Sivard, *World Military and Social Expenditures.*

67. Ariel Dorfman, "Bread and Burnt Rice: Culture and Economic Survival in Latin America," *Grassroots Development* 8 (1984): 3; Roy Preiswerk, "Cultural Identity, Self-Reliance, and Basic Needs," *Development* 3 (1981): 83.

68. Richard Falk et al., eds., *Toward a Just World Order* (Boulder, Colo.: Westview Press, 1982); Nerfin, *Another Development;* Galtung, *True Worlds;* Goulet, *Cruel Choice;* Rajni Kothari, *Footsteps into the Future* (New York: Free Press 1974); Alvin Toffler, *The Third Wave* (New York: Morrow, 1980); Bay, *Strategies of Political Emancipation;* Samuel Kim, *The Quest for a Just World Order* (Boulder, Colo.: Westview Press, 1984).

69. A few governmental organizations, such as the Interamerican Foundation (created by Congress), may have similar potential. See Williams, "Reaching the Poorest"; Hakim, "Lessons from the Interamerican Foundation Experience."

70. Robert Gorman, ed., *Private Voluntary Organizations as Agents of Development* (Boulder, Colo.: Westview Press, 1984); Alfred Katz and David Smith, *Self-Help Groups and Voluntary Action: International Perspectives* (New York: Irvington, 1984); David Horton Smith et al., eds., *International Perspectives on Voluntary Action Research* (Lanham, Md.: University Press of America, 1983).

71. Jorgan Lissner, *The Politics of Altruism: A Study of the Political Behaviour of Voluntary Development Agencies* (Geneva: Lutheran World Federation, 1977).

72. Landrum Bolling with Craig Smith, *Private Foreign Aid* (Boulder, Colo.: Westview Press, 1982).

73. Mario Padrón Castillo, *Cooperación al desarrollo y movimiento popular: Las associaciones privadas de desarrollo* (Lima: Centro de Estudios y Promoción del Desarrollo, 1982).

74. Lissner, *Politics of Altruism.*

75. Ibid.

76. Morss and Morss, *U.S. Foreign Aid.*

77. Eugene Linden, *The Alms Race: The Impact of American Voluntary Aid Abroad* (New York: Random House, 1976).

78. Brian Smith, *U.S. and Canadian Nonprofit Organizations as Transnational Development Institutions* (New Haven: Institution for Social and Policy Studies, 1983); Judith Tendler, *Turning Private Voluntary Organizations into Development Agencies: Questions for Evaluation* (Washington, D.C.: Agency for International Development, 1982).

79. Mervyn Jones, *In Famine's Shadow* (Boston: Beacon Press, 1965); Lappé, *Aid as Obstacle.*

80. Sommer, *Beyond Charity.*

81. Jones, *In Famine's Shadow;* Whitaker, *Bridge of People.*

82. Oxfam America, "Facts for Action"; Jason Clay, "Organizing to Survive: Indigenous People's Organizations," *Cultural Survival Quarterly* 8 (1984).

83. Joe Short, "Aid That Works" (Boston: Oxfam America, 1982).

84. Tim Johnson, "New Director Reflects on Oxfam America's Role, Philosophy," *Oxfam America News,* Winter 1985, 2.

85. Oxfam America, *Program Paper: Latin America and the Caribbean* (Boston: Oxfam America, 1984).

86. Shelton Davis and Julie Hodson, *Witness to Political Violence in Guatemala: The Suppression of a Rural Development Project* (Boston: Oxfam America, 1982); Laurence Simon and James Stephens, *El Salvador Land Reform* (Boston: Oxfam America, 1982).

87. Edward Herman and Frank Brodhead, *Demonstration Elections* (Boston: South End Press, 1984). To contrast this with Nicaraguan elections, see Frank Brodhead, "The Nicaraguan Election and the Problem of Democracy," *RESIST Newsletter* 169 (October 1984): 1; Martin Diskin, "Nicaraguan Elections: Whose Sham?" *RESIST Newsletter* 172 (January 1985): 3; William Robinson and Kent Norsworthy, "Elections and U.S. Intervention in Nicaragua," *Latin American Perspectives* 12 (Spring 1985): 83.

88. Central America Information Office, *El Salvador: Background to the Crisis* (Cambridge, Mass.: Central America Information Office, 1982); Robert Armstrong and Janet Shenk, *El Salvador: The Face of Revolution* (Boston: South End Press, 1982); World Council of Churches, *Human Rights in El Salvador* (Geneva: World Council of Churches, 1984); World Council of Churches, *Human Rights in Guatemala* (Geneva: World Council of Churches, 1984); Cynthia Arnson, *El Salvador: A Revolution Confronts the U.S.* (Washington, D.C.: Institute for Policy Studies, 1982); Marvin Gettleman et al., eds., *El Salvador: Central America in the New Cold War* (New York: Grove Press, 1981).

89. Barry, *Dictators and Dollars.*

90. George Black, "Guatemala: The War Is Not Over," *NACLA Report on the Americas* 17 (1983): 2; William Goodfellow, "U.S. Economic Aid to El Salvador: Where Is the Money Going?" *International Policy Report,* May 1984; Gabriel Aguilera Peralta, "Terror and Violence as Weapons of Counterinsurgency in Guatemala, *Latin American Perspectives* 7 (1980): 91; Edelberto Torres-Rivas, "Guatemala: Crisis and Political Violence," *NACLA Report on the Americas* 14 (1980): 16; Raymond Bonner, *Weakness and Deceit: U.S. Policy and El Salvador* (New York: New York Times Books, 1984); Jim Handy, *Gift of the Devil* (Boston: South End Press, 1984).

91. Frederick Cuny, *Disasters and Development* (New York: Oxford University Press, 1983).

92. Editors, "Guatemala: Women in the Revolution," *Latin American Perspectives* 10 (1983): 103.

93. Oxfam America, "Facts for Action."

94. COPROSAL, *War and Health* (San José, Costa Rica: COPROSAL, 1983).

95. Henri Weber, *Nicaragua: The Sandinist Revolution* (London: Verso, 1981).

96. John Gitlitz, "Hegemony and Dissent: Pluralism and Human Rights in the New Nicaragua," in Peter Schwab and Adamantia Pollis, eds., *Toward a Human Rights Framework* (New York: Praeger, 1982); Amnesty International, *Report of the Amnesty International Missions to the Republic of Nicaragua* (New York: Amnesty International, 1982); Americas Watch, *Report on Human Rights in Nicaragua* (New York: Americas Watch, April 1984); Helena Claudio Fragoso and Alejandro Artucio, *Human Rights in Nicaragua Yesterday and Today* (Geneva: International Commission of Jurists, 1980); Lawyers Committee for International Human Rights, *Nicaragua: Revolutionary Justice* (New York: Lawyers Committee for International Human Rights, 1985); Inter-American Commission on Human Rights, *Report on the Situation of Human Rights in the Republic of Nicaragua* (Washington, D.C.: Organization of American States, 1981).

97. Peter Rosset and John Vandermeer, eds., *The Nicaragua Reader* (New York: Grove Press, 1983); Jaime Biderman, "The Development of Capitalism in Nicaragua," *Latin American Perspectives* 10 (Winter 1983): 7; Deidre English, "Nicaragua under Fire," *Mother Jones,* August/September 1985, 21; "Nicaragua's Foreign Trade: U.S. Tightens the Economic Noose," *Dollars and Sense,* June 1985, 6; Richard Fagen, "Revolution and Crisis in Nicaragua," in Diskin, *Trouble in Our Backyard;* Lars Schoultz, "Nicaragua: The U.S. Confronts a Revolution," in Richard Newfarmer, ed., *From Gunboats to Diplomacy: New U.S. Policies for Latin America* (Baltimore: Johns Hopkins University Press, 1984); John Cavanagh and Joy Hackel, "U.S. Economic War against Nicaragua," *Counterspy,* March/May 1984, 12; Michael Harrington et al., "Democracy under Siege," *Democratic Left,* March/April 1985, 3; Jeanne Gallo, "Plotting the Destruction of Nicaragua," *RESIST Newsletter* (August/September 1983): 1; Joe Collins, "Nicaragua: Bitter Fruits of U.S. Policy," *Food First News,* Fall 1984, 1; John Saul, "Under Fire II," *This Magazine,* Spring 1985, 5; Michael Conroy, "External Dependence, External Assistance, and Economic Aggression against Nicaragua," *Latin American Perspectives* 12 (Spring 1985): 39; Beth Stephens, "The Contra War of Terror: Prelude to an Invasion?" *Nicaraguan Perspectives,* Fall 1984, 21; Center for Defense Information, "Into the Fray: Facts on the U.S. Military in Central America," *Defense Monitor* 13 (1984): 1; Marlene Dixon, ed., *On Trial: Reagan's War against Nicaragua* (San Francisco: Synthesis, 1985); Fred Landis, "CIA Psychological Warfare Operations: Case Studies in Chile, Jamaica, and Nicaragua," *Science for the People,* January/February 1982, 6.

98. Marlene Dixon and Susanne Jonas, *Nicaragua under Siege* (San Francisco: Synthesis, 1984); Thomas Walker, ed., *Nicaragua in Revolution* (New York: Praeger, 1982).

99. Oxfam America, "Facts for Action."

100. Joseph Collins, *What Difference Could a Revolution Make? Food and Farming in the New Nicaragua* (San Francisco: Institute for Food and Development Policy, 1982).

101. Dixon and Jonas, *Nicaragua under Siege;* Rosset and Vandermeer,

Nicaragua Reader; Walker, *Nicaragua in Revolution;* Marvin Ortega, "Workers' Participation in the Management of the Agro-Enterprises of the APP," *Latin American Perspectives* 12 (Spring 1985): 69; Barbara Goldaftas, "Feeding Nicaragua," *Dollars and Sense,* March 1985, 9; Forrest Colburn and Silvio Franco, "Privilege, Production, and Revolution: The Case of Nicaragua," *Comparative Politics* 17 (April 1985): 277.

102. Yarborough, "Central America in Crisis"; Cuny, *Disasters and Development.*

103. Mary Pritchard, "Nicaragua: Farmers Chose Him," *Oxfam America News,* Winter 1984, 3; Phillippe Merchez, "Nicaragua: Harvest Time in the Cooperatives," *Refugees,* February 1985, 30.

104. Collins, *What Difference Could a Revolution Make?*

105. Dixon and Jonas, *Nicaragua under Siege;* Walker, *Nicaragua in Revolution;* Margaret Randall, *Sandino's Daughters* (Vancouver: New Star, 1981).

106. Carmen Diana Deere, "A Comparative Analysis of Agrarian Reform in El Salvador and Nicaragua," *Development and Change* 13 (1982): 1.

107. Barb Hendrie, "Oxfam America Tools for Peace in Nicaragua," *Oxfam America News,* Summer 1984, 1.

2

State Terror as a Complement of Economic Policy: The Argentine Proceso, 1976–1981

Paul G. Buchanan

The military regime that held power in Argentina from 1976 to 1983 is best known for offering an excellent case study of failed authoritarian rule. Even so, as an extended exercise in *dominio* (the term Gramsci used to refer to the coercive "moment of force" by which dominant social groups, as represented by political regimes, use the state to physically control subordinate groups and impose their will on civil society), the self-designated "Proceso de Reorganización Nacional" (Process of National Reorganization) was unprecedented in its systematic use of state terror to achieve regime objectives. At both the external (foreign relations) and internal (domestic program) levels, the military regime's basic approach toward achieving policy objectives was underscored by a prompt recourse to coercion. Internally, this was manifest in the infamous "dirty war" against leftist subversion, which started out as an antiguerrilla campaign and degenerated into the death, "disappearance," and torture of over 30,000 civilians (including scores of children and pregnant women) at the hands of military and paramilitary death squads. Externally, it was evident in the murder, intimidation, and kidnapping of Argentine exiles abroad, the saber rattling that accompanied the territorial dispute with Chile over the Beagle Channel islands in 1978, involvement in the Bolivian military coup d'état of 1978, training of right-wing military and paramilitary forces in Central America from 1979 to 1982, and finally the forcible reoccupation of the Falklands/Malvinas Islands in 1982.

However, while much has been made of the fact that the Falklands/Malvinas debacle proved to be the Argentine Cyprus, and while attention has most often focused on the more overt transgressions of the Proceso—the gross violations of human rights and pervasive corruption under the military regime—less attention has been accorded to two other facets that were integral parts of this exercise in *dominio:* the use of state terror as a complement to a particular economic program, and the subtle use of terror to enforce the acquiescence of those most adversely affected by that program. This chapter will therefore attempt to address both of these subjects and thereby garner a more complete picture of the use of state terror as an economic policy instrument essential for the exercise in *dominio* that was military rule in Argentina from 1976 to 1981.

ARGENTINA UNDER THE PROCESO:
A CONCEPTUAL AND CONTEXTUAL INTRODUCTION

It should not appear incongruous that the Argentine Proceso be considered in neo-Gramscian terms. The context in which Gramsci wrote in many respects resembles the Argentine situation after World War II. The fundamental dichotomy of the agrarian and industrial sectors that resulted from the shift in the Argentine mode of production during the first half of the twentieth century,[1] the ensuing emergence of the urban industrial classes (particularly the domestic bourgeoisie and the organized labor movement) as economic and political actors, and the ongoing situation of chronic political instability marked by frequent regime change and the inability of contending social groups to establish a minimum level of consensus, much less agree to the hegemony of any one of them, combined to produce an ongoing period of "organic crisis" during the postwar years that echoed the Italian experience of the late teens and early twenties. Thus while the fit is by no means hermetic or universally transferable, a neo-Gramscian approach offers a lucid theoretical framework with which to analyze the context in which the Argentine Proceso emerged and subsequently ruled.[2]

With this in mind, it should come as no surprise to see that in many respects Gramsci proved remarkably, albeit unknowingly, prescient in forecasting the conditions surrounding the military's assumption of power in Argentina in March 1976. The period immediately preceding military intervention was "a phase in the class struggle that precedes: either the conquest of power on the part of the revolutionary proleteriat . . . or a tremendous reaction on the part of the propertied classes and governing caste."[3] Its most overt manifestation was a full-scale guerrilla war waged by leftist groups against the army in the northern province of Tucuman, rampant sectarian violence betwen leftist and rightist terrorist groups (some of which were connected to the government) in the cities that resulted in an average of over three politically motivated murders a day, the breakdown of normal party lines, a sustained wave of strikes, work stoppages, and industrial sabotage that paralyzed production, a huge fiscal deficit, an inflation rate exceeding 500 percent, and rapid disinvestment by foreign capital, which aggravated an already-severe balance-of-payments problem.[4] It was, in effect, a period of "organic crisis," that is, "a crisis of authority . . . a crisis of hegemony, or general crisis of the State."[5] With the government of Isabel Perón wracked by corruption and factional infighting that were in essence an internal reflection of the external problems confronting it, by early 1976 the situation had become "delicate and dangerous, because the field was open to violent solutions, for the activities of unknown forces, represented by charismatic 'men of destiny.' "[6]

Faced with the nearly complete disruption of social order and government functions, and already engaged in a violent armed struggle with well-organized groups that proposed to fundamentally alter the basic Catholic, capitalist socioeconomic parameters of Argentine society once they attained power, the armed forces decided to assume the role of "men of destiny" and steer the country away from the Marxist abyss. In the words of Guillermo O'Donnell, the "threat level" confronting society was such that the military could no longer refrain from assuming direct political control of the country.[7] In Gramsci's terms, they were compelled to become a "political force which [moved] into action [because] 'legality' was in danger."[8] To that end, the armed forces stepped in and removed Isabel Perón from office in a bloodless coup d'état on March 24, 1976. These were the circumstances surrounding the advent of this exercise in *dominio* that came to be known as the "Proceso de Reorganización Nacional." As such, we can add "organic crisis" to the types of political climate George Lopez has identified as likely to lead to regime change conducive to state terror.[9]

But what is it about the Proceso that allows its identification as an exercise in *dominio*? After all, state terror and government coercion are long-standing facts of human history.[10] If we accept the definition of terrorism as "the purposeful act or threat of violence to create fear and/or compliant behavior in a victim and/or audience of the act or threat,"[11] and that state terror is "a system of government that uses terror to rule,"[12] then what is there to distinguish the Proceso from other reigns of terror extending back to antiquity? The factors, I suggest, are twofold. The first involves the specific class content of both the regime and the "audience" toward which state terror was directed. The second includes the systematic way in which state terror was utilized in pursuit of specific policy objectives.

For Gramsci, a social group (or groups) is dominant, that is, exercises *dominio,* when "it tends to 'liquidate,' or to subjugate perhaps even by armed force" antagonistic groups, and "leads kindred and allied groups."[13] After the March 1976 *golpe de estado,* this was precisely the relationship of the military regime with the organized working classes and the transnational and agro-export sectors, respectively. Like any other regime (a political regime being the collection of social groups and political actors that gain control of the apex of the state apparatus, or what is commonly known as government), in gaining control of the Argentine state apparatus the military junta formally assumed a monopoly of legitimate violence over a given territory, since "the exercise of repression is juridically absent from civil society. The State reserves it as an exclusive domain."[14] However, in assuming control of the state, the armed forces tacitly accepted

Gramsci's narrowly defined conception of the state as "a political society—i.e. a dictatorship, or coercive apparatus to ensure that the masses conform to the type of production and economy of a given moment."[15] In effect, the armed forces envisioned the state during the Proceso as "the site of the armed domination or coercion of the [here transnational and landed] bourgeoisie over the exploited classes."[16]

In this context, state terror can be conceived of as government repression involving "the use of coercion or the threat of coercion against opponents or potential opponents in order to prevent or weaken their capability to oppose the authorities and their policies."[17] Closer to the specifics of the regime examined here, it can be defined as "any action [such as liquidation or subjugation] taken by the government which reduces the power of social classes."[18] In this case the state terror was directed against the organized working classes and lower bourgeoisie that were the mass political support base of the Peronist regime that had preceded the Proceso and that the military consequently held responsible for the chaotic conditions it inherited. What is significant here is that while coercion is one of several policy instruments available to regimes, during exercises in *dominio* such as the Proceso it becomes the primary policy instrument, to which all others (such as persuasion, exchange, and reasoned, legitimate authority) are subsumed. We should recall that this conception of the state as primarily a coercive instrument of a specific dominant group was facilitated by the severity of the crisis that had confronted it in the period preceding military intervention, when not only were noncoercive policy instruments ineffectual, but the very state monopoly of legal violence within the country was being challenged at a variety of levels. The weakness of the state under the Peronist regime, in other words, is what allowed the military to reduce the very concept of state to its most basic, primitive, and coercive level in an effort to reassert its superordinate national authority.

In the face of the virtual collapse of government and social order, the Argentine military hierarchy envisioned itself in quasi-gnostic terms along the lines Gramsci had once offered for the Italian revolutionary classes. That is, it was "at once a force of movement and a repository of past and present cultural values"[19] that, in the absence of hegemony as the "normal" form of control, was forced to resort to coercion, which becomes dominant only in times of crisis.[20]

The concept of hegemony (*egemonia*) has a long history in Marxist thought and has been the subject of considerable, often bitter debate.[21] This is not the place to engage in further discussion of the precise meaning of the term. What is relevant to our concerns is that, contrary to Leninist conceptions of hegemony as dictatorship of a class, with all the coercive implications it is said to entail, Gramsci conceived of *egemonia* as

a socio-political situation, a moment in which the philosoph[ies] of society fuse or are in equilibrium, an order in which a certain way of life and thought is dominant, in which one concept of reality is diffused throughout society in all its institutional and private manifestations, informing with its spirit all taste, morality, customs, religious and political principles, and all social relations, particularly in their intellectual and moral connotation.[22]

Hegemony therefore requires of dominant social groups that "account be taken of the interests and tendencies of the groups over which hegemony is to be exercised, and that a certain balance or compromise be formed—in other words, that the leading groups should make sacrifices of an economic-corporative kind."[23]

It is obvious that hegemony did not obtain in the period of "organic crisis" preceding the advent of the Proceso. As I shall clarify further on, neither did it afterwards. The point is that without hegemony as the "normal" form of control, and given the magnitude of the crisis at the time, it should not be surprising that the military regime opted for *dominio,* of which state terror is an integral part. As Sergio Zermeño aptly phrases it:

Are not military dictatorships the most obvious manifestation of hegemonic incapacity at all levels, an incapacity that has been reiterated since the demise of the oligarchic order? These military dictatorships, as emergent instruments of coercion without consensual constraints, demonstrate in patent fashion the triple crisis of hegemony that placed them on the scene numerous times, and which today makes them inevitable.[24]

When such moments occur, the balance between integrative and repressive functions within the state apparatus sways inexorably toward the latter.[25]

The coercion associated with state terror, however, comes in many guises and forms. Most obvious is "active coercion," involving the use and threat of use of violent force. Less visible, but often no less effective, is "covert" or "subtle" coercion, where the "power of a class is reduced by changes in the rules of the game which define the structure of socio-economic activity, that is, rules by which power is exercised in the struggle among classes over the direction of society."[26] Moreover, there are differences and gradations within these two types of coercion. John Sloan has called attention to the different types of active coercion known as repression (the use of governmental coercion to control or eliminate actual or potential opposition) and the more extreme variant of repression known as enforcement terrorism, which is more likely to be lethal and cruel.[27]

Similarly, we can distinguish between different types of covert or subtle coercion. Here again, Gramsci understood that "the state had instruments of control far more subtle and effective than dictatorial force, that the threat of force was only one of a number of state functions, and that variations in the legal-political forms of the state were highly significant."[28] Thus measures such as press censorship, rescinding of basic welfare legislation for selected groups, direct government intervention and control of social group organizations such as labor unions, prohibitions on the right to assembly, speech, and thought, bans on literature, changes in school curriculums, outlawing of political parties or social interest groups, economic controls such as wage ceilings and the elimination of collective bargaining, closure of public health facilities, and raises in public transportation rates represent some of the more subtle coercive measures regimes use to control those they view as antagonistic to their rule.

Even the state apparatus itself reflects the different types of coercive approaches. At a broad level, "Concrete reorganizations in the state apparatus reflect readjustments in the balance [or in Gramscian terms, 'relation of forces'] between social classes."[29] That is to say, "The state apparatus, understood as the hierarchy and configuration of specific branches, agencies, and functions of the state, adapts chameleon-like to the mutable strategies used by the dominant classes against the dominated classes, and to the dynamics of the internal balance of power within the dominant bloc."[30] In effect, "It is possible to conceive of the concrete distribution of functions within the state apparatus, their degree of hierarchical-functional concentration or separation, as forms of reproduction . . . imposed by the development of social contradictions."[31]

During an exercise in *dominio,* this becomes most apparent in the expansion and promotion of the internal security apparatus, most notably specialized agencies such as the intelligence services, secret police, border guards, and gendarmes, as well as in the growth of paramilitary groups and the reorientation of the armed forces' role toward internal rather than external security concerns. It is more subtle although no less evident in the transfer or demotion of the institutional referents of specific social groups such as organized labor (most often embodied in a Labor Ministry), as well as in the amount of resources allocated to and character of those employed in each of them. The same applies for those agencies more generally concerned with the provision of basic public goods such as health, welfare, and social security, and social services like water and electricity, and public housing and transportation. In most of these agencies it is in the application of negative measures that coercion becomes apparent. Upgrading of agencies and services in these latter areas is most often used as an incentive, inducement, or reward for cooperation, while the downgrading, elimination, or curtailment of agencies and services is most often used as a disincentive, constraint, or punishment for uncooperative or antagonistic groups. Again, whatever the precise combination of measures used, "It is in the sphere of *dominio* that change in structure becomes immediately apparent, and *dominio* is always associated with coercion, state power, the 'moment of force.' "[32]

During an exercise in *dominio,* the use of coercion—in all of its particular guises—is "designed to force compliance through a climate of fear."[33] Its goal is to intimidate into utter submission the body politic in general, but more specifically those groups that may be opposed to the regime or some of its policies. It is this climate of pervasive fear promoted by the systematic and varied usage of coercion that, regardless of the precise characterization applied, ultimately defines "state terror."

This was, in sum, the underlying rationale of the Proceso. Alain Rouquié characterized it thus: "The amplitude of the repression, the brutality and decentralized character of the methods used . . . the impunity of unit leaders within the armed forces, the use of torture, reprisals, and summary executions, the disappearance of suspects, all point towards creating a climate of dissuasive fear."[34]

This climate of fear was dissuasive in the sense that it was designed to intimidate the economically and politically out-of-favor—the organized working classes and lower bourgeoisie—from pressing vindictive claims that would interfere with the regime's "liberal" or "neoclassic" economic program. As I will detail, this program was oriented toward reasserting the primacy of the agro-export sector and transnational finance capital in the Argentine mode of production, in order to fully exploit those areas where it was believed that Argentina held a competitive advantage in the world capitalist market.

The climate of fear was also dissuasive in the sense that it was designed to intimidate all those who were otherwise predisposed to object to the overt class content and whole-scale abridgment of basic human rights of the repressive campaign, particularly after the guerrillas were defeated in late 1977. This included all non-Peronist political parties, intellectual, legal, professional, and human rights groups, and the resident foreign communities. The sowing of fear was dissuasive, finally, in that it was designed to show international Marxism that it could not and would not find fertile ground in Argentina as long as the armed forces could prevent it.

During an exercise in *dominio* such as the Proceso, the concept and functions of the state are narrowed and reduced to their most primitive form. It becomes "a political society, dictatorship, apparatus of coercion (army, police, administration, courts, bureaucracy, etc.), government (which equals the state in the strict sense), apparatus of power, and domination."[35] As a particular form of dependent capitalist state,

it maintains and structures class domination, in the sense that this domination is rooted principally in a class structure that in turn has its foundation in the operation and reproduction of capitalist relations of production. . . From this perspective the state is, first and foremost, a relation of domination that articulates in unequal fashion the components of civil society, supporting and organizing the existing system of social domination.[36]

More importantly, as a form of "bureaucratic-authoritarian"[37] rule, the Proceso was a response "to important modifications of the relations of production and to important stages of the class struggle."[38] In other words, the Argentine state apparatus under the Proceso reflected a particular type of authoritarian response on the part of a specific coalition of social groups (the so-called "coup coalition" mentioned by Guillermo O'Donnell) to the intense socioeconomic conflicts surrounding their assumption of power. For Dante Caputo, "From the point of view of the dominant social groups that exercised power during these years . . . this process signified an exceptional opportunity to consolidate their social domination."[39]

Because of the gravity of the threat posed by the "organic crisis" leading up to the installation of the military regime, and the fact that the very nature of social relations had changed significantly during the crisis, it was felt that, as Gramsci once remarked, there "must be the political methods used, the resort to violence and the combination of legal and illegal forces."[40] Specifically, it was believed that only through the systematic use of state terror could the challenge to basic societal parameters posed by Marxist subversion be decisively overcome.

Finally, the virtual "colonization of the State by the military" (the details of which will be elaborated upon shortly) was by no means a product of chance.[41] On the contrary, it was done precisely to bestow an aura of professional neutrality on what was basically the transparent intent of the transnational and agro-export elites to reassert their dominance over the rest of Argentine society after a period during which this dominance had been seriously and often violently questioned. The military leaders of the Proceso well understood that the state "best serves the interests of the capitalist class only when members of this class do not participate directly (or at least overtly or as a majority) in the state apparatus, that is to say, when the *ruling class* is not the *politically governing class*."[42] Moreover, the economic interests of these elites were juxtaposed against those of the lower bourgeoisie as well as the working classes, since the former were considered "traitorous" because of their historical identification with the Peronist movement.[43]

Thus the military-authoritarian regime represented just the upper fractions of the Argentine bourgeoisie, the traditional landed and agro-export interests, and the conservative military hierarchy. Both economically and politically the Proceso turned its back on the subordinate fractions of the bourgeoisie as well as the working classes. This was done with the understanding that the "State can only truly serve the ruling class (as manifest in a particular regime) in so far as it is relatively autonomous from the diverse (and here subordinate) fractions of this class, precisely in order to be able to organize the hegemony of the whole of this class."[44] Whether the agro-export elites and transnational sectors of the Argentine bourgeoisie did have a hegemonic project or were instead content to reassert their economic and political dominance over the more national and urban industrial sectors of the bourgeoisie is open to question. What is fact is that during the initial phase of their rule (1976-1979), they and their military allies deemed it necessary to impose a period of *dominio* in order to "cleanse" Argentine society of the economic and political "malignancies" that had brought the country to the verge of collapse.[45]

I will now proceed to develop the details of this project, at least as it was manifest in the varied use of state terror as a complement to economic policy. For the moment, what I have tried to do is conceptualize the context in which the Proceso emerged in terms that are most consonant with the realities of the Argentine experience. One need not hold a strong ideological position to realize that the recent economic and political conflicts between Argentine social groups have been played out both along class lines and in zero-sum fashion. Thus, rather than offer it as a rigidly ideological explanation, I have undertaken this "conceptual-contextual" excursion in order to address three main concerns.

At a general level, I have attempted to show how the notion of state terror can be safely integrated into a broader theoretical framework without suffering appreciable loss of definition. More specifically, I have attempted to demonstrate the viability of a neo-Gramscian perspective as a conceptual framework for understanding the general context and circumstances of the Proceso. Finally, in doing so, I have sought to correct erroneous assumptions that Marxist thought offers little in the way of positive analytic constructs for understanding the nature of state terror in the modern world, particularly as it appeared in Argentina from 1976 to 1981.[46]

THE PROCESO: REGIME AND ECONOMIC PROGRAM

As a type of military authoritarian regime, the "Proceso de Reorganización Nacional" differed substantially from previous Argentine exercises in noncompetitive rule. Whereas other coups during the postwar era had at most resulted in the partial militarization of the apex of the Argentine state apparatus, with most of the uniformed personnel concentrated in defense-related agencies, as provincial governors, or in very high ranking positions,[47] here the extent of militarization of the upper echelons of the state apparatus was unprecedented in that it was virtually complete. With the exceptions of the Ministry of Economy (entirely controlled by civilians) and the Ministry of Education (in which the military shared management positions with like-minded civilians), every major branch of the state was staffed through the department level with military personnel.[48] Rank had its privileges. Flag officers (generals and admirals) were awarded cabinet and subcabinet position (ministers, secretaries, and under secretaries), while upper-rank field-grade officers (colonels, commodores, majors, and captains) were assigned positions down to the director of department level.

Control over lead agencies within the state apparatus, as well as provincial governorships, ambassadorships, and all other high-ranking posts, was divided among the three branches of the armed forces. The army assumed most of the internal control agencies, including the Ministries of Labor and Interior (the latter having jurisdiction over the federal police, customs, internal revenue, and border control agencies) and a variety of specialized intelligence units. The navy took control of the Ministries of Foreign Affairs and Social Welfare. The former was allocated to the navy on the objective criterion that it had the most external orientation of the three services. The latter, however, was awarded to the navy because it had been used by the Peronist regime as a major instrument for cultivating political support and had consequently become a bastion of patronage, political favoritism, and corruption. As the most consistently anti-Peronist of the armed forces,[49] the navy asked for and received authority to undertake the mission of drastically transforming the scope and character of the Ministry of Social Welfare, which included the Secretariats of Housing, Public Health, and Social Security. The air force, as the most politically neutral and professionally detached of the services, supervised the Ministry of Transportation. In an effort to promote interservice cooperation, many posts within each ministry and the provincial governments were further subdivided among the different military hierarchies.[50]

As for the three branches of the federal government, the legislature was disbanded and the judiciary placed under military control. Consequently, the role of the executive became paramount. As the branch under which all the centralized administrative agencies, semiautonomous entities, and public enterprises were grouped, the executive was formally divided among the three services in the form of the military junta of commanders-in-chief. The presidency, however, was reserved for an army officer, since he was the representative of the largest service. General Jorge Rafael Videla was named to the presidency, which was also significant because the main Argentine intelligence agency, SIDE (Servicio de Intelligencia del Estado) was under the the the direct control of the Office of the President. Although representatives of the other military branches were given positions within SIDE, it was the army that retained predominant influence over it during the Proceso.

Most significant in terms of this chapter is the fact that the sole branch of the state controlled entirely by civilians during the Proceso was the economic management branch, under the leadership of the Ministry of Economy. This included all nonmilitary public enterprises and the Secretariats of Commerce, Finance, Industry, and Agriculture, as well as the Central Bank. As such, the Ministry of Economy was the principal, when not sole, articulator of economic policy during this period. Both in that respect and in the broader division of the state apparatus among the three military services, the Proceso represented a considerable "deepening" over previous experiments in bureaucratic-authoritarian rule such as that which had governed Argentina from 1966 to 1973.[51]

This "deepening" was extended to the point where the Ministry of

Economy was placed under the control of a "liberal" economic team headed by former Minister of Economy, Secretary of Agriculture, officer of the large land owners' association (the Sociedad Rural Argentina), Business Council director, and academician, José Martínez de Hoz. More than a man of extensive credentials, Martínez de Hoz "symbolized through his personal interests the unity of agrarian, industrial and financial concerns."[52] As an heir to one of Argentina's best known landed aristocratic names, Martínez de Hoz also demonstrated through his array of activities the tendency of the landed elite to diversify its economic and political interests among a variety of sectors, in order to ensure that their economic and political fortunes were not exclusively tied to any one of them.[53] Once Martínez de Hoz was installed, his policies ensured that the interests of the landed elite took precedence over all others within the regime's economic program.

The convergence of the military hierarchy with the agro-export and transnational sectors responded to the fundamental logic of a shared conceptualization of Argentine society and the evils that afflicted it. For both the military hierarchy and the upper bourgeoisie, the roots of Argentina's demise as a world power harked back to the advent of Peronism as a political and social force in the mid-1940s. Consequently, the underlying premise of their rule was a shared dedication to the eradication of Peronism as a social and political force in Argentina, something that had been repeatedly attempted without success since the overthrow of the first Peronist regime in 1955.[54] More importantly, this alliance presaged the return—although this time in far more drastic and coercive fashion—to the "orthodox" stabilization policies that had been tried, again without much success, several times before.[55]

In essence, the military hierarchy believed that

the grave manifestations of violence, disorder, and conflict of the 1970's were nothing more than the product of a process of distortion within the national life begun in 1946. These distortions—ideological, political, economic—[were believed to be] contrary both to the security and natural potential of the country. This perception led the armed forces to converge in program, and partially in ideology, with the most hardline sectors of the traditional anti-Peronist groups, sectors of the "Liberal" persuasion.[56]

Upon assuming power, the military proposed three main objectives: (1) to eradicate Marxist subversion in all its forms from Argentine life; (2) to restructure and stabilize the national economy in a way that would eliminate and prevent future disruptions of the productive process, and that would make best use of those areas where Argentina enjoyed a "comparative advantage" in the world capitalist market; and (3) after the accomplishment of the first two objectives, to undertake a gradual, yet profound transformation of Argentine society proper, in order to put an end to Peronism and other corrupting influences that detracted from the traditional values of the nation. This included the return to a situation of respect for traditional authorities such as the military and the Catholic church, the elimination of corrupting influences such as feminism, nontraditional religions, and "delinquent" art forms, and the reassertion of the "proper" role of both men and women within the family and society at large.[57] Only in this way, it was believed, could the "cancer" afflicting Argentine society be entirely cured. Moreover, because of the gravity of the situation, the "medicine" to be applied would of necessity be harsh.

The organic perception of Argentine society as seriously ill and in desperate need of a drastic cure was shared, at an economic level, by the "liberals" who assumed control of the economic branch. They believed that a market freed from external interference was the most efficient allocator of resources within society. This belief went hand in hand with an individualistic political philosophy that was opposed to state involvement in social life beyond narrowly defined limits. Throughout the years preceding the Proceso, these individuals, generally identified with the agro-export sector on personal and economic grounds, maintained a position of strict opposition to the expansion of the state's role as expressed through activities such as employment programs, redistributive policies, extension of social welfare coverage, and sectoral development strategies. They were most strongly opposed to the state-sponsored drive toward industrial self-sufficiency that had begun in response to the Depression and World War II and had received its largest boost, along with the aforementioned social programs, during the first Peronist regime of 1946-1955.[58]

Their diagnosis of the economic situation at the time they assumed control of the economic management branch was that the major reason the Argentine economy stagnated was the distortion of relative domestic prices caused by the industrialization program and expansion of the state. That is, the introduction of import tariffs created a protective wall that allowed for the rise and subsequent consolidation of inefficient domestic industries. In parallel, the agro-export sector, which was the repository of the natural comparative advantages of the country, was discriminated against (via export taxes and domestic price controls) in order to serve demagogic, although inefficient, policies of income redistribution. To this were added the monopolistic practices of a corporative labor movement that conspired with the industrial bourgeoisie to structurally adjust prices to costs behind the tariff barriers. This made it possible for them to agree on wages and prices, which created a structural tendency toward inflation and low productivity. Successive governments, finally, wasted resources on an inflated public bureaucracy, inefficient public enterprises, and the maintenance of a huge, costly, and deteriorated social welfare system.[59]

With this diagnosis made, the economic team offered the following prescriptions: (1) to reduce real wages by at least 40 percent relative to those of the previous five years; (2) to eliminate taxes on agricultural exports; (3) progressively to reduce import tariffs; (4) to eliminate subsidies to non-traditional (industrial) exports; (5) to eliminate deficient social services such as health, housing, and sectoral promotion credits, and to raise prices for all public services; (6) to liberalize the exchange and finance markets; and (7) to reduce public expenditures, public employment, and the deficit by reorganizing the state apparatus (along more narrow lines) and by "re-privatizing" state enterprises.[60]

What this economic program was proposing to do was more than merely to stabilize the economy. Stabilization implies returning to the normal state of affairs after a period of abnormality. This project sought to reverse the 35-year logic of industrialization that had preceded it, and to "dismantle the productive structure erected as of the 1930's" in order to restore Argentina to its proper place as a "preindustrial country."[61] To this end, "The traditional program of the agrarian bourgeoisie appeared to be the most appropriate for radically changing the Argentine economic structure."[62]

Reaffirmation of a "liberal" economic outlook that championed the notion that Argentina had a comparative advantage in agro-exports was provided by the objective criteria of rising international prices for basic food products and the incidence of famine (particularly in the Horn of Africa) during the early seventies. All of this buttressed "liberal" arguments that the agro-export and agro-industrial sectors were the only productive activity that could objectively improve Argentina's position in the international economic market.[63] As Martínez de Hoz explained it,

The problem of the world food shortage will be one of the most important confronting humanity over the next few years. . . . Just as the oil exporting nations have become powerful in the international scene, so then will the countries that export food find themselves in the not so distant future in a similar position of predominance within the world concert of nations.[64]

The prescription of Martínez de Hoz and his "liberal" colleagues was awarded further credence by the prestige associated with one of the foremost practitioners of this economic philosophy, Milton Friedman, and by the fact that his policies were being followed with apparent success by the military regime in neighboring Chile. All of this made their program seem eminently rational and objectively advisable, which allowed them to justify the use of coercive measures in pursuit of their economic ends. For the military hierarchy, the "liberal" economic program provided a form of theoretical cement that justified brutal reassertion of its traditional authority over civil society. It offered a technical rationale for using terror as a means of restructuring class relations, since a highly exclusionary approach toward subordinant social groups was required for the repastoralization of the economy. The economic "turning back of the clock" provided a structural foundation for reducing the social arena along historically traditional, pre-Peronist lines. Military-enforced "societal" discipline, hence, was required in order to reimpose the traditional class hierarchy and authority lines that were the social parameters of this nostalgic vision.

Opening the Argentine domestic market was expected to stimulate industrial efficiency via increased international competition. It was believed that agro-industries such as food processing, meat packing, and cereal refineries would experience the most growth, as would related industries such as fishing enterprises and leather and textile manufacturers. On the other hand, heavily subsidized industries such as those involved in consumer durables and heavy manufacturing would be eliminated by foreign competition, which would decrease the financial burden on the public sector. To this would be added the elimination of many social services and the transfer of state enterprises to private hands. Coupled with the freeing of prices (including those of agricultural products) within the domestic market, these measures were deemed necessary for restoring some sense of order to the Argentine economy.

However, in a country that had a 35-year history of sustained industrialization, an extensive public sector providing a wide range of goods and services, and very large and well-organized urban industrial classes, particularly the domestic bourgeoisie and the organized labor movement, this required that coercive measures be applied in order to prevent their interference with the free operation of the market. For that reason, this economic model has also come to be known as "market fascism."[65] In order to fully understand the scope of this project, we must briefly describe some of the structural conditions with which it was confronted.

In Argentina a historically low birth rate has led to a relative scarcity of labor, which has contributed throughout its history to a low rate of unemployment.[66] As a result, labor unions in labor-intensive sectors enjoyed disproportionate strength, since there was no reserve labor pool to draw from in order to avoid meeting their demands. Most of the labor force and their institutional representatives were concentrated in those industries built up during the state-sponsored industrialization drive and in the public sector, be it the centralized state apparatus, state enterprises, or quasi-public entities. The economic program adopted by the Proceso was therefore oriented toward breaking the power of the unions, which was considered a vital step toward eliminating Peronism as an economic and political force (since the vast majority of the organized labor movement was Peronist).

The opening of the domestic market was designed to eliminate those very industries in which the unions had greatest strength. It also punished the "traitorous" domestic entrepreneurs who had allied themselves with the Peronists in previous years. Elimination of these industries would create a large pool of unemployed who could then be used as a reserve labor force with which to break the power of the unions in remaining industries. Moreover, elimination of industries in which the unions were strong displaced labor to the service and agro-industrial sectors, in which they were relatively weak. The more individualized forms of work in the service and agrarian sectors also helped break the sense of collective identity of the working classes, a fact that was reinforced by the elimination of union social service programs and public services expressly oriented toward them. The lowering of import barriers and overvaluation of the peso thus not only fostered competition within the Argentine market, but were also initial steps in the move to diminish the collective strength of the lower industrial classes. Obviously enough, these classes were not about to witness their own destruction without resistance. It was for this reason that coercion became an essential component of the regime's economic program.

Regrettably, it is impossible within the context of this chapter to delve further into the details of this exclusionary "liberal" economic program, particularly the causes and consequences of its ultimate failure. Since our interest is focused on the use of state terror as a complement to economic policy, the reader is advised to examine the specific evaluations of the economic measures implemented by the Proceso available elsewhere.[67] The major point to be underscored with regard to this economic program is that it contained a number of overlapping objectives that made the recourse to terror all the more advisable (in the eyes of those responsible for implementing it) in order to ensure full achievement of all of them. At a social level, the economic program sought to reestablish the dominance of the traditional landed and transnational sectors over the lower bourgeoisie and organized working classes that had enjoyed the favor of the preceding Peronist regime and had been challenging that dominance since the advent of Peronism in the mid-1940s. To do so, the Proceso proposed to reverse the industry-oriented strategy in vogue since 1930 and to reemphasize that area where Argentina was believed to hold its most natural comparative advantage: the agro-export sector and its attendant infrastructural and secondary industries. This was to be done by opening the domestic market to foreign competition, expanding export opportunities for primary goods, reducing the role of the state in the productive process in general and the provision of basic goods and services in particular, and allowing the price of agricultural products destined for export and home consumption to be determined by the international market.

These measures were taken in order to eliminate inefficient domestic industries and state activities where the lower bourgeoisie and organized labor were concentrated, which would displace labor toward less unionized and more "traditional" industries related to agriculture. In this way not only would the position of the agro-export sector be enhanced; the economic and political strength of the lower bourgeoisie and organized labor would be permanently broken as well, which was the first step toward reestablishing the "natural" hierarchy among socioeconomic classes that had been so seriously disrupted by the generalized disorder that characterized the period of "organic crisis" preceding the military coup d'état of March 1976.

Given the severity of this crisis, the scope of the regime's project, and the organizational strength of the groups to be subordinated and excluded, it becomes readily apparent why the systematic use of coercion was deemed vital for the success of the Proceso. It is to the various forms in which state terror was manifest, especially as they related to the economic program, that we now turn.

THE PROCESO AND THE USE OF STATE TERROR

Within days of the *golpe,* all political parties and activities were outlawed. Basic legal rights (habeas corpus, the right to be formally charged and receive a fair trial, and so on) were suspended. All labor unions (including the national labor confederation, the Confederación General de Trabajo or CGT) and the small businessman's association (the Confederación General Económica or CGE) were declared illegal as well, and their headquarters, social and welfare facilities, and financial resources were placed under military control. Strikes, slowdowns, lockouts, and other actions that impeded productivity were declared to be crimes against national security punishable by long prison sentences.[68] Collective bargaining was abolished, and a strict wage freeze in all sectors, as outlined earlier, was imposed. As a result, by late 1976 real wages had dropped an average of more than 50 percent relative to the last year of the Peronist regime, and the workers' share of the national income declined from 48.5 percent to just 29 percent. By 1981 this figure had only risen slightly above 30 percent, and real wages continued at levels half those of six years before.[69] In effect, the "rules of the game" were altered by closing the legal modes of access, redress, and representation normally used by the lower bourgeoisie and the labor movement to press their demands. Thus forced into institutional silence, these classes saw their material standard of living drop dramatically as domestic prices rose and their purchasing power diminished under the regime's exclusionary economic policies.

This was compounded by the "rationalization" of the state apparatus undertaken by the regime after it assumed power. In accord with a principle known as the "subsidiary of the state," a broad range of agencies were either compressed, eliminated, or transferred to the private sector, and their personnel similarly displaced or dismissed. A major instrument used to this effect by the "rationalization" program was a law that authorized dismissal of employees without indemnization or warning for reasons of "service," "national security," or "prescindibility."[70] Most of those fired on these grounds were union activists, as in the case of 300 state utility workers fired en masse in mid-1976.[71] By 1980 the regime claimed to have eliminated more than 200,000 employees from the public payroll.[72] Paralleling these reductions in the public work force were similar decreases in industrial employment, which was a product of the wave of bankruptcies among local enterprises that resulted from the opening of the domestic market to foreign competition. From 1975 to 1981 industrial employment decreased 26.9 percent.[73] Overall, industrial output declined 24 percent relative to the 1974 level, and a full 10 percent of the industrial work force (800,000 people) were without jobs by 1981.[74] Conversely, the agricultural sector maintained the moderate growth levels of previous years.[75] The areas that did show growth, as foreseen, were the financial and agro-industrial sectors.[76]

Elimination of collective bargaining facilitated more than the drop in wage levels. It also prevented workers from having a voice in determining work conditions (which, among other things, resulted in the regime increasing the minimum work week from 36 to 42 hours), allowed for increased salary differences among categories of workers, and prevented the domestic bourgeoisie from reaching wage agreements with the unions that would have undermined the regime's economic program.[77] Along with the outlawing of strikes and other union activities, direct military control of union facilities and resources, massive firings, and the displacement of labor to more individualized or less extensively unionized activities, this was designed to break the collective identity and sense of spiritual affinity of the social classes that were the lifeblood of the Peronist movement.[78] With these measures the Proceso hoped to eliminate the strength of these groups on four distinct, yet interrelated levels: as economic, corporative, social, and political actors.[79]

Eventually, a new Law of Professional Associations was passed that attempted to disarticulate the basic union structure that had existed under the previous regime.[80] Among other provisions, it outlawed the existing national labor federation (the CGT) and allowed for multiple unions per industry, level of activity, sector, and region. This was designed to break the "vertical" structure that was the organizational backbone of the Peronist-dominated labor movement. The new trade union law placed all union activities under strict regulations closely supervised by the Ministry of Labor, which was controlled by the army. In addition, the Registry of Employer's Associations, which had been the institutional referent for small businesses within the Ministry of Economy, was transferred to the Ministry of Labor as a department-level dependency of the National Directorate of Professional Associations.[81]

The significance of this move derives from the fact that it shifted responsibility for an employer's institutional referent to the exclusive jurisdiction of the agency responsible for administering organized labor interests. More importantly, it meant that this referent was being removed from the economic policy-making branch (where it had institutional access to the policy-making process) and placed in a control agency responsible for regulating the activities of groups further down the productive ladder. Coupled with the disbanding of the employers' organizational representative (the CGE), this measure formally marked the exclusion of the lower bourgeoisie as an economic and political actor. With regard to the labor movement, this objective was made explicit by then Secretary of Industry Juan Alemann: "With these policies we attempt to weaken the enormous power of the syndicates . . . [because] Argentina used to have a syndical power that was too strong. . . . [By] . . . weakening it we have created the basis for a future political opening."[82] At an economic, organizational, political, and ultimately social level, the Proceso systematically excluded the lower bourgeoisie and organized working classes.[83]

To the antiorganizational measures and economic constraints were added other subtle coercive restrictions designed to reduce the power of the excluded classes. Ceilings on rents and public transportation rates were lifted, which effectively dislocated large sectors of the working population. Rigid standards of appearance and dress were imposed in the workplace, at school, and on the street. Failure to comply with these standards, even for economic reasons, often resulted in dismissal or arrest. Applications for employment were scrutinized by security personnel in order to determine "subversive" backgrounds, including labor activism. A similar procedure was instituted in many schools, particularly those located in or near working-class districts. On the rationale that, in the reputed words of the military governor of Buenos Aires, General Ibérico Saint Jean, "subversion begins in culture and in education," a general clampdown on these activities was effected. Censorship of the media was universal, and bans on all literature, arts, and other forms of expression considered to be "subversive" were enacted. This included the works of Cortázar, García Marquez, Freud, Marx, Neruda, and Sinclair, among others. The entire educational system was overhauled in order to rid it of "class-oriented," so-called "secular humanist," and other "subversive" subjects, and to reestablish the primacy of traditional Catholic values. Sociology and political science were eliminated from many university curriculums on the grounds that they were "Marxist" sciences. Students and faculty suspected of harboring "subversive" tendencies were expelled and often arrested.[84]

The militarization of the state apparatus complemented these measures. Instead of social workers or professionals in various public service fields, those who sought the assistance of public agencies were confronted by military personnel interested in locating "subversives" and their sympathizers. This was especially evident in the Ministry of Social Welfare, where navy officers took a particularly dim view of the "parasitic" tendencies of the lower classes. A similar situation occurred in the previously union-operated welfare agencies (*obras sociales*), which saw their resources and property transferred to the army-controlled Ministry of Labor. In effect, at the most basic levels of interaction an air of oppression hung heavily over Argentine society.

Two areas that witnessed the promulgation of subtle coercive measures in systematic fashion were those of public health and social security, both located under the jurisdiction of the navy-controlled Ministry of Social Welfare. On a general plane, the amount of financial resources to these sectors was cut by more than half in the period 1976-1981.[85] The total number of beds provided by public hospitals decreased by more than 25 percent.[86] The expropriation of the union-operated social welfare network, including the union-operated hospitals that provided a major portion of the coverage for the organized working classes, furthered the curtailment of basic social services. Public hospitals were ordered to charge fees for basic diagnosis and treatment, the first time this had ever occurred. In lieu of the union social security programs, private retirement plans were offered at rates far above those of the unions. This effectively excluded a large portion of the labor movement from both types of coverage.[87]

As if these general restrictive measures were not enough, there were even more sinister applications of this type of coercion. Public hospitals and medical attention facilities in working-class neighborhoods were systematically closed, most often on the grounds that there was a "scarcity of demand." Simultaneously, people were turned away from those that remained open (often after lengthy trips to reach them) on the grounds that there was an "excess of demand," or because they could not afford the basic service charge demanded for what once had been free. Many hospitals were placed under the control of military doctors, who were more concerned with monitoring the patient population for possible "subversives" than with looking for signs of disease. Union affiliation, either directly or as a relative of a union member, was often used as a ground for denial of service.

Not surprisingly, disease and mortality rates among the working-class population increased dramatically under the Proceso.[88] At the same time, price controls on basic medical products were lifted, and regulations governing the fabrication and dispensation of medicine were relaxed, which forced the least advantaged sectors of the population to use more expensive and inferior (when not ineffectual) medical products in an effort to seek relief.

More generally, the National Integrated Health Plan established by the Peronist regime to ensure comprehensive medical coverage for the entire population was repealed. In its place were offered a number of private health plans established by profit-oriented medical enterprises and insurance agencies. However, the detrimental effects of the regime's economic program on working-class incomes made it impossible to afford private coverage. In turn, the lower bourgeoisie saw a greater part of their income directed toward medical attention, which had an adverse impact on their overall standard of living. In effect, the Proceso removed the minimum health and welfare "floors" previously provided by the state as a form of punishment for those groups it believed to be the causes of the Argentine malaise. Both materially and physiologically, this meant that the lower bourgeoisie and organized working classes were made to pay a heavy price as a consequence of their economic, political, and social exclusion.

The excluded sectors initially attempted to resist the moves against them. In 1976 and 1977, for example, there were over 500 strikes and numerous other protests called against the regime's economic policies.[89] Likewise, certain parts of the media voiced concern over the scope and direction of the repressive campaign.[90] The answer to these and all other forms of dissent, an answer that came to identify the Proceso as unprecedentedly brutal, was an extremely high level of violence. Though this violence touched all sectors of the population, it was most harshly felt by the groups that were viewed as antagonistic or "culpable" by the regime.

If the economic exclusion, political and organizational restrictions, and denial of basic public services represented the rational, systematic, and more subtle coercive aspects of the "liberal" prescription for transforming Argentine society, then the "dirty war" against subversion represented an emotional, cathartic venting of accumulated rage on the part of the military and its allies against those held responsible for the national decline. Hence no rules of war, much less civility, conditioned the unleashing of the repressive apparatus. The end—eradication of subversion—justified any means taken on its behalf. Here too, the campaign of state terror was both rational and systematic.

The armed forces began the "active" part of the state terror campaign by consolidating their hold on society, first by militarily defeating the guerrillas in the northern provinces in 1976-1977 and by simultaneously occupying all major cities and towns. Curfews were declared, restrictions on pedestrian and vehicular traffic imposed (particularly near government and military installations), massive identification checks were instituted, and random searches of individuals and raids on public areas and private property were conducted frequently and without warning. Factories and schools were occupied by military personnel looking for subversives, assemblies of more than a dozen people for nonfamily or non–government-sanctioned reasons were prohibited, and soldiers patrolled the streets, where they were allowed to enforce these security measures as they deemed fit. These were, in the words of Adolfo Perez-Esquivel, "troops of occupation within their own country."

It was in the activities of paramilitary death squads, however, that the climate of terror was most energetically sowed and reached its most vicious expression. Some of these squads were odd mixtures of civilian and military personnel—most notably the Argentine Anti-Communist Alliance (the infamous "Triple-A"), which had been organized under the previous regime by right-wing Peronists under the leadership of former Social Welfare Minister José Lopez Rega. Most, however, were more formally connected to the state by virtue of their being specialized branches of existing military units. Whether formally or informally attached to the state, these decentralized commandos of a half-dozen heavily armed men operated with nearly complete autonomy and in highly amorphous, overlapping jurisdictions. In addition to those of the military high command, each service branch, military district, police district, and police station had its own "operative" unit. Working day and night out of unmarked cars and trucks, these groups would kidnap from a variety of locations—home, school, restaurants, theaters, even churches—individuals previously targeted by the various intelligence services as suspect. Passersby or family members who witnessed the abductions would often be kidnapped as well, or seized later, when they went to report them.

The abducted would first be taken to local detention centers, where they were physically tortured via beatings, electric shock, prolonged immersion in rancid water, excrement, or other vile liquids, burning, mutilation, rape, and attacks by trained dogs. They would also be psychologically tortured in the form of forced denial of sleep, exposure to the torture of other prisoners (often their own relatives), and subjection to prolonged periods of isolation and sensory deprivation, extreme temperature and noise levels, various combinations thereof, and simulated executions.[91]

While many individuals found innocent, or guilty of "minor" infractions, gained their freedom eventually, many others were subsequently transferred to the secret detention centers operated by the different services, SIDE, and the Federal Police. Some of the more notorious sites were located at the Naval Mechanics School (ESMA) in Buenos Aires, at the army installations in Campo de Mayo outside of the capital, and at the Federal Police barracks on the road to the international airport of Ezeiza. Dozens of other centers were located around the country, especially in and around the industrial cities of Córdoba and Rosario. Once in these centers, the prisoners would again be subjected to various combinations of torture while being interrogated, often under the supervision of military doctors who determined their pain tolerance and threshold levels. There were even specialists in different types of torture, such as the infamous "crow" or "white angel of death," Lieutenant Carlos Astiz of the Naval Mechanics School. Astiz was known for his penchant for "turning" prisoners by torturing women and children in front of their families. He subsequently became better known for being the commander of the Argentine force that invaded the South Georgia Islands, thereby starting the Falklands/Malvinas conflict.[92]

After an indefinite period of incarceration without any formal charge having been brought against them, most of these prisoners were killed, either by summary execution or by being sedated, loaded onto aircraft, and dumped out over remote areas and the Atlantic Ocean. Recently, soldiers involved in these dumpings have come forth to reveal that hundreds of victims were disposed of in this and other similarly gruesome and systematic fashions.[93] To cement the bonds of loyalty (and culpability) tying them together, all members of these squads were required to directly involve themselves in the torture and murder of suspects. In some cases "blood pacts" were confirmed by summarily executing prisoners in front of the rest of the squad, as was the case with military officers in the "Sun of May" (Sol de Mayo) lodge operated in Córdoba.

Although the exact figures have yet to be determined, about 10,000 to 15,000 people died at the hands of these military and paramiltary groups; 15,000 to 30,000 disappeared after being abducted and are presumed dead; and another 25,000 were subjected to torture before being released. In contrast, leftist guerrilla and terrorist groups killed less than 5,000 people before being defeated. At most, only 20 pecent of those victimized by right-wing death squads and miltary forces were actively involved in Marxist sub-version; the rest were not directly involved with terrorist or guerrilla groups. The ramifications of the "dirty war" do not end with the acknowl-edgment of "excesses" that led to the disappearance of innocents. During the past few years a number of children of "disappeared" persons have been found in adoptive homes, in many cases those of military personnel in Argen-tina or located abroad. Rather than the "excesses" of an "overzealous" few (as the military leaders have maintained that it was), the "dirty war" provided the framework in which the regime's social transformation project could begin. In this regard, it was a deliberate, extensive, and systematic process of societal subjugation.

It is Gramsci who once again provides perspective on these paramilitary activities: "In the present struggles . . . it often happens that a weakened State machine is like a flagging army: commandos, or private armed organi-zations, enter the field to accomplish two tasks—to use illegality, while the State appears to remain within legality, and thereby to reorganize the State itself."[94] That is to say, "Is the civil guerrilla struggle," these paramilitary groups (in Gramsci's time incarnate in the *squadristi* of the Fascist movement) are "not against the State, but aligned with it."[95] In allowing right-wing paramilitary death squads to roam freely and act with impunity, and by disavowing any formal connection with them (such as by claiming that, at most, any "excesses" were the work of anonymous groups exacting "justice" against leftist subversives), the military regime of the Proceso could continue to justify the need for the legal restrictions on political and other forms of social activity as a means of consolidating the superordinate authority of the state in the face of these external "threats." This also per-mitted it to restructure the state apparatus and implement the more subtle coercive measures deemed essential by the "liberal" theoreticians for the fundamental transformation of Argentine society.

Who, then, were the bulk of those victimized by the "active" part of the state terror campaign? Not surprisingly, the majority of the victims of the "dirty war" were located among the excluded social groups. Forty percent of all those who "disappeared" were trade union activists and union members. Nineteen percent came from other occupations that were directly connected in one way or another with the excluded groups, particularly journalists, medical doctors, and teachers.[96] The remainder were for the most part students. Again, the vast majority of these people were not directly connected with guerrilla or terrorist groups.

The extent of the terror campaign against organized labor is well summarized by Francisco Delich: "[Union] leaders and activists were killed, disappeared, imprisoned, and exiled . . . they numbered in the thousands. There were executions in the factories, and physical and psychological violence designed to terrorize the workers."[97] Because of these actions, many union members were forced to quit their jobs in order to save themselves.[98] As mentioned earlier, strikes and other forms of protest were physically suppressed, most often by sending troops into the factories, where they beat and arrested leaders and forced the rest of the workers back to the job.[99] Many times, as in the case of Public Utility Workers Union president Oscar Smith, vocal protest resulted in permanent "disappearance." Most of the union members who disappeared or were imprisoned came from traditionally strong Peronist unions with histories of politicization and activism, such as the Metalworkers, Autoworkers, Mechanics, Textile, and Public Transportation unions.[100] The regime's reach even extended to union activities overseas, as in the case of the dismissal and intimidation of union members of the national airline (Aéreolineas Argentinas) working in the United States.[101]

While less extensive than the campaign against organized labor (since the lower bourgeoisie was less organized and ideologically united as a group), state terror was selectively applied against the subordinate fractions of the bourgeoisie in order to preclude their interference with the economic program. Leaders of the outlawed CGE were arrested and held for indefinite periods, others were forced into exile, and many were the targets of death threats, beatings, and other intimidating acts. One particularly nasty aspect of the state terror applied against the lower bourgeoisie was the use of anti-Semitism. While Jews occupied a significant position within this class, they received a disproportionately high amount of the terror meted out against it. This was particularly true of Jewish merchants living or working in the Province of Buenos Aires, which was under the control of a faction in the army that had well-known fascist sympathies and viewed the decline of Western civilization as part of an insidious plot by a global Marxist-Zionist conspiracy.[102]

At another level, intellectuals not linked to the regime became the target of an intense ideological examination that was designed to locate and weed out those with Marxist sympathies. Many professions—journalism, psychoanalysis, and law in particular—saw wholesale purges. Moral and ideological censorship covered the full spectrum of creative activity, which significantly curtailed intellectual growth and diminished the free flow of information in society. Furtive behavior, especially reading and writing between the lines, therefore became the primary creative focus within civil society. Finally, the adverse impact of the economic program on their individual fortunes forced thousands of middle-class Argentines into voluntary economic exile. Thus, although relatively selective compared to the coercion directed against the labor movement, this varied application of state terror had its desired effect: the lower fractions of the bourgeoisie were divided and cowed into acquiescent silence or opportunistic support for the regime.

This application of state terror had a dramatic impact on the whole of Argentine society, but particularly on the excluded social groups. The magnitude and intensity of the coercive campaign, in all of its guises, significantly altered the basic forms of interaction among members of these groups. On the one hand, in Gramsci's words, the Proceso "juridically abolished even the modern forms of autonomy of the subordinate classes [such as] parties, trade unions, and cultural associations," and sought to "incorporate them into the activity of the State: the legal centralization of all national life in the hands of the ruling group."[103] On the other hand, at an individual level the "active" part of the state terror campaign imposed a degree of fear that affected the basic textures of sociability within the excluded groups. The individuals who comprised these groups—that is, individual working-class and lower middle-class people—were not only divorced from the sources of power, but also deprived of basic rights and subjected to the continual violence of those who held power. The notion of social power, at least as it was manifest in identification and participation with collective groups, became an alien concept for each of these individuals. They were forcibly alienated by overwhelming fear from the rest of their peers. Group identification, since it was a primary reason for individual victimization, was abandoned in favor of isolation and uninvolvement.

This was most evident in the generalized attitude of *no te metas* (don't get involved) that characterized Argentine society during this period. Such alienation lay at the core of the state and yet was a product of the process of desocialization and identity regression produced by the pervasive atmosphere of fear and terror. It was, in effect, an "infantilization" of each individual member of the excluded groups. Isolated, frightened, powerless, and with no recognizable rights, the individual was deprived of the basic attributes of a "mature" social being.[104]

It was this "infantilization" of individual members of the excluded groups that was the ultimate goal of the Proceso because it ensured the fundamental rupture of the collective identities of those who stood in the way of the transformation of Argentine society and were held mainly responsible for the "organic crisis" that had brought Argentina to the brink of collapse. In a sense, the entire society was reduced to the level of a child's nightmare: better obey, comply, and behave, or "te van a agarrar los hombres del Falcon" (the men in the Ford Falcons will get you).[105] In a very real sense, then, during the Proceso Argentine society reverted to its most primitive form along with the state apparatus.

CONCLUSION

The "Proceso de Reorganización Nacional" was an exercise in *dominio* characterized by the systematic application of state terror to complement an economic program that pursued a particular social vision with an overt class content. The campaign of state terror spanned a range of manifestations that sought to cover the full spectrum of Argentine social life. This included legal and political restrictions designed to weaken the organizational capacity of the excluded social groups to defend their collective interests, "mere" coercion and repression used to enforce these restrictions against those who attempted to defy them, and wholesale enforcement terrorism that sought to disrupt the very fabric of society and break the individual capacity and will of excluded group members to resist the regime's moves against them. Underscoring this broad range of state terror was a basic class content, both in regard to perpetrators and their victims, as well as in its systematic method and uniformity of direction. State terror was, in effect, applied systematically, rationally, multivariously, and extensively in pursuit of a specific socioeconomic project prescribed by the social groups dominant at that time: the agro-export and transnational elites, along with their allies in the military hierarchy.

As an exercise in *dominio,* the Proceso was both a sophisticated and most crude form of authoritarian rule. Moreover, it was a salient manifestation, if not ultimate expression, of the zero-sum nature of economic and political competition that has plagued Argentina throughout the postwar years. Most importantly, it represented a turn backward to the most egotistical, most arrogant, and darkest side of the Argentine psyche. For this reason, it is appropriate that we leave Gramsci with the last word. Whatever its purported intentions, the Proceso ultimately revealed itself to be "the government of an economic class that did not know how . . . to exercise a hegemony beyond dictatorship. . . . It was a reactionary, repressive movement."[106]

NOTES

This chapter had its genesis during my stay as a visiting scholar at the Center for Study of State and Society (CEDES) in Buenos Aires, Argentina, in the fall of 1983. I am grateful to the CEDES staff for their gracious and stimulating hospitality during the course of my visit. I would also like to acknowledge the assistance of Carlos Hugh Acuña in the subsequent collection of data and exchange of ideas that shaped the initial contours of the chapter. Finally, I must thank Margaret Weir and the Center for the Study of Industrial Societies at the University of Chicago for providing congenial work space during the research phase of the study.

1. The phrase "dichotomy of agrarian and industrial sectors" is offered by J. Girling, "Thailand in Gramscian Prespective," *Pacific Affairs* 57, no. 3 (Fall 1984): 386.

2. Such an interpretation is not confined to this particular instance. A number of Latin American analysts have recently used Gramsci's thought to examine political conflict and change in the region, particularly as it applies to national state formation and development. See, for example, E. Laclau, "Teorías marxistas del estado: Debate y perspectivas," and F. Rojas H., "Estado capitalista y aparato estatal," both in N. Lechner, ed., *Estado y política en América Latina* (Mexico, D.F.: Siglo XXI, 1981); M. Kaplan, *Aspectos del estado en América Latina* (Mexico, D.F.: UNAM, 1981), chap. 1; and J. C. Portantiero, "Gramsci para latino-americanos," in C. Sirvent, ed., *Gramsci y la política* (Mexico, D.F.: UNAM, 1980).

3. A. Gramsci, *Selections from Political Writings, 1910-1920,* selected and edited by Quintin Hoare, translated by John Mathews (London: Lawrence and Wishart, 1977), p. 191.

4. The chaotic situation during the last year of Isabel Perón's government is well summarized by Wayne C. Smith, "The Return of Peronism," in F. Turner and J. E. Miguens, eds., *Juan Perón and the Reshaping of Argentina* (Pittsburgh: University of Pittsburgh Press, 1983), pp. 97-146. For a more detailed look at the situation that has a greater sense of immediacy, consult the Argentine daily newspapers *Buenos Aires Herald* (for an account in English), *Clarín,* and *La Nación* for the period July 1974-March 1976.

5. A. Gramsci, *Selections from the Prison Notebooks,* edited and translated by Quintin Hoare and Geoffrey Norwell Smith (New York: International Publishers, 1971), p. 210.

6. Ibid.

7. "The greater the threat level, the greater the polarization and visibility of the class content of the conflicts that precede implantation of the BA [bureaucratic-authoritarian regime]. . . . a higher threat level lends more weight, within the armed forces, to the 'hard line' groups. The end result is "to provoke a more obvious and drastic defeat of the popular sector and its allies." G. A. O'Donnell, "Reflections on the Patterns of Change in the Bureaucratic-Authoritarian State," *Latin American Research Review* 13, no. 1 (Spring 1978): 7. It should be noted that O'Donnell includes the Proceso as a type of bureaucratic-authoritarian regime.

8. Gramsci, *Selections from the Prison Notebooks,* p. 215.

9. In fairness to Lopez, it is probable that he would equate "organic crisis" with his category of "major civil war." The fact is, however, that a period of organic crisis can exist that leads to coercive regime change without first transiting through a full-fledged civil war. Notwithstanding the high level of violence and extent of organization of guerrilla groups in Argentina during the period immediately preceding the military's assumption of power, this challenge never reached the proportions of those confronting, say, Somoza in Nicaragua in 1979, and the outcome in any case was exactly the reverse. See G. A. Lopez, "A Scheme for the

Analysis of Government as Terrorist," in Michael Stohl and George A. Lopez, eds., *The State as Terrorist: The Dynamics of Governmental Violence and Repression* (Westport, Conn.: Greenwood Press, 1984), pp. 59-62.

10. One need only to think back on the genocidal practices of a variety of regimes spread throughout history to get an idea of the prevalence of "official" terror in human society. On this general point and its derivations in the late twentieth century, see M. Stohl and G. A. Lopez, "Introduction" in *The State as Terrorist,* pp. 3-7.

11. Ibid., p. 7.

12. This is the third definition of terrorism given in *The American Heritage Dictionary of the English Language* (Boston: Houghton Mifflin, 1969), p. 1330, cited and emphasized by Stohl and Lopez, "Introduction," p. 7.

13. Gramsci, *Selections from the Prison Notebooks,* p. 57.

14. Perry Anderson, "The Antinomies of Antonio Gramsci," *New Left Review,* no. 100 (1977): 32. "Monopoly of legitimate violence over a given territory" of course refers to Max Weber's basic definition of the state.

15. A. Gramsci, *Letters from Prison,* selected, translated, and introduced by Lynne Lawner (London: Jonathan Cape, 1975), p. 204 (letter written to his sister-in-law Tania from the penal colony of Turi, September 7, 1931).

16. Anderson, "The Antinomies of Antonio Gramsci," p. 26.

17. Stohl and Lopez, "Introduction," p. 7.

18. Steven I. Jackson and Duncan Snidal, "Coercion as a Policy Instrument in Dependent States" (Paper presented at the International Studies Association annual meeting, March 19-22, 1980), p. 25.

19. A. Gramsci, *L'ordine nuovo, 7: Il materialismo storico,* pp. 199-200, cited in Gwyn A. Williams, "The Concept of 'Egemonia' in the Thought of Antonio Gramsci: Some Notes on Interpretation," *Journal of the History of Ideas* 21, no. 4 (December 1960): 594.

20. Williams, "Concept of 'Egemonia' in the Thought of Antonio Gramsci," p. 591.

21. For a good summary of the evolution of the concept of hegemony in Marxist thought, see Anderson, *The Antinomies of Antonio Gramsci,* pp. 15-27.

22. Williams, "Concept of 'Egemonia' in the Thought of Antonio Gramsci, " p. 587.

23. Gramsci, *Selections from the Prison Notebooks,* p. 161.

24. Sergio Zermeño, "Las fracturas del estado en America Latina," in Lechner, *Estado y política en America Latina,* p. 69.

25. See Rojas H., "Estado capitalista y aparato estatal," pp. 158-171.

26. Jackson and Snidal, "Coercion as a Policy Instrument in Dependent States," p. 26.

27. John Sloan, "State Repression and Enforcement Terrorism in Latin America," in Stohl and Lopez, *The State as Terrorist,* p. 83.

28. W. L. Adamson, *Hegemony and Revolution* (Berkeley and Los Angeles: University of California Press, 1980), p. 86.

29. Rojas H., "Estado capitalista y aparato estatal," p. 171. On Gramsci's notion of "relation of forces," see Gramsci, *Selections from the Prison Notebooks,* pp. 180-185.

30. Rojas H., "Estado capitalista y aparato estatal," p. 157.

31. Ibid., p. 166.

32. Williams, "Concept of 'Egemonia' in the Thought of Antonio Gramsci," p. 591.

33. Sloan, "State Repression and Enforcement Terrorism in Latin America," p. 83.

34. Alain Rouquié, "El poder militar en la Argentina de hoy: Cambio y continuidad," in P. Waldmann and E. Garzón Valdez, eds., *El poder militar en la Argentina, 1976-1981* (Buenos Aires: Editorial Galerna, 1983), p. 73.

35. Christine Buci-Glucksmann, *Gramsci and the State* (London: Lawrence and Wishart, 1980), p. 91.

36. G. A. O'Donnell, "Tensions in the Bureaucratic-Authoritarian State," in D. Collier, ed., *The New Authoritarianism in Latin America* (Princeton: Princeton University Press, 1979), p. 287.

37. According to O'Donnell, "bureaucratic-authoritarianism" is a form of rule that has as its principal social base the military and upper bourgeoisie, is directed by specialists in technology and coercion, and involves the political and economic exclusion of the popular sectors, suppression of basic rights of citizenship for much of the population, increased transnationalization of the productive structure, and the depoliticization of social issues. See ibid., pp. 291-294, for a more precise definition.

38. Nicos Poulantzas, "The Problem of the Capitalist State," in R. Blackburn, ed., *Ideology in the Social Sciences* (New York: Pantheon Books, 1972), p. 246.

39. Dante Caputo, "Balance provisorio," in Waldmann and Garzón Valdez, *El poder militar en la Argentina, 1976-1981,* p. 129.

40. Antonio Gramsci, *Quaderni del carcere,* 4 vols., edited by V. Gerratana (Turin: Einaudi, 1975), notebook 7, fragment 80, cited in Buci-Glucksmann, *Gramsci and the State,* p. 99.

41. Alain Rouquié, interview published in *Resumen de la actualidad,* no. 88 (March 23, 1983): 23. For a deeper look at the antecedents and characteristics of this military "colonization" of the Argentine state during the Proceso, see his *Pouvoir militaire et société politique en la Republica Argentina* (Paris: Presses de la Fondation Nationale des sciences Politiques, 1978), also published in Spanish under the title *Poder militar y sociedad política en la Republica Argentina* (Buenos Aires: Siglo XXI, 1982).

42. Poulantzas, "Problem of the Capitalist State," p. 246.

43. The size of the domestic bourgeoisie was first expanded by the import-substitution industrialization program begun before and accelerated by the Peronist regime of 1946-1955. The primary instrument of expansion was exponential growth in the national state bureaucracy and public enterprises. See Julio Mafud, *Sociologia del Peronismo* (Buenos Aires: Editorial Américalee, 1972), especially pp. 131-132. On the growth of the public sector in Argentina, see Juan Lazarte, *La Burocracia . . . sentido y significado* (Buenos Aires: Catedra Lisandro de la Torre, 1960). For an orthodox view of the role played by the import-substitution industrialization program in Argentine economic history, see Carlos Diaz Alejandro, *Essays on the Economic History of the Argentine Republic* (New Haven: Yale University Press, 1970), pp. 67-140.

44. Poulantzas, "Problem of the Capitalist State," p. 247.

45. For a detailed look at the regime's "organic" view of Argentine society as

suffering from the "cancers" of subversion, economic instability, and social disorder, see Republica Argentina, *Documentos básicos y báses políticas de las fuerzas armadas para el Proceso de Reorganización Nacional* (Buenos Aires: Junta Militar de la Nación, 1980). Also see "Acta fijando el propósito y los objetivos básicos para el Proceso de Reorganización Nacional," *Boletín Oficial,* March 29, 1976.

46. I do not, however, claim exclusive market on this point of view. I do believe that better understanding of a given situation is achieved by presenting alternative and hopefully complementary conceptualizations of the problem. For a view that holds that the Marxist tradition deals inadequately with the notion of political repression, see John F. McCamant, "Governance without Blood: Social Science's Antiseptic View of Rule; or, The Neglect of Political Repression," in Stohl and Lopez, *The State as Terrorist,* pp. 25-29.

47. See, for example, the personnel characteristics of the Onganía regime (1966-1970) offered in Mariano C. Grondona, "La estructura cívico-militar del nuevo estado argentino," *Aportes,* no. 6 (October 1967): 66-76; and the personnel descriptions of the regimes that governed from 1955 to 1969 offered in Jorge Niosi, *Los empresarios y el estado argentino (1955-1969)* (Buenos Aires: Siglo XXI, 1974).

48. Data on the extent to which the state apparatus was militarized during the Proceso is found in Paul G. Buchanan, "Regime Change and State Development in Postwar Argentina" (Ph.D. diss., Department of Political Science, University of Chicago, 1985). Also see Oscar Oszlak, "Políticas publicas y regimenes políticos: Reflexiones a partir de algunas experiencias latino-americanas," *Estudios CEDES* 3, no. 2 (1980): 28-33; and Rouquié, *Poder militar y sociedad política en la Republica Argentina.*

49. The anti-Peronism of the Argentine armed forces, and the navy in particular, arose from the social origins and mores of the military hierarchy (in the case of the navy traditionally divided between the landed aristocracy and Buenos Aires–based bourgeoisie) and was compounded by their fundamental disagreement with Perón over the composition and course of Argentine society as well as the character of his rule. Despite divisions within the military hierarchy over the Peronist "problem" (especially within the army), this stance has remained unchanged under non-Peronist regimes throughout the postwar period. On the social origins of the Argentine military hierarchy, see José Luis de Imaz, *Los que mandan* (Buenos Aires: EUDEBA, 1964), pp. 45-84.

50. Oszlak, "Políticas publicas y regimenes políticos," p. 29; Rouquié, *Poder militar y sociedad política en la Republica Argentina.* For a more specific look at national health and labor administration under the Proceso, see Buchanan, "Regime Change and State Development in Postwar Argentina," chaps. 3 and 4.

51. For an initial description of the role of civilian "technocrats" within a bureaucratic-authoritarian regime, specifically the regime that ruled Argentina from 1966 to 1973, see Guillermo A. O'Donnell, *Modernization and Bureaucratic-Authoritarianism: Studies in South American Politics* (Berkeley and Los Angeles: University of California Press, 1973, and his 1960-1973, *El estado burocrático-autoritario* (Buenos Aires: Editorial del Belgrano, 1982).

52. Ronaldo Munck, *Politics and Dependency in the Third World: The Case of Latin America* (London: Zed Books, 1984), p. 298.

53. For a good description of this diversification and the reasons for it, see

A. Rouquié, "Hegemonia militar, estado, y dominación social," and R. Sidicaro, "Poder y crísis de la gran burgesia agraria argentina," both in Rouquié, ed., *Argentina hoy* (Mexico: Siglo XXI, 1982).

54. The bibliography documenting these attempts is too extensive to mention in its totality, but a good idea of their general thrust can be obtained from O'Donnell, *Modernization and Bureaucratic-Authoritarianism;* Gary Wynia, *Argentina in the Postwar Era* (Albuquerque: University of New Mexico Press, 1978); and Joseph Page, *Perón: A Biography* (New York: Random House, 1983).

55. On both the orientation of the "liberal" economic team and the role of "orthodox" stabilization policies under bureaucratic-authoritarian regimes, see O'Donnell, *Modernization and Bureaucratic-Authoritarianism.* For a good examination of previous economic stabilization programs in Argentina as they related to the use of repression, see David Pion-Berlin, "The Political Economy of State Repression in Argentina," in Stohl and Lopez, *The State as Terrorist,* pp. 99-122.

56. Adolfo Canitrot, "La disciplina como objectivo de la política económica. Un ensayo sobre el programa económico del gobierno argentino desde 1976," *Desarrollo económico* 19, no. 76 (January–March 1980): 454.

57. On the objectives of the Proceso, as well as the perceived need to return to the "traditional" values of Argentine society, see "Acta fijando el propósito y los objetivos básicos para el Proceso de Reorganización Nacional" and *Documentos básicos y báses políticas de las fuerzas armadas para el Proceso de Reorganización Nacional.* For a view of what this meant in terms of society itself, with specific reference to the educational system, see A. Spitta, "El 'Proceso de Reorganización Nacional' de 1976 a 1981: los objectivos básicos y su realización práctica," in Waldmann and Garzón Valdez, *El poder militar en la Argentina, 1976-1981,* especially pp. 90-100.

58. For a general look at the move toward industrialization and its ramifications, see Diaz Alejandro, *Essays on the Economic History of the Argentine Republic,* pp. 67-140, 208-276, 309-350. Also see Wynia, *Argentina in the Postwar Era,* for a good general examination of the relationship between economic policy and political behavior during the postwar period.

59. This discussion of the diagnosis and prescriptions offered by the "liberal" economic team during the Proceso is based on Canitrot, "La Disciplina como objectivo de la política económica," pp. 458-461.

60. Ibid., pp. 459-460.

61. Aldo Ferrer, "La economia argentina bajo una estrategia 'preindustrial,' 1976-1981," in Rouquié, *Argentina hoy,* p. 105.

62. Sidicaro, "Poder y crísis de la gran burgesia agraria argentina," p. 89.

63. On this point, see ibid., pp. 90-91, and Rouquié, "Hegemonia militar, estado, y dominación social," pp. 48-49.

64. José A. Martínez de Hoz, speech given on April 21, 1976, cited in *La Prensa,* April 3, 1976.

65. The term comes from P. Samuelson, in a speech given to open the 60th World Economic Congress in Mexico City, August 4, 1980, and cited in F. Delich, "Desmovilización social, reestructuración obrera, y cambio sindical," in Waldmann and Garzón Valdez, *El poder militar en la Argentina, 1976-1981,* p. 104.

66. On the composition and distribution of the labor force in Argentina, see Juan

José Llach, "Estructura ocupacional y dinámica del empleo en la Argentina: Sus pecularidades, 1947-1970," *Desarrollo económico* 18 (October–December 1978): 539-592; and his "Estructura y dinámica del empleo en la Argentina desde 1947," CEIL, *Documento de trabajo,* no. 2 (1978).

67. Besides the collections of essays in Rouquié, *Argentina hoy,* and Waldmann and Garzón Valdez, *El poder militar en la Argentina, 1976-1981,* see Canitrot, "La disciplina como objectivo de la política económica," and his "Teoria y practica del liberalismo. Política antiiflacionaria y apertura económica en la Argentina, 1976-1981," *Desarrollo económico* 21, no. 82 (July–September 1981): 131-190.

68. The primary measures enacted to this effect were Decrees 9, 10, and 11 of March 24, 1976 (which suspended union activities and outlawed all unions and the CGE), Law 21, 261 of March 24, 1976 (which declared illegal all strikes, work stoppages, and so on), Law 21, 270 of March 1976 (which placed over 100 unions under military control), Law 21, 271 of March 24, 1976 (which placed CGT resources under military control), and Law 21, 356 of July 22, 1976 (which declared illegal all unions, congresses, and elections). For these and other related measures, see *Boletín de legislación* 18 and 19 (1976 and 1977).

69. Data on real wages comes from the Instituto Nacional de Estadistica y Censo (INDEC), published in *Clarín Internacional,* October 31, 1982, sec. 2, p. 4; data on workers' percentage of the national income comes from INDEC, cited in *Clarín Internacional,* December 5, 1982, p. 6. It should be noted that Argentine government figures on these economic indicators and others such as unemployment rates during this period are widely believed to be seriously underestimated.

70. Law 21, 274 of March 29, 1976, *Boletín de legislación* 18, no. 4 (April 1976): 119-120. On the effects of this measure and others on public employee unions, see L. E. Dimase, "La política economico-social inagurada en 1976 y sus efectos en los sindicatos que nuclean trabajadores de empresas estatales," *Revista CIAS* 30, no. 301 (April 1981): 33-61.

71. *Argentina Outreach* 1 (November–December 1976): 1-3 has a good description of the events surrounding the firing of these workers.

72. José A. Martínez de Hoz, speech given on January 2, 1980, cited in F. Delich, "Después del diluvio, la clase obrera," in Rouquié, *Argentina hoy,* p. 137. Also see Martínez de Hoz, 1976-80, *Báses para una Argentina moderna* (Buenos Aires: Ministerio de Economia, 1981), pp. 39-58, for a more detailed discussion of the "rationalization" program.

73. Figures derived from INDEC, cited in *Clarín Internacional,* September 20, 1982, sec. 2, p. 7.

74. Ferrer, "La economia argentina bajo una estrategia 'preindustrial,' 1976-1981," pp. 115-116, 117.

75. The growth rate was 2.1 percent annually. See ibid., p. 116.

76. Jorge Schwarzer, "Estrategia industrial y grandes empresas: el caso argentino," *Desarrollo económico* 18 (October–December 1978): 341; Rouquié, "Hegemonia militar, estadó, y dominación social," pp. 48-49.

77. On this point, see Delich, "Después del diluvio, la clase obrera," pp. 138-139; and A. Canitrot, "La disciplina como objectivo de la política económica," pp. 465-466.

78. I am indebted to Carlos Hugo Acuña for clarifying this point.

79. The notion of social groups operating at four different levels, particularly the organized working class, is derived from Delich, "Después del diluvio, la clase obrera," p. 137.

80. Law 22, 105 of November 7, 1979, *Boletín de legislación* 21, no. 2 (July-December 1979): 181-190.

81. Decree 2, 562 of October 17, 1979, *Boletín de legislación* 21, no. 2 (July–December 1979): 197. It was not entirely coincidental that this measure was passed on the day traditionally celebrated by Peronists as their national holiday (October 17, 1945, being the date Perón was freed from prison after a daylong demonstration on his behalf in front of the government house by a huge crowd of working-class supporters).

82. Juan Alemann, statement published in *La Prensa,* October 23, 1979.

83. For a good examination of the full scope of these measures, particularly as they were applied to the labor movement, see B. Gallitelli and A. Thompson, eds., *Sindicalismo y regimenes militares en Argentina y Chile* (Amsterdam: Centro de Estudios y Documentación Latinoamericanos [CEDLA], 1982), pt. 2, "Argentina, sindicalismo, y regimen militar," pp. 91-225 (essays by Falcón, Gallitelli and Thompson, and Munck).

84. On the impact of these more "subtle" forms of coercion on society, and within the educational system in particular, see Spitta, "El 'Proceso de Reorganización Nacional' de 1976 a 1981," pp. 80-83, 90-97.

85. The portion of the national budget allocated to these sectors fell from 6 percent in 1975 to less than 3 percent in 1981. See S. Belmartino, C. Bloch, and Z. T. de Quinteros, "El programa de estabilización económica y las políticas de salud y bienestar social: 1976-1980," *Cuadernos Médico Sociales,* no. 18b (October 1981): 25-26; J. Bello, "Política de salud, 1976/81. Aporte para la evaluación de un proceso," *Cuadernos Médico Sociales,* no. 23 (March 1983): 25-28; M. B. Gonzales, "Health Care: Another Victim of the Junta," *Latinamerica Press* 15, no. 30 (August 3, 1983), p. 6; and Buchanan, "Regime Change and State Development in Postwar Argentina," chap. 4.

86. Belmartino, Bloch, and de Quinteros, "El programa de estabilización económica y las políticas de salud y bienestar social: 1976-1980," pp. 26-30; Bello, "Política de salud, 1976/81," pp. 28-30.

87. For an excellent study of the effects of these measures on individual strategies for securing health and welfare attention, see Juan J. Llovet, *Servicios de salud y sectores populares. Los añós del Proceso* (Buenos Aires: CEDES, 1984). For a general view of the regime's health program and its effects, see S. Bermann and J. C. Escudero, "Health in Argentina under the Military Junta," *International Journal of Health Services* 8, no. 3 (1978): 531-540.

88. Belmartino, Bloch, and de Quinteros, "El programa de estabilización económica y las políticas de salud y bienestar social: 1976-1980," pp. 31-32; Bello, "Política de Salud, 1976/81," pp. 21-26; Gonzales, "Health Care: Another Victim of the Junta," pp. 6-7; and Bermann and Escudero, "Health in Argentina under the Military Junta," p. 534.

89. On these strikes and the regime's response to them, see Ricardo Falcón, "Conflicto social y regimen militar. La resistencia obrera en Argentina (Marzo 1976-Marzo 1981)," in Gallitelli and Thompson, *Sindicalismo y regimenes militares en Argentina y Chile,* pp. 91-139; and Leon E. Bieber, "El movimiento laboral

argentino a partir de 1976," in Waldmann and Garzón Valdez, *El poder militar en la Argentina, 1976-1981,* pp. 116-122.

90. The most prominent case was that of Jacobo Timerman, publisher of the newspaper *La Opinión,* who complained in a number of editorials in 1976 that the scope of the repressive campaign was unwarranted. For his troubles, in 1977 this erstwhile supporter of the military regime (and long-term anti-Peronist and *gólpista*) was arrested and jailed without charge, where he was subjected to physical and psychological torture. Amid intense international pressure he was released and deported to Israel in 1979. For his version of events, see *Prisoner without a Name, Cell without a Number* (New York: Random House, 1981). Unlike Timerman, there were dozens of other journalists who never reappeared after their arrests.

91. The atrocities committed by the military regime have received considerable international attention and have been well documented by various organizations. Among others, see the human rights reports issued periodically by the Asamblea Permanente por los Derechos Humanos, Centro de Estudios Legales (CELS), and Servicio Paz y Justicia, all of Buenos Aires, as well as those of Amnesty International, Americas Watch, the OAS, and the U.S. government during the period 1976-1980. The description of the activities and methods of the paramilitary squads offered here is derived from these sources and others, as well as from personal interviews conducted in Buenos Aires in 1983.

92. Astiz is currently on trial in Buenos Aires on charges of torture and murder. His capture by British forces in 1982 sparked an international uproar, as victims living in exile in Europe, Canada, and the United States tried to have him extradited to stand trial in their respective jurisdictions. As a prisoner of war, he was returned to Argentina in the prisoner exchange that followed the cessation of hostilities. Vivid testimony of his actions at the Naval Mechanics School has been reported extensively in the Argentine press, particularly during the fall of 1984, when his trial began. See *Clarín,* October–December 1984, for an almost daily recompilation of these events.

93. Revelations of these and other methodical applications of terror (existence of concentration camps, use of crematoria, mass executions, secret gravesites, and so on) have been extensively documented by the investigative commission (the Sabato Commission) charged by President Alfonsín with determining the extent of human rights violations and fate of those who "disappeared" during the Proceso. See the *Informe de la Comisión Nacional sobre la Desaparición de Personas* (Buenos Aires: Presidencia de la Nación, Secretaria de Información, September 1984). Additional information on the "dirty war" has begun to surface during the trial of nine former junta members (all military officers).

94. Gramsci, *Selections from the Prison Notebooks,* p. 232.

95. Gramsci, *Quaderni del carcere,* vol. 2, pp. 808-809, cited in Anderson, "The Antinomies of Antonio Gramsci," p. 31.

96. Asamblea Permanente por los Derechos Humanos, *Lista de los detenidos-desaparecidos* (Buenos Aires: 1981), p. 4. Also see B. Gallitelli and A. Thompson, "La situación laboral en la Argentina del 'Proceso,' 1976-1981," in Gallitelli and Thompson, *Sindicalismo y Regimenes Militares en Argentina y Chile,* pp. 152-157.

97. Delich, "Después del diluvio, la clase obrera," p. 140.

98. Falcón, "Conflicto social y regimen militar," p. 98.

99. Gallitelli and Thompson, "La situación laboral en la Argentina del 'Proceso,' 1976-1981," pp. 150-151.

100. Ibid., pp. 155-156.

101. See the petition filed by the Transportation Workers of America (AFL-CIO) before the Civil Aeronautics Board on July 31, 1979, charging Aérolineas Argentinas (which was managed by the air force) with unfair labor practices. Also see "Exporting Repression — Argentine Style," *Soho News* 6, no. 44 (August 2-8, 1979).

102. See Timerman, *Prisoner without a Name, Cell without a Number*, for the role anti-Semitism played in his abduction and subsequent incarceration, as well as within the "dirty war" in general. There is a fairly extensive literature on the subject of anti-Semitism under the Proceso. Among others, see R. Weisbrot, "The Siege of the Argentine Jews," *New Republic* 184 (June 27, 1981): 16-21; and G. W. Wynia, "The Argentine Revolution Falters," *Current History* 81, no. 2 (February 1982): 74-77, 87-88.

103. Gramsci, *Selections from the Prison Notebooks*, p. 54, n. 4.

104. This notion of individual repression under conditions of state terror leading to a widespread condition of alienation within excluded social groups paraphrases the argument developed by Guillermo A. O'Donnell at the "Seminar on Issues on Democracy and Democratization, North and South" held at the Kellogg Institute, University of Notre Dame, on November 14-16, 1983. Any errors of interpretation or misidentification are my own.

105. I first heard this phrase while I was in Buenos Aires in 1983, used by the children of a friend who as a Peronist Youth leader had been forced underground for five years in order to avoid the security apparatus (since he was marked for "disappearance"). I later discovered that it was a phrase commonly used by Argentine children to scare each other, much in the way my three-year-old talks about ghosts and monsters. In their case, however, the monsters were very real.

106. Gramsci, *Letter from Prison*, p. 205 (letter written to his sister-in-law Tania from the penal colony of Turi, September 7, 1931). I must note that in writing about the medieval communes (from which this quote is taken), Gramsci stated that they "did not know how to create [their] own category of intellectuals" and thus could not exercise hegemony. In the case of the Proceso, Martínez de Hoz and his "liberal" cadre were the regime's intellectuals, but they had no interest in exercising hegemony, just class domination.

3

Asian State Repression and
Strikes against Transnationals

David Kowalewski_____

The vicious state repression of popular dissent within Third World countries in the postwar era has tended to make a mockery of the liberal notion of linear historical "progress" toward greater economic and political freedoms. As Third World economic development took place, it was assumed, so too would "political development" in the form of enhanced human rights and liberties. Frequently Third World countries were deemed politically undemocratic because they were at a "lower stage" of economic development. As they progressed toward a "higher stage" similar to that enjoyed by advanced industrial countries, they would become as democratic as the latter. Economic and political progress were viewed as alternate sides of the same development coin.[1]

Yet certainly a number of advanced industrial countries, such as the Soviet Union and East Germany, are well known for their political repressiveness. Also, although a number of Third World nations have developed economically—some indeed becoming newly industrialized countries (NICs)—news of their repressive state practices still finds its way into the pages and circuits of the world's mass media.[2] Clearly the linkage between economic development and repression is far more complex.

DEPENDENCE AND DEVELOPMENT

To explain this contradiction in the liberal global paradigm, dependency theorists have arisen to present their own version of global political economy.[3] Although some aggregate economic development of the Third World is indeed occurring, they assert, this growth is often dependent development. Two types of dependency can be distinguished: macro-level or structural, and micro-level or personal. According to dependency theorists, Third World countries are structurally dependent on First World countries in several respects. Economic production is highly dependent on First

World transnational enterprises (TNEs), which appear more concerned with their own quarterly profit report than with the host country's well-being. The financing for that production is often dependent on loans from institutions dominated by First World countries, for whom the recipient's welfare often takes second place to their own economic and political priorities. The output of that production is frequently dependent upon export trade to a few First World countries and thus upon the vicissitudes of a small number of markets abroad. The actual benefits from that production, finally, are often minimized because of national legal structures (provision of infrastructure, tax holidays, and the like) that favor foreign producers over domestic ones.[4]

In addition to these structural dependencies, Third World state officials are often seen as dependent personally on the First World in terms of their socialization as well as numerous material benefits. Whereas the theory of macro-level dependence stresses the degree to which entire countries in the Third World are tied into the global political economy, the theory of micro-level dependence emphasizes the extent to which the Third World's elite classes have an ideology and material interests virtually identical to those of the elite classes of the First World. Although most of the research on dependency theory focuses on macro-level indicators, a number of theorists have noted the need for "studies more micro-sociological in nature."[5] Seemingly the common and symbiotic class affiliation of Third World state officials and First World elites induces the former to behave as "corporate compradors," "lumpenbourgeoisie," "comprador politicians," in short, a "clientele class" of the First World.[6] Third World "technocrats," for example, are often trained by First World educators who stress aggregate economic growth fostered by TNE investment and the political stability with which to ensure it over economic redistribution and political liberty. Thus development policies become dependently based upon elitist First World economic and political assumptions. According to some observers, state officials in the Third World "have been trained in an educational system bequeathed by the colonial experience which structures their dependency-oriented thinking by training them to work for multinational corporations."[7] This educational socialization is reinforced by heavy TNE advertising for goods that usually only the elites of the Third World can afford, thereby generating "a counterpart bourgeoisie" infused with a First World "culture of commodities."[8] This transnational elite alliance is further cemented by numerous informal socializing processes whereby the "elite classes of the dependent area" enter "into intimate contact with the center economy."[9]

Less charitably, micro-level dependency theorists also point to the numerous personal benefits received by Third World state officials from their First World superordinates. These officials are occasionally described as the "major beneficiaries" of TNE investment in their countries.[10] Johan

Galtung refers to the "joint benefits" enjoyed by First and Third World elites.[11] At least one empirical study has provided evidence of these benefits accruing to Third World elites. According to Vincent Mahler's data, "The coopted elite described by dependency theorists does seem clearly in evidence: it appears that income in [Third World] countries host to considerable foreign investment is confined to a very small group of households."[12] Indeed, a recent United Nations study has suggested that "high income obtained locally from the activities of multinational corporations may accrue largely to domestic elites associated with foreign interests."[13]

A number of micro-level mechanisms are claimed to provide Third World state officials with these material benefits. First, joint ventures with TNEs, it is sometimes claimed, "hasten the incorporation of Third World . . . state managers into the global economy under control by transnational capital."[14] Second, personnel interchange or "revolving doors" between state bureaucracies and TNE subsidiaries in the Third World provide state officials with substantial material benefits while simultaneously creating a public-private "conflict of interest." Finally, TNE bribes to Third World state officials, according to one observer, demonstrate that "these influence-seeking interactions constitute a multinational corporate diplomacy and a foreign policy of the firm."[15] All these mechanisms, in sum, apparently tend to generate an official "commission-agent bourgeoisie" in Third World polities.[16]

DEPENDENCY AND REPRESSION

Both structural and personal dependencies, the argument concludes, result in undemocratic, repressive policies toward Third World nonelites. Structural dependencies render Third World economies especially vulnerable and unstable, thereby inducing state officials to repress any popular dissent that could easily hinder economic development. Likewise, the personal dependencies of Third World state officials on First World elites generate a systematic policy bias away from nationalistic sympathies with their own conational nonelites and in the direction of favoritism toward their foreign First World elite classmates. Viewing themselves as transnational "junior partners" of First World elites in the global game of political economy, they ultimately see their own conational nonelites as mere cogs in the national economic machine, who may ultimately pose a serious threat to their own power and privilege. Personal dependencies and the consequent repressiveness assure that development benefits remain at the top, while few such benefits "trickle down" to nonelites at the bottom.

Crucial to the dependency-repression theory, as is clear from the foregoing discussion, are the TNEs of the First World. Some students of Third World politics suggest that "multinational corporations . . . may be critical elements in the causal chain that induces and sustains authoritarian solutions in a particular society."[17] The International Institute of Human Rights noted that TNEs had "negative impacts" on human rights in the Third World.[18] Another study concluded that TNE-dominated "export-processing zones are enclaves in which foreigners live like an occupying army."[19] In Latin America anti-TNE protests have been found to elicit increasing police and military repression.[20] In Brazil TNEs have been linked to the development of repressive death squads.[21]

DATA FOR THE STUDY

To examine this dependency-repression theory, an expedient sample of 52 labor actions taken against TNEs in underdeveloped Asian countries between 1968 and 1983 was gathered from a wide variety of sources (see the Appendix).[22] Expedient samples are a set of cases gathered from all available sources rather than selected from a total known population of existing cases. Since the total population of labor actions against TNEs in the Third World is presently not known or readily available, an expedient sample was correspondingly drawn as a substitute. Such samples can be useful, depending upon the range and reliability of the sources utilized. For the current sample, several diverse sources were consulted; the great majority were Asian-based publications, some 83 of which yielded data on labor disputes at TNE subsidiaries. The most fruitful sources turned out to be church- and academy-related research groups, whose ideological bias was only occasionally observable. The accuracy of the reports also appeared satisfactory; duplicate reports only rarely contained minor inconsistencies.

As table 3.1 reveals, the actions took place in eleven Asian host countries against TNEs from seven First World home bases (including two transnational joint ventures). The TNEs were involved in banking, agriculture, aquaculture, mining, garments/textiles, electronics, other light manufacturing, heavy industry, and tourism.

Expedient samples automatically raise the question of representativeness and thereby of generalizability of results. Because of the lack of any complete data on strikes against TNEs in Asia or elsewhere, a series of surrogate tests of representativeness was conducted by relating the data to information from other sources concerning the home bases and hosts of TNEs in Asia. If our sample is roughly representative, then assuming no particularly strong strike-proneness against TNEs with certain home bases or in certain Asian host countries, the distribution of the labor actions with respect to TNE home bases and host countries should correspond somewhat with distributions of TNE home-base and host-country involvement in Asia.

With respect to home bases, the ratio of the labor actions against U.S. TNEs to those against Japanese TNEs equals 2.9. This figure accords roughly with the ratio of total stock of U.S. foreign direct investment in

Table 3.1
Sample Characteristics

Home base	Percent	N
United Kingdom	4.0	2
West Germany	8.0	4
Switzerland	2.0	1
Japan	18.0	9
United States	52.0	26
Canada	4.0	2
Australia	8.0	4
Joint venture[a]	4.0	2
Total	100.0	50
Industry		
Banking	3.9	2
Agriculture	5.9	3
Aquaculture	3.9	2
Mining	3.9	2
Garments/Textiles	17.6	9
Electronics	31.4	16
Other light manufacturing[b]	25.0	13
Heavy industry	5.9	3
Tourism	2.0	1
Total	100.0	51
Host		
Singapore	1.9	1
Thailand	5.8	3
Indonesia	5.8	3
Malaysia	7.7	4
Philippines	38.5	20
South Korea	21.2	11
Papua New Guinea	1.9	1
Sri Lanka	1.9	1
Hong Kong	11.5	6
Taiwan	1.9	1
Fiji	1.9	1
Total	100.0	52

[a]Between two or more First World TNEs.

[b]Enterprises outside of garments/textiles and electronics, such as those in toys, food and tobacco processing, plastics, and pharmaceuticals.

Asia to that of Japan (2.4). Further, about one-half of all the labor actions were directed against U.S. TNEs. This relatively equal labor-action proportion between those against U.S. TNEs and those against non-U.S. TNEs corresponds closely with a study of the distribution of the home bases of subsidiaries of the world's 400 largest TNEs in 11 Asian countries: U.S. mean = 78; non-U.S. mean = 79.

With respect to host countries, the data on the number of labor actions in each host country was correlated with (1) the amount of foreign direct investment stock and (2) the total number of employees of TNEs in those countries.[25] The first Pearsonian correlation (labor actions with TNE investment) turns out moderately positive (r = .37), while the second (labor actions with TNE employees) proves even more so (.64). In sum, the sample appears to possess the property of representativeness to at least some measurable degree. Examples include the strike by hundreds of plantation workers against Castle and Cooke's pineapple operations in Thailand in 1978, the formation of a "tent city" by garment workers against Canada's Top Form subsidiary in the Philippines in 1982, and the sit-in by 50 electronics workers at National Cash Register's plant in Hong Kong in 1981.

MEASUREMENTS

The first theoretical question that immediately arises concerns the connection between TNEs and state repression. Dependency theory strongly suggests that Third World states will favor TNEs over workers when TNEs are faced with threats from worker dissidents. Third World state officials, structurally and personally dependent on TNEs for national aggregate growth and individual socialization and emoluments, will tend to intervene repressively on behalf of TNEs and against their workers, lest the TNE "goose that lays the golden eggs" sustain any damage.

Conceptually, in this study state intervention refers to the open and explicit involvement of state employees, acting in their official capacities, in the labor disputes in some role (mediation, imposition of cooling-off periods, arbitration, police actions, and so on) that would likely influence outcomes. By repression is meant that the dispute resulted in monetary, physical, psychological, or other costs being imposed on TNE workers. Costs refer to those phenomena that immediately reflect a reversal in the workers' previously held and commonly accepted values, namely economic well-being, physical security, freedom, self-respect, and the like.

Operationally, a dummy state-intervention variable was first generated. The labor disputes were coded as (1) if the sources indicated that Asian state officials played an active and open role in some official capacity during the dispute. Such a role was indicated by their publicly known interactions with TNE management, labor leaders, or both. Events were coded as (0) if such a role was absent.

In addition, four repression variables (firings, injuries, detentions, and coerced terminations to the disputes) for each of the labor actions were created. All four variables indicate repression as defined above, namely the imposition of some kind of cost to workers' values. Firings reflect at least a short-term economic cost on workers' incomes. In the Third World context, where unemployment rates exceed those in advanced industrial countries, economic costs may well prove more than short term. Injuries directly damage the values of physical security as well as economic well-being of workers. Detentions immediately subvert the value of freedom of physical movement. Coerced termination reduces to some extent the workers' freedom of movement, their ability to bargain further for enhanced well-being in terms of wages, working conditions, and the like, and their relative self-respect in comparison to the TNE's victory in putting an end to their disruption of production.

Firings were coded according to the degree to which the sources reported that worker-participants in the disputes were dismissed from employment following the initiation of the labor action. Included were temporary or permanent dismissals, explicit firings, preventive suspensions, and layoffs. Injuries were measured according to whether or not any of the participating workers sustained any physical suffering because of beatings or other types of physical abuse at the hands of managers, supervisors, foremen, fellow workers, scabs, or coercive organs. Detentions were coded according to the degree to which all the worker-participants in the disputes were physically deprived of freedom of movement. Included were detentions, arrests, and other forms of incarceration at TNE facilities, specially constructed "camps," or state jails and prisons. Coerced termination was coded according to whether or not the labor action came to a forced conclusion against the expressed will of the worker-participants through lockouts, cessation of production, effective introduction of scabs, physical dispersal, and the like. In addition, a more general dummy repression measure (whether or not the sources reported the occurrence of any of the four repression indicators just listed at the events) was also created.

Asian states intervened directly in slightly over one-half (51.9 percent) of the labor actions. Workers experienced firings in 49.0 percent of the events; detentions in 12.2 percent; injuries in 8.2 percent; and coerced terminations in 32.7 percent. At least one form of repression occurred in two-thirds (67.3 percent) of the cases (table 3.2).

To assess the validity of the repression indicators, they were correlated with an opposite measure of event outcomes, that is, the degree to which workers attained concessions to their demands. If the indicators validly measure repression, then we should expect negative correlations with concessions at the events. Occasionally, of course, those responsible for applying repression or the "stick" may also grant concessions or the "carrot." Yet concessions can minimize the fear induced by repression,

Table 3.2
Repression Indicators ($N = 49$)

Frequency of repression

Dummy repression variables	Percent of all cases
Firings	49.0
Detentions	12.2
Injuries	8.2
Coerced termination	32.7
Any type of repression	67.3

Pearsonian correlations of repression indicators and concessions

Repression variables	Concessions [e]	Significance
Firings [a]	-.40	.002
Detentions [b]	-.25	.004
Injuries [c]	-.17	.123
Coerced termination [d]	-.39	.003

Pearsonian correlations of repression index

Repression variable	Repression index [f]	Significance
Firings	.65	.000
Detentions	.53	.000
Injuries	.60	.000
Coerced termination	.56	.000
Concession variable	-.47	.000

[a]Proportion of total number of worker-participants terminated following the initiation of the action. Includes temporary or permanent dismissals, firings, preventive suspensions, and layoffs. (0) = None reported by sources; (1) = Reports of "some" or less than 50 percent of worker-participants; (2) = Reports of "most" or "many" or 50 to 99 percent; (3) = Reports of "all" or 100 percent.

[b]Degree to which the total number of worker-participants experienced deprivation of freedom of physical movement. Includes detentions, arrests, and other forms of incarceration. (0) = None; (1) = Reports of a "few," less than 20, less than 10 percent; (2) = Reports of "some," 20 or more but less than 100, 10 percent or over but less than 50 percent; (3) = Reports of "most" or "many," 50 percent or over, 100 or more, "all."

[c]Physical suffering sustained by participating workers. Includes bodily damage because of beatings or other types of physical abuse conducted by managers, supervisors, foremen, fellow workers, scabs, or coercive organs. (0) = None; (1) = Some.

[d]Forced conclusion to the action against the expressed will of the worker-participants. Includes lockouts, cessation of production, effective introduction of scabs, physical dispersal. (0) = No; (1) = Yes.

[e]Degree to which workers achieved fulfillment of their demands during the dispute. Demands concerned grievances regarding wage compensation, nonwage compensation, prior repression of fellow workers, unions, working conditions, and sexual harassment or discrimination. (0) = No concessions reported by sources; (1) = Concessions to only a small part of total demand(s); (2) = Concessions to most of total demand(s); (3) = Complete concessions to demand(s). On the utilization of similar concession scales at dissident events, see David Kowalewski and Paul Schumaker, "Protest Outcomes in the Soviet Union," *Sociological Quarterly* 22 (Winter 1981): 57-68.

[f]Additive index of the four repression variables in (a) through (d) in dummy form.

while repression can undermine the good will secured from concessions. Hence concessions and repression appear to coincide only rarely. Table 3.2 shows that all four repression indicators are indeed negatively correlated with the concession variable, three of them significantly and the fourth almost so. The mean correlation turns out a moderately negative – .30. In short, the repression variables appear validly to measure the costs experienced by TNE workers during labor disputes.

To obtain a more general and exact measure of repression experienced by TNE workers at the events, the four repression measures in dichotomous or dummy form were added to form an overall repression index for each labor action. Thus each event was subsequently coded on a scale ranging from zero (no type of repression reported) to four (all four types reported). Table 3.2 indicates that the repression index is strongly and positively correlated with all four specific repression variables (mean correlation = .61) and strongly and negatively correlated with the concession variable (– .47).

TRANSNATIONALS AND ASIAN STATE REPRESSION

To specify the dependency theorists' proposition more exactly, we should expect that when Asian states intervene in worker actions against TNEs, repression will prove higher than when they refrain from intervention. As transnational "dependents," Asian state officials should wield their power on behalf of their "senior partner" TNEs but against the welfare of their conational worker nonelites. In short, when they intervene, TNEs will tend to benefit through the suppression of an unruly and profit-threatening workforce. Workers, in contrast, will suffer the costs of firings, detentions, injuries, and forced returns to work.

Table 3.3 presents Pearson correlations between Asian state intervention and repression of TNE workers. If dependency theorists are correct, then we should expect strongly positive correlations between intervention and repression. The dependency proposition fares poorly, however, when firings of workers are considered (r = .03). Workers are fired by TNE management regardless of whether Asian states intervene in the dispute. Seemingly, Asian state officials are insufficiently dependent on TNEs to exert a repressive occupational outcome on TNE workers. On the other hand, dependency theorists might argue that the near-zero correlation indicates that state officials do little to prevent TNE firings of dissident workers.

Dependency theory seems closer to the mark, however, when the other repression measures are considered. The three correlations turn out far more positive, and all significantly so. When Asian state officials intervened in the labor actions, workers suffered substantially more injuries, detentions, and coerced terminations than when state intervention was absent. In short, TNEs fared better, and workers worse, when Asian states became involved in the actions than when they eschewed intervention. The correlation between intervention and the more general repression index emerges moderately strong and statistically significant (r = .40).

Some specific examples illustrate these relationships. In September 1980 workers at Canada's Top Form garment subsidiary in the Philippines went on strike, demanding recognition of their union as a collective bargaining agent. Workers picketed the plant and slept in the street outside in tents. Yet after negotiations with the Ministry of Labor, firemen arrived, spraying the

Table 3.3
Intervention and Repression (*N* = 49)

	State intervention	
Repression indicator	r	Significance
Firings	.03	.412
Injuries	.27	.031
Detentions	.31	.016
Coerced termination	.37	.005
Repression index	.40	.002

workers with fire hoses, while police inflicted a number of injuries on the strikers.[26]

At Century Textile in Indonesia in April 1972, the entire labor force of 487 workers struck for a wage increase, transportation and food allowances, and other issues. After mediation by the Labor Inspection Bureau, police forced the strikers to return to work, arresting 12 of their leaders.[27] National Cash Register's workers in Hong Kong experienced a similar fate during their sit-down strike for severance pay in April 1971 after mediation by the Labor Department. TNE security guards dispersed the strikers.[28]

South Korean police likewise dispersed a strike and demonstrations by 1,000 Mattel workers demanding improvement in working conditions and other concessions in June 1977. Yet South Korean workers at Control Data in the spring and summer of 1982 fared even worse at the hands of the state. Workers conducted sit-ins at the plant as well as the Ministry of Labor's offices, struck for two days, and took a number of TNE executives hostage, demanding an end to work-related illnesses, firings of workers, and high quotas. Police interrogated union leaders during which beatings occurred. Several were arrested and later imprisoned. TNE managers broke into workers' homes. Five women workers were attacked by supervisors; three of them were pregnant, and the fetus of one woman died as a result of the attack. Workers reported being blacklisted by the Korean Central Intelligence Agency.[29]

Yet this repression associated with Asian state intervention may well be due simply to the degree of militancy expressed by TNE workers. The laborers may have "brought the repression on themselves" by a high level of tactical and demand militancy during the events. To test for this possibility, two militancy variables were generated for each event: a seven-point tactical militancy scale ranging from simple wearing of protest garb up to physical damage to persons or property; and a six-point additive demand militancy index comprising the total number of distinct demands made by workers. Multiple regression statistics were generated for the relationships between state intervention and the repression index while controlling for each of the two militancy variables. Yet the beta-weights indicate that state intervention is positively associated with repression of TNE workers regardless of their tactical (.38) or demand (.41) militancy.[30]

In sum, the findings indicate that Asian states, presumably because of their dependence on TNE operations, follow a repressive policy that goes against the interests of their own conational nonelites. Some connection appears to exist between Third World state repression and TNE-sponsored economic development. But is it due to dependence?

STRUCTURAL DEPENDENCE AND STATE REPRESSION

Dependency theorists would suggest that both the structural and personal dependencies of Asian state officials should help account for this repression of TNE workers. Because of macro- and micro-level dependence, the argument claims, Asian state officials will repress TNE workers in the interests of their foreign co-elite "senior partners" in the transnational development game. The aggregate and individual benefits to be obtained from their TNE partner-guests will direct the policies of Asian state officials toward the repression of disruptive TNE workers.

Statistically the labor-action data should show that when dependency indicators are introduced into the analysis, the correlations between intervention and repression will be seriously reduced. If state intervention leads to repression because of dependency, then intervention itself should reveal a near-zero relationship with repression. In short, the dependency measures themselves should account for variation in repression and thus reduce the correlations between state intervention and repression to insignificance. The repression of TNE workers should occur simply because some Asian states are more dependent than others.

If, on the other hand, dependence fails to account for Asian state repression of TNE workers, then the correlations between intervention and repression should remain robust. When we control for measures of dependency, we should still find a strong connection between state involvement and repression of TNE workers. In short, Asian state intervention should lead to repression regardless of how dependent those states may be.

As noted earlier, dependency theory claims that both macro- and micro-level dependencies are operative in Third World state repression. The first or structural set of dependencies, those at the macro level, can easily be measured. The four dimensions of macro-level dependence discussed above (productive, financial, trade, and legal) are often described as leading to repressive state actions. Production dependence on TNEs, bolstered by legal guarantees, should encourage repression by state authorities. According to some observers, "Transnational corporations in Southeast Asia . . . enjoy power that has no link with foreign armies . . .; governments are prepared with weapons . . . to assure that the transnationals can operate profitably."[31] TNE executives themselves have been found to exert pressure on governments to repress unions.[32] Interviews conducted in the Philippines have indicated that TNEs prefer to work with authoritarian regimes.[33] According to Robert Wales, president of Mobil Oil Philippines, "If martial law will instill some discipline and solve the law and order problems, the temporary loss of freedom of speech is not important."[34] Thus the higher the level of TNE productive dominance and legal shelters thereto attached, the greater should be the pressure for Asian state coercion.

Likewise, financial dependence as indicated by a high level of foreign debt should also induce a greater level of repression. According to some observers, repression becomes necessary to enforce discipline for the sake of generating foreign exchange in order to meet financial obligations. Workers for TNEs should experience particular repression since their employers are usually major exporters and thus earners of needed foreign exchange.[35]

A high level of trade dependence in terms of export structure and partner concentration has frequently been linked to repressive policies in the Third World. A high and growing level of exports suggests not only a desire for foreign exchange and hence the requisite "labor discipline," particularly among workers for export-oriented TNEs, but also a lower preference for the internal market, whose low consumption must frequently be enforced by repression.[36] As the Asian Development Bank put it, "law and order and political stability" comprise an "important factor in export expansion in Southeast Asia."[37]

Data on all four structural dependence dimensions were gathered for the labor actions. Measures of productive dependence include TNE penetration and importance of TNE-dominated free trade zones in the Asian host economy. The former indicates the degree to which TNE investments dominate the country in relation to its total stock of capital and population, while the second measures the extent to which the country's labor force is employed in free trade zones, which are virtually always dominated by TNEs. Financial dependence is indicated by absolute foreign debt as well as foreign debt relative to the country's exports. Trade dependence is measured by exports as a proportion of gross domestic product, the growth rate of exports, and the degree to which the country's trade is concentrated on a single country's market abroad. Finally, legal dependence of Asian states on foreign enterprises is indicated by the extent to which the country's laws impose controls (such as foreign content and import restrictions) and provide incentives (such as tax holidays and research services) concerning TNE investment.

If dependency theory is valid, then when we control for these structural dependency variables, the intervention-repression correlation should fall to zero. Asian states should intervene repressively only because these macro-level "constraints" will minimize the possibility for state intervention in behalf of TNE workers and against TNE management.

Yet the data in table 3.4 cast some doubt on macro-level or structural dependency theory. In no case is the original positive relationship between the intervention variable and the general repression index influenced by the macro-dependency measures. The relationships stay remarkably robust, indeed statistically significant. For example, regardless of the foreign debt structure of Asian states, intervention still results in repression of TNE workers (beta-weights = .36 and .35). The findings may suggest that even if Asian states reduce their structural dependence, they will still intervene repressively against TNE workers and in behalf of TNE management. Apparently the Asian state tends to favor TNEs and repress their workers for reasons other than structural dependence. But why?

Table 3.4
Intervention, Repression, and Dependence

Structural dependence control[a]	Intervention and repression	N
Productive dependence		
TNE domination[b]	.42 **	40
FTZ domination[c]	.38 **	48
Financial dependence		
Absolute debt[d]	.36 **	48
Debt ratio[e]	.35 **	48
Trade dependence		
Export proportion[f]	.41 **	41
Export Growth[g]	.41 **	47
Trade concentration[h]	.39 **	36
Legal dependence		
TNE controls[i]	.37 **	46
TNE Incentives[j]	.36 **	46

[a]Figures represent beta-weights for the relationship between intervention and the repression index under controls for the specific structural dependence variable. Double asterisks show that the unstandardized regression coefficient exceeds 2.0 times and error.

[b]Stock of capital invested by TNEs in relation to the total stock of capital and the population; equals TNE stock divided by the square root of the total stock of capital times the population of the host country in 1967.

[c]Relevance of TNE-dominated free trade zones in relation to the labor force of the host country; equals number of workers employed in FTZs as a permillage of the total labor force in 1975.

[d]External public debt of host country, outstanding net of undisbursed, and net of past repayments in millions of current U.S. dollars in 1973.

[e]Amortization and interest payments on host country's external debt as a percent of the value of its exports of goods and nonfactor services, each in current U.S. dollars converted at average annual exchange rates in 1973.

[f]Exports of goods and nonfactor services as a percent of gross domestic product (both in domestic currency and at current market prices) of host country in 1973.

[g]Annual average growth rate of merchandise exports as derived from exponential trend of host country in 1970-1975.

[h]Value of host country's goods exchanged with its most important trade partner as a percent of its total foreign trade in 1972.

[i]Host-country government's economic policy toward TNEs based on an additive measure of its control interventions, restrictions, and inducements to investments in 1977.

[j]Host-country government's incentives for TNEs, based on an additive measure including corporate and personal taxes, tariffs, capital, research and development, training/information/housing services, siting, production, and local content, for 1977.

Source: All dependence data is derived from Volker Bornschier and Peter Heinz, *Compendium of Data for World-system Analysis* (Zurich: Soziologisches Institut der Universität Zürich, 1979).

PERSONAL DEPENDENCE AND STATE REPRESSION?

Yet dependency theory may still be useful in explaining the linkage between Asian state intervention and repression of TNE workers. Although structural, macro-level dependency measures fail to explain Asian state repression against TNE work forces, perhaps personal, micro-level ones can. Asian state officials may intervene repressively against TNE workers because of personal socialization and benefits derived from First World elites. Certainly the data necessary to test this explanation are not readily available and indeed at present almost defy any kind of systematic collection without enormous research costs. Thus our ability to link these personal dependence processes to our sample of labor actions is unfortunately impossible.

However, considerable contextual evidence can be found that suggests that Asian state officials, because of personal socialization and material benefits derived from connections with TNEs and related First World elites, should have substantial motivation to repress disruptive TNE workers. Both formal and informal socialization mechanisms have been found to instill in Asian state officials a developmental preference for TNE-based production. The Economic Development Institute of the World Bank, for example, socializes Asian technocrats into TNE-dominated export-oriented investment programs. Similar educational courses have been sponsored by the Asian Development Bank. Given the lending leverage these institutions have over Asian state officials, one must assume that the instruction is taken seriously.[38] Likewise, the Ford Foundation provides essential funds for educational systems in Asian countries as well as scholarships for students and military officers.[39] Indeed, university education in First World institutions has given birth to such appellations as the "Berkeley Mafia" for state officials in Indonesia and the "Ivy League Mafia" for those in the Philippines.[40]

Informal socialization mechanisms linking Asian state officials with TNEs are evident as well. U.S. TNEs in the American Chamber of Commerce in Taiwan have been found to have close social ties to high-ranking public employees.[41] In Indonesia the overseas Chinese partners of TNEs are closely linked to several state officials.[42] Indonesian generals have been discovered "hobnobbing with foreign oil magnates."[43] The generals are said to feel "at home" with TNE executives.[44] Unilever reportedly has "powerful" social "contacts" with military officials in Asia.[45] A former Philippine ambassador to Japan, Roberto Benedicto, has been known in Tokyo and Manila as "Marubenedicto" because of close social ties to Marubeni.[46] President Ferdinand Marcos had extensive social contacts with Toyota executives, while his wife Imelda cultivated similar connections with those of Ford.[47] Union Carbide, Hoechst, Monsanto, and other pesticide manufacturers and distributors, according to reports, enjoy a "cozy relationship with the government" of the Philippines.[48] Del Monte's Delta Farms had close social ties to the provincial commander of the Philippine Constabulary, whose forces worked hand in hand with the TNE's own security guards.[49] Castle and Cooke's Dole subsidiary in the Philippines provided President Marcos with a home at its plantation in southern Mindanao.[50]

In addition to these socializing mechanisms, at least three personal benefit connections link Asian state officials with TNEs in Asia. First, joint ventures of TNEs in Asian countries provide substantial benefits to state officials.[51] The managers of Asian state enterprises are often personally dependent on TNEs for financing and technology and thereby become a "consolidated [economic] power" in their own right. The economic "state bureaucracy," it is said, "forges an alliance with foreign interests . . . and makes ample use of political repression."[52] In the countries of the Association of Southeast Asian Nations, one observer found a "new social class which bases its economic position on the synchronization of . . . the direct or indirect interest of foreign capital and . . . their own . . . control over . . . state resources."[53] In nonmanufacturing subsidiaries in Indonesia, the partners of TNEs tend to be politicians and generals who benefit substantially thereby.[54] According to a survey of 87 Japanese TNE joint ventures in Indonesia, a significant proportion of their partners have close government contacts.[55] Military partners of TNEs have been referred to as the "local puppets" of the transnationals.[56] Among Castle and Cooke's Dole Thai pineapple plantation shareowners are several family members of Thai state officials.[57] In the Marcos Philippines, since the state often owned a share of large private corporations with which TNEs were linked, joint ventures allowed TNEs useful access to state politicians and bureaucrats.[58] The Record Company of America established a joint venture communications partnership with Defense Minister Juan Ponce Enrile. In 1971 Enrile was also a Dole shareholder and corporate lawyer.[59] Similar joint ventures have been found between Philippine military officers and TNEs.[60] These linkages, according to some scholars, have become a "fruitful source of corruption."[61]

Second, personnel interchange or "revolving doors" between state and TNE employment also operate to enhance the personal benefits of Asian state officials. According to the TNE-based Pacific Forum, Asia's military rulers are often hired by TNEs for their "administrative talents."[62] In the Pacific islands a number of government leaders are TNE directors.[63] Gulf Oil in Korea has employed former high-ranking members of the Ministry of Defense and Central Intelligence Agency.[64] Current and former state officials in Malaysia are "often heavily sought after by foreign . . . enterprises . . . in order that their current or previous political connections may be used to expedite tasks."[65] For example, Sime Darby and Dunlop have employed former officials of the Finance Ministry and Central Bank.[66] Similar revolving doors swing between TNEs and the Thai government.[67] In the Philippines, Castle and Cooke's Stanfilco subsidiary hired local barrio officials and mayors as labor contractors on its banana plantation.[68] Under

Marcos, employment connections between Philippine military officers and agricultural TNEs produced joint meetings designed to "pacify" Muslim dissidents in Mindanao.[69] At one of Castle and Cooke's operational sites, the TNE hired the local mayor and chief of police as head of its security force.[70] A former Philippine ambassador to Japan later became the chair of Mariwasa-Honda and a director of Porcelana-Mariwasa and Electro Alloys.[71] A number of former Indonesian officials and current "government advisers" are employed by Australian TNEs.[72] Several military officials serve as TNE brokers and consultants and are reportedly well paid for their services.[73] The president, directors, and general manager of General Foods in Indonesia are high-ranking military officers.[74] Some TNEs employ active-duty military officers, up to the rank of brigadier general, to "keep discipline" among workers.[75]

Finally, TNE bribes provide substantial personal benefits to Asian state officials. According to one study, in Southeast Asia "kickbacks to government figures [occur] on such a scale that they have become an organic segment of the international marketing and distribution network."[76] Japanese TNEs have been found to "bribe without hesitation" and are "incredibly crude" in their methods.[77] TNEs in Sri Lanka have also been discovered exerting a "corruptive influence on political power."[78] Research has uncovered TNE bribes to labor inspectors in Malaysia.[79] In South Korea the huge Japanese trading TNEs claim that bribery "payments are part of usual business practices."[80] In Indonesia TNEs make "contributions" to the military generals' pension fund.[81] According to extensive interviews with various elites in the Philippines, corruption has played an important role in TNE-state relations.[82] Castle and Cooke, for example, "donated" to several projects of the wife of President Marcos.[83] Local state officials in the Philippines received "special allowances" from agricultural TNEs.[84] One study found that U.S. silvicultural TNEs donate funds to state officials issuing cutting licenses. The same TNEs have been discovered giving bribes to state forest rangers in order to facilitate the repression of indigenous peoples displaced by their operations.[85]

In sum, a wide array of research reports suggests that micro-level or personal dependencies may exert a significant impact on Asian state repression. According to one observer of Indonesian politics, "Even if it is a legal strike, the military-police will be introduced to suppress it, as transnational corporations are in collusion with the repressive state."[86] Formal and informal socialization into TNE objectives, as well as the enhancement of personal material benefits, suggest that dependency theory, at least in its micro-level form, may prove useful in explaining the repression of TNE workers and others perceiving themselves disprivileged by their operations.

IMPLICATIONS

Third World economic development has certainly failed in many cases to lead to greater human rights for masses of people. Yet some Third World citizens—various elites, prominent among them state officials—have indeed developed and enjoy more human rights than a number of their fellow citizens. Most citizens in the Third World, however, remain in squalid underdevelopment, and their dissent against this kind of "existence" is often repressed by those very citizens who have indeed developed.

Dependency theorists would explain this anomaly in the global liberal paradigm by positing another conceptual framework. Because Third World political elites are dependent on First World elites, particularly TNEs, for development—structural and personal—they are led to repress any destabilization by nonelites that might annoy or threaten the source of these development "eggs" by which they are constrained and to which they have become, willingly or unwillingly, addicted.

Our study of labor actions in Asia suggests that indeed state officials do tend to repress nonelite threats to the TNE development "geese." The TNE worker in Asia suffered repression more frequently when state officials intervened than when they refrained from intervention. For their part, TNEs were able to achieve the suppression of an unruly work force more often when their Asian state hosts became involved. "It is in our own selfish interest," stated one U.S. TNE executive in South Korea, "to have a strong government that controls . . . labor so everything will blossom and we can continue to make profits."[87] According to a survey of U.S. TNE executives in Hong Kong in 1975, no less than 94 percent of the respondents expressed satisfaction with the state's handling of labor disputes.[88]

Yet we also saw that these repressive outcomes emerged regardless of the structural dependence of Asian state officials on the First World for aggregate national development. When the data were controlled for structural or macro-level dependency indicators, intervention still led to repression of TNE workers.

However, substantial evidence was uncovered that suggested that the personal or micro-level dependence of Asian state officials on First World socialization and material benefits may help explain the intervention-repression connection. A mutually beneficial transnational alliance system between state officials and TNEs may help explain the frequently favorable repression climate that TNEs find in Third World Asia. Conceivably, individual state officials can be psychologically and materially dependent on TNEs regardless of the degree of their countries' macro-level dependence. The objective structural dependence faced by Third World state officials may be less salient than their subjective personal dependence in explaining their repressiveness in behalf of First World interests. Hence, regardless of any current level of structural dependence, such state officials may act repressively simply to continue or expand their existing mutually beneficial relationships with TNEs.

The findings suggest that researchers might usefully examine more thoroughly and systematically the micro-level dependency linkages between Third World state officials and First World elites, particularly TNEs.

Whereas macro-level dependency theory at times ignores the transnational elite class alliances forged within Third World polities, the evidence presented here suggests that such symbiotic relationships may be ignored only at the risk of theoretical poverty. Whereas macro-level dependency theory occasionally hints that Third World state officials may be "forced" to repress popular dissent, the micro-level dependency perspective suggests that they may indeed be "willing" perpetrators of repressive behaviors. Socialized into TNE priorities and obtaining personal emoluments from TNE connections, Third World state elites may have every personal motivation to orient their policies toward repression of popular dissent that threatens their worldview and material enhancement. Perhaps for these reasons, for example, former President Marcos told U.S. petroleum TNEs after martial law was declared: "We'll pass the laws you need—just tell us what you want."[89] Conversely, TNEs have much to gain in the short run from Third World state repression. Immediately after martial law was declared in the Philippines, the American Chamber of Commerce in Manila cabled Marcos wishing him "every success" in his endeavors.[90]

Thus macro-level dependency theory, which has certainly proven theoretically enlightening in some respects, might gain a number of useful insights by integration with micro-level theory. While structural dependency theory often leaves open the possibility that Third World state officials are truly "nationalist" policymakers simply compromised by aggregate economic and political realities, micro-level data suggest that in many cases the "compradorial" perspective may prove more theoretically useful. Certainly the collection of such data poses numerous difficulties. Yet the widespread violations of human rights across the Third World by state officials indicate that a humanitarian concern as well as a theoretical one should provide sufficient motivation to make the quest a top research priority.

NOTES

1. Paul Stevenson, "Accumulation in the World Economy and the International Division of Labor," *Canadian Review of Sociology and Anthropology* 17, no. 3 (August 1980): 214-215.

2. For a good discussion of the issue, see Bruce Russett and Harvey Starr, *World Politics: The Menu for Choice,* 2d ed. (New York: Freeman, 1985).

3. See Fernando Cardoso and Enzo Faletto, *Dependency and Development in Latin America* (Berkeley and Los Angeles: University of California Press, 1979); Frank Bonilla and Robert Girling, *Structures of Dependency* (East Palo Alto, Calif.: Nairobi Bookstore, 1973).

4. On these four dependency dimensions, see George Lopez, *Dependence and Interdependence in the International System* (Columbus: Consortium for International Studies Education, Ohio State University, 1979); James Lee Ray, "Economic Dependence and Domestic Political Instability in Latin America" (Paper presented to the annual meeting of the International Studies Association, Los Angeles, March 1980).

5. Christopher Chase-Dunn, Richard Rubinson, and Volker Bornschier, "Cross-National Evidence of the Effects of Foreign Investment and Aid on Economic Growth and Inequality," *American Journal of Sociology* 84, no. 3 (November 1978): 679.

6. See Trevor Farrell, "Multinational Corporations, the Petroleum Industry, and Economic Underdevelopment" (Ph.D. diss., Cornell University, 1974), p. 137; Ernst Utrecht, *Transnational Corporations in South East Asia and the Pacific* (Sydney: Transnational Corporations Research Project, University of Sydney, 1978), vol. 1, p. 87; Andre Gunder Frank, *Lumpenbourgeoisie: Lumpendevelopment. Dependence, Class, and Politics in Latin America* (New York: Monthly Review Press, 1972); Hans Luther, "Grassroots Control and Compliance Patterns in Singapore," in Bruce McFarlane, ed., *Political Economy of Southeast Asia in the 1980s* (Adelaide, South Australia: Veriker, 1979), p. 3; Susanne Bodenheimer, "Dependency and Imperialism," in Michael Smith, Richard Little, and Michael Shackleton, eds., *Perspectives on World Politics* (Chatham, N.J.: Chatham House, 1981).

7. Alexander Hicks and Leonard Hirsch, "Dependence Change and Dependency Reversal" (Paper presented at the annual meeting of the Midwest Political Science Association, Chicago, April 1980), p. 16.

8. David Apter, "Charters, Cartels, and Multinationals," in Apter and Louis Goodman, eds., *The Multinational Corporation and Social Change* (New York: Praeger, 1976), p. 34.

9. Tim McDaniel, "Class and Dependency in Latin America," *Berkeley Journal of Sociology* 21 (1976-1977): 60.

10. Ernest Feder, *Dependency in Mexican Agriculture* (N.p.: Institute of Social Studies, 1977), p. 119.

11. Johan Galtung, "A Structural Theory of Imperialism," *Journal of Peace Research* 9, no. 2 (1971): 81.

12. Vincent Mahler, "Mining, Agriculture, and Manufacturing: The Impact of Foreign Investment on Social Distribution in Third World Countries," *Comparative Political Studies* 14, no. 3 (October 1981): 284.

13. United Nations, Department of Economic and Social Affairs, *The Impact of Multinational Corporations on Development and on International Relations* (New York: United Nations, 1974), p. 35.

14. Philip McMichael, "Social Structure of the New International Division of Labor," in Edward Friedman, ed., *Ascent and Decline in the World-System* (Beverly Hills: Sage, 1982), p. 140.

15. Steven Holloway, "Transnational Politics of the Aluminum Multinationals" (Paper presented to the Annual Meetings of the International Studies Association, Philadelphia, March 1981), p. 3.

16. Eduardo Galeano, *Open Veins of Latin America: Five Centuries of the Pillage of a Continent* (New York: Monthly Review Press, 1973), p. 14.

17. Richard Falk, *A World Order Perspective on Authoritarian Tendencies* (New York: Institute for World Order, 1980), p. 8.

18. T. E. McCarthy, *Transnational Corporations and Human Rights* (Geneva: Division of Human Rights, United Nations, 1979), p. 2.

19. Ahamed Idris-Soven et al., *The World as a Company Town* (The Hague: Mouton, 1978), p. 26.

20. Ibid., p. 33.

21. Martha Huggins, "Multinational Corporations and Brazilian Death Squads" (Paper presented to the Annual Meetings of the Society for the Study of Social Problems, Washington, D.C., August 1985).

22. Ted Robert Gurr, *Politimetrics* (Englewood Cliffs, N.J.: Prentice-Hall, 1972).

23. Data for 1973 from Yoshi Tsurumi, *The Japanese Are Coming: A Multinational Interaction of Firms and Politics* (Cambridge, Mass.: Ballinger, 1976), p. 252.

24. Data for 1967 from Volker Bornschier and Peter Heinz, *Compendium of Data for World-System Analysis* (Zurich: Soziologisches Institut der Universität Zürich, 1979), pp. 116-117.

25. Data for 1979 from Obie Whichard, "U.S. Direct Investment Abroad in 1980," *Survey of Current Business* 61, no. 8 (August 1981): 31-32.

26. See Ibon Research, 1981b; and Christian Conference on Asia/Urban-Rural Mission, 1981b, 1981c, 1981f, and 1981g, in the Appendix.

27. See "Japanese Transnational Enterprises," 1980; and Ibon Research, 1981b, in the Appendix.

28. See Christian Conference on Asia/Urban-Rural Mission, 1982b; and Tse, 1981, in the Appendix.

29. See Robbins and Siegel, 1980; "Mattel in Korea," 1979; Australia-Asia Worker Links, 1981; and all references on Control Data in the Appendix.

30. The tactical militancy scale was coded as (1) wearing of protest garb; (2) orderly march; (3) boycott of overtime; (4) sit-in or hunger strike; (5) labor strike; (6) lockout of managers and supervisors, occupation of premises, hostage taking; and (7) physical damage to persons or property. The demand militancy scale was constructed as an additive index of dummy variables with regard to whether or not workers made demands concerning the following six grievances: wage compensation, nonwage compensation, working conditions, prior repression of workers, unionization, and sexual harassment or discrimination.

31. Charlotte and Stewart Meacham, *Imperialism without Invading Armies* (New York: Amber, 1976), p. 21.

32. Krishna Kumar, *Transnational Enterprises: Their Impact on Third World Societies and Cultures* (Boulder, Colo.: Westview Press, 1980), p. 11.

33. Robert Stauffer, *Transnational Corporations and the Political Economy of Development,* Research Monograph no. 11 (Sydney: University of Sydney, 1980), p. 46.

34. "Philippines: A Government That Needs U.S. Business," *Business Week,* November 4, 1972, p. 42.

35. See Cheryl Payer, *The Debt Trap* (New York: Monthly Review Press, 1974).

36. See Theotonio dos Santos, "The Structure of Dependence," *American Economic Review* 60 (1970): 231-236.

37. U. Hla Myint, *Economy: Development Policies in the 1970's; A Study Sponsored by the Asian Development Bank* (New York: Praeger, 1972), p. 24.

38. World Bank, *Annual Report, 1982* (Washington, D.C.: World Bank, 1982), pp. 42-43.

39. Pacific-Asia Resources Center, *Free Trade Zones and Industrialization of Asia* (Tokyo: AMPO, 1977), pp. 193-195.

40. David Ransom, "The Berkeley Mafia and the Indonesian Massacre," *Ramparts,* October 1970, pp. 27-29, 40-49; Walden Bello, "The World Bank in the Philippines," *Southeast Asia Chronicle* 81 (December 1981): 4.

41. Tingko Chen, "The Role of MNCs in Taiwan's Future Economy," in Michael Skully, ed., *A Multinational Look at the Transnational Corporation* (Sydney: Dryden, 1978), p. 110.

42. Robert Pringle, *Indonesia and the Philippines: American Interests in Island Southeast Asia* (New York: Columbia University Press, 1980), p. 207.

43. Cheryl Payer, "The IMF and Indonesian Debt Slavery," in Mark Selden, ed., *Remaking Asia: Essays on the American Uses of Power* (New York: Pantheon, 1974), p. 67.

44. Harold Crouch, "Generals and Business in Indonesia," *Pacific Affairs* 48, no. 4 (Winter 1975-1976): 530.

45. Corporate Information Service, *Unilever's World* (London, n.d.), p. 82.

46. Joel Rocamora, "Japanese Capital in the Philippines," *Southeast Asia Chronicle* 88 (February 1983): 11.

47. Pacific-Asia Resource Center, *Free Trade Zones,* p. 180; Robyn Lim, "Multinationals and the Philippines since Martial Law," in Skully, *Multinational Look,* p. 133.

48. Walden Bello, David Kinley, and Elaine Elinson, *Development Debacle: The World Bank in the Philippines* (San Francisco: Institute for Food and Development Policy, 1982), p. 83.

49. Eleanor McCallie and Frances Moore Lappé, *Banana Industry in the Philippines* (San Francisco: Institute for Food and Development Policy, 1978), p. 19.

50. Henry J. Frundt, *Agribusiness Manual* (New York: Interfaith Center on Corporate Responsibility, 1978), p. I-9.

51. On the significance of joint ventures in the dependency debate, see Raymond Duvall and John Freeman, "State and Dependent Capitalism," *International Studies Quarterly* 25, no. 1 (March 1981): 99-118.

52. See Russett and Starr, *World Politics,* p. 460.

53. Richard Tanter, "The Militarization of ASEAN," *Alternatives* 7, 4 (Spring 1982): 524-525.

54. Franklin Weinstein, "MNCs and the Third World: The Case of Japan and Southeast Asia," *International Organization* 30, no. 3 (Summer 1976): 394-395.

55. Yoshi Tsurumi, "Japanese Investments in Indonesia," in Gustav Papanek, ed., *The Indonesian Economy* (New York: Praeger, 1980), p. 306.

56. Pringle, *Indonesia and the Philippines,* p. 280.

57. Commission on Justice and Peace in Thailand, *The Impact of MNCs in Thai Society: The Case of Dole Thailand* (Bangkok, 1979), p. 10.

58. Stauffer, *Transnational Corporations,* p. 40.

59. Guy Whitehead, "Philippine-American Economic Relations," *Pacific Research* 4, no. 2 (January–February 1973): 6.

60. Gerald Sussman, "Philippine Information System Geared toward Multinationals and Security," *Multinational Monitor,* June 1983, pp. 6-7.

61. Robyn Lim, "The Philippines and the Dependency Debate," *Journal of Contemporary Asia* 8, no. 2 (Spring 1978): 204.

62. Jiro Tokuyama, "The New Pacific Era and Japan's Role," in Robert Hewett, ed., *Political Change and the Economic Future of East Asia* (Honolulu: University Press of Hawaii for the Pacific Forum, 1981), p. 56.

63. James Winkler, *Losing Control: INCs in the Pacific Islands Context* (Suva, Fiji: Pacific Conference of Churches, 1982).

64. American Friends Service Committee, *The U.S. and Korea* (Philadelphia, 1980), p. 10.

65. Toh Kin Woon, *The State, Transnational Corporations, and Poverty in Malaysia,* Research Monograph no. 16 (Sydney: University of Sydney, 1982), p. 3.

66. Cynthia Enloe, "State-Building and Ethnic Structures," in Terance Hopkins and Immanuel Wallerstein, eds., *Processes of the World-System* (Beverly Hills: Sage, 1980), pp. 273-274; Corazon Siddayao, *ASEAN and the Multinational Corporations* (Singapore: Institute of Southeast Asian Studies, 1978), p. 68.

67. Commission on Justice and Peace in Thailand, *Impact of MNCs,* p. 10.

68. Arvada Mennonite Church, "Agribusiness in the Philippines," *Newsletter* 25 (January 1979): 4.

69. Geoffrey Arlin, "Martial Law in the Philippines," *Bulletin of Concerned Asian Scholars* 6, no. 4 (November–December 1974): 44-45.

70. Henry Frundt, "Corporations and Human Economic Rights," *Interfaith Center for Corporate Responsibility Brief,* October 1979, p. 3-C.

71. Mamoru Tsuda, *A Preliminary Study of Japanese-Filipino Joint Ventures* (Quezon City, Philippines: Foundation for Nationalist Studies, 1978), p. 130.

72. Kate Short, "Australian-Based Manufacturing Corporations in Indonesia," in Utrecht, *Transnational Corporations,* vol. 1, p. 176.

73. Ibid., vol. 1, p. 97.

74. Christian Conference on Asia/Urban-Rural Mission, *In Clenched Fists of Struggle* (Hong Kong, 1981), p. 101.

75. Short, "Australian-Based Manufacturing Corporations," pp. 141, 160; Bob Wyrick, *Hazards for Export* (Long Island, N.Y.: Newsday Special Report, 1981), pp. 24-25.

76. Frederick Clairmonte and John Cavanagh, "Food as Corporate Commodity," *Southeast Asia Chronicle* 86 (October 1982): 10.

77. Ingrid Palmer, *The Indonesian Economy since 1965* (London: Frank Cass, 1978), p. 165; Franklin Weinstein, *Indonesian Foreign Policy and the Dilemma of Dependence* (Ithaca, N.Y.: Cornell University Press, 1976), p. 284.

78. Tissa Balasuriya, "Multinationals and Christians," *Logos* 15, no. 2 (July 1976): 25.

79. Utrecht, *Transnational Corporations,* vol. 3 (1981), p. 98.

80. Christian Conference on Asia/Urban-Rural Mission, *Minangkabau: The Story of People vs. TNCs in Asia* (Hong Kong, 1981), p. 75.

81. Fox Butterfield, "U.S. Law against Bribes Blamed for Millions in Lost Sales in Asia," *New York Times,* June 26, 1978, p. D10.

82. Stauffer, *Transnational Corporations,* p. 62.

83. International Documentation and Communication, *Castle and Cooke in Mindanao* (Rome, 1978), p. 9.

84. Ernst Utrecht, *The Social and Cultural Impact of the Activities of Transnational Corporations in Southeast Asia,* Working Paper no. 14 (Sydney: University of Sydney, 1982), p. 22.

85. Anti-Slavery Society, *The Philippines: Authoritarian Government, Multinationals, and Ancestral Lands* (London, 1983), p. 64.

86. Yohinori Murai, "Japanese Corporations and Their Impact on the People of Indonesia," *Center for Christian Response to Asian Issues Documentation Series* 2, no. 1 (March 1983): 9.

87. "Quote of the Month," *Multinational Monitor,* December 1982, p. 10.

88. Michele Kay, *Doing Business in Hong Kong* (Hong Kong: South China Morning Post and American Chamber of Commerce in Hong Kong, 1976), p. 42.

89. Stephen Shalom, *The United States and the Philippines* (Philadelphia: Institute for the Study of Human Issues, 1981), pp. 176-177.

90. Ibid.

APPENDIX: DATA SOURCES

American Friends Service Committee. 1980. *The U.S. and Korea.* Philadelphia.

Australia-Asia Worker Links. 1981. *Mattel: Moonlighting the World.* Case Study no. 3 (June). Fitzroy, Australia.

_____. 1982. *World Car.* Fitzroy, Australia.

_____. 1983a. *Denzil Don in the Philippines.* Fitzroy, Australia.

_____. 1983b. "James Hardie Workers Strike in Indonesia." *Asian Workers Organizing* 1, no. 3 (May): 2.

_____. 1983c. "Safcol in the Philippines: Dispute Continues." *Asian Workers Organizing* 1, no. 2 (March): 1.

Bello, Walden. 1981. "Building on Martial Law." *Multinational Monitor* (February): 8-11.

_____, David Kinley, and Elaine Elinson. 1982. *Development Debacle: The World Bank and the Philippines.* San Francisco: Institute for Food and Development Policy.

Brooks, Philip. 1982. "Nestle Is Declared 'Vital' by Marcos in Attempt to Break Strike." *Multinational Monitor* (April): 18-19.

Cantwell, Rebecca, Don Luce, and Leonard Weinglass. 1978. *Made in Taiwan: A Human Rights Investigation.* New York: Asian Center, Clergy and Laity Concerned.

Chen, Yu-hsi. 1981. "Dependent Development and Its Sociopolitical Consequences: A Case Study of Taiwan." Ph.D. diss., University of Hawaii.

Christian Conference on Asia/Urban-Rural Mission. 1977. *Captives on the Land.* Colombo, Sri Lanka.

_____. 1981a. "Fairchild." *Voices* 5, no. 3 (August): 8-9.

_____. 1981b. *In Clenched Fists of Struggle: Report of the Workshop on the Impact of TNCs in Asia.* Hong Kong.

_____. 1981c. *Minangkabau: The Story of People vs. TNCs in Asia.* Hong Kong.

_____. 1981d. "Penang Women Strike Back." *Voices* 5, no. 1 (March): 4.

_____. 1981e. "Rama IV." *Voices* 5, no. 1 (March): 2-3.

_____. 1981f. *Struggling to Survive: Women Workers in Asia.* Hong Kong.

_____. 1981g. "A 'Top Form' Strike." *Voices* 5, no. 1 (March): 9.

_____. 1982a. *From the Womb of Han: Stories of Korean Women Workers.* Hong Kong.

_____. 1982b. *Plight of Asian Workers in Electronics.* Hong Kong.

_____. 1982c. "Women in Action." *Voices* 6, no. 3 (May–June): 3.

Cohen, Walter. 1977. "Oceania in the World System: Part II." *Pacific Research* 8, no. 5 (July–August): 1-12.

Commission on Justice and Peace in Thailand. 1979. *Impact of MNCs in Thai Society: The Case of Dole Thailand.* Bangkok.

_____. 1981. *More Information about the Impact on Thai Society of Dole Thailand.* Bangkok.

"Control Data." 1982a. *Voices* 6, no. 3 (May–June): 2-3.

_____. 1982b. *Korea Key Contact* 50 (16 July): 1-7.

"Control Data Dispute Continues." 1982. *Human Rights Internet Reporter* 7, no. 5 (June–August): 1044.

"Control Data Fires Labor Activists in South Korea." 1982. *Multinational Monitor* (May): 4.

"Control Data Korea Three in Gaol." 1983. *Voices* 7, no. 1 (May): 12.

"Control Data Korea Withdraws and Attacks Follow on Other Unions." 1983. *Maryknoll Justice and Peace Office News Notes* (March): 20.

De Silva, Douglas. 1980. "Are Workers outside the Pale of the Just Society?" *Logos* 19, no. 2 (April): 77-81.

Dimasupil, Leon. 1981. *Neo-Colonialism and Filipino Industrial Workers.* Washington, D.C.: Friends of the Filipino People.

Friends of the Filipino People. 1980. *U.S. Employment and Corporate Profits: The Philippine Connection.* Washington, D.C.

Gallin, Dan. 1973. "Counter-Strategies of the Employees." In Tudyka, *Multinational Corporations,* 31-38.

Grossman, Rachael, and Lennie Seigel. 1977. "Weyerhaeuser in Indonesia." *Pacific Research* 9, no. 1 (November–December): 1-11.

Hamilton, Saralee. 1982. "Korean Women Fight Union-Busting Tactics." *Women and Global Corporations* 3, no. 1-2: 1-2.

Ibon Research. 1981a. *Primer on the Fishing Industry.* Manila.

_____. 1981b. *Primer on the Garment Industry.* Manila.

_____. 1981c. *Primer on the Oil Industry.* Manila.

_____. 1982. "Japan in Northern Luzon: Issues Raised by Japanese Corporate Activity in the Philippines." *Ampo* 14, no. 3: 38-50.

International Documentation and Communications Center. 1981. *Impact of TNCs on the Quality of Work.* Rome: IDOC for the World Council of Churches.

Japan Emergency Christian Conference on Korean Problems. 1982a. "Crushing Free Labor: Wuonpoong and Control Data." *Korea Communique* 45 (15 October): 40-47.

_____. 1982b. "Labor Disputes: Control Data." *Korea Communique* 44 (15 June): 40-41.

"Japanese Transnational Enterprises in Indonesia." 1980. *Ampo* 12, no. 4: 1-73.

Kelly, Tom. 1982. "Purifying South Korea's Workforce." *Christianity and Crisis* (4 October): 275.

"Korea: Control Data." 1983. *Asian Rights Advocate* 7, no. 4 (April–May): 1-3.

Lee, Patricia. 1981. "Hotel and Restaurant Workers in the Philippines." *Southeast Asia Chronicle* 78 (April): 33-35.

"Life on the Global Assembly Line." 1981. *Korea Report* 10 (June): 12-13.

Lim, Robyn. 1978a. "Multinationals and the Philippines since Martial Law." In Skully, *Multinational Look,* 126-139.

_____. 1978b. "Philippines and the 'Dependency Debate': A Preliminary Case Study." *Journal of Contemporary Asia* 8, no. 2 (Spring): 196-209.

_____. 1982. "Foreign Investment and Philippine 'Development.' " In Utrecht, *Transnational Corporations,* vol. 4: 97-120.

Luther, Hans. 1978. "Strikes and the Institutionalization of Labor Protest: The Case of Singapore." *Journal of Contemporary Asia* 8, no. 2 (Spring): 219-230.

McCarty, Vern. 1972. "Philippine Copper." *Pacific Research* 3, no. 3 (March-May): 20-21.

"Malaysia: What Price 'Success'?" 1980. *Southeast Asia Chronicle* 72 (April): 1-23.

"Mattel in Korea." 1979. *Korea Report* 4 (January): 9-10.

Millar, Ron. 1982a. "Bechtel Workers Strike in Indonesia." *Multinational Monitor* (December): 10.

_____. 1982b. "Caltex: Indonesian Workers Demand Nationalization." *Multinational Monitor* (October): 7.

Neumann, A. Lin. 1978. " 'Hospitality Girls' in the Philippines." *Southeast Asia Chronicle* 66 (July): 5-6.

_____. 1980. "Unrest Spreads in the Philippines." *In These Times* (1-7 October): 7.

"News Briefs." 1979. *Korea Report* 4 (January): 18.

Pacific and Australasian Consultation on TNCs. 1981. "TNCs, Governments, and Churches Listen to the Voice of Our Peoples." In *World Council of Churches Programme on TNCs, Struggling for the Sharing of Wealth and Power,* 18-41.

Pacific-Asia Resources Center. 1977. *Free Trade Zones and the Industrialization of Asia.* Tokyo: Ampo.

Paglaban, Enrico. 1978. "Philippines: Workers in the Export Industry." *Pacific Research* 9, no. 3-4 (March–June): 1-31.

"Penang Women Workers on Strike." 1981. *Australia-Asia Worker Links* (January): 4.

"Philippines: Profile in Underdevelopment." 1982. *One Sky Report* (January): 1-24.

"Resistance at Control Data." 1982. *One Sky Report* (September): 22.

Robbins, Linda, and Jenny Siegel. 1980. "Mattel Toys Around with Foreign Workers." *Pacific Research* 11, no. 2 (Spring): 3-8.

Rothschild, Matthew. 1982. "Women Bear Up at Control Data Korea." *Multinational Monitor* (September): 14-16.

Skully, Michael. 1978. *A Multinational Look at the Transnational Corporation.* Sydney: Dryden.

Stokes, Henry. 1981. "Unions Are Battered in Seoul Sweatshops." *New York Times* (1 March): 8.

_____. 1982. "Two Americans Held Hostage by Seoul Workers Nine Hours." *New York Times* (7 June): A3.

Tadem, E. 1980. *Mindanao Report: A Preliminary Study in the Economic Origins of Social Unrest.* Davao City, Philippines: AFRIM Resource Center.

_____. 1983. "Japan's Presence in the Philippines." *Alternative Studies* 3: 1-12.

Transnational Cooperative. 1980. "Asian Workers: A New Threat from the North?" *Transnational Brief* 2 (September): 1-28.

_____. 1981. *Pacific Changes.* Sydney.

Tse, Christiana. 1981. *Invisible Control: Management Control of Workers in a U.S. Electronics Company.* Hong Kong: Center for the Progress of Peoples.

Tudyka, Kurt. 1973. *Multinational Corporations and Labour Unions: Selected Papers from a Symposium in Nijmegen.* Nijmegen, Netherlands: Werkuitgave SUN.

"Update on Control Data Korea." 1983. *Human Rights Internet Reporter* 9, no. 1-2 (November): 130.

Utrecht, Ernst. 1978-1983. *Transnational Corporations in South East Asia and the Pacific.* 5 vols. Sydney: Transnational Corporations Research Project, University of Sydney.

_____. 1982. *The Social and Cultural Impact of the Activities of Transnational Corporations in Southeast Asia.* Working Paper no. 14. Sydney: Transnational Corporations Research Project, University of Sydney.

Wenkam, Robert. 1974. *The Great Pacific Rip-Off.* Chicago: Follett.

"Workers No Different in Other Free Trade Zones." 1980. *Logos* 19, no. 2 (April): 79-81.

World Council of Churches Programme on TNCs. 1981. *Struggling for the Sharing of Wealth and Power: Regional Reports—Asia, Pacific, Australasia, Africa, North America.* Geneva: Bulletin no. 7 (December).

4

Internal and External Aspects of Repression by a Lame Leviathan: The Case of Zaire

Thomas M. Callaghy

THE POSTCOLONIAL STATE IN AFRICA:
REPRESSION BY LAME LEVIATHANS

The modal African state is conceived here as an organization of domination controlled with varying degrees of efficacy by a ruling group that competes for power and compliance, for sovereignty, with other political, economic, and social organizations both internally and externally. It is a partly autonomous, partly dependent structure of control in which a dominant elite or class seeks to cope with constraints and uncertainty, to manage its dependence on all groups, internally and externally, in its search for sovereignty.[1]

This political class struggles simultaneously on two fronts against universalistic and particularistic elements for unity and power. It does so in order to expand the domain of the state at the expense of both infrastate and suprastate institutions and actors and to protect its own interests. Internally, chief concerns are ethnic, regional, and personalistic particularisms, strongly rooted universalistic religions, emerging class structures that manifest some universalistic characteristics, and the quasi-autonomous activities of a variety of external actors. On the external front, the state combats the universalistic legacies of the colonial state—strong linkages to the world capitalist system increasingly dominated by transnational corporations and the pervasive influences of a wide variety of international organizations and of competing ideologies and blocs in the international state system. Yet the international system also has important particularistic characteristics as its constituent states and organizations pursue their own interests and values. This allows African states some room for maneuver. The two fronts of the battle interact in complex and shifting, but persistent ways, such that they are the two sides of the same fragile coin.

Most African countries are centralizing, but distinctly limited authoritarian, patrimonial-bureaucratic states that operate within an organic-statist tradition clearly distinct from both liberal democracy and totalitarianism, but possessing pseudoelements of each. These characteristics are weakly institutionalized, but nonetheless important supportive elements. These states manifest low levels of development and penetration and limited coercive and implementation capacities. Central to their state-formation strategy are prefectoral forms of territorial administration and coercive instruments that are used both to control a complex and fragmented society and to extend the state's limited domain. Of particular concern are rural particularisms resulting in large part from fluid but powerful forms of ethnicity and localism and the dispersed power conditions of traditional political structures that remain partially viable.[2] The single-party or military-controlled corporatist structures are employed primarily in an attempt to control a limited societal pluralism resulting from a modest level of socioeconomic modernization and an economy in the early stages of dependent capitalist development.

Precapitalist economic elements also remain important.[3] Weakly institutionalized arms of the state, these state structures maintain only a very limited mobilization of the subject population. The most heavily institutionalized structures and processes are those of prefectoral territorial administration and the coercive instruments used by it, both of which were inherited from the colonial state but partially patrimonialized by highly personalized civilian or military leadership. Thus politics is highly personalized, and ruling elites are consolidating their power within the structures of the state while the stratification gap between the rulers and the ruled grows. Of increasing importance are emerging, but still very fluid, class structures that are affected by both the state and external actors and forces. The colonial state has been adapted to new realities and is influenced by precolonial notions of authority and conflict, but it has not been basically restructured.

From this perspective, a central thrust of contemporary African reality is attempted state formation—the slow and uneven consolidation of central political and economic authority out of dispersed power conditions internally and dependent conditions externally. African reality is thus heavily state-centric, and state repression is central to this reality. The state is a potentially semiautonomous actor internally vis-à-vis particularistic groups and less particularistic emerging classes and externally vis-à-vis the powerful forces of the world capitalist system and the major actors of the international state system. The degree of autonomy must be empirically investigated in each case, not dogmatically denied or proclaimed. The process of establishing and consolidating these states has been facilitated by an international system that supports the primary existence of these states, even keeping particular regimes in power, but without necessarily being able to dictate their nature and structure in systematic ways.[4]

While the nature of the international system appears to maintain, with a few exceptions and alterations, the persistence of new states in their basically artificial boundaries, the search for internal and external sovereignty, authority, and unity remains very incomplete in most African countries. For African ruling groups of all ideological and policy persuasions, the need and desire for greater authority over their societies and territories is a primary concern. Central to the efforts to achieve greater authority are the coercive functions of armies and police forces. To a large extent the authoritarian forms of rule result not from high levels of power and legitimacy, but from the tenuousness of authority and the search for it. This search for sovereignty takes place within the context of weak, poorly organized and institutionalized states attempting to rule distinctly early modern societies.

In early modern states, a single political system simply does not exist. Central authorities do not have binding, intensive, continuous, and direct jurisdiction over all persons and actions taking place within a unified territory; they do not monopolize the means of administration, adjudication, and extraction within their territory. In short, power is dispersed; there are coexisting and partially competing traditional, quasi-traditional, and nontraditional political and legal systems in the local areas beyond the complete control of central officials. This situation is further complicated by a fluid class situation. A single "national" and "modern" political structure does not hold sway in a direct and unmediated way via a fully bureaucratized administration, unified legal system, and coercive apparatus over all people in all localities. In the typical situation, local, decentralized, usually patrimonial, forms of rule compete with central authorities for compliance, legitimacy, and resources from the same set of people. Intermediary authorities of various types thus prevent the maintenance of a direct state-subject or "citizen" relationship.[5]

The basic argument here is that most African ruling groups, civilian and military alike, have responded to the early modern nature of their societies in the context of the first or primary-product–exporting phase of the delayed-dependent development syndrome by relying on a centralist and corporatist colonial tradition and a wide variety of authoritarian techniques to create centralizing patrimonial administrative states with organic-statist orientations. Early modern armies, police, and secret police forces constitute crucial but often precarious pillars of these efforts. This syndrome is similar in many ways to early modern state formation efforts in Europe and in nineteenth-century Latin America, and in fact, via the colonial state, has some of its roots in these efforts. African authoritarianism falls within the organic-statist vision of politics that stresses the organic harmony and order of the political community as guaranteed and structured by a relatively autonomous state. Such an elitist and statist orientation adopts an intermediary position between liberal pluralist and Marxist views of politics by emphasizing the need for and legitimacy of unity in order to achieve the common good. In so doing, it rejects individualistic, autonomous-group, and class-based forms of conflict in favor of state-structured and controlled interaction. The state is seen as necessary to regulate conflict, and this regulation is achieved in large part by the "archi-tectonic action" of rulers and the control efforts of the territorial adminis-trative apparatus and the armies and police forces that support it.[6]

Thus two major thrusts of these early modern state formation efforts are (1) the control of a limited societal pluralism in small relatively modern sectors by depoliticization or departicipation using inclusionary corporatist structures of a single-party apparatus or exclusionary corporatist measures of military regimes without party structures; and (2) the attempted exten-sion and strengthening of highly authoritarian and centralizing territorial structures to control ethnic, regional, and linguistic particularisms as they mix in complex ways with emerging class factors and the uneven effects of modest levels of socioeconomic modernization. The military and the police are central to both thrusts. This repressive patrimonial-administrative state constitutes the underlying form of domination in Africa today, above which floats a host of varying and changing regime types.[7]

MOBUTU SESE SEKO AND THE ZAIRIAN STATE: PATRIMONIALISM, STATE FORMATION, AND REPRESSION

The Zairian state is an emerging organization of domination seeking to expand its domain in a very hostile and uncertain environment, both inter-nally and externally. The survival of this patrimonial-administrative state never appears assured; uncertainty remains a pervasive fact for the ruler and his political aristocracy.

The state of Mobutu Sese Seko can be conceptualized as an African variant of early modern European absolutism. Responding to a severe crisis of order and authority in Zaire in the early 1960s, Mobutu seized power in a military coup d'état in November 1965. Over time his regime evolved from a relatively typical military autocracy with striking *caudillo* and Bonapartist characteristics into an African version of an absolutist state with key elements of single-party corporatism, departicipation, and military despotism. The extra-absolutist characteristics of the regime are weakly institutionalized, but nonetheless important supportive elements. This evolution of the regime took place haltingly and unevenly, but surely, and was greatly facilitated by considerable external assistance.[8]

The Zairian absolutist regime is an authoritarian state organized around a presidential monarch who adopted the Belgian colonial state structure and patrimonialized it by creating an administrative monarchy that was then used to recentralize power. In this state, patriarchal patrimonialism and patrimonial forms of administration, mixed with emerging bureaucratic ones, are both salient characteristics.[9] But like all absolutist states,

Mobutu's kingdom has distinctly limited capabilities. Old forms and structures of authority continue to operate. Mobutu has increased his personal discretion beyond the confines of both traditional (precolonial) restraints and modern, legal ones, but has used elements of both for legitimation purposes. He has appropriated the coercive, administrative, and financial means to increase his patriarchal patrimonial power. He has used police and military forces and a cadre of territorial administrators or prefects—the king's men—to control all key societal groups via the corporatist elements of the single party, the Popular Movement of the Revolution (MPR), and to emasculate the power of all traditional and quasi-traditional intermediary authorities.

With these coercive and administrative instruments Mobutu has sought to "whittle away traditional rules and practices"[10] and limit the power of workers, students, churches, and other groups. This has been an uneven and halting process, but the distinction between state and subject has become increasingly sharp. Like its European predecessors, Zairian absolutism "c'est tout d'abord l'expression d'une *volonté* de puissance qui s'est exercée dans tous les domaines."[11] It is a will to dominate, a desire for unification, obedience, and glory; it is an impulse to overwhelm doubt. The authoritarian control structures of absolutism have been so grandiosely promulgated because the reality is often so shallow. Success has been both remarkable and limited. Basic order has been maintained, but with periodic and sometimes significant external assistance. Some have considered this to be an achievement, though a brutal one, given the country's history, but the authority of the Zairian absolutist state still often appears like a "sort of authoritarian bragging which drowns in an often mocking passivity."[12]

In the depths of the regions, the norm is disobedience tempered by absolutism. Centralized administrative control has increased, but it is still far from being unlimited. It is just unsupervised. Authority relations are still mediated to a significant degree. Tocqueville's statement holds true for the Zairian absolutist state: "Centralized administration was established *among* the ancient powers, which it supplanted, without, however, detroying them."[13]

The Mobutu strategy of state formation is highly organic-statist in orientation and entails (1) the consolidation and use of coercive force (with considerable external assistance) to reestablish general political order and prevent or contain overt political unrest; (2) an intense personalization (patrimonialization) of power; (3) a recentralization of power along the lines of the authoritarian colonial state using a territorial administrative apparatus to dominate the population in various ways; (4) the emasculation or elimination of all alternative sources of autonomous authority, traditional or modern; (5) the maintenance of severely constricted and channeled political participation (departicipation) in which a single highly corporatist state party is recognized as the only legitimate political arena; (6) the establishment of an "ideology" (Mobutuism) that consists of an eclectic blend of legitimating doctrines, a set of expectations of what the state requires of its "citizens" (actually subjects), and a political religion built around the presidential monarch; and (7) neomercantilist economic policies designed to increase the economic and political power of the state, its ruler, and his political aristocracy.[14]

These elements are held together and guided by highly personalistic ruler-ship and politics, resulting in a patrimonial-administrative state controlled by a presidential monarch and a political aristocracy and using an eclectic blend of legitimating doctrines. In pursuing his state-formation strategy, Mobutu has both relied heavily on external support and sought to limit external influence when it impinged on his interests and those of his political aristocracy.

In the process of carrying out this strategy of state formation, a ruling class, here characterized as a political aristocracy, has emerged that is both the child of the state and its principal internal support. As in seventeenth-century France, the Zairian absolutist state has created its own political aristocracy—a *noblesse d'Etat*—which in turn supports its creator.

EXTERNAL ASPECTS OF STATE REPRESSION IN ZAIRE

Zaire was born in the international arena and has remained there. Inter-national assistance has been a continuous and pervasive factor supporting the emergence, consolidation, and survival of the Mobutu regime in Zaire. Such support was crucial to Mobutu's control of the armed forces from the earliest days, crucial to his first "coup" in September 1960, crucial to his seizure of full power in 1965 as an African *caudillo,* crucial to the emer-gence and consolidation of an absolutist state with its political aristocracy, and crucial to its ability to survive a severe debt and economic crisis and two external invasions in 1977 and 1978. External military and intelligence support to the regime is still vital for its survival. A word of caution is neces-sary, however, for although external assistance has been essential, it has not been all-determining. The Mobutu regime would not exist today without ex-ternal support, past and present, but its ruler and his political aristocracy have successfully fought off important challenges to their relative autonomy.

Since his earliest days in the turbulent crucible of Zairian politics, Mobutu has shown a Machiavellian flair for establishing and manipulating shifting coalitions of support, both internally and externally. Other states, international organizations, transnational corporations, and external groups such as the Catholic church have complex, shifting, and often com-peting sets of economic, politico-strategic, and normative interests to pursue in the Zairian arena. The interstices created by these multiple sets of interests often permit some room for maneuver, some autonomy for the absolutist ruler and his political aristocracy. External influence does have its limits.[15]

The international system usually operates to maintain the basic integrity and boundaries of a state as they were agreed upon at the time of independence. Powerful actors in the international system can also work to maintain a particular leadership group in power or work to replace it, but the power of actors in the international system is much more restricted at the level of the regime. In short, it is possible to keep a state together; it is even possible to help dictate who rules it. But it is very difficult to effectively dictate, or even to influence in major ways, the structure and process of a country. The Mobutu regime emerged in Zaire as a result of the complex interplay of internal and external political, economic, sociocultural, historical, personal, and idiosyncratic factors. Altering its basic structure is extremely difficult.

This authoritarian and rather ineffective patrimonial regime clearly served many of what might be called neocolonial economic interests (but also politico-strategic ones) until the onset of a severe economic and fiscal crisis in 1975. Since then several different types of actors in the international system have attempted to change the very nature of the regime, with minimal results so far. At the same time, and for a variety of reasons, some of the major actors fear the politico-strategic and economic consequences of any attempt to replace the current authorities. From the logic of the neocolonial position, it might be possible to argue that if "foreign capital" had been able freely to structure the Zairian regime, it would have designed something quite different from the regime that now exists or would be able effectively to restructure the regime now. The Soviets may be learning some of these same lessons in Africa, particularly in regard to the difficulties of creating viable Leninist transformation regimes in Angola, Mozambique, and Ethiopia.

Since 1965 external actors have focused on maintaining the Mobutu regime in power, but the nature of the regime, its structure, plays a positive or negative legitimating role in these external support efforts. As a result, external actors have tried to induce changes at the regime level that would facilitate their support efforts to current authorities. Mobutu, on his own, has taken steps to portray his regime in a favorable light to external actors from whom he needs crucial support, among other things by stressing his anticommunism (or anti-Sovietism in the case of China) and politico-strategic and economic importance. He has also acquiesced, at least superficially, in a number of externally induced changes in order to increase his external legitimacy with Western states (and their domestic and international constituencies), international organizations, and banks. But he has gone only as far as necessary to obtain such support, and when events changed or the composition of the support coalition could be altered, he backed off from changes that did not suit his needs or desires. In the process the absolutist state has so far remained intact and in power.

In this regard Arthur Stinchcombe delineates a conceptualization of legitimacy that concentrates on whether other centers of power view a regime as legitimate and worth supporting: "A power is legitimate to the degree that, by virtue of the doctrines and norms by which it is justified, the power-holder can call upon sufficient other centers of power, as reserves in case of need, to make his power effective."[16] He terms this backup a "nesting of reserve sources of power" that allows a regime to overcome opposition where the legitimacy of the regime as viewed by its subjects is low or non-existent. This type of assistance has always been crucial to Mobutu's survival and that of his political aristocracy.

Most recently this pattern has been vividly demonstrated by the aftermath of the two invasions of the Shaba Region in 1977 and 1978 and by the ongoing debt crisis. Economic and fiscal reform, military reorganization, and political liberalization efforts have all been initiated in Zaire as a result of direct pressure by external actors following internal crises caused to a substantial degree by the nature of the regime. The intent of the external actors was to alter certain key characteristics of the absolutist state, but the reform efforts have had only marginal effect.[17] The core of the absolutist state—Mobutu's personal discretion and the power of the political aristocracy—remains, thanks in large part to the assistance of external supporters and despite their efforts to induce change in the nature and structure of this state.

INTERNAL ASPECTS OF STATE REPRESSION IN ZAIRE

Consolidation of Coercive Power

After the 1965 coup d'état a major process in the development of Zairian absolutism was the consolidation of coercive power undertaken with considerable external assistance. Mobutu has invariably maintained his direct and personal control of military affairs. In the context of this chapter, the military means both the army and the gendarmery/police forces. The military has always been a major pillar, if a shaky one, of the regime, more prominently in the beginning, but still very important in the succeeding years. Immediately after the coup in 1965 states of emergency and exception were instituted that allowed extensive intervention of the military into politico-administrative affairs. Initially the provinces remained effectively under military administration and control. Provincial police units were brought under the supervision of the army until 1966, when they were organized as a national police force under the control of the Ministry of the Interior.

During the colonial period the Belgian-created and officered Force Publique combined the functions of an army and a police force. There were, however, also territorial or provincial police and local collectivity or chief's police; the latter were quasi-traditional forces. In August 1972 Mobutu returned to the colonial pattern of the Force Publique by dissolving the national police and turning its functions over to a greatly enlarged national gendarmery. In short, the national police simply became the national gendarmery and one component of the Forces Armées Zairoises (FAZ), which also includes the army and the small navy and air forces. By the late 1970s the army had a strength of about 30,000, and the gendarmery was at about 20,000.

Right after the coup the Sûreté, or secret police, was reorganized and brought under the control of Colonel Singa, a close collaborator of General Mobutu. In August 1969 the Sûreté was again reorganized, becoming the National Center for Documentation (CND); a National Security Council was also formed the same month to assure coordination between all the forces of order. In 1981 the secret police was again reorganized partially, the internal section of it becoming the CNRI (Centre National de Recherche et d'Investigations) with its functions little altered.

Repression as an Instrument of Order and Political Control

Our masses must understand that if every person does what pleases him and seeks to satisfy his ambition, anarchy will be the inevitable result.[18]

In this one sentence Mobutu captures the major thrust of his absolutist state—order and control. After the severe crisis of the first five years of independence, order and control have remained the top priorities of the regime. The state of emergency declared at the time of the coup d'état was lifted for all areas of the country except Kivu and Haut-Zaire in July 1966. But as the minister of the interior warned: "The enemy is still within our walls and the danger remains." He urged constant vigilance and, in an interesting aside, commented that state personnel must prove to the world that the country is one "of order and discipline."[19] The prefects of the eight regions incessantly exhort their subjects to be vigilant in the search for "antirevolutionary" persons or groups. After listening passively, the subjects usually go about their own business, for after all, the struggle is with the state itself and its prefects and forces of order.

The gendarmery is the principal security tool at the disposal of the prefects. They constantly complain that they need more gendarmes, that the ones they have are poorly equipped and badly disciplined, and that because of insufficient transport the gendarmes are sometimes of little use in emergencies. The prefects can requisition the use of the gendarmery for a wide variety of tasks in addition to its routine security and patrol functions. For example, prefects from Bas-Zaire and Kivu requisitioned gendarmes for the following tasks in the early 1970s: to control land disputes between various clans and town factions in Mbanza-Ngungu Zone in late 1970 (and in early 1979); to enforce a decision to remove a corral so that a dispensary could safely be built in Kimvula Collectivity in September 1973; to maintain order in the Mbanza-Ngungu Zone court in early 1975; to help collect the head tax and other taxes in the town of Mbanza-Ngungu in December 1974; to guard the guest house of a visiting Chinese vice minister of agriculture in August 1973; to guard administrative offices and prefects' houses; to guard businesses recently "Zairianized" in Cataractes Sub-Region in February 1974 to prevent damage and theft until the new owners (many of them administrative officials) could take over their new benefices; to protect foreign teachers from bandits in Gombe-Matadi, Mbanza-Ngungu Zone, in September 1973; to search for bandits; to guard the railroad and ports of Matadi and Boma in response to a tract threatening sabotage in June and July 1969; to transport prisoners in Walikale Zone, Nord-Kivu, in December 1972; and to help control the widespread smuggling in Nord-Kivu during the period 1971-1974.[20]

The gendarmery uses a wide variety of measures to assure order and security, including roving patrols, fixed surveillance posts, roadblocks, checks of identification cards, and encirclement and dragnet operations called *ratissages*. These activities are frequently carried out in collaboration with the Disciplinary Brigade of the JMPR, the youth wing of the MPR. For example, in early 1973 the Cataractes Sub-Region suffered from a wave of banditry, murder, armed robbery, and disorder that included widespread attacks on Europeans, including several murders. The sub-regional committee met in extraordinary session on 29 January 1973 and ordered the gendarmery to undertake special measures. In conjunction with the JMPR and the CND and with the logistical assistance of the Presidency, the local gendarmery proceeded to conduct mobile patrols, establish barricades on the roads and control posts in towns and villages to seek out the bandits, carry out a number of *ratissages,* and assign guards for Europeans living in 20 isolated spots. Daily reports were sent to Mbanza-Ngungu and Kinshasa.

Elaborate measures of population control exist that seek to increase the state's power over its subjects. For example, every Zairian must constantly carry an identification card, which is a principal instrument of population control. In order to increase its control capabilities, the regime decided in 1972 to issue new identification cards that would include "all information useful in facilitating administrative control in various domains."[21] These "citizen" cards had to be purchased. Zairian administrative and security personnel constantly check the cards of their subjects. If there is some "irregularity," the person can be arrested or be forced to pay a "fine." Harassment over these cards is a pervasive source of uncertainty for the population.

The regime spends considerable time and resources trying to stem the rural exodus into towns and cities. In an attempt to slow this massive flow, the regime announced in 1975 that it was establishing a permit control system that would regulate the influx of the rural population to the cities and prevent rural villagers from staying on. Although the regime did not admit it, the announced measures were almost identical to those imposed by the Belgian colonial state in 1933. Even the forms were identical. Prior to 1975 the gendarmes periodically rounded up vagabonds and the unemployed and returned them to their regions of origin. Bas-Zaire had a particular problem with Kinshasa youth who came into the region and created security problems. These young people were rounded up by the gendarmes and sent back to Kinshasa.

Explicitly subversive movements or tendencies receive top priority from the prefects and the gendarmery. One prefect stressed to his staff that "the authority of the State cannot be contested; it does not defer to any group whatever its interests or opinions." In late 1972 army and gendarmery units were still attempting to eradicate the last remnants of opposition to the new regime in the Walikale Zone of Nord-Kivu Sub-Region. The zone prefect observed that "the population of Walikale Zone, more precisely the operational zone of Wassa, has been greatly contaminated by the mulelist rebellion." Assassinations, kidnappings, and human sacrifices were still being practiced, according to administrative and military officials. About the same time four "antirevolutionary" men were arrested by the police for opposition activity in Beni Zone, interrogated by the CND, and turned over to authorities for prosecution.[22]

All political meetings held in secret or not sanctioned by the administration are illegal. The prefects and their gendarmes are constantly on alert for what they call "illicit or clandestine political meetings." Most of these secret meetings have to do with conflicts between traditional authorities at the village and collectivity levels or between these and the administration of the absolutist state that is trying to slowly weaken their power.

Sentiments of regionalism or local particularism are displayed in a variety of other ways, such as boycotting or attempting to sabotage regime celebrations and meetings or openly disagreeing with pronouncements of regime officials. An example of the latter took place in the town of Kintanu in May 1972. In a mass meeting the regional commissioner, or prefect, had ordered the destruction of two local monuments. A local electrician who worked for the state voiced his opposition to this order:

The governor and the authorities who represent him are strangers here; no matter what they think, they have no right to dictate orders here. As a man of the region I have land here, and I am going to do whatever I want. The destruction of these two monuments interests only the governor. The officials who come from elsewhere wish to take our lands.

This incident was investigated by the police, and the police report indicated that other influential local people felt the same way and often held secret meetings. Appropriate action was taken by the prefects and the police.[23]

The prefects and the forces of order must also cope with the possibility of more overt and violent opposition. In February 1974 the zone prefect for Kimvula warned his sub-regional prefect by cable that he feared that an uprising was imminent because of arbitrary arrests and widespread abuse by the gendarmery. Prefects in Nord-Kivu Sub-Region warned of a similar possibility in early 1973 because of poor administration of the coffee-purchase program by the National Coffee Office.

As a result of a series of economic, military, and political crises in the 1970s, opposition to the Mobutu regime increased substantially after 1975. The most dramatic manifestations were the two invasions of Shaba Region from Angola in 1977 and 1978, both of which were put down only as a result of massive external assistance. More localized forms of opposition have been successfully dealt with by the army and the gendarmery. In January 1978 a small uprising took place near the town of Idiofa in the Kwilu area of Bandundu Region, near the native village of Pierre Mulele, an early 1960s revolutionary figure. Followers of a local millenarian religious sect attacked two villages, and the army and gendarmery were brought in to stop them. Fourteen leaders of the uprising were publicly executed without trial, and Amnesty International estimated that about 500 other people were killed. In July 1979 about 200 young people were killed by soldiers and gendarmes near the city of Mbuji-Mayi in the Kasai Oriental Region, apparently for failing to pay the army for permission to engage in illegal digging for diamonds and for refusing to cease digging when so ordered by the troops.[24]

Students of the university system have periodically staged violent strikes and riots. The specific causes have usually been related to the conditions of student life, but these incidents have also had heavy political overtones. For example, in April 1980 university students mounted a major strike at all three university campuses. In addition to university-related demands, the students called for the removal of the entire Political Bureau and the establishment of a multiparty system. The army and the gendarmery violently stopped the demonstrations and closed the campuses, the students were evacuated to the interior, and the university was shut down until October. The gendarmery has also been used to end a series of illegal strikes by workers and teachers.

Disputes between traditional authorities and groups pose serious contingencies for the prefects. In late 1975 one Bas-Zaire prefect stated that "the spirit of separatism still reigns here, hate, jealousy and tribalism abound." Revolving most often around land and traditional power issues, these intense disputes often go on for decades and may occasionally "lead the population to armed conflict." Thus one of the major order and control tasks of the prefects and the gendarmery is to "put a definitive end to the traditional disputes which spill so much ink."[25]

Sorcery and fetishism are additional sources of uncertainty related to local particularism. A wide variety of superstitious practices pose a threat to order and stability because they stir up turmoil in local populations. In 1973 a Cataractes prefect reminded one of his zone prefects that "sorcery is a shameful practice," while another prefect called people who stirred up his population with such practices "these occult malefactors." The most common administrative response is to arrest and expel sourcerers and fetishers from the local area where they are disturbing the peace. Such was the case with a "prophet" Munzemba in the Collectivity of Gombe-Sud in Bas-Zaire in 1968. Dealing with these problems often proves difficult because of conflicts between state and local traditional courts about how these matters should be treated.[26]

Major societal groups are also key sources of concern for the prefects and the police forces. Some of the more important ones, such as the unions, the youth movements, and the press, have been integrated directly into the state-party apparatus. The prefects and the forces of order spend considerable time monitoring the activities of these groups and of important groups that have not been directly integrated into the party, such as teachers, businessmen, missionaries and other foreigners, refugees, the churches, and "social and cultural" organizations. The latter two are of particular concern because the administration sees them as fronts for opposition activities. In a letter to all his prefects in August 1970, the regional commissioner for Bas-Zaire expressed concern about the recent appearance of several new organizations. He warned that antiregime individuals often hide "behind the social character of these associations" and reminded his prefects that no organization could operate in the region without his accord. The gendarmery has been systematically used to close down illegal syncretic religious or church movements because they are seen as threats to order and control.[27] Finally, the gendarmes have taken an active role in organizing and supervising the Mobutu regime's version of corvée labor, called *salongo*.

SALONGO

In January 1973 Mobutu announced what was, in effect, a major new coercive activity, namely *salongo*. Although enveloped in a thick cloud of "revolutionary" cant, it is really corvée labor, albeit described as an educational way of mobilizing the population. According to regime officials, however, it has its roots in the communalism and solidarity of traditional society rather than in the coercive nature of the colonial state:

In effect we have examined traditional society and there discovered collective work which is done with enthusiasm and without constraint; colonial society on the other hand had to force people to work, to compel them to the point of devaluing the work and thus stripping it of all its ennobling content.[28]

The people are said to participate in *salongo* freely, with joy, and "without constraint," for "only the civic sense of the citizen persuades him to participate in the collective work." The emphasis is on collective labor in the interest of national development. *Salongo* is also proclaimed to be a way

that the masses can commune with Mobutu. In launching this policy the
president appears to have been influenced by a visit to Peking. It is
interesting to note that he was impressed by the Chinese emphasis on work,
discipline, and control, but not by their stress on equality and distributive
justice. His authoritarian state is congruent with the former, but antithetical
to the latter.[29]

The Zaire regime referred to *salongo* in 1973 as "collective work in the
public interest and field work" with the stress on its voluntary, noncoercive
nature. This theme is reiterated constantly in administrative reports. For
example, in May 1973 the Cataractes sub-regional commissioner noted that
"all the militants performed the work with joy." At the end of 1974 one
zone commissioner wrote that "all aspects of *salongo* are carried out in a
spontaneous and regular manner in all nooks and crannies of Songololo
Zone." On the whole, however, *salongo* is anything but voluntary. Occasionally some enthusiasm can be generated if the project has particular local
interest—a hospital, for example—but generally this is not the case. In
administrative correspondence and regulations the prefects refer to *salongo*
as "work *imposed* on the people" and "*obligatory* civic work." Indeed,
this was made very clear by the Kivu regional commissioner in June 1975
when he stated that "several unthinking militants do not respond to the fulfillment of *salongo* work," and that it is "not well understood by the militants." As a result, he decreed that "all Zairian citizens living in Kivu Region
are obliged to respond to the civic work of *salongo*." Failure to comply can
bring sanctions of 8 to 30 days in jail and/or a fine of five zaires.[30]

Corresponding to the colonial varieties of corvée labor, there are two
basic types of *salongo:* agricultural and general. The first may be either
individual or collective and is a direct descendant of the colonial policy of
obligatory cultivation, except that cash crops for export are not stressed.
The forced cultivation of food crops was reimposed in Bas-Zaire in
February 1968 and reorganized by a December 1972 decree. Citing the
assertion that agriculture is the regime's "priority of priorities" and that
Bas-Zaire did not have enough food, the decree established "obligatory
agricultural work." Under this program all unemployed men must plant a
minimum of 50 *ares* (an *are* is 10 square meters) in manioc, maize, rice,
beans, bananas, and groundnuts. Women must plant a minimum of 30 *ares,*
and all employed adults must plant at least 2 *ares.* Failure to comply carries
possible sanctions of one to six months in jail and/or fines ranging from 10
to 25.5 zaires. With the advent of *salongo* in early 1973 came the establishment of collective fields by schools, businesses, state offices, and local
administrative jurisdictions.[31]

The second or general type of *salongo* normally takes place on Saturday
afternoons from two to five o'clock, but sometimes a whole day is set aside,
and everything else comes to a halt. Markets and stores close, and all movement and traffic stops. Apart from special personnel, such as on-duty

doctors, gendarmes, and foreigners, everyone is obliged to undertake tasks assigned by the local administration. The workers are usually required to bring their own hoes, machetes, shovels, and pickaxes, while local businesses are forced to provide vehicles, heavy equipment, and other tools. The work is controlled and supervised by state officials, although this is often made difficult by lack of transportation. Regular reports on these activities must be sent up the administrative hierarchy.

Despite all the pronouncements about *salongo* being oriented toward developments that benefit large numbers of people, almost all of the projects are state related. They are the traditional tasks of corvée labor: building and repairing roads and bridges, constructing and maintaining offices and houses of state personnel, and generally cleaning up. The following is a list of typical projects taken from over 50 reports on *salongo* activities for both Cataractes and Nord-Kivu sub-regions spanning the period from February 1973 to June 1975: (1) building, repairing, cleaning, and painting a whole host of state buildings, namely, offices of the collectivity, the zone, the sub-region, the JMPR, the civil registry, the courts, and the gendarmery, as well as prisons, administrative guest houses, and residences for officials at all levels; (2) building and repairing roads, streets, bridges, fences, drainage canals, and erosion barriers, as well as cutting away and removing a great deal of debris; (3) general cleanup operations for administrative compounds, markets, parks, and aseembly fields or arenas; (4) making bricks for construction purposes; (5) erecting party monuments; and (6) occasionally building or repairing hospitals and schools.

From considerable personal observation in Kinshasa, Bas-Zaire, Kivu, and Shapa over a 15-month period, it was apparent that there is not much enthusiasm for the Zairian form of corvée labor. Lassitude would be a much more accurate word, resulting not just from the compulsion involved, nor from the inconvenience, but rather from the realization that all the work goes to reinforce the power of the consolidating state. Passive resistance and minimum compliance are the norms.

The Gendarmery and the Army as Occupying Forces

The Zairian absolutist state has a gendarmery and an army that are clearly early modern in character. They are poorly trained, armed, fed, housed, paid, and disciplined. In short, they constitute an occupation force that lives "on the backs of the population," and their major task is the "muzzling of the people." The army has not been particularly effective when opposed by another organized armed force, but it and the gendarmery have proved to be effective, if brutal, population control instruments. Mobutu, "better than most, knows that his army has never confronted another military force and achieved victory without external help."[32] This was certainly the case during the 1960-1967 period when Mobutu used both

United Nations troops and white mercenary armies to fight his most important battles, and the situation has not changed, as was demonstrated by the
poor performance of the army during the Angolan civil war in 1975-1976
and the invasions of Shaba Region in 1977 and 1978. Significant outside
military assistance has had little impact on the performance of the military.
As a result, there is now a quasi-permanent, albeit low-profile, presence of
foreign military personnel with Zairian units of all types and at most levels.
The two principal traits of the Zairian military are rapaciousness and
relative loyalty to Mobutu. Mobutu's mechanisms for controlling the military, particularly the periodic purges of the officer corps, assure its basic
loyalty, but also greatly weaken its fighting capabilities. This is not true,
however, of its capabilities as an occupation force, as an instrument of
internal order and extraction.

The Zairian military (meaning both the army and the gendarmery) abuses
the subject population in a whole host of ways: theft, extortion, and armed
robbery of all kinds; arbitrary arrests, illegal fines, setting up of
unauthorized barricades, kidnappings, beatings, rapes, forced labor,
harassment of businessmen, physical attacks and extortion in village open-
air markets, and scavenging and pillage of crops, fruit, goats, and chickens;
attacks on missions; and even fishing with dynamite, which destroys local
fishing grounds. The local populations view the military as a foreign conquering force. One resident of the Cataractes Sub-Region put it this way:
"Such completely barbarous acts deeply disturb the people and they often
wonder why our military brothers who are supposed to look after our
security perform their duty as if they are in a conquered land."[33] The
traditional chief of Gombe-Sud complained in 1972 that the current situation was worse than it had been under colonial domination:

My people truly suffer in a situation that we never thought we would see, even in the
period when the colonial troops sowed panic. But the situation of my people, which
is now the work of Zairians, seems unnecessary. If such a situation continues
without a solution, we will see some regrettable consequences because our military
brothers make old people from sixty to eighty carry sacks filled with beans and
march more than twenty kilometers on foot and the girls and even old women are
often violently raped. The slightest resistance to these things results in a beating. It is
truly inhuman citizen Commissioner. The protectors of the Zairian people fiercely
attack their own brothers![34]

The soldiers and the gendarmes usually come from other regions of the
country, particularly from areas most loyal to Mobutu. A great deal of
inherent hostility exists between the military and the local populace. The
former are "strangers" who believe that the latter are "still savage and
backward"; the reverse is also true. Complaining about the brutal treatment of his people by the army and the gendarmery, a village chief

recounted a "talk" he had in 1968 with a group of soldiers from Haut-Zaire: "These soldiers . . . did not hesitate to say that in Haut-Zaire where they come from, few people survived [the chaos of the early 1960s], while here [Bas-Zaire] there were no slaughters and that they would try in every way to provoke this area and if successful they would be the first to exterminate us all." With increasing separation of state and society characteristic of absolutist regimes, officials do not want state agents to come from the local area. For example, speaking in 1973 to a local unit, a gendarmery commander commented that "if the performance of the Gombe-Matadi section had not been very productive up to now, it is because of the familiarity of the gendarmes with the population; they are for the most part natives of the area."[35]

In order to appreciate this aspect of absolutist domination, let us examine a few concrete cases of abuses of the subject population. As the Cataractes sub-regional commissioner put it in December 1971: "When the population sees the gendarmes, it no longer feels safe, in fact, quite the contrary." In the first six months of 1970 a police officer and eight of his men committed a whole series of abuses against the villages of the local collectivity of Mfidi that included illegal fines, extortion, beatings, theft, the illegal arrest of the collectivity chief and others, and general harassment of the villagers by confiscating identification cards. For example, a man "from the village of Sadi was truly treated like a savage beast; he was beaten, bound and forced to pay a seven zaire fine without a receipt." During this period, these police agents extracted 1,213 zaires, 313 chickens, and 25 pigeons from 137 villagers. The Zairian regime rarely has to take public opinion into account, but these incidents took place just prior to the 1970 presidential "election." Mobutu was the only candidate, but the prefects wanted to make sure that the election took place without incident. As a result, the local prefect took the unusual step of administratively removing the police officer himself.[36]

In late 1971 and early 1972 the zone prefect for Kimvula reported serious problems with the local police contingent. One police agent raped several women, stole numerous possessions including 9 goats, 78 chickens, and 2 pigeons, and severely beat a mason; another raped a 14-year-old girl and then coerced her parents into dropping charges against him; a third regularly arrested people illegally and extorted money from them; a fourth severely beat a young girl of 14 for refusing to have sexual relations with him; two others regularly collected illegal "fines" in a local village; a seventh demanded a goat in the name of the zone prefect, and when the village refused he simply took one; an eighth stole several things from a state office; a ninth physically attacked the wife of an assistant zone prefect while drunk, and finally, this same policeman, along with two others, set up an unauthorized road barricade, extracted two-zaire fines from all passing businessmen, and stole merchandise from some of them. Similar things happened in Nord-Kivu as well.[37]

Over a seven-month period in 1968, soldiers stole more than 45 goats from a local village group near Kimpese in Bas-Zaire. Using an army truck with the license plate removed, they would simply move into a village and load up the truck. Reports of rapes appeared to be unfounded, but the soldiers did force the women to "sell" them food for token prices. One woman, for example, was forced to take only 30 makuta for 30 sacks of manioc. Along the Angolan border near the villages of Kinsitu and Kindompolo, soldiers in early 1971 were forcing local women to grow crops for them, arresting their daughters, and pillaging local food supplies. Because the army and the gendarmery are poorly and irregularly fed and paid, this scavenging and pillaging activity is common. In short, the soldiers and gendarmes eat off the fields and the plates of the subjects.[38]

The zone prefect for Songololo in Bas-Zaire was forced to suspend nightly patrols by the military in September 1971 because the soldiers and gendarmes were setting up unauthorized barricades, demanding "drinking money" from people, and raping women at will. These practices of coercive appropriation are endemic to the Zairian absolutist state. Similar activity was reported to the regional commissioner in October 1971. Near Kimpese and Madimba soldiers and gendarmes were stopping trucks on the Matadi-Kinshasa road and inflicting "fines" of 10 to 25 zaires on the drivers. Often these trucks carried food bound for the hungry Kinshasa markets. Those who were not able or willing to pay these "fines" were not allowed to pass for at least three days. If the truck contained food, it usually rotted in the tropical sun and humidity.[39]

On 19 June 1972 the Bas-Zaire regional commissioner received an administrative cable on four recent incidents involving the army. Several soldiers severely beat a school director who had tried to stop the rape of a 13-year-old girl and a male nurse who had tried to prevent the rape of hospitalized women. A 12-year-old girl was raped in her village, and a soldier fired shots into the village to scare away the inhabitants, then helped himself to all the chickens he wanted.[40]

In April 1973 a village chief wrote to the commander of Camp Ebeya in Bas-Zaire and described how his soldiers harvested fruit, cut down trees, and pillaged crops that belonged to the local population. The soldiers and their wives would move into the fields planted by the villagers and fill up huge sacks with food that did not belong to them. In addition, the soldiers demanded food directly from the villagers. Those who refused were threatened. The village chief asked, "We who live by farming, how will we live?"[41]

Soldiers are responsible for much of the armed robbery. Bas-Zaire is oppressed by soldiers and gendarmes from Kinshasa who come into the area and terrorize the local population. For Kasangulu Zone this is a particular problem because of its proximity to Kinshasa, and May 1973 was an especially bad month. On the seventh of the month soldiers and gendarmes from

Kinshasa harassed and illegally arrested a village chief. On the thirteenth a group of soldiers traveling in a Toyota jeep without a license plate kidnapped a mechanic in Sonta-Bata and took him to Kinshasa. But the worst incident took place on the night of 22-23 May when seven soldiers moved in and terrorized the residents of Kibuanga village. The soldiers pillaged the village, beat up its inhabitants, fired shots into the air to scare people, demanded money, destroyed a bar after consuming all the beer they wanted, looted several houses, illegally arrested or detained people, and then demanded money for their release. Anyone who resisted was arrested; several people fled into the forest. The soldiers took 381 zaires from the village chief and extracted 162 zaires from nine other people. Finally they kidnapped six villagers and took them to Kinshasa.[42]

Two months later another major incident took place in Kasangulu. Soldiers and gendarmes stationed on the Zaire River at Zongo to guard a power station attempted to pillage the village of Sefu, and "a riot broke out between the soldiers and the inhabitants of Sefu which resulted in two civilians dead and two soldiers gravely wounded."[43] Sometimes the subjects do fight back.

In addition to their brutal treatment of local populations, the soldiers and gendarmes often do not perform the tasks assigned to them. In July 1973 the Zairian head of the Chinese agricultural center at Mawunzi in Bas-Zaire complained to officials at Camp Ebeya that men assigned to protect the center and its Chinese advisers were simply not doing their job. Instead, they drank too much and spent most of their time with their women, to the point of standing guard only two to five hours a night. An insane person invaded the living quarters of the Chinese experts one night because no soldiers were standing guard. He was detained and removed by Zairian residents of the camp.

Finally, businessmen are favorite targets of the soldiers and the gendarmes. In September 1973 a Cataractes businessman complained to the sub-regional commissioner that soldiers were a major source of trouble in a bar he owned. They extorted money and beat up and arbitrarily arrested customers and staff alike. In one incident the local commander arrested the bartender and closed the bar because the bartender did not play the record he requested. The bar did not even own that particular record.[44]

Extraction in an Early Modern State: The *Ratissage*

The *ratissage* is a major control and extraction tool of the Zairian absolutist state carried out by the gendarmery and the army. Let us look at some examples. On 27 May 1973 a major *ratissage* was conducted as a joint operation by the army and the gendarmery in two Bas-Zaire collectivities— Kwilu-Ngongo and Lufu-Toto. It was supervised jointly by one of the assistant sub-regional prefects and the local commanders of the army and gendarmery. On 25 May two prefects visited the officials of the two collectivities to inform them secretly about the *ratissage;* the same was done with the heads of the local sugar works. They too were sworn to secrecy. It now being late at night, the two prefects returned to Kwilu-Ngongo to wait. About 1 A.M. troops and gendarmes started to arrive in trucks. As they arrived, they were distributed to various assembly points.

The *ratissage* began at about 6 A.M. The troops and gendarmes moved systematically from house to house, street to street, from one locale to another demanding that people "present their identification cards in order to see if they had paid their taxes and fulfilled other requirements." Both collectivities were completely shut down; nothing functioned normally. All businesses and offices were closed, and the local outdoor market was put out of operation. Above all the troops and gendarmes were looking for *irréguliers*—those who had not fulfilled all of their "civic" duties. According to the sub-regional commissioner, the operation took place with complete discipline and calm. In Kwilu-Ngongo 439 people were rounded up; there were 174 in Lufu-Toto, for a total of 613. A sizable number of them were Angolans. All of the detained were trucked to administrative offices for sorting and processing. The "irregularity" for each detainee was determined by administrative officials. Most of these *irréguliers* fulfilled their "obligations" by buying the identification card or paying the head tax and other taxes and fines. Some had not paid their taxes since 1968 or 1969, and about 50 had no piece of identity at all.

The *ratissage* is clearly an extractive measure. A total of 1,393 zaires was collected, 470 zaires in Lufu-Toto and 923 zaires in Kwilu-Ngongo. This came from the purchase of identification cards and the payment of the head tax, other local taxes, and fines for various "infractions." After this process had run its course, the 42 people who remained were arrested "because they seemed suspicious to us." Two escaped prisoners were returned to prison.

The sub-regional commissioner observed that the *ratissage* "took place under our direct supervision and to our very great satisfaction." He did find two dark clouds, however. The local judicial police officer manifested an "indifferent attitude" by not showing up until 6 P.M.; he then showed up drunk and quickly disappeared again. Most likely a local man, he did not want to be identified with this exploitative operation against "his" people. He presumably got drunk because he knew that he would be punished by his supervisors for not participating. The prefects, the army and gendarmery commanders, and the troops and gendarmes were probably not from Bas-Zaire. This is a classic example of the man caught between the strong pressures and attachments of local particularism and the demands of a consolidating state. The second dark cloud had to do with the ability to maintain permanent control after the *ratissage,* particularly for Lufu-Toto. The sub-regional commissioner noted that the collectivity had only five gendarmes attached to it, and given the importance of the collectivity, the number "is plainly insufficient; it is high time we reinforced it."[45]

That is an official version of a *ratissage*. Let us now look at an unofficial version of a *ratissage* by a victim of one. It was held three weeks earlier (6 May 1973) in the town and collectivity of Kimpese in Bas-Zaire. This one was supervised by the sub-regional commissioner himself. Six hundred people were rounded up, most of whom fulfilled their "civic" duties and were released; 22 were repatriated to their regions of origin. According to the commander of the local gendarmery, the population and businessmen of Kimpese were quite satisfied with the operation of the *ratissage,* and, in fact, no abuses were committed: "The attitude of our men, soldiers and gendarmes alike, towards the civilian population was irreproachable . . . no violence took place."

A local resident presents quite a different picture, however. He wrote a detailed letter of protest to the zone prefect with copies to the sub-regional and regional prefects, the Departments of Defense and Political Affairs (Interior), and the Presidency. He signed it "an observer." In the letter our observer refers to the *ratissage* as "this dirty operation" and asserts that the soldiers and gendarmes committed robberies and rapes, beat people, committed "other abuses about which one does not dare reveal the secret because it is shameful," and arbitrarily arrested people whether their papers were in order or not. He avers that people were arrested solely "to be sent to the Zone offices to put money in the State coffers because, according to the Zone Commissioner, they were empty." For our observer, the *ratissage* was clearly an extractive and exploitative operation by an alien state. Our local subject notes that the taxes collected were way above the amount they legally should have been, and he charges that this was because the officials and gendarmes pocketed most of it, leaving only some for the state. He claims that this same procedure was followed with the "fines" collected for often imaginary infractions. Because the town was completely shut down, the population was not permitted to eat the entire day, children included. Speaking directly to the zone prefect, our observer states that all these abuses show that "you make your population suffer and you do the opposite of what the Father of the nation expects of you as his representative."[46]

Finally, the observer recounts that after the departure of the soldiers, the zone prefect gave the gendarmes "an important sum" from the money collected during the *ratissage* so they could buy drinks. This led to a drunken rampage in which the gendarmes generally mistreated the local population. They insulted people, slapped them around, stopped the trucks of businessmen, pulled out the merchandise and beat up the drivers and the businessmen without any hesitation, and demanded "tips" from all the passersby. Those who refused were detained. The observer concludes by saying: "This is what we the Zairian people of Kimpese have suffered this 6 May 1973, a date which is engraved in our hearts like the one of 4 January 1959."[47] The date of 4 January 1959 refers to the suspension by the Belgians of a Bakongo political meeting in Leopoldville (Kinshasa), which led to three days of burning and pillaging. The Belgians reacted with force to put down the disturbance at the cost of 42 killed and over 200 wounded, all Zairians. The day became known as "la journée des martyrs de l'indépendence." It is highly indicative that the observer of the *ratissage* equated it with this detested symbol of Belgian colonial oppression.

This impassioned letter of protest did reach central regime officials. It was read by the director general of the Department of Political Affairs, who wrote to the sub-regional commissioner asking for an investigation. The latter responded with a terse letter in which he noted that he had directed the *ratissage* himself and that no abuses had occurred. In concluding, he noted that "the letter must be considered an unwelcome annoyance imposed on officials burdened by so many tasks."[48] It was the perfect response of an absolutist prefect.

Controlling Early Modern Police Forces

The gendarmery is thus a crucial instrument used by Zairian prefects to control the local population, but as is quite apparent from the previous sections, it is an imperfect instrument, one that is often difficult to control. Despite these problems, however, the prefects constantly complain that they do not have enough soldiers and police at their disposal. The bad relations that frequently exist between these groups usually result from the army, gendarmery, and CND being unwilling to submit to the prefects under the principle of unity of territorial command. For example, Kivu officials complained frequently in the 1970s that the CND was sending patently inaccurate information to Kinshasa. These problems have been common to other areas as well. Witness the following statement by the regional commissioner for Bas-Zaire made in August 1968:

We note with regret that certain security agents, especially the lower level ones, do not wish to submit to proper administrative authority under the pretext that they report to the central government. Certain of you do not hestitate to arbitrarily arrest local authorities with the sole aim of ridiculing them.[49]

In the 1971 annual meeting of all the regional commissioners, control of the police was a major preoccupation. A police commission was established to investigate ways of increasing central control of the police. It wrestled with the difficult problem of the often-acrimonious relations that exist between the territorial administration and the army, the gendarmery, and the CND. It also decried the fact that there were too few national police and that they were poorly equipped, trained, and disciplined. The commission also spent considerable time discussing the problem of increasing central control of the collectivity police, who were characterized as unqualified, incompetent, poorly paid, and, above all, "supported by the chiefs of the local collectivities because of kinship ties which unite them."[50] In short, the collectivity police were frequently beyond the control of the centralizing state. It is a characteristic of early modern states that not all coercive forces come under the direct and continuous control of the central administrative apparatus.

This problem is particularly acute in areas of the country where traditional political structures remain the most coherent, especially in traditional states that remain quasi-autonomous. For example, in 1975 Mwami (king) Ndeze Rubago II (Daniel) of Ruthshuru Zone in Nord-Kivu was still the ruler of a traditional ministate. In the late 1960s and early 1970s his power remained so great that he served as both collectivity chief and zone prefect, that is, both traditional ruler and the representative of the centralizing absolutist state. As *mwami* and collectivity chief, he had his own traditional or collectivity police, which he used to run his state his way. The sub-regional prefects constantly complained about "Mwami Ndeze's attitude of insubordination . . . the obtruseness [*sic*], stubbornness and the arrogant and insulting attitude of this chief make the administration of his region quite difficult." One prefect complained about the illegal removal of locality chiefs by the *mwami,* his giving the zone police court "the air of a true popular tribunal held in the open air in front of the zone office," and the inability of central state-appointed assistant zone prefects to sit on the police court or to handle administrative correspondence. The latter was handled only by the *mwami*'s private secretaries. From 1967 to 1972 there was not a single state inspection of local traditional courts, and the *mwami* replaced judges at will, despite repeated warnings and complaints.[51]

In 1969 an article in a Kinshasa newspaper accused Mwami Ndeze of grossly mistreating his subjects: "The absolutism of this traditional chief is felt in all areas." For example, the peasants, according to this article, "do not see why they must divide the fruits of their sweat with the officials of the chiefdom." The *mwami* exiles and confiscates the property of anyone who seriously opposes him. He also imposes outrageous traditional fines ranging from 10 to 50 zaires. If the peasant does not pay, he "becomes a slave of the chief." The *mwami*'s police, rather than those of the central state, arrest his subjects for any infraction. These arrests take place as they did in the days of the Suzerains:

Before being conducted to prison, an arrested villager is spit upon in the face and is required not to wipe it off until he is in the depths of the prison, that is, not in the presence of the *mwami.*[52]

For his part, the *mwami* was forever loudly proclaiming his undying loyalty to Mobutu and his absolutist state. In itself this was a way of keeping the encroaching central state at a distance. When the state began to push too hard, however, the *mwami* would take decisive action. In 1970, for example, the activities of the local CND agent clearly crossed the boundary of what the *mwami* thought was appropriate. As a result, in October he expelled the CND agent from Ruthshuru and allowed his office to be sacked, after which several dossiers were missing. After this incident the sub-regional CND administrator noted that "it is the very presence of the CND in his zone that he refuses to accept in a barely disguised manner no matter what agent we send there."[53] If this incredible act of resistance had been tried by a collectivity chief in any area of the country where traditional ministates no longer existed, the individual would have been instantly arrested, imprisoned, and removed from his position. None of these things happened to Mwami Ndeze. In short, there were two layers of state repression here.

Consequences of Repression by a Lame Leviathan

In this type of early modern state, the extension of central political control over complex and turbulent societies is a highly coercive and extractive process. The absolutist state whittles away the powers of traditional authorities while maintaining basic control of most societal groups. Ultimately the power of the state is impressive, given the context, but is nonetheless limited in character. The current Zairian state is an early modern Leviathan, but a lame one.

Mobutu's absolutist state does maintain basic order, but at a very high cost. It brutally exploits the population and weakens or destroys liberty, local autonomy, intermediary authorities and associations, and community spirit. Moreover, it creates inequality, fosters dependence on the state, and prevents incremental political change. Absolutist rulers divide and manipulate societal groups, and most sociopolitical and economic issues become administrative matters. In short, such a regime creates and widens a gap between state and society.

Above all, the cost in terms of human suffering is substantial, and the major victims are the peasants and the urban poor. In short, most of the population is subjected to organized repression and extraction. The rulers of this type of authoritarian state are not greatly concerned with mass welfare. Not only does the state not assist its subjects to improve their welfare, it often prevents them from improving their lot on their own. In addition, the administrative monarchy destroys popular rights, makes a mockery of justice, and provides few services. Its forces of order and extraction are everywhere, and the latter is a full-time and often brutal business. Absolutist rules have a tendency to overreach themselves, and the resulting exploitation of resources and human suffering can reach staggering proportions. With the development of the French absolutist state in the seventeenth century, the "conditions of life among the lower classes—the great majority—worsened as the century progressed."[54] This also appears to be happening in Zaire under Mobutu's absolutist state.

In a courageous pastoral letter in March 1976, Catholic Archbishop Kabanga of Lubumbashi discussed the sad state of affairs in Zaire: "Whoever obtains a scrap of authority, or some means of pressure, profits from them to pressure and exploit people, particularly in the rural milieu. All methods are good to obtain money or to humiliate the human person."[55] As one of the most famous opposition tracts of seventeenth-century France asserted: "If we examine the use that is made of these immense sums that are collected with such abuses and extortion, we shall find all the characteristics of oppression and tyranny."[56] Zaire today is much like old-regime France, where "everything was calculated to discourage the law-abiding instinct."[57] As a result, no sense of community exists or is allowed to develop. The stratification gap between the rulers and the ruled widens, facilitating class formation and the division of societal groups from each other. Finally, what the great French historian Georges Pages said of Louis XIV's absolutist state also holds true for Mobutu's:

But although she achieved a work of national significance, she was unable to give her authority a national basis. . . . She . . . was unable to develop without emptying of substance the institutions that might have sustained her. She committed the irreparable error of believing that it suffices for a government to be strong. The administrative institutions created by Louis XIV and Colbert provided no remedy; they increased the strength of royal power but did not associate it with the nation.[58]

CONCLUSION: THE STATE AS LAME LEVIATHAN

Recent discontent with the notions of the state and state formation in the African context and an accompanying preoccupation with the "decline of the state" has much to do with the way that the state and state formation have been conceptualized. There has been much recent discussion of the "overdeveloped," "underdeveloped," or "soft" state, and of "uncaptured" populations and "exit options." These notions are a reaction to the shattered illusions of a postcolonial voluntarist view of the state that was held by many analysts and actors alike. It had various modernization, democratic, neocolonial, socialist, and revolutionary versions. There was an assumption of malleability of both state and society, of linear success and increasing strength that has been increasingly belied by evidence of uneven and even diminishing control, resilience of traditional authority patterns, poor economic performance, debt and infrastructure crises, the emergence of *magendo* or second economies, reductions in administrative performance, curtailment of capacities, political instability, and resistance and withdrawal. Underlying these new discussions is often a tone of surprise and bewilderment. Based on the belief that a broader historical, comparative, and analytic perspective is useful, this chapter has presented the notion of a repressive patrimonial-administrative state as the underlying form of domination in Africa today, above which floats a host of varying and changing regime types.

Much of the writing on the state in Africa in the immediate postcolonial period suffered from both a voluntarist and a nonhistorical view of the state and the processes of state formation. The state was perceived to be strong, or at least strong enough to put into action the desires of those who controlled it. On the side of liberal or "bourgeois" social science, the state, under the wise and legitimate leadership of modernizing elites, was to serve the new nation by pursuing policies of development and democracy. On the Marxist side, radical leadership groups were to combat neocolonialism and underdevelopment by constructing socialist states in the interests of the oppressed masses; or, comprador elites served the interests of international capitalism and/or fostered the development of capitalism in the periphery.

I believe that both views have proved to be inaccurate. Analysts of Africa, of all varieties, now talk about state decay, state decline, the withering away of the state that has been run into the ground by external actors and forces and/or local ruling classes, or even the fact that a state no longer exists. I suspect, however, that reality has not changed as much as our views and conceptualizations of it. Many of the processes that now attract our attention have been under way since the day of independence, if not before. Certainly expectations by both actors and analysts were far too high.

Both of these views of the state are also essentially functionalist. The liberal view is that the state is an arbitrator and provider of services, a performer of certain necessary functions. The Marxist view has usually been that the state functions to serve the interests of a given class, either to construct socialism or foster capitalism, international, local, or both. A broader conceptual and historical approach to the state may help. There is another basic view of the state, a Weberian one, which sees it simply as an organization of domination and control.[59] This state can serve a variety of interests, even a variety of surface political forms, but it does not have to serve any of them well or at all. The mix and balances can also vary rather dramatically over time, and all the while the basic nature of the state, the underlying structure of domination, may change little or not at all.

The underlying nature of the state in Africa is quite clearly that of an authoritarian organization of domination, a repressive but weak one. The state is a Leviathan, but a lame one, a weak patrimonial-administrative state, and it is not likely to change very fast. The modal African state is a weak, blunt instrument of domination in whomever's hands it is perceived to be—the IMF and monopoly and finance capital, a modernizing elite, radical populists, African socialists, Afrocommunists, a comprador ruling class, a state bourgeoisie, absolutist presidential monarchs and their political aristocracies, or an emerging capitalist bourgeoisie. The state in post-colonial Africa has never functioned as well as many actors or analysts assumed, or it has functioned in ways that people did not approve.

The likelihood of major, guided or unguided, socioeconomic or political structural change in Africa, including the lessening of state repression, in the medium run is not high. But as the historical record of seventeenth- and eighteenth-century Europe and nineteenth-century Latin America suggests, changes do take place, albeit very slowly, very unevenly, and in ways that did not at first appear to go in any given direction. Our task is to look closely at current reality and then try to sort out the up and down cycles of surface change from the longer-run changes that appear quietly, but that, cumulatively and eventually, do gather social, economic, and political weight and alter the basic design of the underlying structure of repression and of socioeconomic reality.

NOTES

1. On the renewed emphasis on "domination and subordination" in the study of African politics, see John Lonsdale, "States and Social Processes in Africa: An Historiographical Survey," *African Studies Review* 24, no. 2/3 (June/September 1981): 139-225.

2. Ibid., p. 154: "States are a fabric of ordered tension between 'a variety of competing forms of authority,' each with different myths of legitimacy and principles of allegiance." For an excellent analysis of particularisms and their complex impact on politics, see Crawford Young, *The Politics of Cultural Pluralism* (Madison: University of Wisconsin Press, 1976).

3. On the nature of African economics, see Frederick Cooper, "Africa and the World Economy," *African Studies Review* 24, no. 2/3 (June/September 1981): 1-86; and Thomas M. Callaghy, "The State and the Development of Capitalism in Africa: Some Theoretical and Historical Reflections," in *The Reordering of the State in Africa,* ed. Naomi Chazan (Boulder, Colo.: Westview, 1987).

4. Aristide Zolberg, "A View from the Congo," *World Politics* 19, no. 2 (October 1966): 144. See also Thomas M. Callaghy, "External Actors and the Autonomy of the Political Aristocracy in Zaire," in *State and Class in Africa,* ed. Nelson Kasfir (London: Frank Cass, 1984), pp. 61-83.

5. Early modern is a typological concept with specific characteristics, not necessarily a historical or chronological notion, much less an evolutionary one. Seventeenth- and eighteenth-century absolutist states in Europe were early modern, as were most nineteenth-century Latin American states. Although many African states have superficial similarities with current authoritarian regimes in Latin America, most of the latter can no longer be considered predominantly early modern in character. Pseudomodern authoritarian forms of rule in Africa only partially mask the solid core of a patrimonialized colonial state structure that must contend with traditional and quasi-traditional politics, powerful forms of particularism, and emerging class consciousness.

6. On the concept of organic-statism, see Alfred Stepan, *The State and Society:*

Peru in Comparative Perspective (Princeton: Princeton University Press, 1978), chaps. 2 and 3. On the limited possibilities for democratic rule in Africa, see Thomas M. Callaghy, "Politics and Vision in Africa: The Interplay of Domination, Equality, and Liberty," in *Political Domination in Africa,* ed. Patrick Chabal (Cambridge: Cambridge University Press, 1986).

7. For the full elaboration of this argument, see Thomas M. Callaghy, "The State as Lame Leviathan: The Patrimonial Administrative State in Africa," in *The African State in Transition,* ed. Zaki Ergas (London/New York: Macmillan/St. Martin's, 1987).

8. For a more detailed version, see Thomas M. Callaghy, *The State-Society Struggle: Zaire in Comparative Perspective* (New York: Columbia University Press, 1984); also see Crawford Young and Thomas Turner, *The Rise and Decline of the Zairian State* (Madison: University of Wisconsin Press, 1985).

9. Max Weber states that "patriarchal patrimonialism is mass domination by one individual" that requires an administrative apparatus and a coercive capacity; *Economy and Society,* ed. G. Roth and C. Wittich (Berkeley and Los Angeles: University of California Press, 1978), vol. 2, p. 1106.

10. F. Dumont, "French Kingship and Absolute Monarchy in the Seventeenth Century," in *Louis XIV and Absolutism,* ed. R. Hatton (Columbus: Ohio State University Press, 1976), p. 66.

11. Robert Mandrou, *Louis XIV en son temps* (Paris: Presses Universitaires de France, 1973), p. 205.

12. Pierre Goubert, *L'ancien régime* (Paris: Armand Colin, 1973), p. 19; my translation.

13. Alexis de Tocqueville, *The Old Régime and the French Revolution* (Garden City, N.Y.: Doubleday, 1955), p. 57; emphasis added.

14. On the notion of African neomercantilism, see Thomas M. Callaghy, "The Difficulties of Implementing Socialist Strategies of Development in Africa," in *Socialism in Sub-Saharan Africa: A New Assessment,* ed. C. G. Rosberg and T. M. Callaghy (Berkeley: Institute of International Studies, 1979), pp. 126-128.

15. In a review of the recent world-system literature, particularly the work of Immanuel Wallerstein, Aristide Zolberg suggests that it is unwarranted theoretically to contend that "the position of countries in the world economy *determines* the character of their political regimes" and reminds us that the development of states is affected as much by a plurality of international politico-strategic actors as it is by international economic forces; "Origins of the Modern World System: A Missing Link," *World Politics* 33, no. 2 (January 1981): 266. This point is graphically illustrated by Zaire's long-standing debt crisis; see Thomas M. Callaghy, "The Political Economy of African Debt: The Case of Zaire," in *Africa in Economic Crisis,* ed. John Ravenhill (London: Macmillan, 1985).

16. Arthur L. Stinchcombe, *Constructing Social Theories* (New York: Harcourt, Brace, 1968), p. 162.

17. See Callaghy, "External Actors and Autonomy" and "Political Economy of African Debt"; and Thomas Turner, "Zaire: Stalemate and Compromise," *Current History* 84 (April 1985): 179-183.

18. Mobutu quoted on the first page of a major MPR document, "Rapport d'activités, 1967-1972," Kinshasa, 1972.

19. Administrative instructions, Kinshasa, 12 July 1967.

20. All the examples come from administrative correspondence, meetings, and police requisitions from the sub-regions of Cataractes and Nord-Kivu, 1969-1974, and from an interview with a Cataractes assistant sub-regional commissioner, Mbanza-Ngungu, 16 January 1975.

21. Letter from the minister of the interior to all regional commissioners, Kinshasa, 28 August 1972, and administrative correspondence, August 1972-September 1974.

22. Minutes, Sub-Region Committee meetings, Goma, 28 December 1972 and 13 April 1973.

23. Confidential police report, Mbanza-Ngungu, 19 May 1972.

24. Amnesty International, *Human Rights Violations in Zaire* (London: Amnesty International, May 1980).

25. Annual report, Luozi Zone, 1974; sub-region monthly report, June 1974; inspection report, January 1975; meeting of zone commissioner, Mbanza-Ngungu, 16 July 1968; Nord-Kivu Sub-Region Committee meeting, 28 December 1972.

26. Administrative correspondence, 28 December 1972, 12 October 1973, 12 February 1974; administrative reports, March–September 1968.

27. Administrative correspondence, Matadi, 11 August 1970.

28. Speech by State Commissioner Kithima, "La philosophie de *salongo,*" Kinshasa, 3 May 1973.

29. Speech by State Commissioner Engulu, "La territoriale et la radicalisation du MPR," Kinshasa, 5 September 1974; and Sebisogo Muhima, "Le role du 'Salongo' (travail manuel) dans les écoles," in *Zaire-Afrique* 95 (May 1975): 273.

30. Cataractes Sub-Region monthly report, May 1973; annual report, Songololo Zone, 1974; and "Arrêté no. 01/RTE/75 du 3 juin 1975," Bukavu, emphasis added.

31. "Arrêté no. 909/CAB(REGICOM)40/BZ/72 portant imposition de cultures," 28 December 1972; and administrative correspondence, January 1973-December 1974.

32. Nsi yi Betu-Kulu, "L'armée Zairoise: mercenaire de la naissance," *Politique aujourd'hui,* March-April 1976, pp. 1, 37.

33. Administrative correspondence, 28 January 1970.

34. Administrative correspondence, Gombe-Sud, 26 March 1972.

35. Administrative correspondence and reports, Kimvula, 13 December 1971, and Mbanza-Ngungu, 24 June 1968 and 9 October 1973.

36. Administrative correspondence, 9 December 1971 and 22 August 1970.

37. Administrative report, Kimbula, February 1972; sub-region administrative meeting, 28 December 1972.

38. Administrative reports, 3 September 1969 and 31 October 1969; administrative correspondence, 25 March 1970 and 4 June 1971.

39. Administrative correspondence, 7 October 1971 and 29 October 1971.

40. Administrative cable, 19 June 1972.

41. Administrative correspondence, Zamaba, 9 April 1973.

42. Administrative correspondence, reports, and cables, 24-30 May 1973.

43. Cataractes Sub-Region monthly report, July 1973.

44. Administrative correspondence, 3 July-3 August 1973, 14 September 1973.

45. Administrative report on the *ratissage* by the assistant sub-regional commissioner, Mbanza-Ngungu, 28 May 1973.

46. This account is based on the sub-regional commissioner's brief report, Mbanza-Ngungu, 6 May 1973; a letter from the gendarmery commander to the sub-

regional commissioner, Kimpese, 8 May 1973; and the private letter from the "observer," Kimpese, 12 May 1973.

47. "Observer" letter, Kimpese, 12 May 1973.

48. Administrative correspondence, 19 September 1973 and 21 December 1973.

49. "Mémorandum à l'intention du Ministre de l'Intérieur et des Affaires coutumières," Matadi, 24 August 1968.

50. "Réunion des Gouverneurs tenue à Kisangani du 16 au 20 août 1971," p. 54.

51. "Attitude du *Mwami* NDEZE," administrative letter to the minister of the interior, Goma, 17 July 1968; an undated administrative evalution of Mwami Ndeze; administrative memorandum, Rutshuru, 11 December 1969; annual report, Rutshuru Zone, 1972.

52. *L'Etoile* (Kinshasa), 4 and 5 October 1969.

53. Letter from CND sub-region chief to the sub-regional commissioner, Goma, 30 November 1970.

54. William F. Church, *The Impact of Absolutism in France* (New York: John Wiley, 1969), p. 2.

55. Quoted in Michael G. Schatzberg, *Politics and Class in Zaire* (New York: Africana, 1980), p. 161.

56. *Les soupirs de la France esclave, qui aspire après la liberté,* 1690, quoted in Church, *Impact of Absolutism,* p. 104; this tract was written by a leading French Calvinist pastor while in exile in Amsterdam and then smuggled into France.

57. Tocqueville, *Old Régime,* p. 67.

58. Quoted in Church, *Impact of Absolutism,* p. 158.

59. John McCamant, "Governance without Blood: Social Science's Antiseptic View of Rule; or, The Neglect of Political Repression" in *The State as Terrorist: The Dynamics of Governmental Violence and Repression,* ed. Michael Stohl and George A. Lopez (Westport, Conn.: Greenwood Press, 1984), pp. 11-42, has charged that the political science literature and its theoretical models tend to ignore "the awful and bloody deeds of governments" (p. 11). The charge is overdrawn, but his critique of the "antiseptic" nature of the major models and particularly of the lack of salience of political repression in them, analytically or descriptively is appropriate. He looks at interest group models, systems theory, structural functionalism, Marxism, dependencia, elite theory, and geopolitics. The first three overstress consensus, and while Marxism and dependencia discuss oppression, political repression is not a central analytic aspect of them. This results from conceptual difficulties regarding the nature of the state and of politics. McCamant asserts that we must lay aside our models and begin afresh, and he makes suggestions for doing so. Strikingly, however, he leaves out one important model altogether—the Weberian one. Although undergoing a resurgence now, the Weberian perspective has not been important in American political science in large part because of the severe damage done to it by Talcott Parsons. Parsons simply left out most of its major elements, and it is precisely these elements that are most pertinent here. In fact, all of McCamant's suggestions for a new model are already central to the Weberian perspective. See Jere Cohen, Lawrence E. Hazelrigg, and Whitney Pope, "De-Parsonizing Weber: A Critique of Parsons' Interpretation of Weber's Sociology," *American Sociological Review* 40, no. 2 (April 1975): 229-241; Randall Collins, "A Comparative Approach to Political Sociology," in *State and Society,*

ed. Reinhard Bendix (Boston: Little, Brown, 1968), pp. 42-67; idem, *Conflict Sociology* (New York: Academic Press, 1975); and Callaghy, *State-Society Struggle,* chaps. 1-3.

5

An Archaeology of State Terrorism:
The Philippines under Marcos

Lester Edwin J. Ruiz

> The poignant wish for a tranquil life will find no sanctuary in today's
> world. We live in a revolutionary era. It is an era of swift, violent, often
> disruptive change, and rather than lament this vainly, we have to decide
> whether we should be the masters or victims of change.
> —Ferdinand E. Marcos, *Today's Revolution: Democracy,* 1971

In his work *Knowledge and Politics,* Roberto M. Unger suggests rather
cryptically that "legalism and terrorism, the commitment to rules and the
seduction of violence, are rival brothers, but brothers nonetheless."[1] Disci-
ples of the "liberal democratic" tradition would undoubtedly dismiss such
a claim. The sole guarantee of freedom, they argue, is the unequivocal
commitment to the "rule of law." This claim, unfortunately, may conceal
more than reveal the truth of Unger's suggestion when considered in the
light of particular situations, such as the reign of Ferdinand E. Marcos of
the Philippines (1969-1986).

The period between 1972 and 1983, the Marcos "martial law years," saw
an increase in the arbitrary arrests, detentions, torture, and murder of the
"enemies of the state," the "barbaric campaign of genocide" against the
Moro people, and the exploitation of the already poorest of the poor by the
Marcos dictatorship.[2] In order to operationalize this attack on the Filipino
peoples, the Marcos regime needed a working ideology to both guide its
adherents and legitimize their political program. Marcos pleaded that the
current challenge of the development cycle in the Philippines demanded the
"primacy of order" as the nation moved to democracy via martial law.[3]

This chapter is concerned mainly with the politico-philosophical and
sociomoral logic of Philippine constitutional authoritarianism, the
rationale if not the ideology that sustained the Marcos rule. It explores the
theoretical and practical relationship between the "primacy of order" and
the emergence of "state terrorism," the "purposeful use or threat of

violence [by a state] to create fear and/or compliant behavior in a victim and/or audience."[4]

The chapter unfolds in three interrelated parts. First, I show that Philippine constitutional authoritarianism, rooted as it was in an organicist, hierarchical order, emerged within the historical and "revolutionary" process of modernization and therefore viewed political disorder as the fundamental political problem to be overcome. Second, I demonstrate that contrary to those who viewed it as an aberration of the "liberal democratic" tradition, Philippine constitutional authoritarianism understood itself as a particular expression of this tradition, synthesizing some aspects of natural rights theory with positivism in its attempt to develop a coherent ideology for the Filipino peoples. Third, I argue that Philippine constitutional authoritarianism privileged the "primacy of order" as constitutive of political life and, therefore, construed the primary task of politics as the creation and/or imposition of order.

Throughout the chapter I begin to suggest some connections between Philippine constitutional authoritarianism and the logic of state terrorism. I conclude that the former not only provided the legitimation for a practice of domination, but also set the Philippines under Marcos on the path toward a form of state terror and violence, the reality of which can now be thoroughly examined in the post-Marcos era.

MODERNIZATION AND REVOLUTION: POLITICAL DISORDER AS THE PROBLEM OF PHILIPPINE CONSTITUTIONAL AUTHORITARIANISM

On September 21, 1972, Ferdinand E. Marcos, then president of the Republic of the Philippines, placed the entire Philippine archipelago under martial law. The immediate reasons for what some "liberal democratic" thinkers considered a constitutionally questionable measure[5] were meticulously stated in Proclamation no. 1081, "Proclaiming a State of Martial Law in the Philippines." The document read, in part:

It is definitely established that lawless elements . . . have entered into a conspiracy . . . for the prime purposes of . . . undertaking and waging an armed insurrection and rebellion against the Government . . . in order to . . . forcibly seize political and state power . . . overthrow the duly constituted government, and supplant our existing political, social, economic, and legal order with an entirely different one. . . . [Their activities] have seriously endangered and continue to endanger public order and safety and security of the nation . . . [and] have assumed the magnitude of an actual state of war against our people and the Republic of the Philippines.[6]

Martial law, it was argued, was a response to a profound crisis in the Philippines, in which the events enumerated in Proclamation no. 1081 were of no small significance. As early as 1970 theorists of what later came to be known as "Philippine constitutional authoritarianism" already noted the existence of a "revolutionary situation" in the country. Marcos himself stated that Filipinos were living in a revolutionary era of "swift, violent, often disruptive change." "Rather than lament this vainly," he proclaimed, "we have to decide whether we should be the masters or victims of change."[7]

This "revolutionary situation" was dramatically portrayed by the "First Quarter Storm," a period of massive and intense confrontation between a broad student-peasant-labor coalition on the one hand, and government military and paramilitary forces on the other. The Marcos government, along with most of its critics, acknowledged this confrontation as an expression of a deeper societal crisis.[8] The confrontation, called by many the "rebellion of the poor," became a full struggle to achieve fundamental changes in the political, economic, and cultural life of the nation.

The "rebellion of the poor" was recognized by the Marcos government, at least rhetorically, as the most serious challenge to its existence. It was exacerbated by the alleged and immediate threat posed to the Republic by a conspiracy of leftist Communist and rightist oligarchic elements on the one hand, and by a Muslim secessionist movement supported by foreign groups on the other.[9] Significantly, Marcos excluded the "leftist conspiracy" and the "Muslim secession" from the "rebellion of the poor," which he recognized as "legitimate." The imposition of martial law had two interrelated goals. First, it sought to prevent these so-called "lawless elements" from throwing the country into chaos by destroying the "duly constituted government."[10] Second, Marcos employed martial law as a tool to address the issues raised by the "rebellion of the poor."[11]

This "rebellion of the poor" was also understood by the Marcos government within a larger historical process that the Philippines, like many other nations of the so-called developing Third World,[12] was experiencing, namely, the "inevitable outcome of the modernizing process."[13] Because sweeping changes in its political, economic, and cultural life were required in order to meet the imperative of development, the Philippine experience of the process of modernization was a "disquieting, at times convulsive, undertaking." While Marcos agreed with his nationalist-Marxist critics that the Philippines was caught in a "revolutionary situation," he argued further that the uniqueness of the Philippine situation lay in the convergence of the revolutionary process with the process of modernization. Because Philippine society required "drastic, fundamental changes" in order to enter the modern era, modernization made revolution inevitable.[14] Modernization required revolution; conversely, revolution presupposed modernization. Thus

there are two reasons for [revolution]: the modern temper and the actual conditions of societies themselves. The power to control and change his environment is a cardinal belief of modern man, and revolution is the ultimate expression of this outlook. On the other hand, societies that have experienced economic and social changes exercise tremendous pressure on their political authorities, which makes for a "revolutionary situation . . ." in actuality and by definition, modernizing societies are revolutionizing—indeed, revolutionary societies.[15]

For Marcos theorists, then, the convergence of modernization and revolution was not only the historical context of the "rebellion of the poor" nor simply its consequence; the convergence itself constituted the crisis. In the context of this "swift, violent, often disruptive" change, a choice was posed between chaos and order, between being the "masters or victims of change," which demanded the unilateral assertion of political will by the sovereign not only to preserve political order but to guarantee that change itself would be mastered. Thus the crucial question for the Marcos government as it faced the crisis of 1971, in the words of Samuel Huntington that it cited approvingly, was whether or not the "processes of political modernization and political development have lagged behind the processes of social and economic change."[16] In this context two fundamental questions needed to be faced. First, Why was modernization necessary? Second, What kind of revolution was necessary?

Philippine political, economic, and cultural life was correctly perceived by the Marcos theorists, themselves schooled in the Western "liberal democratic" tradition, as primarily oligarchic in character. They recognized that political inequality rested on the existence of social inequality. However, unlike its nationalist-Marxist critics, the Marcos government viewed the problem of political and social inequality as being rooted in the "irresponsible exercise of public and private power."[17] The principal issue was not the existence of an oligarchy as such, but the abuses of that oligarchy.

This oligarchic structure was historically rooted in the Spanish *encomienda* system, which established an aristocracy built on an inequitous land-ownership structure. This was modified into a client-elite structure at the turn of the century by the "American experiment in democracy." The modification had two fundamental consequences for latter-day "liberal democratic" politics. On the one hand, the aristocracy-turned-client-elite viewed the established "liberal democratic" institutions and processes as vehicles for maintaining its position of political, economic, and cultural privilege. On the other hand, the "masses" viewed the oligarchy as guarantors of their survival and well-being. Thus a "culture of patronage," one of the consequences of the *encomienda* system, became the operative principle of contemporary Philippine politics. This, in turn, it was argued, led to a politics of status quo maintenance and a politics of dependence.[18] "Liberal democracy" was transformed into an "oligarchic democracy."[19]

Undergirding this oligarchic political-institutional arrangement was a political culture that was "populist, personalist, and individualist." This type of politics, the Marcos theorists maintained, undermined public institutions. Public resources and offices become viewed as spoils for the winners and their supporters, jeopardizing thereby the public and collective goals of the nation. Coupled with an absolutist view of private property, defended at that time by the Philippine Supreme Court, this nepotistic, symbiotic relationship between patron and client corrupted political authority and militated against any kind of innovation or change. The maintenance of the status quo meant that the privilege of the oligarchy would be preserved, whereas modernization meant the possible loss of these privileges. For the oligarchy, Marcos theorists argued, modernization had to be avoided.

Moreover, this view of public institutions as instruments of privilege required a "minimalist" view of the state. "Oligarchic democracy" preferred a "weak state," subordinated to the interests of the oligarchy, that acted primarily to safeguard its privileges and guarantee the conditions that would enhance these privileges. Not surprisingly, postwar Philippine political institutions were built on a liberal, Lockean philosophy; similarly, economic institutions were organized around the philosophy of laissez-faire capitalism.[20]

Thus the Marcos theorists, at least in rhetoric, repudiated the old oligarchic politics that "intervened in government to preserve the political privileges of [its] wealth, and to protect [its] right to property."[21] On the other hand, they rejected not only the "weak politics" of Western "liberal democracy" but especially the political consequences of its economic ideology that left the Philippines a dependent client state. Marcos theorists asserted:

Philippine society reached a point where we could not keep up the design of a limited, representative and democratic political order that we had tried to foster. . . . For a time the Philippines seemed to have made democracy work. But its stability was founded on insecure ground. Patronage—and demagoguery—met people's seasonal expectations. Elections, held every two years, kept the poor cyclically content—while all the laws for social reform remained on the books. National politics continued to be a game of musical chairs. The personalities shifted around, the policies remained the same. So, for more than 20 years as an independent Republic, we blithely played at democracy—and some of us at revolution. Finally, of course, we had to set aside these playthings and face the facts of real life.[22]

Philippine constitutional authoritarianism, in fact, was the Marcos answer to "facing the facts of real life." Whether the Marcos government successfully carried out its claim to revolution and modernization, however, has now been practically settled. The transformation of "oligarchic democracy" to "crony capitalism," for example, belies the Marcos claim that the repudiation of the "old oligarchic politics" was done in the name of his "new democratic politics." In fact, the Philippines under Marcos was an example of a capitalist client state. Moreover, the events of 1985-1986 have underscored the failure of his authoritarian, elitist conception of politics. Unfortunately, while Marcos and most of his loyal cronies have left the Philippines, the legacy of authoritarian politics remains a very real option in the nation. Not only are there "Marcos loyalists" who wish to return the country to an unabashedly authoritarian rule, but the "liberal democratic" underpinnings of the Aquino government, which it shares with the Marcos regime, when set within the global context of a capitalist world political economy, predispose it toward authoritarian politics.[23] It is important, therefore, to continue to examine, however partially, the politico-philosophical legacy of the Marcos government, if only to more fully understand the choices with which the Filipino peoples are confronted today. It is to this necessary task that this chapter now turns.

THE POLITICAL PHILOSOPHY OF PHILIPPINE CONSTITUTIONAL AUTHORITARIANISM: A "LIBERAL DEMOCRATIC" PROBLEM

The Nature of Revolution

Theorists of the Marcos government argued that democracy was the only form of government that recognized the people's inherent right to revolution. The people's right to rebel, an argument that they drew from Locke, is an "elemental human right" that is inviolable.[24] The people have the right "to cast out their rulers, change their policy, or effect radical reforms in their system of government or institutions, by force or by a general uprising, when the legal and constitutional methods of making such changes have proved inadequate or so obstructed as to be unavailable."[25] Revolution is not simply the "violent confrontation of two national groups having irreconcilable interests,"[26] but the process by which radical changes are sought, where the "total re-orientation of the instrumentalities of the government and other institutions of society" is effected in order to achieve the goals and aspirations of its people.

This "right to revolution" was grounded in what the Marcos theorists called, again echoing Locke, the "egalitarian ideal," a prescriptive social value that "urges those persons who occupy positions of power and responsibility—in government or the private sector—to treat equally every individual in society."[27] Located within a broader "humanistic credo" that affirms both human creativity and rationality as the driving forces of democratic ideals, this egalitarian ideal is the moral basis for all public and private "transactions." When a government's institutions violate this ideal, rebellion against it becomes justified.[28] Equality is the impetus for "revolution," which, in turn, is founded on human creativity or freedom.

The "right to revolution" was balanced, however, with the public "right to suppress rebellion," which is the right and obligation of the "duly constituted" political authority to defend itself and preserve the public good.[29] Three decisive premises were implied in this public right. First, rebellions are of two kinds: those that are legitimate challenges posed by the people to the political authority, and those that are illegitimate assaults on it. Second, because it is "duly constituted," the government has the right to "protect" the people by suppressing those rebellions that are illegitimate. Third, that the "right of revolution" is never absolute.

Philippine Constitutional Authoritarianism: A "Liberal Democratic" Revolution

When the "consciousness of the political authority coincides with the revolutionary demands of the masses," a "revolution initiated by the government becomes a matter of necessity."[30] For the Marcos theorists, the necessity for this "revolution from the center" arises historically because of the "rebellion of the poor." By their existence in the midst of an affluent oligarchic minority, the poor challenge the existing polity and its legitimacy and make revolution necessary. Thus Marcos argued that "revolutions begin when the political order must respond to economic and social change, when, for example, it is challenged to integrate into the society the so-called oppressed groups who now have developed a political consciousness."[31]

Truly democratic revolutions are rooted in the historical aspirations and experience of the people and are enacted by the people themselves. For the Marcos theorists, however, it is the "duly constituted Government," the state apparatus, that wages this revolution. Presupposing, without having demonstrated, that the "revolutionary demands of the masses" had, in fact, coincided with the political consciousness of the Marcos government, its theorists pointed out, "It is *for* the people that we embark on the democratic revolution in order to alter or transform society."[32] The dubious identification of his government with the Filipino peoples was never acknowledged by Marcos. Constitutional authoritarianism, in fact, rested on an illusion of unity. It took the events of February 1986 not only to finally demystify this illusion, but more important, to call into question the viability and desirability of this elite conception of politics.

"Democratization of Wealth": The Problem of Economic versus Political Rights

That this "democratic revolution," waged by the government on behalf of its people, viewed the "democratization of wealth" as the central question to be addressed by the revolution was quite understandable. In theory the "democratic revolution" was waged primarily against an "oligarchic democracy" that was built on the concentration of wealth in the hands of a few, who through their wealth controlled the political institutions of governance. In practice, however, the Marcos government failed to destroy the politico-economic structure of this "oligarchic democracy." Marcos replaced the "old oligarchy" with his own cronies. Their presence in and out of government underscored the rise of a new oligarchy that later came to be popularly known as "crony capitalism." The investigations of the Presidential Commission on Good Government under the Aquino government have begun to uncover the pervasiveness of Marcos' now de-legitimated "new oligarchy."

Nevertheless, on a politico-philosophical level the "democratization of wealth" was seen as a problem of the relationship between political and economic rights, the distinction between which became crucial to the political philosophy of Philippine constitutional authoritarianism. While advocating a broad notion of the "rights of man," Marcos theorists argued for the primacy of economic rights as a programmatic strategy for the "democratic revolution." In a discussion obviously intended as a polemic against "liberal democratic" human rights activists, Marcos deplored the emphasis on political rights:

It is unfortunate that in the context of our political experience the concern for human rights has always been a concern for "political" rights: the right to free speech, of assembly, and so on. . . . [But] is it possible . . . that for the masses of Filipinos themselves, the primordial concern is the economic right to survive with dignity?[33]

This rhetorical question was rooted less in the concrete observation that the poor were deeply concerned with their economic situation than in the political understanding, shared ironically by both "liberal democrats" and nationalist-Marxists, that only within a society where basic needs are met can political rights have any substantive significance.[34] For this reason the Marcos theorists rejected the "liberal democratic" emphasis on political and procedural rights, since it failed to acknowledge that they presupposed the fulfillment of basic needs. Formal (political) equality had to be undergirded by substantive (social and economic) equality.

Thus the question of rights posed a deeper political-institutional problem. The challenge to the democratically elected leadership was not simply to "achieve and maintain an authentic democratic process which rests on such ideals as freedom of speech, of the press, of assembly," but "to establish first of all, the credibility of government as an institution oriented to working for the welfare of the many and not just the few,"[35] that is, to establish a government that was responsive to the basic needs of its people. For the Marcos government, this meant institutionalizing the economic rights of the people.

The failure of "oligarchic democracy," it was argued, rested precisely on its unwillingness to honor the commitment to improve the people's situation, for whom the question was not simply one of political rights but of economic rights as well. The task, then, was to "create the [economic] institutions and the milieu that would make the exercise of political liberties the privilege not only of the few but of all."[36] The restructuring of the oligarchy, or the "democratization of wealth," became the central duty of the "revolution from the center." For the Marcos theorists, this meant primarily the redistribution of wealth, not the restructuring of the means for producing wealth.

The Necessity of a Strong State

Marcos argued that the necessary institutional precondition and consequence of the challenge of revolution posed by the "rebellion of the poor" against an "oligarchic democracy" was the establishment of a strong government fully committed to the welfare of the majority of its people. Without negating the importance of "realistic" considerations that make a strong government necessary, it is crucial to note that the move to a "strong government," clearly a shift from a Lockean to a Hobbesian understanding of the state, was rooted in two fundamental assumptions of what government is and ought to be: first, that rightly understood, government is an advocate of its people; second, that government is a (relatively) autonomous institution of society. Thus Marcos theorists judged both "the liberal Lockean umpire state" and the Marxist-Leninist "vanguard of the proletariat" inadequate to the modernizing and revolutionary society. The former was a "weak" institution incapable of carrying through the "democratic revolution," the latter so ideologically determined by class interests that it was unable to encompass the whole democratic constituency.

At the first level, having presupposed the legitimacy of government vis-à-vis its people, itself a dubious assumption, Marcos theorists hastened to argue that "the government . . . does not conceive of itself as the head, the crown, the apex, of the national community. It is not at the summit but at the core; it is the power surrounded by the people, to whom it proposes and whom it leads."[37] Moreover, in response to the cry for social transformation, the government initiates the "radicalization of existing social arrangements." It does so not only because it is a "duly constituted authority," but because it is "the only authority morally bound to act in behalf of the people."[38] A democratic government by its very nature "is obliged to make itself the faithful instrument of the people's revolutionary aspirations."[39]

Despite this rather overstated and largely dubious claim, the construal of government as the advocate of its people evidenced a shift away from the "liberal democratic" notion of an "umpire state" that views government as an impartial, autonomous institution whose function is limited to the adjudication of competing claims. As Marcos theorists have argued, "We can no longer accept the Jeffersonian dictum that the best government is that which governs least."[40] Such a repudiation recognizes that the historical circumstances that occasioned the forging of an "umpire state" no longer exist. The increasing complexities of human community, domestically and internationally, necessitated new obligations and, consequently, increased authority for government.[41]

At the second level, arguing against those who viewed the state as merely the instrument of class interests, Marcos theorists proposed the concept of an "autonomous state" as a political and philosophical linchpin of the "democratic revolution." This they did even while recognizing that the oligarchic government of the Philippines historically has been "party to a grand conspiracy of the rich against the poor." It was argued that

the concept of an autonomous government—one able to exert its own will—is central to our theory of democratic revolution . . . even if . . . we single out only two major power groups—the rich and the poor—in national society, government is the third entity whose role we cannot ignore.[42]

The (relatively) autonomous state, however, unlike the classical Marxist-Leninist theory that Marcos theorists understood as seeking to destroy the existing socio-political structure and establish a "dictatorship of the proletariat," was viewed as an institution that "will not favor one and injure the other." "Our theory," they argued, "requires a conscientious government that will preside over the interaction between the rich and the poor, or among various sectors of society, in the spirit of justice and fair play."[43] Rather than being the "umpire" of competing interests or the instrument of one class, government became the guardian and implementor of policies that sought to equalize opportunities among the people as a whole. This view tried to affirm both the Marxist-Leninist insight into the necessity of a "vanguard of the proletariat," while avoiding what was perceived to be its distorted view of a "captive state," and the liberal Lockean principle of the primacy of the citizen, while repudiating its ineffective view of an "umpire state."[44] What the Marcos theorists failed to ackowledge was the centralizing logic of a strong, "autonomous state" that tends not only to identify the "spirit of justice and fair play" with its own interests but also to shift the terrain of politics from civil society to the state.

A Different Conception of Liberty, Freedom, and Rights

The argument for the necessity of a "strong state" is legitimated by a conception of liberty, freedom, and rights that is largely different from that of the classical "liberal democratic" tradition. In an essay entitled "Liberty and Government in the New Society," Onofre D. Corpuz posed the dilemma of the contemporary Filipino intellectual as having to choose "between the socio-political concepts of the old and those of the new social order" to ground the politics of the "New Society."[45] This dilemma, it was argued, was rendered acute since the historical milieu in which the concepts of liberty, freedom, and rights arose had been fundamentally altered.

The first significant encounter of Filipino intellectuals with modern political thought, that is, the ideas of "national self-determination," "popular sovereignty," "liberty," and "political rights," was with the ideas of Voltaire, Rousseau, Paine, and the "later European Enlightenment." This was eclipsed at the turn of the century by the Anglo-American political tradition that has since shaped the Philippine tradition of jurisprudence.[46]

Corpuz argued that this Anglo-American political tradition, which was essentially the "paraphrasing of the political ideas of the seventeenth century English philosopher John Locke,"[47] was concerned primarily with the preservation of individual life, liberty, and property, particularly as they are threatened by government. Its view of liberty, therefore, was construed largely as "autonomy" from government, particularly of the propertied classes. Contrasting this to the more populist understanding of *liberté, égalité, fraternité* of the French Revolution, Corpuz argued that the Lockean tradition not only excluded the vast majority of the people, but also became the most "powerful or respectable justification in western political thought of the oligarchic domination of society."[48] Thus the Lockean notion of liberty could not provide the basis for a truly democratic society.

In a different though related context, Marcos argued that if the notion of political liberty was to be adequate to the realities of the Philippines, it had to be enlarged by a commitment to the normativity of equality. Agreeing with Corpuz that the fundamental demand of the "rebellion of the poor" was for equality and not liberty, Marcos proclaimed that the former was the more powerful motive force in a developing society. Citing Leslie Lipson in order to expose the inadequacy of the Lockean understanding of liberty, Marcos asserted: "The interrelationship between liberty and equality is obvious. Differences of status produces [sic] differences in liberties. Some individuals are more free than others, and such differences are also inequalities. When equality of opportunity is provided, liberties are equalized. To abolish differences of status is . . . to enlarge the freedoms of those at the bottom."[49]

The emphasis on political liberty, Corpuz further argued, led to an unwarranted, if not erroneous, emphasis on the Bill of Rights as the primary source of liberty, security, and welfare. While a necessary dimension of governance is the protection of the citizen from arbitrary acts of government, this "Bill of Rights tradition" that emphasized "rights" as limitation was unable to provide the foundations for a broader vision of the national community, for a political community cannot be founded exclusively on negative rights. Such a view offered nothing substantive to the propertyless class—in the Philippines, the larger portion of the population. Corpuz observed:

There are also other citizens, comprising the larger number of our people, who are daily beset by the afflictions of poverty, ill health, and lack of opportunity. These citizens . . . understandably place their expectations on the government, believing that it ought to be obligated, rather than forbidden, to act in their behalf, to ameliorate their lot, and emancipate them from misfortune. It is these citizens for whom government must . . . intervene beyond keeping the law, in order that . . . our national community become more of a community.[50]

Marcos theorists therefore sought to establish a government that was allowed to act on behalf of the less fortunate. Indeed, for them, it was more important that the government be formally obligated to promote the common welfare and that it be authorized and adequately empowered to promote the well-being of all citizens in a manner that was beyond the capacity of factions and class interests to frustrate.[51] The necessary task was to ensure that government worked for the common welfare and not to limit its powers. This became the fundamental moral justification for a "strong state" that championed the common welfare.

In this view of a "strong state," political liberty is enlarged to mean human capacity, that is, the ability to attain one's full potential. Corpuz argued that "full humanity" was the heart and soul of liberty.[52] Thus that which diminished human capacity, such as abusive government and socio-economic deprivation, must be repudiated. In the context of the "democratic revolution," the political authority had the "moral obligation to use the community's substance and intelligence to defend the dignity of every citizen." Political liberty as human capacity implied a collective, communitarian responsibility.

At its core, however, the notion of liberty as capacity rested on the idea of human freedom. Drawing on the Aristotelean ideal of the fully human being as one who has attained excellence of body, mind, and soul, which thereby endows the individual with virtue as a citizen, Corpuz argued that this excellence "requires that man be free . . . in the sense that he is free from violation of other men . . . that his capability is not destroyed by the afflictions of bodily infirmity, intellectual ignorance, and moral depravity."[53] To be fully human, one must be fully free.

Elsewhere this philosophical notion of freedom was given political meaning by Marcos. Drawing on Richard Godwin, he argued that freedom must be understood within the structural and material relations that tend either to restrict or to promote human liberty. Freedom constitutes a description of human possibilities rather than an a priori assertion of rights and values. It does not mean pursuit of private desires, the condition of which permits each person to constitute himself or herself as a society of one. Rather, it becomes the pursuit of common interests and desires. As a description of social relations, freedom is constituted by participation in a common life.[54]

This was a decisive point for Philippine constitutional authoritarianism. Not unlike the Marxists who contented that freedom is inextricably related to the material relations of society, the Marcos theorists rightly understood that the struggle for freedom required "altering and improving upon the structures and institutions that confine or diminish human possibility of fulfillment." The "democratic revolution" had to be translated into a socio-political task. Indeed, for Corpuz, this meant that all human institutions, including government, had to be placed in the service of the political community to "restore, promote, or enhance human capability." Rather than representing a limitation on human freedom, government must reflect the people's enlightened conscience, assisting rather than hindering the attainment of their full human potential. "In other words," Corpuz concluded, "government becomes the community's instrument of liberation and freedom because the government helps men to become free and human."[55]

In their repudiation of the classical Lockean conception of liberty, freedom, and right with its concomitant commitment to an "umpire state," the Marcos theorists rightly underscored the inadequacy of the "liberal democratic" tradition for a modernizing and revolutionary Philippines. Such a truncated view of social and political life indeed tends to eclipse other equally important dimensions of human life. Corpuz has rightly pointed out, for example, that other matters like "sustenance and shelter . . . faith and religion . . . cooperation and conflict . . . revenge and hatred, and the gentle emotions of affection and love" occupy the common Tao more than the matter of political liberty.[56]

It is ironic, therefore, that such a sensitivity to the need for addressing the larger questions of political and economic life failed to recognize, perhaps deliberately so, that one of the decisive linchpins on which the theory of a state-led "democratic revolution" rests, namely, the unity of civil society and the state, the confluence of the "will of the people" and the "will of the state," was precisely that which, theoretically and practically, could not be sustained. In retrospect, despite its claims of legitimacy and the appeals to its "duly constituted authority," the Marcos government as early as 1969 began to lose its "legitimacy." By 1971 the rupture between state and civil society in the Philippines was practically irreversible. In the context of this fundamental rupture, the political project of Philippine constitutional authoritarianism, particularly its adherence to the "primacy of order" as its operative foundation, quickly provided the foundation for the practice of state terrorism.

THE PRIMACY OF ORDER: THE OPERATIVE FOUNDATION OF PHILIPPINE CONSTITUTIONAL AUTHORITARIANISM

The conviction that government is the instrument of liberation and freedom was not rooted solely in the pragmatic recognition that only a "strong state" can successfully wage a democratic revolution against a deeply entrenched oligarchic minority in a rapidly modernizing world. The Marcos theorists shared a more profound underlying philosophical assumption, namely, that "order" is constitutive for political life. "Order" was seen as a concrete structure and pattern of governance that privileges the state as the prime mover of political life.

It bears repeating that for the Marcos theorists the imposition of martial law in the Philippines was due largely to the threat posed by "lawless elements" seeking to destroy the "duly constituted government." Marcos himself argued:

When, however, the duly established or legitimate government is attacked by a force that aims at its overthrow and take over through force or violence . . . then the new leader's principal concern is to make sure that his government can enforce the law. . . . usually he ends up with an authoritarian government, in the sense that he must be compelled to proclaim Martial Law because the extent of disorder and violence has rendered the ordinary militia or police powerless to enforce civil law.[57]

Drawing on U.S. constitutional law, to which Philippine law is indebted, Marcos theorists argued that martial law entailed "the military merely being utilized to strengthen the civil government in the enforcement of existing law." They cited approvingly the consensus of Burdick, Willis, and Willoughby, U.S. authorities on constitutional law, that martial law "is not a substitute for the civil law, but is rather an aid to the execution of the civil law."[58]

Marcos argued, therefore, that the imposition of martial law was not a surrender of the civilian authority to the military. Rather than being alien to the democratic heritage, martial law was an extraordinary measure provided by democracy to protect itself.[59] Marcos went further, however. He argued early on that martial law in the Philippines

has not established a military regime and its purpose is not to restore the status quo. Its character and purposes have been shaped by the historic need . . . which is the reconciliation of established liberal democratic aspirations with the social and economic conditions of the people. . . . The intervention of Martial Law must . . . be viewed as a creative, if extraordinary, measure to break this circle of futility [the inhospitable social and economic conditions of the people].[60]

Implicit in this extraordinary, though not unprecedented, use of martial law was the valuation of the primacy of order for the existence of political community. Drawing on Samuel Huntington's observations of the problems confronting developing countries, Marcos theorists noted that "the primary problem is not liberty but the creation of a legitimate public order [since] men may have order without liberty, but they cannot have liberty without order."[61]

Not insignificantly, Marcos theorists appeared unwilling to define what constituted "order" as such. They preferred to argue for its necessity. Implicit in the argument was a fundamental assumption, namely, that particular structures and patterns of relationships, universal and continuous over time, are constitutive of human life. The argument for the primacy of order in political and social life turned out to be grounded in the assumption that "order" was a constitutive element of the universe. "To seekers of essential truths," Marcos had argued,

one proof that God exists [is] the obvious presence of order in the constellations of the universe. . . . The withdrawal of the design for this order and harmony would be instantly followed by collision, fire and wreckage. The proposition has a moral content: the price of order is destruction.[62]

What is interesting, however, is the almost ontological consequence that Marcos drew for politics from this theological assertion. "On the plane of human society," he continued,

this correspondence of order and moral value has a counterpart in government and community. No matter how numerous the individuals . . . and regardless of the variousness of their wants and interests . . . they have a collective interest in the preservation of order . . . [for] the supreme and eternal good, the highest morality, is the avoidance of self-destruction. To assure itself that this high moral duty is performed, human society has instituted law and fashioned the instrument of government with which to enforce it.[63]

This "collective interest in the preservation of order" became rooted in the organic human instinct for self-preservation that, for the Marcos theorists, served as the "prime mover of peace and order in society." In Thomas Hobbes' atomistic view of self-preservation and survival, one finds this fundamental assumption foreshadowed.[64] Striking was the collectivization and institutionalization of this view. Like Hobbes, Marcos held that self-preservation comprised the moral justification for the necessity of order in society. Unlike Hobbes, Marcos interpreted "order" as constitutive rather than regulative. On the one hand, Marcos argued that society had an implicit order beyond the self-interests of individuals, although he understood it as not being self-regulating or self-enforcing. On the other hand, Marcos recognized that political reality was comprised of the perpetual struggle of individuals and individuals-writ-large committed to the preservation and enlargement of their self-interests. He therefore argued for the necessity of enforcing "law and order" to protect these individuals not only from the ravages of self-interest, but especially from the threat of destruction. "The collective rights of the citizens to protect themselves from destruction," wrote Marcos, "becomes, to a government of laws, an obligation to impose order—as the maxim goes, public welfare is the highest law."[65]

The argument for the primacy of order drew on a particular notion of authority and law. Marcos theorists exposed their "liberal democratic" affinities in their construal of "authority" as legal authority.[66] Not surprisingly, Marcos consistently grounded his actions in the judicial process,[67] unequivocally affirmed the "rule of law,"[68] and constantly defended his government's legitimacy.[69] The primacy of law, of what Unger calls the "legal mentality," became construed as a principle of public order.[70] It is noteworthy that to this day Marcos continues to insist that he is the "duly elected" president of the Philippines.

The notion of authority as such, however, was an elusive one. Marcos theorists simply presupposed it. They determined that only in its expression as "legitimate public order," to borrow Huntington's phrase, could authority be identified. Not only authority but legitimate public authority was at stake for Marcos and his government. In practice this meant the creation of public order. The authority initially proclaimed as rooted in "the people's will" or the Constitution in reality was transferred to the structures of public order. Moreover, within these structures, of which law was the underlying principle and the instrumentalities of government (the military, the police, and the bureaucracy) the institutional expressions, authority became understood as command. Echoing Hobbes' conception of authority, Marcos asserted that "martial law necessarily creates a command society. But a new society cannot emerge out of sheer command alone."[71] Despite his recognition that the "democratic revolution" could not be reduced to "sheer command," Marcos held on to the assumption that a "command society" where "order," "law," and "authority" were embodied in a single "duly constituted authority" was necessary. Without institutional form, authority was an illusion.

Convinced by Huntington's grave reservations about the indifference to political development of the "Lockean American," Marcos theorists argued that the fundamental problem that most developing societies like the Philippines face has less to do with "holding elections" than with "creating organizations" that will meet the goals of development. What is decisive for these countries, they argued, is the existence of stable public institutions that can guarantee the meaningfulness of any electoral process.

Sounding the warning that a government administered by persons over persons must first "enable the government to control the governed" before it "obliges it to control itself," Marcos theorists applied to the Philippines Huntington's argument that the primary problem was not liberty but the creation of legitimate public order. As Huntington put it, "Authority has to exist before it can be limited, and it is authority that is in scarce supply in those modernizing countries.[72]

Within this framework, politics, despite the rhetoric that proclaimed it as the practice of freedom,[73] became the practice of creating public order. Authority was no longer understood as the ongoing deliberative relationship between the government and its people in the context of their shared values. Rather, authority was construed as the prerogative of government to command its people. Rather than "the law" being an expression of authority, it became that which conferred it. Thus the Marcos government continually sought to create and sustain structures and patterns of governance designed to maintain "domestic stability."[74] The increased militarization and bureaucratization of the state, both of which greatly increased its repressive and coercive powers, comprised significant aspects of this process.[75] Somewhat ironically, what originally had been conceived as an institution created to safeguard the very source of authority on which legitimacy rested, namely, the people, evolved as the primary agent of its destruction. The consequence of politics became its condition; what was regulative became constitutive.

For the Marcos theorists, the creation of "legitimate public order" essentially involved balancing the claims of the individual vis-à-vis those of the society. Having asserted, for example, that "all politics begins by recognizing the need to maintain an effective balance between the claims of the individual and those of the community," they argued that the problem was how one could combine "that degree of individual liberty without which law becomes tyranny with that degree of law without which liberty becomes anarchy."[76] Politics is reduced to the adjudication of competing interests.

The fundamental issue, of course, was not whether "legitimate public order" was necessary or even desirable, nor was it the adjudication of competing claims. Rather, as both "liberal democratic" and nationalist-Marxist critics of the Marcos regime jointly noted, the issue was whether the creation of public order encompassed, in a meaningful way, the participation of the people, for whom it had been created.[77] Despite Marcos' insistence that participation had been guaranteed through institutions like the Sanggunian Bayan (Citizens' Assemblies) and the Batasang Pambansa (National Assembly), in practice there were no effective institutional mechanisms for such participation.[78]

The reason for the absence of effective mechanisms of participation was not simply "institutional." Despite the claim that it had succeeded in freeing "our people from their role as a mere gallery of consent . . . by enrolling the overwhelming majority of our people in the political process,"[79] the Marcos government primarily conceived of participation as the inclusion of those who had been excluded from the decision-making processes of the state into already-defined patterns and structures of governance. Government had already predetermined the nature and extent of participation. The state acted on behalf of its people by creating the institutions in which the people might participate. Participation was reduced to assent.[80]

In retrospect, this particular conception of participation resulted, at least on the level of electoral politics, in what Ellen Trimberger called the "depoliticization of the masses."[81] Given the Marcos government's monopoly of the political terrain, most Filipinos developed a cynical attitude toward traditional political institutions. The sense of "belonging," crucial to political community, was eclipsed. On a deeper, clandestine level, however, the absence of meaningful and efficacious participation in the governance of the body politic resulted in the creation of peoples' organizations. The "February 1986 Rebellion" that saw the eruption into Philippine politics of peoples' movements, from the spontaneous though relatively unorganized "liberal bourgeois" sector to the more highly organized nationalist/leftist-inspired "cause-oriented" groups, suggests that the "depoliticization of the masses" was more apparent than real. With the demise of Marcos, peoples' direct participation in the creation of the structures and patterns of governance is being rediscovered with a passion.

Moreover, the question of "legitimate public order" cannot be reduced to the question of the adjudication of competing claims. The question of "public order," then as now, is fundamentally a problem of civil society, that is, what it means to be constituted as a political community. What the Marcos theorists failed to fully understand was that the crisis of Philippine political life was less the loss of authority or legitimacy than it was the disintegration of the relational structures that constituted political life. No doubt this disintegration paved the way for the imposition of order as a compensatory principle of "common life." In the absence of this "common life" brought about by the complex process of modernization and revolution, "law and order" became the only structure for the "common." Because they emphasized the creation of public order as the central task of politics and focused on exclusive legitimacy as its primary goal, Marcos theorists did not address the question of political community at the fundamental, transformative level of "the common." Political community, if it has disintegrated internally, cannot simply be "restored" by circumscribing the disintegration with an external "system of laws."[82] Nor can formal legitimacy replace substantive legitimacy without undermining the latter's emphasis on consensus from the ground up.

The discussion of "dissent" during the Marcos regime further illustrates the consequence of reducing politics to the creation of legitimate public order. After affirming the "right of political dissent," including the implied repudiation of any claim to absolute political authority, as fundamental to democratic society and the concept of political liberty, Marcos theorists moved immediately to domesticate political dissent. They specified it as "dissent through free expression"—not dissent as such—within the larger framework of the political community. This dissent would thereby imply the existence of an authority, for them residing in "duly constituted government." Thus, reechoing Hobbesian logic, they argued that

where there is no government there can be no law. Where there is no law there can be no legal rights. Where there are no legal rights the only "rights" that are operational are the rights of brute force and cunning. . . . If, therefore, dissent is claimed as a right, it must be claimed within the framework of law.[83]

Procedurally, the "right of political dissent" was balanced with the "right of government to preserve itself" in order that it might continue to preserve "the system of law that guarantees rights."[84] Any threat to the law and order it sought to preserve, therefore, became a threat to those rights that were initially valued. Consequently, the former had to be preserved at all cost. In this sense the "right of political dissent," and the freedom to dissent it presupposed, required that it be subordinated to the government when by its exercise it threatened what the latter construed as the public welfare. Yet the determination of what constitutes not only the "public welfare" but "political dissent" as well was left, again, to the Marcos government. Political life was defined primarily by government, not by the people. Accountability to the people disappears into the mandate supposedly given once and for all.

This state-centric construal of "political dissent" was challenged by critics of the Marcos government ranging from the nationalist-Marxist opposition to the "liberal [Lockean] democratic" opposition. In the mid-1970s, for example, the latter questioned the legitimacy of the Marcos government from a juridico-procedural perspective that challenged Marcos' interpretation of the law, that is, the identification of law with the state. Unfortunately, because they shared Marcos' premise of "the rule of law" as the Archimedian point from which all laws are understood, they blunted the goal of their criticism. With the gradual emergence of popular criticism, particularly in the early 1980s, this formal/procedural challenge was relocated within the context of the substantive opposition to the Marcos government. Thus Jovito Salonga argued:

In the final analysis, our hope is not in any foreign power, nor in a Constitution, nor in any statute or law, nor in any court of justice. Our true hope is in our own people, who, thanks to current developments, including the so-called lifting of Martial Law, are asserting their right to be free—with increasing boldness and courage.[85]

In short, Salonga was challenging the formal/procedural basis on which the Marcos government built its argument for the "rule of law." More importantly, he implied that the proper locus of politics was civil society, that social transformation ultimately rested with the people who were struggling for justice and freedom. This was a direct challenge both to the central assumption of Philippine constitutional authoritarianism and its destructive consequences. Marcos theorists assumed that the state was the *primum movens* of political life. Consequently, the state had to have the capacity to impose its will absolutely. This not only led to the "depoliticization of the masses," but also to the contraction of political space under the Marcos regime. The state as the *locus politicus* meant that those who dissented "outside the law" were branded subversive. They were disenfranchised from the "legitimate" body politic, their claims given no credence whatsoever. Where disorder prevailed, coercion became not only the sole prerogative of the state, but necessary. Locke surrendered to Hobbes.

State coercion, of course, was not limited to its overt expression as political and military oppression. For the most part, the coercive character of Philippine constitutional authoritarianism rested on its adherence to a particular understanding of the "rule of law." Not only were the presidential commitment orders (PCOs), presidential detention actions (PDAs), and Proclamation no. 1081 coercive and arbitrary,[86] the "legal mentality," undergirding the "rule of law," was more profoundly destructive of political life. Since it valorized formal equality over substantive equity, it legitimated uniformity of persons "before the law" as the fundamental principle of government. This formal conception, partly because it rested on the premise of arbitrary command, gave impetus not only to the levelling of status in society, but more importantly, it reinforced the view of social life as being mediated by "calculable rules." Such levelling of status in the context of a society of rules first meant the equal subjection of all citizens to the state. It also meant, and with equal significance, the reduction of the plurality of meanings inherent in any political reality to that which the impersonal rules stipulated. The "legal mentality" was a consciousness of order transformed into the practice of coercion. Unfortunately, such a truncated view of political life failed to recognize the plurality of political forms, structures, and expressions that were necessary for a democratic society. Philippine constitutional authoritarianism reduced democracy to a system of rules and ignored the fact that at its most profound level democracy is a way of life.

Implicit in the understanding of the necessity of absolute "state power" for the creation and maintenance of public order is the assumption that social transformation on an institutional level, not unlike the Marxist-Leninist theory of social change, requires a minority within society that initiates and sustains revolutionary activity. Adopting a perspective not entirely different from the Marxist-Leninist "vanguard," though more like that of Hobbes' Sovereign who is the Great Definer of political life, Philippine constitutional authoritarianism identified this "revolutionary minority" with the Marcos government. It affirmed a theory of state and social change that was thoroughly modern. As Marcos himself asserted: "The power to control and change his environment is a cardinal belief of modern man, and revolution is the ultimate expression of this outlook—the modernizing outlook."[87] "We have to decide whether we should be the masters or victims of change."[88]

These values of "mastery" and "control" converged with the statist structure and pattern of governance of the Marcos government. As the "unilateral assertion of political will" that coalesced with the monopoly of violence and legitimacy asserted by the Marcos government, the "authority to govern" as well as the process of governance became understood as the power to control and master the social and ecological environment. This was effected through the legal and military instrumentalities of the state.[89] The world is only beginning to realize the human and ecological costs that the Marcos regime exacted from the Filipino people. Perhaps more importantly, we are only beginning to realize that the outcome of social change is inescapably shaped—even determined—by its historical and institutional mediation. That is, the political choice of the state as the sole agency of social change turned out to be its own contradiction. The political, economic, and cultural legacy that the Marcos government left, including the foreign debt, a practically nonexistent domestic infrastructure of production, distribution, and consumption, and a highly politicized and fractious military, to mention only a few concerns, underscores its vision of a "democratic revolution" as nothing but an illusion. That which was seen as the bearer of transformation, the state, was in the last analysis that which devoured not only its children but its creator.

CONCLUSION

This chapter has argued that Philippine constitutional authoritarianism embodies a logic of domination that sets it on the path of state-sponsored terrorism. Not unlike the Jacobin phase of the French Revolution (1793-1794), which represented a major watershed in the history of both state-sponsored terrorism and intrastate violence, the Marcos government utilized terror and violence to effect social change. In contrast to those who have construed both "revolutions" as examples par excellence of the complete abandonment of the "rule of law,"[90] however, I have suggested in this chapter that at least in the case of the latter, it was its ideology, which privileged the "rule of law" and the "primacy of order," that provided not only the legitimation for state-sponsored terrorism, but also its normative and encompassing vision.

The causal link, if any, between the "rule of law" and state-sponsored terrorism remains at the very least, elusive. No attempt has been made to establish one. However, my excavations into the "liberal democratic" tradition in the Philippines suggest the rather disturbing conclusion that when politics in a revolutionary and modernizing world is construed within a statist, militarist, and corporate-capitalist horizon, the centralizing logic of the "primacy of order" and its concomitant commitment to the "rule of law" that is at its core may be one of the politico-philosophical and socio-moral sources of terrorism and violence and for that reason may prove to be one of the most deceptive and elusive obstacles to radical democratic politics anywhere.

NOTES

1. Roberto M. Unger, *Knowledge and Politics* (New York: Free Press, 1975), p. 75.

2. Teodoro A. Agoncillo and Milagros C. Guerrero, *A History of the Filipino People,* 5th ed. (Quezon City, Philippines: R. P. Garcia Publishing Co., 1977), p. 642. See also Amado Guerrero, *Philippine Society and Revolution,* 3d ed. (Oakland: International Association of Filipino Patriots, 1979); Robert Stauffer, "The Political Economy of Refeudalization," in David Rosenberg, ed., *Marcos and Martial Law in the Philippines* (Ithaca, N.Y.: Cornell University Press, 1979), pp. 180-218; Richard Vokey, "Islands under the Gun," *Far Eastern Economic Review* 8 (May 1981): 36-42; Southeast Asia Resource Center, "400 Year War—Moro Struggle in the Philippines," *Southeast Asia Chronicle* 82 (February 1982): 1-28; Southeast Asia Resource Center, "The Philippines in the 1980s—From Normalization to Polarization," *Southeast Asia Chronicle* 82 (April 1982): 1-28; Amnesty International, *Report of an Amnesty International Mission to the Repubic of the Philippines, 11-28 November 1981* (London: Amnesty International Publications, 1982); Permanent Peoples' Tribunal, *Philippines: Repression and Resistance* (London: Zed Press, 1983); Lawyers Committee for Human Rights, *The Philippines: A Country in Crisis* (New York: Lawyers Committee for Human Rights, 1983); Lawyers Committee for Human Rights, *Salvaging the Philippines: Violations of Human Rights under Marcos* (New York: Lawyers Committee for Human Rights, 1985); Guy Sacerdoti and Philip Bowring, "Marx, Mao, and Marcos," *Far Eastern Economic Review* 21 (November 1985): 52-62; and John Bresnan, ed., *Crisis in the Philippines: The Marcos Era and Beyond* (Princeton: Princeton University Press, 1986).

3. A number of studies have been made of the particular ideological underpinnings of those regimes that engage in state-sponsored terrorism. For the more comprehensive theoretical treatments, see Herbert Kelman, "Violence without Moral Restraints: Reflections on the Dehumanization of Victims and Victimizers," *Journal of the Social Issues* 29 (1973): 21-62; George A. Lopez, "National Security Ideology as an Impetus to State Terror," in Michael Stohl and George A. Lopez, eds., *Government Violence and Repression: An Agenda for Research* (Westport, Conn.: Greenwood Press, 1986), pp. 73-95.

4. Michael Stohl and George A. Lopez, eds., *The State as Terrorist: The Dynamics of Governmental Violence and Repression* (Westport, Conn.: Greenwood Press, 1984), p. 9. Unger argues in *Knowledge and Politics* that "terror [is] the systematic use of violence unlimited by law" (p. 75). The argument of this chapter, however, is that Philippine constitutional authoritarianism understood the use of state-sponsored violence as being sanctioned by the law, not limited by it.

5. Diosdado Macapagal, *Democracy in the Philippines* (Ontario, Canada: Ruben J. Cusipag, 1976), pp. 28-29; Raul Manglapus, *Philippines: The Silenced Democracy* (Maryknoll, N.Y.: Orbis Books, 1976), pp. 12-20. See also Rolando del Carmen, "Constitutionality and Judicial Politics," in Rosenberg, *Marcos and Martial Law in the Philippines,* pp. 85-112.

6. Proclamation no. 1081, "Proclaiming a State of Martial Law in the Philippines," in Ferdinand E. Marcos, *The Democratic Revolution in the Philippines,* 2d ed. (Englewood Cliffs, N.J.: Prentice-Hall, 1979), pp. 335-351.

7. Ferdinand E. Marcos, *Today's Revolution: Democracy* (Manila: National Media Production Center, 1971), "Introduction," p. i.

8. Ferdinand E. Marcos, *Revolution from the Center: How the Philippines is Using Martial Law to Build a New Society* (Hongkong: Raya Books, 1978), pp. 32-35. See also Marcos, *Democratic Revolution*, pp. 140-150; Guerrero, *Philippine Society and Revolution;* José Maria Sison, *Struggle for National Democracy* (Manila: Amado Hernandez Memorial Foundation, 1972).

9. Marcos, *Democratic Revolution*, pp. 111-131; Proclamation no. 1081, ibid., pp. 335-351.

10. Ibid., p. 114; see also Ferdinand E. Marcos, *Progress and Martial Law* (Manila: National Media Production Center, 1981), pp. 1-20.

11. This was suggested by the Mansfield (Valeo) Report to the U.S. Senate, which read, in part: "Beyond the ostensible objective of restoring law and order, martial law had paved the way for a reordering of the basic social structure of the Philippines. President Marcos has been prompt and sure-footed in using the power of presidential decree under martial law for this purpose." Cited in Marcos, *Democratic Revolution*, p. 141; see also Macapagal, *Democracy*, pp. 18-19.

12. Thus the 1960s saw two major United Nations conferences on trade and development, Geneva in 1964 and New Delhi in 1968, during its First United Nations Development Decade. See "1967 Report on the World Situation," U.N. Document E/CN.5/417; and "Trends and Problems in World Trade and Development, Charter of Algiers," U.N. Conference on Trade and Development, Document TO/38, 3 November 1967. Compare also the influential social teachings of the Roman Catholic church, "Mater et Magistra," "Pacem in Terris," and "Gaudium et Spes," in Joseph Gremillion, *The Gospel of Peace and Justice* (Maryknoll, N.Y.: Orbis Books, 1979), pp. 143-335.

13. Marcos, *Today's Revolution*, "Introduction," p. v. See also note 12, and Cyril E. Black, *The Dynamics of Modernization: A Study in Comparative History* (New York: Harper and Row, 1966).

14. Marcos himself noted in *Democratic Revolution* (p. 2): "It can bear repeating that the only immutable object in human life is the principle that everything is susceptible to change. . . . we provoke and welcome change to survive the shocks and tensions of man's headlong flight to technology. . . . we live in a time of revolution. Mankind is in a ferment of change . . . *in the democracies, change has the special property of volition*" (emphasis added). For the substance of this "modernization," see Marcos, *Democratic Revolution*, "Introduction," pp. ii-iii; *Progress*, pp. 38-45.

15. Marcos, *Progress*, pp. 65-66.

16. Samuel Huntington, cited in Marcos, *Democratic Revolution*, p. 70.

17. Marcos, *Democratic Revolution*, pp. 93-94.

18. Marcos, *Revolution from the Center*, pp. 19-22.

19. Ibid., p. 22; Marcos, *Democratic Revolution*, p. 94.

20. Ferdinand E. Marcos, *In Search of Alternatives: The Third World in an Age of Crisis*, 3d ed. (Manila: National Media Production Center, 1980), pp. 83-92.

21. Marcos, *Revolution from the Center*, p. 21.

22. Marcos, *In Search of Alternatives*, p. 22.

23. Post–February 1987 events seem to bear this argument out. See Lester Edwin

J. Ruiz, "Philippine Politics as a Peoples' Quest for Authentic Political Subject-hood," *Alternatives: Social Transformation and Humane Governance* 11, no. 4 (October 1986): 505-534; Edicio de la Torre, "On the Post-Marcos Transition and Popular Democracy," interview by Lester Edwin J. Ruiz, *World Policy Journal* 4, no. 2 (April 1987).

24. Marcos, *Today's Revolution,* p. 2.

25. Ibid., p. 1.

26. Ferdinand E. Marcos, *An Ideology for Filipinos* (Manila: National Media Production Center, 1980), p. 23.

27. Ibid., p. 13.

28. Ibid., p. 17; Marcos, *Today's Revolution,* pp. 1-3.

29. Marcos, *Democratic Revolution,* p. 218.

30. Marcos, *Today's Revolution,* p. 7.

31. Ibid., p. 20.

32. Ibid., p. 86.

33. Marcos, *Ideology for Filipinos,* pp. 15-16.

34. Ibid., p. 17.

35. Ibid., p. 19.

36. Ibid., p. 21. As theorists of Philippine constitutional authoritarianism asserted elsewhere: "Equality is the fundamental demand of the rebellion of the poor: It should be the ideological force behind the New Society." Marcos, *Democratic Revolution,* p. 151.

37. Marcos, *Today's Revolution,* pp. 11-12.

38. Marcos, *Ideology for Filipinos,* p. 29.

39. Marcos, *Today's Revolution,* p. 12. Thus Marcos wrote: "Governments are now judged according to their willingness and capacity to act as instruments of social change. The people—the governed—look to their governments for leadership not only in the political order but also in the social and economic orders." Ibid., p. 9.

40. Ferdinand E. Marcos, Blas Ople, O. D. Corpuz, et al. *Toward the New Society: Essays on Aspects of Philippine Development* (Manila: National Media Production Center, 1974), p. 57.

41. Ibid., p. 57.

42. Marcos, *Ideology for Filipinos,* p. 26.

43. Ibid., p. 27.

44. The notion of a "relatively autonomous state," particularly in the case of the Marcos government, flies in the face of the actual situation. See note 8; William Branigin, "The Philippines: A Society Adrift," *Washington Post,* 16 August 1984; Robin Broad, "Behind Philippine Policy-Making" (Ph.D. diss., Princeton University, 1983).

On the theoretical level the Marcos argument for a "revolutinary state" and "autonomous state" may be seen as part of a growing scholary corpus, both Marxist and non-Marxist, that seeks to reevaluate the relationship between state and society in terms of the theory and practice of social and political change. See, for example, Theda Skocpol, *States and Social Revolutions: A Comparative Analysis of France, Russia, and China* (New York: Cambridge University Press, 1979); Ellen Kay Trimberger, *Revolution from Above: Military Bureaucrats and Development in Japan, Turkey, Egypt, and Peru* (New Brunswick, N.J.: Transaction Books, 1978); Nicos Poulantzas, *Political Power and Social Classes* (London: NLB, 1973).

Still more recent discussions, particularly in the neo-Marxist/Gramscian tradition, while not explicitly dealing with the "revolutionary potential" of the state and state system, address the issues that are implicit in the discourse of the "autonomous state." Of course, the radicality of these later discussions (for example, the notion of hegemony and the repudiation of the dichotomy between "base and superstructure") was never seen by the theorists of Philippine constitutional authoritarianism. See, for example, Ernesto Laclau and Chantal Mouffe, *Hegemony and Socialist Strategy: Towards a Radical Democratic Politics,* trans. by Winston Moore and Paul Cammack (London: Verso, 1985).

45. Marcos, Ople, Corpuz, et al., *Toward the New Society,* p. 46.

46. See, for instance, Cesar Adib Majul, *The Political and Constitutional Ideas of the Philippine Revolution* (Quezon City, Philippines: History of the Philippines Press, 1967); Renato Constantino, *A History of the Philippines: From the Spanish Colonization to the Second World War* (New York: Monthly Review Press, 1975); Renato Constantino, *The Filipinos in the Philippines and Other Essays* (Quezon City, Philippines: Filipino Signatures, 1966); Agoncillo and Guerrero, *History of the Filipino People;* Onofre D. Corpuz, *The Philippines* (Englewood Cliffs, N.J.: Prentice-Hall, 1965). It is not surprising to note that the 1935 Philippine Constitution, for example, had large portions lifted verbatim from the U.S. Constitution.

47. Marcos, Ople, Corpuz, et al., *Toward the New Society,* p. 49.

48. Ibid., p. 53.

49. Marcos, *Democratic Revolution,* p. 278. For the most explicit discussion of the meaning of equality in the Marcos corpus, see "Equality and Politics," ibid., pp. 151-167.

50. Marcos, *Democratic Revolution,* p. 55; see also Marcos, "The Conquest of Poverty," ibid., pp. 168-180. For the Marcos theorists, therefore, the "Bill of Rights tradition," as "rights of limitation," had to be not merely subsumed under social and economic rights, but repudiated. Marcos himself argued: "We have seen in our preceding analysis that 'human rights' conceived mainly in terms of political liberty is finally a limitation on human freedom. . . . I will go further now to say that the mantle of protection given by our Bill of Rights did not only conceal from view the real inequalities and oppression in our society; *it also served to preclude all possibility of liberation*" (p. 174; emphasis added).

51. Marcos, *Democratic Revolution,* "The Constitution and Martial Law," ibid., pp. 217ff.

52. Marcos, Ople, Corpuz, et al., *Toward the New Society,* p. 57.

53. Ibid., p. 59.

54. Marcos, *Democratic Revolution,* p. 259.

55. Ibid.

56. Thus Marcos theorists asserted: "The achievement of equality [and therefore of 'political liberty'], if it is to contribute at all to human freedom and to social good, must not be seen merely in terms of possession, but more important, in terms of power and potential. The abiding faith is that where men enjoy equal rights and opportunities in the social order, where they are not weighed down by structures that inhibit or discourage their action, they will be able to create and contribute to their personal welfare and dignity, and to the growth and strength of their community." Ibid., p. 279.

57. Marcos, *In Search of Alternatives,* p. 140.

58. Burdick, Willis, and Willoughby, cited in Marcos, ibid., pp. 140-142.

59. Thus Leslie Lipson argued in his book *The Democratic Civilization:* "As a system of government in existence, democracy has a right to preserve itself. Liberty can be protected against abuses committed in its name. While all liberties depend on maintaining some order, and too many orders mean sacrificing too much liberty, democracy is not required to commit suicide." Cited in Ferdinand E. Marcos, *The Philippine Experience: A Perspective on Human Rights and the Rule of Law* (Manila: National Media Production Center, n.d.), p. 37.

60. Marcos, *Philippine Experience,* p. 36.

61. Samuel Huntington, cited in Marcos, ibid., p. 31.

62. Ferdinand E. Marcos, "Martial Law and Human Rights," in *Democratic Revolution,* pp. 1-2.

63. Ibid., pp. 1-2. Nowhere in the Marcos corpus more clearly than here is the confluence of positivism and natural rights theory, of "premodern" and modern thought, articulated. The argument, as Unger has noted, is that so-called premodern societies draw a clear line between what is immutable in the social order and what falls under the discretion of the rulers. In contrast, modern states tend to construe every aspect of social life as being subject to political will. See Unger, *Knowledge and Politics,* pp. 305-306. Philippine constitutional authoritarianism, in fact, cannot be reduced to either premodern or modern. It is both. See Henry Maine, *Lectures on the Early History of Institutions,* 7th ed. (London: Murray, 1897), pp. 373-386.

64. Thomas Hobbes, *De Cive; or, The Citizen,* ed. Sterling Lamprecht (New York: Appleton-Century-Crofts, 1949), pt. I, chap. 1, secs. 2-3. The rational principle of "self-preservation" in Hobbes is rooted in the prerational fear of violent death. The distinction is crucial, attesting to the dichotomy of reason and desire in Hobbes. See the persuasive argument of Unger, *Knowledge and Politics,* pp. 38-54.

65. Marcos, "Human Rights under the New Society," in "Martial Law and Human Rights," in *Democratic Revolution,* p. 25. Cf. Unger's argument that "the less one's ability to rely on participation in common ends, the greater the importance of force as a bond among individuals. Punishment and fear take the place of community." Unger, *Knowledge and Politics,* p. 75.

66. Marcos, *Democratic Revolution,* pp. 1-24.

67. See, for instance, Marcos, *In Search of Alternatives,* pp. 38-83; Marcos, *Ideology for Filipinos,* pp. 23-25.

68. See Marcos, "A Perspective on Human Rights and the Rule of Law," in *Democratic Revolution,* pp. 237-301.

69. Marcos, "My Fighting Faith," in *Democratic Revolution,* pp. 25-40.

70. Unger, *Knowledge and Politics,* pp. 83-100. See also Iredell Jenkins, *Social Order and the Limits of Law: A Theoretical Essay* (Princeton: Princeton University Press, 1980), pp. 3-30. Marcos often cited the jurist Benjamin Cardozo, who wrote: "Law is the expression of a principle of order to which man must conform in their conduct and relations as members of society." Benjamin Cardozo, *The Growth of the Law* (New Haven: Yale University Press, 1924), p. 140.

71. Compare, for example, Thomas Hobbes, *Leviathan; or, The Matter, Forme & Power of a Common-Wealth Ecclesiasticall and Civill,* ed. C. B. Macpherson (New York: Penguin Books, 1968), chap. 26, p. 312. In this context, Philippine constitutional authoritarianism shows affinities with the national security state system ideology. See, for instance, Jose Comblin, *Le pouvoir militaire en Amérique Latine:*

L'idéologie de la sécurité nationale (Paris: Jean Pierre de Large, 1977); Augusto Pinochet Ugarte, *Geopolitica,* 2d ed. (Santiago de Chile: Andres Bello, 1974). For an explicit discussion of the similarities between Philippine constitutional authoritarianism and the national security state system ideology, see my essay, "Power, Justice, and the Concept of Human Development" (Paper presented at the 23rd Annual Convention of the International Studies Association, Cincinnati, Ohio, 26 March 1982, mimeographed, available from the Center for Research and Education, Lawrenceville, New Jersey).

72. Samuel Huntington, *Political Order in Changing Societies* (New Haven: Yale University Press, 1968), pp. 7-8; cited also, in part, in Marcos, *Philippine Experience,* p. 31.

73. Marcos, *Ideology for Filipinos,* pp. 13-22, 75-84; Marcos, *Democratic Revolution,* pp. 151-167.

74. Cf. Marcos, *Democratic Revolution,* pp. 335-351; Ferdinand E. Marcos, "Optimism Resurgent in Country Today," The President's Report to the Nation during the 5th Anniversary of Martial Law, 21 September 1977, p. 8; Marcos, *Progress and Martial Law,* pp. 49-52.

75. Herbert Feith, "Repressive-Developmentalist Regimes in Asia," *Alternatives: a Journal of World Policy* 7, no. 4 (Spring 1982): 491-506; Delia Miller, "Memorandum on U.S. Military Assistance to the Philippines" (Washington, D.C.: Institute for Policy Studies, 1979); Walden Bello and Severina Rivera, eds., *The Logistics of Repression and Other Essays: The Role of U.S. Assistance in Consolidating the Martial Law Regime in the Philippines* (Washington, D.C.: Friends of the Filipino People, 1977); Noam Chomsky and Edward S. Herman, *The Washington Connection and Third World Fascism: The Political Economy of Human Rights,* vol. 1 (Boston: South End Press, 1979).

76. Marcos, *Philippine Experience,* p. 1.

77. Guerrero, *Philippine Society and Revolution,* pp. 129-169; Renato Constantino, *The Nationalist Alternative* (Manila: Foundation of Nationalist Studies, 1979), pp. 65-90; United Democratic Organization (UNIDO), "A Program for a Just Society in a Free and Democratic Philippines" (Manila, n.d., Mimeographed); National Democratic Front, *Ten-Point Program of the National Democratic Front in the Philippines* (Oakland: Union of Democratic Filipinos and the International Association of Filipino Patriots, 1978).

78. Macapagal, *Democracy,* pp. 30-37. For a fuller understanding of the Philippine situation in relation to the politico-philosophical argument that is being made in this chapter see my dissertation, "Towards a Transformative Politics: A Quest for Authentic Political Subjecthood" (Ph.D. diss., Princeton Theological Seminary, 1985), pp. 1-46. See also notes 2 and 89.

79. Marcos, *Ideology for Filipinos,* p. 50.

80. Ibid., pp. 37-53.

81. Trimberger, *Revolution from Above,* pp. 110-115. Cf. Benjamin Barber, *Strong Democracy: Participatory Politics for a New Age* (Berkeley and Los Angeles: University of California Press, 1984).

82. See, for example, the insightful remarks of Unger on the relationship between the disintegration of community and the dominance of the "legal mentality" in *Knowledge and Politics,* pp. 72-76. Cf. Marcos, *Democratic Revolution,* pp. 305-306.

83. Marcos, Ople, Corpuz, et al., *Toward the New Society*, p. 60; cf. Hobbes, *Leviathan*, p. 188.

84. Marcos, Ople, Corpuz, et al., *Toward the New Society*, pp. 61-62.

85. Jovito R. Salonga, "The Democratic Opposition and Its Vision of the Society Our People Want" (Speech delivered before the Manila Rotary Club, Manila Hilton, Manila, Philippines, 9 October 1980, Mimeographed), p. 7.

86. P. N. Abinales, *Militarization in the Philippines* (Manila: Nationalist Resource Center, 1982); Association of Major Religious Superiors (Philippines), *Political Detainees in the Philippines,* bks. 1 and 2 (Los Angeles: Anti-Martial Law Coalition, 1976, 1977); Jim Zwick, *Militarism and Repression in the Philippines,* Working Paper Series no. 31 (Montreal: McGill University Press, 1982); E. San Juan, *Crisis in the Philippines: The Making of a Revolution* (South Hadley, Mass.: Bergin and Garvey, 1986). See also note 2.

87. Marcos, *Democratic Revolution,* p. 65.

88. Marcos, *Today's Revolution,* "Introduction," p. i.

89. Jim Zwick has argued that the structure and pattern of governance of Philippine constitutional authoritarianism is militaristic, which he understands as the confluence of "militarism" and "militarization" in the organization of the state. This view, while extremely helpful and cogent, tends to reduce the notion of "law and order" to a function of the military, obscuring the central place of the former in the larger Western "liberal democratic" tradition, of which the Philippines is a part. Thus Zwick seems to suggest that the Marcos regime was an aberration in the "liberal democratic" tradition. My own argument in this chapter seeks to locate the phenomena of "militarism" and "militarization" within the larger notion of "law and order" and consequently suggests that Philippine constitutional authoritarianism is a logical expression of the "liberal democratic" tradition. I am not proposing a causal link, however. See Zwick, *Militarism and Repression;* Ruiz, "Towards a Transformative Politics," pp. 45ff. See also note 2.

90. Maximilien Robespierre, "Rapport sur les principles du gouvernement revolutionnaire," in *Discours et rapports de Robespierre,* ed. C. Vellay (Paris: Charpentier, 1908), pp. 332-333. Cf. Crane Brinton, *A Decade of Revolution, 1789-1799* (New York: Harper and Brothers, 1934), pp. 139-140, 158-163; Robert A. Friedlander, "The Implausible Dream: International Law, State Violence, and State Terrorism," in Stohl and Lopez, *Government Violence and Repression,* pp. 235-268.

6

State Repression and Development: The Case of Turkey

Adamantia Pollis

A forceful argument has been made in recent years that gross violations of human rights in Third World countries are a consequence of the priority given to economic growth. The implicit underlying presumption of such a contention—that there is a trade-off between economic development and human rights—is that human rights are contingent on industrialization.[1] It is unfortunate, the argument contends, that human rights are violated in many Third World countries and that repression prevails, but this may be a precondition for economic growth, which in turn is a prerequisite for the flourishing of human rights. An argument that repressive regimes are the inevitable by-product of the process of industrialization is an argument that economic factors are determinants of rights. It thereby challenges the philosophic underpinnings of the Western doctrine of human rights and their claim to universality. The liberal doctrine of rights that is rooted in the theory of natural rights conceives of civil and political rights as inherent, inalienable attributes of man independent of the level of economic development or socioeconomic structure.

Controversy surrounding the issue of universalism versus cultural relativism as it pertains to human rights frames the dialogue in erroneous terms. It is ontologically unsound and obfuscates the critical interrelationships among the substance of human rights, their practice, state repression, and other socioeconomic forces. A multifaceted issue, human rights, has been dichotomized, resulting in an oversimplification that ignores dimensions such as power and national goals. Recent debates on human rights versus economic development, if nothing else, point to the inadequacy of the cultural relativism versus universalism dichotomy by making rights not an issue of universality or of cultural specificity but a consequence of a particular socioeconomic order inclusive of cultural patterns. It is this latter issue of whether rights are contingent on industrialization that this chapter addresses.

The pervasiveness of the view that freedoms are contingent on a certain level of economic development and that repression may be a necessary instrument for attaining growth, not only among scholars but also among political leaders of peripheral countries, is revealed in the argument made by Turkey's Justice Party and its leader, Suleiman Demiral. Demiral claimed in 1970 that the 1961 Turkish constitution "allowed political freedoms far in excess of those Turkey's socio-economic environment warranted" and thus justified limitations and restrictions on freedom.[2]

Efforts to modernize Turkey date from the latter decades of the Ottoman Empire, but it was with the formation of the modern Turkish state in 1922 that both civilian and military leaders articulated the goals of growth and industrialization. The Atatürk revolution, in part a revolution of the incipient bourgeoisie to gain political power, to embark on capitalist development, and to form a bourgeois state, was accompanied in the decades that followed by the repeated use by the state of repression as an instrument of policy. In the post–World War II era Turkey has experienced three military interventions, most recently a coup in September 1980. Moreover, while during civilian semiparliamentary rule a greater degree of freedom existed, as did a competitive party system, violations of individual human rights, including the right to life, were massive, as were restrictions on dissent and the repression of minorities. Furthermore, while the ideological substratum of Atatürk's legacy of modernization incorporated elements derived from the liberal bourgeois state, the notion of economic rights or development for human needs was and remains alien to the rulers of modern Turkey.[3]

The analysis that follows focuses on the relationship between economic development and repression, but it is important to state that a contributing factor to the repressiveness of the Turkish state in the post–World War II years has been its military and strategic importance to the United States. Although Turkey remained neutral during the war, it was included with Greece in the Truman Doctrine because of an alleged threat from the Soviet Union.[4] It also was a recipient of Marshall Plan aid and became a member of NATO at the insistence of the United States. As a client of the United States, Turkey's integration into the Western orbit was not only politico-military, but also economic. In addition to military loans and grants that reached a record high in 1984, economic aid in the form of both grants and loans has been continuous.[5] The United States' hegemony over Turkey, established after World War II with the onset of the cold war, became more thoroughgoing following the Iranian revolution of 1979 when Turkey replaced Iran as the United States' firmest ally in the Middle East.

Turkey, with Israel, serves as the United States' policeman in the Middle East. Thus while repression has been a feature of the Turkish state's goal of economic growth, U.S. national interests in the region and U.S. concern with stability and order have served to reinforce this repression.[6] The economic crisis confronting Turkey in the 1970s, including a huge foreign debt and the attendant domestic discontent at austerity programs in conjunction with U.S. strategic interests, has made repression a tool for preserving the status quo and obtaining foreign aid. An analysis of U.S. policy, particularly of the form and terms of its military and economic aid, would provide an additional dimension to the issue of repression and human rights violations in Turkey. But the fact that historically repression was a feature of the modern Turkish state prior to its politico-military domination by the United States justifies an analytic focus on the relationship between repression and economic development rather than on U.S. policy.

Considerably more than 50 years have passed since the foundation of the modern Turkish state. Atatürk's goal of "westernization" has not been achieved despite radical transformations in Turkish society. Over the decades Turkey has undeniably undergone considerable economic growth, but economic development has remained an elusive goal. Growth has changed the class structure, created a limited industrial base, and deepened capitalist development, but it has not propelled Turkey into the core of the world economy. Turkey remains a peripheral economy with all the attendant dependencies that this entails. At different times Turkey has pursued both the policy of an open economy and that of protectionism with import substitution, but neither has succeeded in creating a self-reliant economy or one that has alleviated the conditions of life for the majority of Turks. Thus economic development has not materialized in Turkey despite the pursuit of varying economic policies and despite the greater or lesser degree of state repression. It is to a more detailed and in-depth analysis of the economy and polity in the post–World War II years that we turn after a brief overview of Turkey's historical development.

HISTORICAL BACKGROUND

Turkey is distinctive in that, with the possible exception of the Bolshevik revolution a few years earlier, its was the first revolutionary nationalist movement whose stated goal was the modernization of a "traditional" society. Led by a military officer, Mustafa Kemal (later Kemal Atatürk), in 1920, at a time when the sultan of an inept, disintegrating Ottoman Empire was signing a treaty with the victorious Allied powers further partitioning the empire and when invading Greek armed forces under the tentative aegis of the Allied powers were moving from Smyrna (Izmir) into the hinterland of Anatolia, the revolution symbolized the transformation of an empire into a Turkish nation-state. Atatürk's program of "westernizing" Turkey was multileveled, and his reforms were designed to permeate the entire fabric of Turkish society. Secularism was to replace Islam, thus destroying the foundations of the sultanate's and the caliphate's legitimacy. Prohibition against the wearing of the fez, disestablishment of the *ulema,* restrictions on the freedom of the mosques, abolition of religious schools and their replacement by secular ones, and changing the written language from the Arabic script to the Latin alphabet were among numerous measures adopted as a strategy for distancing the new Turkish state from the East and identifying it with the West.

The nationalist revolution in Turkey, as was the case in many Third World movements following World War II, was inextricably intertwined with the goal of economic modernization. The Ottoman Empire had already been penetrated by the more advanced capitalist states of Western Europe. This led to the emergence of a predominantly non-Muslim commercial bourgeoisie and the decline of indigenous artisan products, which were replaced by imported factory goods from the industrialized countries of the West.[7] Politically, the rise of a commercial bourgeoisie and pressures toward modernization resulted in the Young Turk revolt of 1908, which adopted severely repressive measures but failed to implement significant reforms.

The newly formed modern Turkish state of 1922, which replaced the sultanate, was quickly recognized by the Allied powers. On one level the revolution was an assertion by the bourgeoisie of their intent to form a capitalist state that would work for their benefit and would facilitate the replacement of the Greek, Armenian, and Jewish commercial bourgeoisie by a Muslim-Turkish one. More fundamentally, the state was to be the agent for the transformation of the precapitalist society into one dominated by the capitalist mode of production. Thus modernization meant the creation of modern centralized state structures, secularization of society, and industrialization through the use of state power.

The society on which Atatürk was determined to impose modernization was a precapitalist one in which familial and localized loyalties predominated. The central authority in Constantinople (Istanbul) had governed an extensive empire, particularly in the earlier centuries, through a vast, highly trained professional bureaucracy and the intellectuals in conjunction with the military elite.[8] There was considerable autonomy in the provinces, except insofar as the sultan's agents, primarily in the form of tax gatherers, extracted surplus from the provinces in order to provide for the financial and economic needs of the sultanate, the caliphate, and the bureaucratic and military institutions in Constantinople. Given the underlying religious precepts of the empire, whereby even the non-Muslim population was organized in *millets* governed by their own clerics, there was no presumption of individual loyalty to or identity with the Ottoman state. In fact, a person's identity was in terms of kinship and/or village and in terms of religion as personified by the local *ulema* or priest. Loyalties were circumscribed by one's group membership and identity.

Atatürk's nationalist revolution was geared precisely to changing these identities and loyalties by transposing them to the nation as embodied in the state. A Turkish, as distinct from an Ottoman or Islamic, nationality was propagated. Turks were defined as historically originating with the Sumerians and Hittites located in the central plains of Anatolia.[9] National integration was the major task confronting the new state leadership. It should also be emphasized that the nationalist revolution and the articulation of a Turkish nationality were promoted by the bourgeoisie as a means of gaining political power and further integrating their economy with those of the more advanced capitalist states of the West.

The Ottoman legacy of a ruling bureaucratic and military elite was incorporated into the new Turkish state, in part because the revolutionaries themselves were of the Ottoman elite and in part because Ottoman historical experience provided no other model of political rule. The modern state, from its legal foundation in 1924 with the adoption of a constitution until the end of World War II, in fact throughout Atatürk's rule, was highly authoritarian. Reforms were imposed from the top down, while opposition and dissent were prohibited and suppressed. In 1925 an emergency "Law for the Maintenance of Order" was promulgated by Atatürk in response to what was labelled a counterrevolutionary uprising by the Kurds in the eastern provinces.[10] This law, which also provided for the establishment of "independence tribunals" to try and sentence those who resisted or opposed the reforms, became the legal justification for the use of force, often resulting in death, against actual or suspected regime opponents. Indicative of the authoritarianism and repressiveness that was to characterize the modern Turkish state was Kemal's statement at the time of the Kurdish rebellion that "we did it [the abolition of the fez] while the Law for the Maintenance of Order was still in force. Had it not been we would have done it all the same."[11]

Atatürk created a one-party state, with the party, the Republican People's Party (RPP), functioning both as a socializing mechanism to gain acceptance for the Atatürk reforms and as an integrative structure. Delegates to the representative body, the Grand National Assembly, were selected from among the members of the RPP. But there was no pretense of democratic rule; the members of the RPP and the delegates were cadres of the party, invariably elites, at first from the new governing center at Ankara, and as the years passed increasingly from the provinces and from the bourgeoisie.[12] The priority was "westernization," to use Atatürk's term, including economic modernization. However, democratic principles and freedoms, of concern because of their identification with westernization, were relegated to the future. Moreover, the notions of individualism, of individual rights, and of freedom of choice, which in the West constitute the underpinnings of democracy, were neither relevant to the overwhelming majority of Turks, whose values and conceptual framework were devoid of such notions, nor were they incorporated as principles of the new Turkish state.

The authoritarian, bureaucratic state, with severely restricted political participation, therefore became the vehicle through which Turkey was to catch up with the West. Reinforcing the historical legacy of administrative rule by an elite—now buttressed by the imperative of creating national integration—was the absence of an independent source of capital or of an entrepreneurial class. The state, as in Ottoman times, extracted surplus value, but it was to be used for the development of the Turkish economy rather than for provisioning the sultanate. Thus the bureaucratic-military apparatus of the modern Turkish state, in coalition with the small commercial bourgeoisie, became the agents of capitalist accumulation. Initially Turkey's international economic position did not differ significantly from that which it held in the latter decades of the Ottoman Empire, namely that of a peripheral merchant capitalist state. Now, however, the national goal of this new modern state was to industrialize by furthering the interests of the bourgeoisie rather than enhancing the power and prestige of the sultan.

At first, Atatürk expected to achieve modernization by pursuing a policy of an open economy, a policy designed to enable the growth and profitability of the commercial bourgeoisie. However, the numerical weakness of the domestic bourgeoisie, due in part to the exodus and decline of the Greeks and Armenians, their limited capital, and most importantly the impact of the worldwide depression of the 1930s, resulting in a decline in exports, adversely affected the commercial bourgeoisie. In 1931 Atatürk added etatism to his fundamental principles governing the Turkish state. With the adoption of etatism, state direction rather than the private sector would propel Turkey to industrialize. Accordingly, the State Economic Enterprises was formed as the agent of capital accumulation mandated to invest in productive ventures.[13] Atatürk's state-directed reforms were thereby extended to the economic sphere, thus strengthening the bureaucratic apparatus and the prominent role of the technocrats and the intellectuals.

The traditional cultural legacy of authoritarianism and, as stated earlier, a value system devoid of notions of individualism and individual rights did not mean that dissent was absent. The dissent, however, was a reflection of class conflict rather than an ideological commitment to individual freedoms or to political and civil rights. As Walter Weiker has stated in his study of the modernization of Turkey, for the Turks "democratic institutions are seen by many as a means of bargaining."[14] The political arena is to be used by competing interests or classes as a forum in the struggle for political power unrestrained by a prevailing consensus on the operative democratic rules of the game. Conflicts among bureaucratic elites, the military, and different segments of the bourgeoisie—the commerical, industrial, and agricultural—and, somewhat later, the workers, were played out within the institutional framework initially set forth in the constitution of 1924 and in subsequent civilian and miltary regimes. Pressures for "democracy" and liberalization most frequently reflected demands for political power rather than any ideological commitment to freedom. From 1924 until the end of

World War II, except for one short-lived experiment at officially establishing an opposition party, Turkey was a one-party authoritarian state. It was during these years, nevertheless, that domestic strife emerged whose public manifestation was controversy over alternative policies to be pursued for growth. Acute social tensions were frequently camouflaged.

It is worth noting that the changing composition of the delegates to the Grand National Assembly in terms of social origin was reflective of shifts in power among different segments of the bourgeoisie—at times in conflict with and at times in coalition with the state administrative apparatus. The initial dominance of the assembly by government officials and military officers declined over the years, although it was not until the post–World War II years that this decline was dramatic and that a new class of landed bourgeoisie became important.[15] Though Atatürk's reforms permeated the social fabric, significantly he had not advocated or introduced any land reform measures. This facilitated the emergence in later decades of a commercial landed capitalist class that over time was reflected in the changed composition of the Grand National Assembly.[16] In the eastern provinces, in addition to the emergence of the Kurdish separatist movement, traditional cultural patterns of religious values, deference to the local authorities, and patron-client relations remained overpowering and resulted in political conservatism.

If, as some writers contend, modern liberalism and the related notions of individualism and individual rights were an outgrowth of the rise of capitalism in the West and the attendant severing of communal ties that resulted in the atomization of the person both in urban and rural settings, no equivalent socioeconomic conditions were extant in modern Turkey.[17] In Great Britain it was the industrial bourgeoisie, and not the state, who were "the agents of modernization"; in Turkey it was the state. In Great Britain the capitalist mode of production became dominant; in Turkey it coexisted with precapitalist forms while its economic development was that of a peripheral capitalist state. Moreover, while in Great Britain it was the bourgeoisie that demanded a liberal state with its plethora of individual civil and political rights as the institutional framework for furthering their interests, in Turkey repressiveness was considered essential for the growth of capitalism. As social transformation took place, it was class consciousness and class conflict that emerged, rather than notions of individual rights and of a democratic ideology, further justifying the use of repression by the state.

DEPENDENCY IN THE POSTWAR YEARS

During the decades of the post–World War II era Turkey has frequently been cited as one of the few less developed societies in which democracy has become deeply embedded in the ethos and values of the people. Military interventions in 1960, 1971, and even in 1980 by and large have been dis-

missed as transient, ephemeral parentheses in Turkey's road to modernization within a democratic political framework. One analyst, in fact, views
the military coup of 1980 as probably another short-run "structural 'repair
job' to preserve the fabric of Turkish democracy."[18] Such an optimistic
view of Turkish democracy neglects several factors that are critical for an
evaluation of Turkey's democratic foundations: the historical legacy of
authoritarianism and the dominance of the bureaucratic state; the fragility
of representative institutions that have been repeatedly undermined by
repressive state actions; the role of the military as guardian of Kemalism;
the pervasiveness of acute class conflict; the separatist movement of the
Kurds and more recently the dissidence of the Alevis; the failure of different
models of economic growth to bring about meaningful economic development; and, as a consequence of Turkey's greater integration into the world
system, the role of the United States and of international financial institutions.

The dismantling of colonial empires at the end of World War II and particularly the onset of the cold war, accompanied by fierce international
competition for the loyalty and alliance of newly independent states,
prompted the development of massive multinational and binational
programs, particularly in the United States, aimed at the modernization of
countries deemed underdeveloped. These programs were grounded in
theories of political and economic modernization that advocated a pluralist
society and envisaged industrialization through the development of capitalism. Moreover, the underlying assumption of these theories was that
modernization involved a more or less linear progression.[19] Foreign aid, in
turn, would provide the needed stimulant by providing the infrastructure,
the capital needed for embarking on industrial projects, and the loans for
importing goods to build an industrial base and, at times, to feed the bur-
geoning urban centers. In other words, as W. W. Rostow argued, foreign
aid would enable underdeveloped economies to reach "take-off" for self-
sustained economic growth.[20] Although the absence of a domestic entrepreneurial class frequently mandated that the United States deal with the
state, the long-term goal was encouragement of private enterprise. In time,
aid programs were extended to include transfers of technology, agricultural
aid primarily geared to increasing the productivity of export products, and
training programs to increase the skills of the working population.

While these aid programs were ostensibly aimed at economic assistance
designed to industrialize Third World countries in a manner replicating the
capitalism of the West, of equal importance from the United States' perspective was the effectiveness of aid in integrating and consolidating the
new states into the Western orbit, thereby strengthening the West's position
vis-à-vis the Soviet Union and hopefully precluding the rise of socialism. In
fact, U.S. State Department documents attest to the fact that the impetus
for including Turkey in the Truman Doctrine and even in the Marshall Plan
as a recipient of economic aid was military considerations. Economic aid

would enable Turkey to devote more of its budget to military expenditures while it would buttress the modernization of the Turkish military and strengthen its defenses.[21] The United States' much-vaunted infrastructure aid for road building was in fact primarily designed to meet U.S. military needs. Concurrently the United States was pressuring Turkey to abandon protectionism and pursue policies that would encourage private enterprise and foreign private investment.[22] And it was the United States in the immediate aftermath of World War II that encouraged Turkey to look to international lending institutions as a way of dealing with strains on its national budget and the deficits in its balance of payments that would follow adoption of the military and economic programs and policies recommended by the United States.[23]

On the whole, foreign aid programs, within the context of pluralist societies, did not result either in economic development or in democratic polities in the Third World generally, including Turkey. Turkey remains a peripheral economy that continues to receive massive economic aid for development purposes, and its formal, semiparliamentary institutions hardly camouflage its repressive military regime. Faced with these realities, the United States abandoned the pretense of furthering democracy and freedom and elevated security considerations to the primary, if not exclusive, criteria for determining foreign policy and granting military assistance.[24] Economic aid, however, remained to speak to the aspirations of Third World peoples while it maintained the international division of capital established in the post–World War II period. At the same time, theoreticians such as Samuel Huntington provided an analytic rationale for the support by U.S. policymakers of dictatorships and military rule by contending that authoritarianism and even overt military rule were inevitable in economically modernizing societies, such as Turkey.[25]

Turkey, despite its neutrality during the war, entered the postwar world firmly entrenched in the Western camp, its position as a dependency within the world system consolidated through the formation of various structural mechanisms. Domestically it underwent radical transformations in both the political and economic spheres. The one-party state of the Atatürk and the İnönü years—the authoritarian state—and the periodic imposition of martial law, in force during World War II, were apparently giving way to a multiparty system when several members from the leadership of the RPP defected and formed the Democratic Party.[26] Moreover, in the first few years, at the prompting of the United States, economic policies comparable to those instituted immediately following the Atatürk revolution were adopted that were geared toward the encouragement of private enterprise and an open economy.

The initial steps toward institutionalizing a liberal state in the late 1940s, in part a result of prodding by the United States after the war in exchange for military and economic aid, more fundamentally reflected pressures from a fraction of the bourgeoisie opposed to the etatism of the Turkish state, whose policies they believed were inimical to capitalist accumulation by the industrial bourgeoisie and inimical to the emerging landed capitalists of the eastern provinces. The formation of the Democratic Party, which won the elections of 1950 and 1954, was in part a consequence of the adversity experienced by the wealthy rural landed class and signaled the collapse of the ruling coalition among several fractions of the bourgeoisie and the state. Power relations among them changed, perceived interests began to diverge, and state-directed industrialization versus private enterprise became a contentious issue.[27]

As stated earlier, as a consequence of the war and its immediate aftermath, Turkey, after years of neutrality and dependence on Germany for aid, became integrated into the politico-military bloc of the West in its confrontation with the Soviet bloc. Of equal if not greater significance in the context of the impact on state repression were the economic changes that took place both in the domestic economy and in Turkey's position in the world economy. The worldwide decline in trade during the war reduced imports of industrial products to Turkey while spurring growth in the domestic industrial sector. However, the decline in exports of Turkey's agricultural products resulted in significant economic hardship that fueled growing support for the Democratic Party, particularly in the rural agricultural areas.[28] It was under these conditions that Turkey's international economic position was redefined and consolidated within the newly structured world capitalist economy that emerged under U.S. hegemony after the war.

The auspicious beginning toward increased freedoms did not materialize. Instead, during the ensuing 40 years, the most striking feature in the evolution of the Turkish state has been the recurring cycles of political liberalization followed by increased repression and military intervention, cycles that have paralleled those of economic growth and economic crises. Political liberalism, in the form of expanded freedoms, failed to assuage pressures from below, precipitating the growing militancy of the labor movement. Class conflict became endemic as vociferous workers' demands, in reaction to the low wage scales characteristic of peripheral states, precipitated massive state repression. State violence, including the use of the military, was directed not only against workers but also against students and in later years was extended to the revived Kurdish movement and most recently to the peace movement. Repression of other dissidents, such as intellectuals and political opponents, was usually accompanied by a more cautious and limited use of force.

The decline of liberalism and the use of repressive measures, including violence against strikes and demonstrations, accompanied each economic crisis. Neither the policies of an open or closed economy nor massive foreign economic aid has led to sustained growth and modernization or to the transformation of Turkey into a modern industrial state, a development that could have sustained a liberal state. On the contrary, periodic economic crises have ensued. Repeatedly the state's response, a response supported by at least one segment of the bourgeoisie, has been increased repression, justified as a measure essential for the maintenance of the stability and order needed for dealing effectively with the periodic economic and political crises as well as for economic development.

The military in Turkey has played a critical role in each successive crisis, thereby defining the nature of the polity. Just as it had viewed itself as the vanguard of Islam in Ottoman times, it perceived itself in the modern Turkish state as the defender of Kemalist principles and of the republic founded on Kemalism. Although Atatürk, the officer, civilianized the government, the military officer class retained a distinctive role—guardian of the Kemalist state. Hence as tensions and conflicts in Turkey periodically became acute in the decades following World War II, the military elite considered it its responsibility to intervene. In essence the military exercised a veto power over the actions and policies of elected governments. Moreover, this guardian function was institutionalized with the formation of the National Security Council, the majority of whose members have been top commanders who have exercised oversight, in addition to the existence of informal military "councils" that exercise considerable power.[29] Periodically when the restraints inherent in the very existence of this shadow military government and the repressive actions by the civilian government were considered insufficient and inadequate to control dissidence, the military intervened directly.

In the decades since World War II Turkey has received massive military aid from the United States that has been justified by the ongoing need for modernizing and upgrading the Turkish military (see table 6.1). Although the specific rationale has varied over the years, Turkey has consistently been considered, albeit with varying degrees of intensity, as critical for U.S. strategic interests. Invariably, in addition to international developments that affected U.S. support for Turkey, any domestic upheaval or perception of instability has been seen as threatening to U.S. interests. Each time military assistance began to decline,[30] the downward trend was reversed when Turkey confronted an economic crisis leading to increased repression and a military coup. This was the case prior to both the 1971 and 1980 coups. Particularly revealing is the United States' failure to phase out specific military grant programs, contrary to the original intention. It should be stated that in Turkey, in accordance with general U.S. policy, direct grants have in part been replaced by military sales purchased by credits guaranteed by the U.S. government.

In addition to massive military aid, economic aid from the United States, from various international financial agencies, and later from the European Community has been massive. Foreign aid began in 1947 when the United

Table 6.1
U.S. Military Aid to Turkey, 1950-1983
(Thousands of Dollars)

Year	Military Assistance (Grants)	MAP Excess Defense Items (Grants)	FMS Deliveries Credits	TOTAL
1950-65	2,397,410	156,246	--	2,553,656
1966	113,087	38,798	460	152,345
1967	131,337	77,181	252	208,770
1968	93,081	40,175	432	133,688
1969	98,805	83,061	396	182,262
1970	89,228	110,942	3,333	203,503
1971	98,724	76,475	139	175,338
1972	60,082	66,856	566	127,504
1973	67,302	103,446	7,924	178,672
1974	78,093	110,750	16,973	205,816
1975[a]	16,253	28,461	93,656	138,370
1976	--	--	106,224	106,224
1977	--	--	35,011	35,011
1978	6,432	--	158,666	165,098
1979	16,695	237	129,334	146,266
1980	39,994	10,776	136,417	187,187
1981	12,984	3,412	107,873	124,269
1982	10,650	3,029	187,900	201,579
1983[b]	5,446	--	152,777	158,223
			TOTAL:	5,383,781

[a]These were the years of the congressional embargo on military assistance to Turkey. It should be kept in mind that the Reagan administration has been lobbying intensively for an increase in aid to Turkey since 1980. It has been defeated by Congress, which maintains the 7:10 ratio with Greece.

[b]The figures for 1983 are incomplete.

Source: U.S. Department of Defense, *Foreign Military Sales and Military Assistance Facts* (Washington, D.C., 1973, 1983, 1985).

States encouraged Turkey to apply to the International Bank for Reconstruction and Development for financial assistance for development projects and to other financial institutions for loans to cover deficits in the balance of payments that would result as Turkey increased defense expenditures.[31] Through 1984 it is estimated that Turkey received a total of $6.5 billion in economic aid from various international agencies[32] and approximately $4 to $5 billion in loans and grants from the United States.[33] The economic assistance was for a variety of projects, including infrastructure development such as transportation, agricultural projects geared toward increasing productivity, and the development of basic metals. It is important to realize that despite all this aid illiteracy in Turkey as of 1983 remained at 33 percent of the population, and 65 percent of its exports were agricultural. Per capita income was estimated at $1,200, a figure that hides both income distribution and enormous regional disparities.[34] Unemployment was officially estimated at 18 percent in 1982 but is undoubtedly far higher.[35] Moreover, Turkey has in part exported its unemployment problem, since there are over three-quarters of a million Turks who still remain as guest workers in Western Europe, particularly Germany.[36] Remittances, which were $2.5 billion in 1981, have begun to decline.[37]

Turkey, it is clear, has not been transformed into an advanced capitalist state despite decades of massive economic aid. None of the aid has been directed at meeting basic needs. Rather, it has been modeled on mainstream notions of economic development with emphasis on expanding Turkey's export potential, which in turn would enable it to purchase the goods needed for its industrialization. Nor has the aid program achieved its ostensible goal of making the capitalist mode of production the predominant form in the domestic economy, a characteristic of the advanced capitalist states. As stated earlier, Turkey's exports were and are heavily agricultural, while the composition of its labor force as of 1982 was 9.5 million engaged in agriculture by comparison to 1.8 million in industry.[38] Turkey, despite decades of economic aid, remains an integral part of the capitalist world system as a peripheral state. In fact, foreign economic aid has reinforced its dependent position in the international division of labor.

In light of its subservient role within the world economy, possibly of greater consequence for Turkey than economic aid per se has been its increasing reliance on international financial institutions to finance mounting deficits in its balance of payments. In turn, as a condition for providing loans the International Monetary Fund and various international banking consortiums in cooperation with Western governments, in particular the United States, have imposed severe austerity programs on Turkey that have worsened the economic position of the majority of Turks. The continuing adverse financial situation in which Turkey has found itself during the post–World War II years and the consequent dependence on international financial institutions has ensured its further incorporation into the periphery of the world economy.

The process started in the first decade after the war when Turkey's balance-of-payments deficits mounted precipitiously. By 1958 it was forced to devalue the lira by 300 percent in addition to obtaining external loans, principally from the IMF, to finance the deficit. As a condition for loans the international financial community, ignoring the issue of basic human needs, imposed stabilization and austerity programs on Turkey. These resulted in devastating economic and social consequences for the people. Nevertheless, balance-of-payments difficulties persisted, and the IMF again came to the "rescue" in 1970. But the deficit kept mounting, particularly after the oil crisis, and by the mid-1970s Turkey was in increasingly dire financial straits. In 1978 the IMF in consortium with private banks adopted a rescue package to save Turkey from "bankruptcy." The terms imposed on Turkey made it clear that its autonomy in formulating national economic policies was to be severely curtailed. The political and economic consequences of the austerity program of 1978, in conjunction with domestic class conflicts, had wide-ranging repercussions leading to a series of developments that culminated in the military coup of 1980 and the later attempt in 1983 to institutionalize a repressive regime under the facade of formal parliamentarianism with highly restricted political participation, the outlawing of several political parties, a marked increase in political prisoners, and the vigorous pursuit, for the first time in Turkey, of the policies of an open economy.

DEMOCRACY AND REPRESSION

The external mechanisms that integrated Turkey into the world economy were reinforced by domestic economic developments determined in part by the state's position in the world system. In particular, the evolution of the class structure, its articulation with the political system, and the intensification of class conflict heightened the repressiveness of the Turkish state. The moves toward liberalization and the establishment of a multiparty system signaled by the formation of the Democratic Party in 1946 were inevitably accompanied by increased political dialogue in the public forum. This move toward the legitimation of political debate, however, did not evolve into the institutionalization of democracy and the acceptance of the principles of individual freedoms. In fact, groups considered socialist remained illegal, and throughout the 1950s labor leaders and other political activists were repeatedly arrested and imprisoned.[39]

Instead of freedom expanding over time, quite the opposite occurred. The historic legacy of authoritarianism, Atatürk's institutionalized ruthless suppression of dissent, and the notion of the military as the guardian of the Republic persisted and resulted in the increased use of repression by the state as the way of imposing order when it confronted pressures from one or another segment of the bourgeoisie for political power and in the face of vociferous discontent from the masses. Periodically, the failure of economic development programs to improve living conditions and the consequent upheavals in society culminated in military intervention. Thus Turkey's history in the postwar years is one of alternating periods of liberalization, when both in law and in practice freedom of speech, press, assembly, and nonviolent dissent and protest were recognized as legitimate, followed by periods of state repression. As attested to not only by human rights organizations such as Amnesty International, but by analysts of Turkish politics sympathetic to military interventions, massive violations of basic human rights, including arbitrary arrests of perceived "trouble-makers," accompanied each economic crisis. The latter precipitated mass discontent that threatened the ruling classes, justifying state repression.

Although democratic institutions have failed to consolidate and acquire legitimacy in Turkey, it is contended by some analysts that a semblance of parliamentarianism was maintained for periods of time due to the absence of significant foreign private investments. As Çaglar Keyder states, "The absence of foreign capital on any significant scale seems to have been one of the necessary conditions making for the survival of democracy within this peripheral capitalist country."[40] As a consequence, the intrabourgeois conflicts and the class conflict between the bourgeoisie and the workers that emerged in the era of rule by the Democratic Party did not include foreign capital as a principal determinant of Turkish politics. Parliament became one of the arenas in the struggle for domination of the state by the commercial, agricultural, and industrial bourgeoisie. In light of conflicting interests, the failures of economic development, and intensifying labor discontent, the recourse to force, intimidation, and military rule, often supported by the United States, seemed consistent with traditional styles of political rule.

The trend toward political liberalization, begun at the end of World War II, was challenged and reversed within a decade. By the mid-1950s not only was Turkey heavily indebted to international financial institutions, but the expectations of both the landed and industrial bourgeoisie were not materializing. On the one hand, the Democratic Party's emphasis on export-oriented growth through the encouragement of agricultural exports concurrent with the importation of goods essential for industrial development had resulted in a growing foreign debt as exports reached a limit, while on the other hand, the ruling Democratic Party, despite its commitment to private enterprise, had not tampered with the bureaucratic structure and continued to divert resources to the support of state enterprises. Simultaneous with the mounting discontent of the urban bourgeoisie and with the financial crisis of 1958, urbanization began as peasants from rural areas migrated to urban centers. An estimated one million migrated to Istanbul alone in the decade 1950 to 1960.[41] The city's population doubled, and the *gecekondus* that surround the cities were established.[42] An urban lumpen proletariat, these rural migrants settled in compact communities composed of those from their province or village of origin. Many remained underemployed or unemployed, particularly during periods of economic crisis, becoming in later years adherents of right-wing and left-wing terrorism.

The military coup of 1960 was precipitated by several factors, most immediately the 1958 devaluation and the stabilization program imposed by the IMF, which intensified the economic crisis by depressing incomes of all sectors except the farmers.[43] The military action, however, was the culmination of a series of authoritarian and repressive measures adopted by Prime

Minister Adnan Menderes as his Democratic Party government faced increasing opposition. Restrictions were placed on freedom of the press and on dissent, while the armed forces were called out to crush antigovernment demonstrations. Finally, Menderes declared martial law when students demonstrated against the gradual erosion of freedoms and the government's unconstitutional actions. The process of accelerating state repression climaxed with the military coup of May 1960. The military acted in accordance with its self-perceived role as guardian of the Republic and defender of Kemalism, one element of which was abhorrence at what was seen as societal anarchy and the disintegration of the bureaucratic tradition. Furthermore, several sectors of Turkish society, including leftist intellectuals, committed to an ideology of reform from the top, welcomed the military coup, as did the RPP, which has been suspected of complicity in the coup. The fragility of notions of basic rights was transparent in the acceptance of the legitimacy of military intervention and in the treatment accorded the overthrown civilian leaders by the National Unity Committee (NUC), as the military officers called themselves. A few months after the officers assumed power, approximately 600 government officials were arrested and charged both with political crimes and with embezzlement. After a trial that has been uniformly labelled absurd, 400 were convicted and imprisoned, while 3, including former Prime Minister Menderes, were executed. This pattern of political liberalization, economic crisis, failure of economic modernization, resort to repression, and military coup was to be repeated several times in subsequent years.

The 1961 constitution, which has been hailed as the most liberal Turkey has experienced—one that guaranteed individual rights and freedoms, legalized all political parties, including the socialist Turkish Labor Party, and established a constitutional court—should be seen against this historical background. The NUC that had usurped power, albeit sharply divided on strategy,[44] was committed to economic development and modernization, which was perceived to be the most severe problem facing Turkey. In line with another traditional Ottoman legacy, that of looking to intellectual elites, the NUC appointed several university professors to draft a new constitution that, after adoption by a Constitutional Assembly, was approved by referendum in October 1961. After eighteen months the NUC proclaimed elections and turned the government over to civilian rule, thus initiating a decade of pluralist politics and relative economic prosperity.

It is contended by Keyder that democratic institutions have been in existence in Turkey for periods of time not only because of the absence of foreign capital but also because of intrabourgeois conflict in which no faction succeeded in becoming dominant.[45] The 1960s did witness a high rate of economic growth under import-substitution policies that resulted in an industrial growth rate of approximately 11 percent between 1963 and 1969,[46] while the continuing deficit in the balance of payments was compensated for by remittances from the *gastarbeiter* in Europe. Protectionism was leading to industrialization, which in turn was enlarging the industrial labor force, resulting in a significant growth of the trade union movement. While the economy was seemingly expanding, the class conflict among the bourgeoisie was somewhat muted. But by the end of the decade the rate of economic growth began to decline rapidly. The industrialization fueled by import substitution was coming to an end, the industrial sector was incapable of absorbing the rural migrants to cities, and the foreign trade deficit had reached an all-time high. The conflicts among the industrial, commercial, and landed bourgeoisie, all vying for control of the state apparatus, which in the early 1960s had been fought within parliamentary rules of the game, in conjunction with extensive strike activity on the part of the growing workers movement under conditions of economic decline, intensified social conflict and led once again to military intervention in 1971. And once again the IMF's stabilization program, including a 65 percent devaluation, was the direct precipitating event.

Politically, the 1960s witnessed the flowering of democracy in Turkey concomitant with the mobilization and politicization of various sectors and classes. The liberal democratic constitutional framework guaranteed both individual and organizational freedoms, enabling the proliferation of political parties and nongovernmental associations, particularly trade unions. By 1963 the right to strike was legalized. As stated earlier, politics in Turkey was partly class based and partly clientelist whereby leaders exploited traditional values. Moreover, the demarcation between clientelist and programmatic parties was not sharp, so that ideological parties concurrently were also clientelist. Thus politics in the 1960s was an admixture of the modern and the traditional, with the latter operative largely in rural areas[47] and in the *gecekondus*,[48] having been modified to conform to the realities of dependent capitalist development. The freedoms embodied in the new constitutional order facilitated the articulation of the socioeconomic transformations that were taking place, which in turn engendered political ferment.

A multiparty system developed. The Justice Party, after a few years of uncertainty, under the leadership of Suleiman Demirel emerged as the descendant of the Democratic Party. It claimed to represent the entire bourgeoisie by making efforts to reconcile their sharply clashing interests. In the early years of the 1960s the RPP still retained its ideological commitment to the administrative tradition, to reform from the top, and to state-directed modernization. In the second half of the decade, as Bülent Ecevit gained prominence in the party, it redefined its ideological stance, positioning itself as left of center, committed to redressing social injustices and appealing to urban workers. The Marxist Turkish Labor Party (TLP), which had been legalized, as had all parties, represented a significant part of the workers, some intellectuals, and some from the middle class. In addition to the TLP, numerous small left-wing parties and groups emerged, some Marxist, some vaguely socialist. Extreme right-wing parties were also formed in the late 1960s, particularly the National Salvation Party, which propagated a conservative Islamic philosophy appealing to the traditional peasantry. Still later a neofascist party, the National Action Party, came into existence. These minor parties played a critical political role in the 1970s as political instability increased.

Simultaneous with the numerical increase in political parties was the appearance of numerous associations, most significantly the trade union movement. The combination of the growth in the industrial labor force, the migration from rural areas to cities, and the explicit sanction given to the right to strike in the 1961 constitution facilitated the development of trade unions.[49] The first significant labor federation, the Türk-Iş, had been organized in 1952 primarily as a mechanism for social control of labor. Its membership consisted principally of public-sector employees, and it claimed to be nonpartisan although it was supported by the Democratic Party. Efforts to form a left-wing trade union had been made earlier, but it was not until 1967 that the militant, leftist Revolutionary Workers Union Confederation (DISK) was organized to represent the interests of the workers in the private industrial sector. The increasing demands of the workers' movement, the organization of youth associations, and the dissemination of various strands of socialist thought contributed to the intensification of class conflict in Turkey toward the end of the 1960s.

The conjunction of several developments led ineluctably, particularly in light of the military's conception of its role as guardian of the state, to another military intervention in March 1971. Among the workers militancy was increasing, and particularly as of 1968 both official and unofficial strikes were on the increase. Student activism was in full swing, and teachers organized a general strike in 1970. At the same time, conflicts among the different factions of the bourgeoisie were intensifying as the era of economic expansion ended. Prime Minister Demirel and the ruling Justice Party were incapable of adopting policies to deal with pressing economic issues or to resolve the intraclass and interclass conflicts. They retained the support only of the petty bourgeoisie and alienated the industrial bourgeoisie. Ineptness and paralysis characterized the Demirel government. Concerned with not alienating the military officers and possibly suffering the same fate as Menderes, the Demirel government was minimally receptive to military intervention. Meanwhile, many officers themselves had developed capitalist interests through their integration into the industrial structure. Not surprisingly, an officers' pension fund had been established that invested heavily in manufacturing,[50] which gave them a military and nationalist stake in capitalist expansion.

The pattern of increased repression as a prelude to military intervention was repeated: arrests, restrictions on freedom of speech, and finally the declaration of martial law in June 1970 in response to a massive worker's demonstration. As in 1960, the austerity measures imposed by the IMF and the economic decline fueled domestic discontent. While the Demirel government argued that Turks, under the 1961 constitution, had too much freedom, in March 1971 the military officers issued a memorandum notifying the legislature and the Demirel government that they had been unable to cope with "anarchy, internecine strife, social and economic discontent."[51] A technocratic government was formed that lasted until new elections were held in October 1973. The elections, however, did not signify a return either to the freedoms or the economic prosperity of the 1960s. They signaled instead the entry of Turkey into an era of considerable social strife, political instability, violence, deepening economic and financial difficulties, and repeated condemnation for violations of human rights by various international bodies and human rights organizations.

The persistence of a political culture that led to expectations that reforms and radical change could and should be imposed by a bureaucratic state and the military was reflected in the reaction of many sectors of Turkish society to the events of 1971. Despite the immediate institution by the military of massive repressive measures, the initial reaction from the bourgeoisie, the intellectuals, and the various left-wing movements was favorable, since they anticipated that the political and economic impasse had been overcome and that the state would undertake the particular reforms advocated by one or another group. The pervasiveness of the Kemalist ideology, which provides legitimacy for military takeovers and the central role of the state as reformer, was true even of the Marxists, who did not abandon efforts to legitimate themselves within this ideological framework until the late 1970s.[52] Acceptance of the military seems not to have diminished despite the continuation of martial law, the establishment of military courts to try those charged with crimes against the state or of leftist ideology, the abolition of freedom of the press, the prohibition against strikes, restrictions on the right of association, and the arbitrary arrest and imprisonment of thousands, including those associated with the TLP, which was banned. It was at this juncture that the Council of Europe, of which Turkey is a member, began its criticism of violations of basic human rights and of the prevalence of torture in Turkey. Since then numerous human rights organizations, most pointedly Amnesty International, have investigated ongoing charges against Turkey and have condemned it for a gross pattern of human rights violations. With the military coup of 1980 the massiveness of the repressive measures precipitated an international outcry against arbitrary arrests and imprisonment, torture, and denial of freedoms.

Politically, during the 1970s there was a systematic erosion of democracy; a repressive apparatus was institutionalized within the framework of a modified formal parliamentary system. Constitutional revisions were enacted. Though guarantees of freedoms were retained, they were qualified by restrictive provisions such as the powers given to the Security Courts to try those arrested and accused of a variety of crimes against the state. The decade of political liberalism was coming to an end, as was the spurt of industrialization of the early 1960s. A further proliferation of political parties took place as the different factions of the bourgeoisie fragmented into separate parties despite the Justice Party's efforts to claim that it spoke for the entire bourgeoisie. Moreover, the right wing of the RPP, unhappy with the party's ideological shift toward social democracy, split and formed its own party. Neither of the two major parties, which continued to dominate the political scene, won a majority in the elections of 1973 or 1977. As a consequence, coalition governments characterized the 1970s, reflective not only of political instability but of continuing intrabourgeois conflict regarding the nature of the bourgeois state, who should have the dominant political power, and what strategies the state should pursue. In 1973 the RPP formed a short-lived coalition with the National Salvation Party, the party of Islamic revivalism, only to be replaced shortly thereafter by Demirel's National Front government, a coalition of right-wing parties. After the 1977 election Demirel again attempted a National Front government. This effort failed, and Ecevit and the RPP, whose electoral support had increased, replaced it. The economic tensions and conflicts among factions of the bourgeoisie and the workers remained unresolved, while the labor movement, DISK in particular, despite restrictions, was becoming increasingly militant. It was also in the 1970s that nonstate terrorism emerged. The most active bands to be formed were right-wing and were attached to the neofascist National Action Party. In reaction, left-wing bands emerged, particularly active in the *gecekondus*. It is difficult to estimate their support, both because of the absence of reliable data and because of the fact that the terrorists pitted one *gecekondu* against another.

Over the 1970s Turkey's economic problems severely worsened. They were aggravated by the invasion of Cyprus by the Turkish army in 1974, the ongoing expense of financing both the military in Cyprus and the Turkish Federated State of Cyprus, and the subsequent U.S. arms embargo, imposed by Congress, which lasted until 1978. Turkey's balance-of-payments deficit, worsened by the oil crisis, grew again. While imports were far in excess of exports, the full impact of the problem was moderated somewhat by remittances from overseas Turkish workers. Moreover, the era of industrialization through import substitution geared to a domestic market had come to an end, both because the existing distribution of income provided a limit to the possible expansion of the domestic market and because of the necessity for accelerated importation of capital and intermediate goods to sustain growth. Importation of intermediate goods in turn worsened the deficit. Beginning in 1978, to meet a condition for loans from the IMF, a series of devaluations was instituted, and significant restrictions were placed on imports. The final stage in the IMF package for saving Turkey from "bankruptcy" was Demirel's adoption of the IMF stabilization program negotiated by his economic adviser, Turgu Özal, later prime minister. This program included another devaluation, abolition of price controls and subsidies to state economic enterprises, and a commitment to end deficit spending.[53] Inevitably these measures reduced purchasing power and living standards.

Repression again became widespread just as insurgent terrorist activities increased. As a consequence of spreading nonstate terrorism, specifically the massacre in K.Maras apparently instigated by the neofascist National Salvation Party (NSP), the Ecevit government imposed martial law in 1978. Arbitrary arrests were again on the increase. Concurrently the Kurdish nationalist movement intensified, as did resistance by the Alevis. Moreover, sectors of the bourgeoisie were becoming increasingly discontented with the policies of the government, the increasing unrest, and the existence of terrorism. The generals' military coup on September 12, 1980, was inevitable. With this action, Turkey's consolidation into the Western orbit as a peripheral capitalist state was assured. An open economy was imposed, and stability as a condition for the encouragement of foreign private investment was promised. Turkey's position as the West's firm military ally in the eastern Mediterranean was strengthened, a particularly crucial development in light of the collapse of the shah's Iran and the socialist victory in Greece's 1981 elections.

PERIPHERAL CAPITALISM AND REPRESSION

The generals' coup of 1980 and the subsequent establishment of Turkey's Third Republic in 1982 culminated nearly 40 years of socioeconomic transformation. However, the national goal of "catching up" with the West has not been achieved. Periodic efforts to industrialize through policies of import substitution, at times by diverting state resources to private industrialists and at times to the State Economic Enterprises, have not succeeded in developing a relatively self-sufficient industrialized society. In fact, these economic policies resulted in the further integration of Turkey into the world economy in a dependent position. Export markets for its agricultural goods are critical in order to earn the foreign exchange to import the goods necessary for industrialization. Subject to the vagaries of international trade and to the limits on its export potential, Turkey was unable to earn enough from exports, even with remittances from workers in Western Europe, to prevent severe balance-of-payments deficits. Nor did extensive economic aid from the United States and later from the European Community, particularly West Germany, improve matters. Perforce, Turkey resorted to loans from international financial agencies that periodically subjected its economy to control by the IMF. Turkey thus found itself in a vicious cycle of needing additional loans to repay past loans and the accrued interest. The economic policies instituted by Premier Özal, consonant with the prescriptions of the IMF, most likely signify the end of the modernizing bureaucratic state in its traditional form and the consolidation of the peripheral bourgeois state in which a free market economy and private enterprise reign supreme, all in conjunction with the preconditions for increased penetration of Turkey by foreign capital.

The strategic importance of Turkey to the Western defense alliance, in particular the United States, should not be overlooked. Military, political, and economic dependency, as in the case of Turkey, are often interlinked. Particularly with the growing anti-Americanism in Greece and the presumed unreliability of its prime minister, Andreas Papandreou, Turkey's strategic importance has grown. This is evident from the sharp increase in military assistance in the past few years[54] and the building of additional U.S. bases in eastern Turkey. Thus since the most recent military coup Turkey appears to have become firmly consolidated as a peripheral society in the world system, serving the military and economic interests of the West and hopefully free of the periodic domestic threats that existed in the past.

Ensuring the further consolidation of Turkey necessitated not only the structural mechanisms for economic dependency but a political framework that would lend itself to the goals of the new bourgeois state, eliminate class conflict, and ensure stability and order. This was precisely the purpose of the new constitution promulgated in 1982. It was clearly designed to eliminate the alternating cycles of liberalization and authoritarianism that had characterized post–World War II Turkish history by institutionalizing the repressive apparatus.

The process that led to military intervention in 1980 did not differ materially from that of the earlier interventions. Beyond the restrictions on democratic freedoms incorporated in the revised constitution of 1971 and the less tolerant attitude of the political authorities, repression had accelerated. By the second half of the 1970s, under the pretext of containing nongovernmental terrorism, martial law was imposed on several provinces, persons were arbitrarily arrested for participating in strikes or demonstrations or for being labelled as potential risks, and many were imprisoned without trial, while others were tried by military tribunals in violation of due process of law. As economic conditions deteriorated, as unemployment increased, as the foreign debt mounted, as inflation skyrocketed, and as the limits of industrialization were reached, discontent spread and repression increased. Both intrabourgeois and class conflict intensified. The new ingredient in the political scene was the violence of the right-wing and left-wing nongovernmental terrorists, a development that became the rationale used by the National Security Council when it overthrew the civilian government.

Immediately after the National Security Council, under the leadership of Kenan Evren, also chief of the Turkish General Staff, executed the coup, it declared martial law, already operative in some provinces, to be nation-wide. All political leaders were taken into custody, and massive arbitrary arrests of lawyers, members of Parliament, intellectuals, and journalists took place. The trade unions were the hardest hit, particularly officials and members of DISK, with an estimated 5,400 imprisoned. Several of the local affiliates of the conservative federation, Türk-İş, were also closed. Further-more, a massive sweep was made of the Kurdish nationalist movement in the eastern provinces. Strikes were banned, all political activity was prohibited, judicial review of legislative and executive actions was suspended, and universities were purged. The estimated number arrested in the first week after the military coup was 10,000.[55]

Since the military justified its coup on the grounds that terrorism had to be contained, it should be emphasized that state repression was on the rise prior to the spread of nonstate terrorism and was directed not only at terrorists or suspected terrorists but at all opponents of the regime. Docu-mentation of human rights violations is extensive. As early as 1976 Amnesty International was investigating allegations of torture of those arrested for political crimes, which allegedly had begun in 1973, and simultaneously was protesting the mass arrests of trade unionists who had demonstrated against the establishment of "extraordinary tribunals for political crimes."[56] Furthermore, Amnesty criticized articles of the penal code that enabled the imprisonment of nonviolent political opponents of the government, an act proscribed by the provisions of the European Convention of Human Rights, to which Turkey was a signatory. From then on Amnesty's reports of violations of basic human rights in Turkey and in particular of the increased use of torture were continuous. By July 1980, a few months prior to the military coup, its findings, based on the report of an investigative mission to Turkey, were that "torture was widespread and systematic."[57]

The "return to democracy," as Evren called it, symbolized by the elec-tions of November 1983, following a referendum "legitimating" the new constitution and concurrently "ratifying" General Evren as president for seven years, was under conditions of severely restricted political participa-tion. Traditional political parties such as the RPP and the Justice Party and their leaders were prohibited from participating, and only new party formations and candidates approved by the National Security Council could take part in the electoral process.

Turkey's post–World War II pattern of expanded rights and freedoms following military rule, constrained somewhat after the 1971 coup, has finally been broken completely. Traditional Turkish authoritarianism, this time in the service of the restructured bourgeois state, has been revived. The gradual emergence of a civil society in recent decades has been crushed. State Security Courts, mandated to control trade union activity, have been formed. A State Supervisory Council has been vested with investigative powers over public and private bodies and organizations. Constitutional rule has created the institutional framework whereby the president, a general, and the National Security Council in the form of the Presidential Council can legally exercise their function as ultimate arbiters of politics. It was under these conditions that the elections, which resulted in a victory for Özal's Motherland Party, a coalition composed of elements from the several earlier conservative parties, took place. With Özal as premier, the continuation of the economic policies initiated by the IMF prior to the military coup was assured.

Symptomatic of the radical transformation of the Turkish state embodied in the 1982 constitution and the institutionalization of repressive apparatus is the clause that affirms that the economy is based on private enterprise. By contrast, the 1961 constitution emphasized the duty of the state to encourage economic development.[58] The traditional role of the Turkish state as the modernizing agent has thus been abandoned. The army, however, retains its self-image as an autonomous force, above classes, and its role as the guarantor of law and order and of the nation in its quest for growth and development. Both the military rulers and the civilian leaders are determined to impose labor discipline so as to facilitate the restructuring of the economy in the interests of the bourgeoisie. Strains and conflicts, however, have not been overcome; they have only been submerged. The ruling Motherland Party is composed of elements from the Justice Party and other conservative political factions, including the neofascists, each of them representing different factions of the bourgeoisie. How long the coalition will persist among them and with the military, and how long the labor movement will remain quiescent, are open questions. An inherent tension exists between the etatist ideology of the well-entrenched military and Özal's bourgeois ideology.

The current regime believes that to attain its economic goals, repression is essential. Immediately after the military coup, the European Community and the Council of Europe, particularly the delegates to the European Parliament, expressed their concern about the abolition of democracy and violations of basic human rights.[59] Violations persisted; the European Economic Community froze its associated agreement with Turkey, Amnesty International continued its condemnation of human rights violations, the International League for Human Rights submitted a communication to the United Nations charging a pattern of gross violations of human rights, torture in particular, and in January 1984 France, Denmark, Norway, Sweden, and the Netherlands brought charges against Turkey for violating the human rights convention, of which it is a signatory, to the Human Rights Commission of the Council of Europe.[60] Human rights organizations continue to document the repression of Syrians, Greeks, Armenians, Kurds, members of the peace movement, intellectuals, and trade unionists. Moreover, the documentation of torture, at times resulting in death, particularly during police interrogation and in military prisons, is voluminous.[61]

The new regime, in its determination to restructure Turkish society, to eliminate class conflict through the use of force, and to reinforce a bourgeois state integrated into the world economy by opening Turkey up to foreign private investment, feels compelled to employ repressive measures on a massive scale.[62] The conjunction of U.S. economic, political, and strategic interests, moreover, makes it imperative that there be law and order, that the threat to the status quo be eliminated, and that conditions favorable to the furthering of U.S. interests prevail. Although it is not possible to judge the extent of U.S. involvement in the coup, it is known that General Evren notified the United States of his intentions prior to the overthrow of the civilian government.

CONCLUSION

The development of the modern Turkish nation vividly illustrates a relationship between the state's professed goal of economic modernization and state repression. The Turkish experience invalidates the widespread presumption that state repression may be a necessary precondition for economic modernization. On the contrary, a more valid hypothesis is that the failure of economic development that is ostensibly modeled on the experience of the West, with industrialization as the major goal, leads to broadly based discontent that in turn prompts state repression. Development in Turkey and in other similarly situated countries is that of dependent capitalism. Hence the state's role is to maintain structural integration with the center, which severely limits the state's autonomy not only vis-à-vis the domestic bourgeoisie but vis-à-vis foreign political and economic interests. Economic development differs markedly from the historical processes that the capitalist states of the West underwent centuries ago. Turkey and other peripheral countries such as Brazil, Argentina, and South Korea who periodically appear to have reached "take-off" for self-sustained growth have undergone similar cycles of political liberalization followed by widespread state repression as economic crises develop. Human rights are sacrificed not because of the priority attributed to economic development, but because of the particular form of development, which mandates exploitation of the working class and state repression to maintain the parameters of the existing order. Thus one determinant of human rights appears to be the dependent economy and not a policy decision geared toward rapid economic growth.

Moreover, the absence of the Western notions of individualism and inalienable rights in Turkey and other peripheral states and of the structural conditions leading to atomization has facilitated the ideological prevalence and the actuality of etatism, whereby the state has prior claims and the individual is submerged within it. Since the cultural forms in Turkey lack notions of individualism, they will not emerge under existing conditions, where the socioeconomic structures militate against their emergence.

It was stated at the outset that no Turkish regime in the last 40 years has formulated an economic development program geared toward fulfilling basic human needs. Rather, the state has attempted to reconcile the conflicts among different factions of the bourgeoisie and to be the agent of industrialization. In order to maintain Turkey's position as a peripheral state in the world system and as a client of the United States, the use of repression is a veritable sine qua non, a repression whose severity has not been modified by the attainment of economic and social rights and the fulfillment of basic human needs. In conclusion it should be emphasized that the issue of human rights and of state repression must be viewed, not only in Turkey but in many peripheral states, within a broader international and societal context in order to elicit the determinants of these phenomena.

NOTES

1. For a discussion of some of the arguments as expressed in UN documents, see Stephen P. Marks, "The Use and Misuse of the Concept of Development in Relation to Human Rights," in Karel Vasak and Philip Alston, eds., *The International Dimensions of Human Rights* (Westport, Conn.: Unesco and Greenwood Press, 1982).

2. Çaglar Keyder, "The Political Economy of Turkish Democracy," *New Left Review,* no. 115 (May–June 1979): 30.

3. Some international agencies, including the World Bank, have begun funding economic development projects geared toward basic needs. Among the works relevant to basic needs issues, see Johan Galtung and Andres Wirack, "Human Needs and Human Rights—A Theoretical Approach," *Bulletin of Peace Proposals* 8, no. 3 (1977): 251-258; P. Alston, "Human Rights and Basic Needs: a Critical Assessment," *Revue des droits de l'homme,* 1979; Christian Bay, "Peace and Critical Political Knowledge as Human Rights," *Political Theory* 8, no. 3 (August 1980): 293-318.

4. For a discussion of U.S. support of Greece, Turkey, Spain, and Portugal, see Adamantia Pollis, "United States Foreign Policy towards Authoritarian Regimes in the Mediterranean," *Millennium: Journal of International Studies* 4, no. 1 (Spring 1975): 33-34.

5. The total U.S. military assistance to Turkey from 1950-1979 was nearly $5.4 billion. In this time period only South Vietnam, Israel, and South Korea exceeded this amount. Michael T. Klare and Cynthia Arnson, *Supplying Repression: U.S. Support for Authoritarian Regimes Abroad* (Washington, D.C.: Institute for Policy Studies, 1981), p. 42. For 1984 alone, military aid in the form of loans and grants totaled nearly three-quarters of a billion dollars, as reported in *Country Reports on Human Rights Practices for 1984* (U.S. Department of State, February 1985), p. 1118.

6. The precise role of the United States in the various military interventions in Turkey might well be a revealing study.

7. For a significant study on the rise of the Orthodox merchants, see Traian Stoianovich, "The Conquering Balkan Orthodox Merchant," *Journal of Economic History* 20 (June 1960): 234-313.

8. The best study of Ottoman administration remains A. R. Hamilton Gibb and Harold Bowen, *Islamic Society and the West,* vol. 1, 2 parts (London: Oxford University Press, 1950, 1957).

9. For a brief discussion of Atatürk's efforts to articulate a Turkish nationality rooted in Anatolia as distinct from an Ottoman or Islamic nationality, see Bernard Lewis, *The Emergence of Modern Turkey,* 2d ed. (New York: Oxford University Press, 1968), pp. 357-361.

10. Ibid., p. 266.

11. Cited in Lewis, *The Emergence of Modern Turkey,* p. 270.

12. For a discussion of the changing occupational composition of the Grand National Assemblies, see Frederick W. Frey, *The Turkish Political Elite* (Cambridge, Mass.: M.I.T. Press, 1965), pp. 180-192.

13. The creation of this state sector in conjunction with the adoption of national economic plans reflected the dominance of state capitalism. It is state capitalism that the current regime is attempting to eliminate. For a discussion of the strength and importance of the public sector in comparison to the private from 1950 to 1976, see Walter F. Weiker, *The Modernization of Turkey from Atatürk to the Present Day* (New York: Holmes and Meier, 1981), pp. 192-195.

14. Ibid., "Introduction," p. xv.

15. For a discussion of the relationship of rural areas to the center from Ottoman times to the present, the RPP efforts to recruit local notables in the first decades after the war, and support from the rural areas for the Democratic Party, see Şerif Mardin, "Center-Periphery Relations: A Key to Turkish Politics?" *Daedalus* 102, no. 1 (Winter 1973): 169-190. For a further discussion of the political role of the wealthy farmers in the more developed of the eastern provinces, see Keyder, "Political Economy of Turkish Democracy," pp. 17-19.

16. Frey, *Turkish Political Elite,* chap. 7.

17. For the argument that notions of individual, inalienable human rights in the West were an outgrowth of the rise of capitalism, see Adamantia Pollis, "Liberal, Socialist, and Third World Perspectives of Human Rights," in Peter Schwab and Adamantia Pollis, eds., *Toward a Human Rights Framework* (New York: Praeger, 1982), pp. 4-8.

18. Weiker, *Modernization of Turkey,* "Introduction," p. xv, note.

19. A vast literature appeared, often paralleling theories of economic modernization. Among them are A.F.K. Organski, *The Stages of Political Development* (New York: Knopf, 1965), and Gabriel A. Almond and G. Bingham Powell, Jr., *Comparative Politics: A Developmental Approach* (Boston: Little, Brown, 1966).

20. Walt Whitman Rostow, *The Stages of Economic Growth: A Non-Communist Manifesto,* 2d ed. (Cambridge, Eng.: Cambridge University Press, 1971).

21. A report sent by the U.S. ambassador to Turkey to the State Department makes clear the primacy of the goal of modernizing the military forces over and above economic modernization. See "Report of the United States Ambassador Concerning Assistance to Turkey," Secret, Ankara, 15 July 1947, *Foreign Relations of the United States, 1947,* vol. 5, pp. 233-236. For a discussion of the activities and the control exercised by the Joint American Military Mission for Aid to Turkey, set up by the Truman Doctrine, see Daniel Lerner and Richard D. Robinson, "Swords and Ploughshares: The Turkish Army as a Modernizing Force," in Henry Bienen, ed., *The Military and Modernization* (Chicago: Aldine, Atherton, 1971), pp. 129-133.

22. *Foreign Relations of the United States, 1947,* vol. 5, p. 234.

23. Ibid., vol. 5, pp. 233-236.

24. Even President Carter, despite his human rights policy, felt constrained to give priority to national security considerations regardless of the repressiveness of the regime. For a discussion of both the principles and the practice of Carter's human rights policy, see David P. Forsythe, *Human Rights and World Politics* (Lincoln: University of Nebraska Press, 1983), pp. 93-110. Only in Latin America was there some limited success; see Lars Schoultz, *Human Rights and United States Policy toward Latin America* (Princeton, N.J.: Princeton University Press, 1981), pp. 113-119, 361-362.

25. Samuel P. Huntington, *Political Order in Changing Societies* (New Haven: Yale University Press, 1968).

26. For a descriptive discussion of the Democratic Party, see Weiker, *Modernization of Turkey,* pp. 128-131.

27. For an excellent discussion of this issue in relation to intrabourgeois conflict, see Keyder, "Political Economy of Turkish Democracy"; for an analysis of the extraction of rural surplus for industrial accumulation and the ties between landlords and the rural bourgeoisie that thwarted land reform, see Turgut Taylan, "Capital and the State in Contemporary Turkey," *Khamsin: Modern Turkey; Development and Crisis* 11 (1984): 12-21.

28. For a discussion of the class coalition in rural areas that supported the Democratic Party, see Ergun Özbudun, *Social Change and Political Participation in Turkey* (Princeton: Princeton University Press, 1976), pp. 46-48.

29. Weiker, *Modernization of Turkey,* p. 103.

30. It should be stated that table 6.1 does not include other forms of military assistance such as training of military personnel, some AID programs, commercial exports licensed under the Arms Export Control Act, and the education of military students.

31. *Foreign Relations of the United States, 1947,* vol. 5, p. 236.

32. *Country Reports,* p. 1118.

33. This figure is an estimate derived from several sources, but principally from Agency for International Development reports; interestingly, economic assistance declined significantly, from $300 million in 1982 to $140 million in 1984.

35. The statistics are taken from the OECD Economic Surveys, *Turkey,* April 1983; per capita income is the lowest in Europe, p. 47.

35. Ibid., p. 36. These figures are undoubtedly underestimated, even if underemployment is not taken into consideration. By 1984 unemployment had apparently more than doubled; see *Bulletin of Labour Statistics, 1984* (United Nations, 1985), p. 60.

36. Cited in Demetrios G. Papademetriou, "A Retrospective Look at Mediterranean Labor Migration to Europe," in Carl F. Pinkele and Adamantia Pollis, eds., *The Contemporary Mediterranean World* (New York: Praeger, 1983), p. 239.

37. See OECD, *Turkey,* p. 5.

38. Ibid., p. 15.

39. There is no adequate study of the violations of fundamental rights such as arbitrary arrest, imprisonment without trial, and torture in Turkey prior to the 1970s. All historical accounts, however, contain sporadic references to repression.

40. Keyder, "Political Economy of Turkish Democracy," p. 24.

41. Ibid., p. 23, taken from a compilation of Turkish census data; see also

Özbudun, *Social Change,* pp. 83-84, for a discussion of geographic mobility up to the middle 1970s.

42. See Özbudun, *Social Change,* pp. 187-188, for a description of the *gecekondus.*

43. Cheryl Payer, *The Debt Trap: The IMF and the Third World* (New York: Monthly Review Press, 1974), p. 45. The author attributes the 1960 military coup directly to the IMF stabilization program.

44. Keyder, "Political Economy of Turkish Democracy," p. 25.

45. Ibid.

46. Weiker, *Modernization of Turkey,* p. 185. Most analysts agree that the 1960s was a decade of economic growth for Turkey; see also Altan Yalpat, "Turkey's Economy under the Generals," *Merip Reports,* no. 122 (March/April 1984): 17; and Keyder, "Political Economy of Turkish Democracy," pp. 22-27.

47. For an interesting discussion of the nature of Turkey's rural peripheral integration with the center, the resultant perpetuation of patron-client relations, and the political conservatism of the peasantry, see Dani Rodrik, "Rural Transformation and Peasant Political Orientations in Egypt and Turkey," *Comparative Politics* 14, no. 4 (July 1982): 417-442.

48. Although Özbudun, *Social Change,* pp. 118-128, argues that with urbanization party machines tend to replace patron-client relations, it should be pointed out that many political parties, particularly in peripheral states, are themselves clientelist.

49. For a discussion of the rise of the labor movement and the left in general, see Mehmet Saläh, "The Turkish Working Class and Socialist Movement in Perspective," *Khamsin* 11 (1984): 86-116.

50. Ahmet Kemal, "Military Rule and the Future of Democracy in Turkey," *Merip Reports,* no. 122 (March/April 1984): 17-18.

51. Keyder, "Political Economy of Turkish Democracy," p. 29; Weiker, *Modernization of Turkey,* p. 103.

52. Kemal, "Military Rule," p. 13, argues that the Marxist movement only began disassociating itself from the Kemalist ideology in the late 1970s.

53. For discussions on the impact of the IMF stabilization policies and Özal's economic policies, see Taylan, "Capital and the State," pp. 31-32, and Kemal, "Military Rule," p. 19.

54. After the lifting of the embargo against military aid to Turkey as a consequence of the Turkish invasion of Cyprus, an informal arrangement was made for a 7 to 10 ratio of aid to Greece and Turkey. The pressure on Congress by the current administration to abandon this ratio and significantly increase aid to Turkey has been intense.

55. Donald Sherblom and Adamantia Pollis, *Report Prepared for the International League for Human Rights, 1980* (New York: International League for Human Rights, 1981), data compiled from various U.S. and European newspaper accounts.

56. *Amnesty International Newsletter,* London, October 1976.

57. Amnesty International, *Report on Torture in Turkey* (London: Amnesty International, July 1980), p. 2.

58. For a discussion of the 1982 constitution, see John H. McFadden, "Civil-Military Relations in the Third Turkish Republic," *Middle East Journal* 39, no. 1 (Winter 1985), in particular pp. 70-73. For a critical analysis of the constitution that

emphasizes the conditions surrounding the adoption of the new constitution, the subsequent elections, and the restrictions on freedoms in the 1982 constitution, see Bülent Tanar, "Restructuring Democracy in Turkey," International Commission of Jurists, *Review,* no. 31 (December 1983): 75-86.

59. Various news releases from the Council of Europe, principally the European Parliament, Strasbourg and Brussels.

60. Press release, Human Rights Commission, Strasbourg, January 27, 1984, announcing that the charges lodged by the five countries were admissible for consideration. In April the commission sent an investigation team into Turkey.

61. In June 1982 the International League for Human Rights in an official communication to the secretary general of the United Nations requested an investigation of the allegations of widespread torture. Periodically there are reports of hunger strikes among political prisoners protesting prison conditions and torture. The most recent, beginning in January 1985, was reported in *Amnesty Action,* U.S. section of Amnesty International, April 1985.

62. The Turkish periodical *Nokto* 3, no. 4 (February 1985) reported on an international symposium held in Istanbul, January 21-23, 1985, to discuss the rehabilitation of political prisoners. The participants were American and Turkish psychologists. The thrust of the conference, as reported by the periodical, was to consider what kinds of treatment would successfully rehabilitate the "terrorists" and stop further activities. Among the participants was Paul Henzi, the alleged CIA station chief.

7

Repression, Dependence, and Political Decay: The Case of Poland

Robin Alison Remington _____

At midnight on December 12, 1981, a military coup in Poland pushed aside the staggering Polish United Workers Party (PUWP) and handed over administration of the country to a Military Council of National Salvation composed of 21 ranking military officers. General Wojciech Jaruzelski spoke to the nation as "head of the Polish government and the armed forces," downplaying the Communist Party and virtually ignoring his own position as first secretary.[1] The general proclaimed "a state of war." He justified martial law as necessary to save the country from civil war and economic collapse.

Thus Poland became the first Communist country in which the "leading role of the Party" was taken over by the armed forces. Military commissars moved into local government posts and managed factories. In "workers'" Poland, enterprises were militarized; refusal to work was a military offense risking court-martial.[2] Selective repression crushed the disorganized resistance of striking miners and street demonstrators.

Western observers and Solidarity activists alike were caught flat-footed, stunned that after 16 months of negotiation and compromise the effort to arrive at a political solution should be aborted by military intervention. Within Poland fears of Soviet invasion had subsided before the coup. In the West, Communist societies were still considered almost magically immune from the epidemic of praetorianism that has swept developing countries around the world. Faith in Leninist organizational theory and party-building techniques had become central to the authoritarian/penetration model of Communist civil-military relations.[3] Now the Polish gun commanded the Party, legalizing repression, suspending "socialist legality."

This analysis attempts to put this turning of Leninist party-army relations on its head into perspective. The focus is on repression as a function of dependence—political/ideological obligations flowing from integration of Poland into the Soviet postwar sphere of influence and economic pressures generated by the country's growing interpendence with Western economies—and political decay symbolized by the declining capacity of political institutions to make and implement decisions.[4] It tentatively hypothesizes the following:

1. The collapse of Poland into martial law came about due to weaknesses of the country's economic and political development and resulting crises of distribution and participation.

2. Notwithstanding the July 1983 lifting of martial law, prior to the 1986 10th Party Congress militarization of the Polish United Workers Party essentially substituted for institutionalization.

3. Consequently, repression functioned both as a reaction to underground Solidarity's potential political challenge and as a weapon of elite struggle within the party-army coalition surrounding Jaruzelski.

4. The extent of such repression related to international pressures on the Jaruzelski regime as well as to indigenous factors.

5. The cluster of attitudes generally attributed to the "military mind"[5] may be more relevant to understanding the trials and tribulations of Polish party "renewal" than Marxist-Leninist prescriptions.

However, these propositions are meaningful only in the context of Polish political culture and its relationship to the postwar efforts at Communist consolidation.[6]

THE REMNANTS OF HISTORY AND POLISH POLITICAL CULTURE

An organized Polish state has existed from the tenth century when Prince Mieszko I accepted Christianity and allied with the Czechs to hold back the German drive to the east. With the reign of Boleslaw I (992-1025) Poland was established as an independent kingdom, yet the Polish monarchy was never absolute or even fully in control. Rather, Poland was a land of strong princes and weak kings, with no tradition of a strong central authority. Nonetheless, when Polish Queen Jadwiga married Grand Duke of Lithuania Wladyslaw Jagiello in 1386, there began a "golden age" of territorial expansion to the east and a renaissance in the arts and society. There was even a legal code giving Poles protection under the law in 1430 that Englishmen were not to have for another 200 years, until the Habeas Corpus Act of 1685. In this period one could already identify a Polish national character devoted to individualism, honor, personal dignity, and national pride. The resistance of the gentry to subordination and a distaste for organized collective activity were already apparent.

Subsequent Polish history is an epic of repression, shattered hopes, and heroic deeds. Russian domination, 150 years of partition, Nazi occupation, and cultural genocide: Poland survived it all. Given centuries of deep popular distrust of authority, even that of Poland's own elected kings (1572-1795), it is not surprising that Polish Communist leaders faced massive hostility in attempting to transform their postwar power into legitimate authority. Although any regime would have had to overcome the Poles' traditional dislike of centralized power and the Polish tendency to fragment democratic institutions, the Communists had an additional handicap stemming from the fact that Moscow was undeniably the Mecca of the world Communist movement. To the ordinary Pole the distinction between their "fraternal Soviet allies" and the former Russian oppressors was academic. Nor was Soviet "liberation" marketable in view of the treacherous behavior of Soviet security forces against the Polish Home Army and common knowledge that Soviet troops sat on the other side of the Vistula for 63 days while the Germans defeated the August 1944 Warsaw Uprising and destroyed the city.

Moreover, in the battle for the hearts and the minds of the Polish population the Polish United Workers Party was no match for the Church. Communist systems go beyond secularism to official atheism. Official atheism is an affront to the basic spiritual conviction of the Poles. For the majority of Poles, to be Polish is to be Catholic. Indeed, for many the line between nationalism and their religious conviction is almost indistinguishable. Governments come and go; the Church and the nation remain.

Often called "the Christ of nations"—implying both divine calling and martyrdom—Poland is symbolized by the fabled phoenix that dies only to rise again. In their struggle for national independence the Poles have alternated between two survival strategies: "romantic insurrectionism," in which the nation's youth died in seemingly hopeless uprisings, and "organic work," dedicated to preserving the nation through persistent grass roots political/economic/social efforts. These strategies of rebellion and accommodation, sometimes characterized as idealism versus realism,[7] served different ends. Polish romanticism sacrificed the lives of independence fighters to perpetuate the heroic myth, thereby indelibly seared into the psyche of a generation. Organic work served to protect the body politic, developing skills and tactics to expand the room for maneuver within existing restraints. Both strategies functioned to preserve the nation. However, the tensions flowing from the conflicting legacies of those who fought under the banner of "freedom or death" and those determined to live to fight another day further complicated the Party's efforts to consolidate control.

In short, the Polish Party had to deal with a population individualistic to the point of anarchy, with a long history of successfully resisting state penetration, prone to factionalism, intensely religious and anti-Russian, generally unpredictable and sometimes suicidally patriotic. Poland was and is a political mine field. Perhaps predictably, during Stalin's lifetime the Soviets essentially ran the Polish armed forces and security services with

Russian officers. More than any of the other tokenly independent East European countries, Poland was treated as an occupied nation.

Throughout World War II Poland was systematically subjected to state terror in both the German- and Soviet-occupied territories. Reportedly, of the 6 million Poles who died in the war, 89.3 percent were executed or died in "pacification" campaigns. Massive transfers of population also occurred during the war years. One and one-half million Poles in Soviet-occupied eastern Poland were deported to the Soviet interior. Two million were expelled from the areas incorporated by Germany in 1939 and another million sent to Germany proper for forced labor. Nor did the end of the war bring peace to Poland. The Polish civil war continued for another two years. Soviet security forces, the Polish military, and security troops attempted to repress the Home Army, which had gone into underground resistance. Official figures for 1945-1948 refer to some 30,000 armed actions and 15,000 victims.[8] Whether or not the figure is reliable, the magnitude of the resistance led to military rule throughout large parts of Poland.

As Poland was forcefully incorporated into the Stalinist interstate system,[9] repression was massive and can be seen as a continuation of the state terror of the war years, with the difference that the official Polish politico-military leadership essentially acquiesced and participated in brutalizing their real and suspected opponents. This repression was a function of both the intensity of the Polish resistance and Soviet determination to neutralize historic anti-Russian sentiments. Although it essentially eliminated the Polish underground and prevented open anti-Sovietism, in retrospect it is fair to say that the desired attitudinal changes did not result, if indeed they were ever actually expected.

Yet notwithstanding Poland's de facto occupation status, when the anti-Tito hysteria swept the Soviet bloc after the Yugoslavs were expelled from the Cominform in 1948 for what Stalin correctly claimed were "conceptions different from our own," the Polish Party largely avoided the show trials and persecutions that convulsed other East European regimes. The head of the newly reconstituted United Workers Party, Wladyslaw Gomulka, lost his job for Titoist deviations (a euphemism for nationalist tendencies) and was put under house arrest. However, unlike Laszlo Rajk in Hungary or Rudolf Slansky in Czechoslovakia, he lived to be rehabilitated. It was an oversight that Stalin undoubtedly would have corrected if he could have foreseen the drama of the 1956 Polish October and the role that Gomulka himself would subsequently play in the collapse of the Stalinist interstate system.

SYSTEMIC TRANSFORMATION: THE NEW COURSE

By definition the Stalinist empire in Eastern Europe required Stalin. When the Soviet dictator died in March 1953, the elaborate infrastructure of Soviet control mechanisms weakened. The Soviet bloc cracked under imperatives of the submerged power struggle that followed his death. The Stalinist empire could not withstand the destabilizing impact of Malenkov's New Course, Khrushchev's concessions to woo Tito back into the socialist camp, and the precipitous de-Stalinization following the Communist Party of the Soviet Union (CPSU) 20th Party Congress in 1956.[10]

Malenkov's New Course was tailored to fit the needs of the post-Stalin collective leadership during a succession process in which there were no formal rules in the Hobbesian world at the top of the Soviet political hierarchy. The emphasis on collective leadership, consumerism, and socialist legality was as much to protect Stalin's successors from each other as to win popular support. It was to buy time while Soviet domestic politics emerged from the shadow of Stalin's personality cult and found a substitute for his charismatic authority.

For our purposes the importance of "socialist legality" and the subsequent attacks on Stalin as a murderous tyrant who had almost destroyed the Soviet Party is that they radically altered the role of the secret police in Soviet society.[11] By eliminating the head of the KGB, Lavrenti Beria, and making him the scapegoat for their own complicity in Stalin's crimes, Stalin's successors broke the stranglehold of the security apparatus on the Party. They also perhaps inadvertently deprived themselves of the use of terror as a legitimate instrument of control. Rehabilitation of Stalin's victims was a logical consequence, indeed, a necessary justification of de-Stalinization.

Throughout this Byzantine political struggle, the Soviets pressed East European Communist leaders to follow the zigzags of Moscow's policies. If socialist legality and de-Stalinization were good for the Soviet Union, they must also be good for Eastern Europe. East European imitation was considered essential validation of Soviet domestic choices. Stalin was gone, but it was assumed that the feudal subordination of East European parties to Soviet direction would remain the same.

Conversely, East European Communists greeted the new order of Soviet priorities with exceedingly mixed emotions. Stalin had created mini-Stalins in his image, who had not died and were not enthusiastic about collective leadership. Moreover, whatever positive feelings might have existed for regularizing their own economic relationship with Moscow, the demands for rehabilitation of purge victims threatened their domestic stability. With Khrushchev's revelations at the 20th Party Congress, East European Communists were faced with the trauma of attacking the myth that had been used to legitimize their entire painful postwar transformations. As an anguished Czechoslovak appeal attempting to stem the tide of disillusionment among the Czechoslovak Communist Party (KSC) rank and file put it:

Much has happened this year. Much that was dear to us has been smashed. . . . Our souls are full of pain because strings have suddenly been touched which we thought inviolable and feelings which were dear to us. Side by side with joy about recent rapid developments many old Communists will feel sadness. They may even feel bitter.

We too feel in the same way, comrades, but one is unthinkable without the other. And if we believe in the Party we believe in it firmly! Only a Party for which revolutionary truth is everything is in a position to plunge the knife of self-criticism so deeply into its own flesh.[12]

In a sense the Polish Party must be considered fortunate that Boleslaw Bierut returned from the CPSU Congress that denounced Stalin and died of a heart attack. He was succeeded by Edward Ochab, a truly remarkable politician in that he is one of the few leaders in any political system to accept his own inability to deal with national crisis and skillfully negotiate his own replacement for the good of the country. This is not the place to recount the drama of the Polish October. Yet the legacy of 1956 is crucial as a milestone in the politicization of the Polish workers' movement, a factor in the PUWP's permanent identity crisis, and a determinant of future party-army relations in Poland.

THE POLISH ROAD TO SOCIALISM

For more than a quarter of a century, Polish workers have been the primary change agent in Communist Poland. Ever since rioting workers in Poznan set off the chain of events that brought Gomulka back to power in 1956, the rise and fall of party leaders in Poland has been a function of worker opposition to party policies.

The sequence of events is clear. On June 20, 1956, the Declaration on Relations between the League of Yugoslav Communists and the Communist Party of the Soviet Union was signed, giving Khrushchev's blessing to "national roads to socialism." Eight days later Polish workers took to the streets in Poznan. Their complaints centered on economic conditions, condemned Party policies, and were openly anti-Soviet. The army was ordered in to disperse the demonstrators. Nonetheless, the Polish Party rejected the Soviet interpretation that Poznan was the work of hooligans and Western saboteurs. Recognizing that legitimate grievances had led to worker violence, the Poles began their own agonizing reappraisal. Many of the arrested workers were quietly released. Those who were tried received comparatively light sentences. Despite a visitation by virtually the entire Soviet Politburo and some tense moments when Soviet troops began moving toward Warsaw, the PUWP was reorganized with Wladyslaw Gomulka at its head.

What were the lessons of Poznan? For the first time Polish workers had struck out as an anomic interest group, and although their demonstration was repressed and individual workers jailed, the Party listened. As a result of Poznan, there began a renationalization of both the Polish Party and armed forces. The Party leadership clearly responded to Polish rather than Soviet interests. In doing so, Polish Communists became among the first to demonstrate Alfred Meyer's assertion that "throughout the European Communist world the societal base is tending to reassert its sovereignty over the political superstructure; the native political cultures are regaining some influence; the political systems are forced to adjust themselves to their several political cultures and social structures."[13]

In the trauma of Poznan, Polish Communists took their role as representatives of the Polish working class seriously. The Party also showed considerable reluctance to resort to extensive repression to protect its position. Yet Polish soldiers had shot Polish workers. The resulting demoralization raised questions about the reliability of the Polish military as an instrument of internal repression, or to put it differently, about the impact of such activity on the Polish military. Moreover, although Soviet Marshal Konstantin Rokossovsky was still Polish defense minister, the support of Polish units commanded by General Waclaw Komar had been instrumental in bringing Gomulka back over Soviet objections.[14] Gomulka's political comeback was made possible by a party-army coalition of forces. While it might be stretching a point to say that Gomulka owed his job to the army, the Polish military had undeniably been drawn into Polish domestic politics on the side of expanded autonomy vis-à-vis the Soviet Union. Although officially on the sidelines, in reality from 1956 the Polish military was a political actor.

Gomulka came in on a wave of hope. Although an orthodox Leninist, he was accepted as a Polish national leader as well. There was a time of cultural and political experimentation. Collectivization was abandoned and Polish agriculture largely restored to private land holdings. The dialogue with the Church led to a "normalization" of party-church relations that substantially increased the power of the Church in both political and religious life. The Polish October fostered a proliferation of literary and artistic efforts. Soviet reluctant acceptance of Polish autonomy was ratified in the treaty governing Soviet troops temporarily stationed in Poland. That treaty, in turn, strengthened the domestic legitimacy of the Polish Party.

Yet in a sense Gomulka was overrated. He was in favor of party reform, but never of restructuring so as to allow for genuine pluralism within or outside the Party.[15] Basically he followed a two-pronged strategy: silencing the advocates of sweeping change, while working systematically to restore both party cohesion and his own control. As Gomulka's fundamental conservatism reasserted itself, economic reform bogged down. The political and literary renaissance fizzled out. Gradually the Party clamped down on the cultural sector. Then in reaction to demands for "socialism with a human face" in neighboring Czechoslovakia, there was a wholesale retreat. The fate of the Czechoslovak reform movement known as the Prague Spring touched off an inner party struggle in Poland, undermining the position of Polish reformers. A wave of repression and anti-Semitic purges followed Warsaw student strikes in 1968.[16] Gomulka played off the nationalistic, anti-Semitic partisans associated with the powerful head of Polish security forces, Mieczyslaw Moczar, against the party technocrats seeking to overhaul Poland's stagnating economy. It was a formula for political and economic paralysis.

Moreover, Gomulka was blinded to the seriousness of the situation by his genuine foreign policy success. In November 1970 the Polish leader signed the Polish–West German Nonaggression Pact. For the first time the Federal Republic of Germany recognized Poland's western border as established after World War II.[17] Swept forward in the euphoria of this accomplishment, Gomulka made a fatal miscalculation (undoubtedly due to his shortsighted policy of not having a Polish housewife among his economic advisers). He raised the price of meat sharply two weeks before Christmas. Rioting broke out in Gdansk and other coastal cities.

By December 17 the Council of Ministers called upon the militia to fire if necessary to get the situation under control. Once again Polish soldiers shot Polish workers. There is considerable confusion about who did and did not give what order; there is none about the political repercussions. Within three days Edward Gierek replaced Gomulka as head of the Polish United Workers Party.

GIEREK'S DILEMMAS

Given the speed with which the transition took place, it is likely that Moscow was informed rather than consulted. A regional party secretary from Katowice, Gierek was selected largely on the basis of his successful economic record, perhaps with the hope that as a former miner he could communicate with the striking workers. The new first secretary took over a leaking, if not sinking, ship of state. Work stoppages continued, backed by threat of general strike. He inherited a declining economy with little or no reserves. This serverely restricted the concessions that he could make to an increasingly suspicious Polish proletariat, less and less willing to be represented by the Party. At the grass roots level the Party itself was divided. Indeed, factory strike committees in Gdansk and Szczecin were as often as not headed by party members from the shipyards, calling for reform of the Party itself as well as of the economy.

Domestically Gierek faced a credibility gap between the Party and the Polish working class, a deeply divided party, and a potentially serious challenge from Moczar's partisan faction advocating repression and then reform. Internationally he had to worry lest his Soviet and East European allies decide that Polish socialism was in sufficient danger to activate the Brezhnev doctrine put forward to justify the "allied socialist" invasion of Czechoslovakia in 1968.[18] To allay Soviet fears in this regard, he was teamed with Prime Minister Piotr Jaroszewicz. An old pro-Moscow warhorse, Jaroszewicz had spent World War II in the Soviet Union serving as defense minister in the Soviet-sponsored Government of National Unity in the 1940s. There is little reason to assume that the Brezhnev leadership would have preferred Moczar's nationalistic law-and-order approach to Gierek's technocratic pragmatism in any case. But such considerations did not silence suggestions from Czechoslovakia and East Germany to the effect that Warsaw was an obvious candidate for the Red Army's "fraternal assistance."[19]

Gierek personally negotiated with the workers in Gdansk and Szczecin, reportedly in exhausting nine- to twelve-hour sessions. Prime Minister Jaroszewicz flew to Lodz to convince the women textile workers of that historically revolutionary city of the Party's good faith. A general strike was averted by a hairbreadth. Gierek openly admitted the crisis of confidence between the Party and the Polish working class. In exchange for their return to work, he accepted a package of political/economic concessions that included a price freeze, subsidies to the poorest families, more freedom of the press, expanded autonomy for the Church, and most importantly, party reform.

Given the ugly prospect of fighting Polish workers in the factories and perhaps unsure as to whether the Polish army would be fighting with them or against them, the Soviets wisely decided that the Brezhnev doctrine could be implemented by economic as well as military means. Moscow reportedly paid the bill for Gierek's compromise to the tune of $100 million in hard-currency credits.[20] Subsequently that would become a factor in the thinking of Solidarity and Polish party leaders alike.

No matter how these events were formally rationalized, the fact was that a de facto vote of no confidence on the part of Polish workers had brought down the Gomulka government. Unlike Poznan, the initial violence was combined with increasingly effective political organization. This time the Party negotiated with the workers instead of debating about them. The Polish workers had demonstrated their ability as a powerful, if uninstitutionalized, political actor. The workers had gotten rid of an unpopular regime, achieved a virtual veto in matters of price policy, and won implicit partnership with the Party in the promised "political renewal." The Party had reestablished substantial credibility with its most fundamental constituency and peacefully avoided a general strike that had every prospect of requiring either massive repression or precipitating invasion of the country. The Polish military appears to have advised negotiation rather than force and to have stayed on the sidelines. All of the parties involved had reason to be pleased with themselves.

Great expectations accompanied the Gierek regime. He had demonstrated considerable political skill in outmaneuvering the Gomulka holdovers, neutralizing Moczar's partisans, and putting together the youngest, best technically trained political team in Eastern Europe.[21] A series of commissions staffed with party and nonparty experts were directed to chart needed economic/political/educational reforms. In May 1971 I was in Poland. Warsaw was alive with political optimism. Change was in the air.

Ordinary people felt their political system was on the move and were willing to give the Party still another chance.

But as with the Polish October of 1956, the euphoria did not last. By my return trip in the spring of 1974 much of the enthusiasm had dwindled. The Poles that I talked with were disappointed, once again disillusioned with the substance of "political renewal." Gierek was surrounded by cronies. The top of the Party had lost its sense of direction. Factions squabbled among themselves trading accusations of favoritism and corruption. Reformers could not agree either. Still worse, Gierek had failed to dislodge the middle strata of bureaucratic Stalinists within the Party that stubbornly opposed implementation of any genuine reform. As long-standing advocate of reform Mieczyslaw Rakowski bitterly described the problem:

On various levels in the government and especially the intermediate level, there exists indolence, inertia, organizational paralysis, inability or unwillingness of men in the positions of responsibility to abandon routine, disregard of human needs, and infringement on the rights of citizens. There are those who say to themselves . . . "never fear, we shall also outlast this reform."[22]

Meanwhile the economic vise tightened. Committed to heavy food subsidies, the government hestitated to raise prices for fear of setting off another round of worker protests. Gierek's strategy of avoiding unpopular austerity programs by borrowing in the West could not survive the combined blows of rising Soviet oil prices and Western stagflation. In an increasingly export-driven economy, the poor quality of Polish exports could not stand the competition. Moreover, even if the imported technology and borrowed capital had been more wisely used, that would not have helped agricultural production, for the shortsighted policy of withholding government investment from the private sector that produces some 80 percent of Poland's agricultural products had predictably negative results.

Economic pressures mounted. The government responded in 1976 with another steep increase in food prices. Once again the workers took to the streets. As in 1970, the Party backed down.[23] Yet some workers had died; others had been arrested. The half-hearted repression that followed the 1976 riots only managed to reinforce the emerging alliance between frustrated workers and alienated intellectuals, who had been brought back into the picture by proposed constitutional revisions that would have written an unacceptably close Soviet-Polish relationship into the Polish constitution. Among the proliferating dissident organizations, the Committee in Defense of the Workers (KOR) is perhaps the best known.[24] Founded in September 1976 to provide assistance for jailed workers and their families, KOR was explicitly not an opposition group and initially avoided ideological theorizing.

In an uneasy truce, the regime ignored the committee until the following spring, when the death of a Cracow university student last seen collecting signatures for a brutality inquiry sent 5,000 students marching in his memory. The authorities reacted atavistically by arresting the most prominent members of KOR, only to precipitate more protests and hunger strikes. In July the regime retreated, declaring a general amnesty for all those involved in the 1976 riots. KOR founder Jacek Kuron triumphantly declared, "No totalitarian power can afford to move against both the workers and the intelligentsia."[25] Events would prove him to be overly optimistic. Yet on the more basic issue Kuron was right. A government as demoralized and increasingly paralyzed as the Gierek regime could not stem the tide or save itself.

Gierek responded to the escalating demands for political access with promises of better communication and more commissions. He moved futilely to stave off the inevitable by going still deeper into debt. By 1979 Polish debts to the West totaled $20 billion, 10 times those of 1971. Debt servicing took 54 percent of the government's hard currency. Real wages had doubled in the past 10 years; food subsidies consumed 40 percent of the entire Polish budget. To even stay afloat, he would have needed to borrow an estimated $4.6 billion in 1980, another $6.5 billion in 1981.

Moreover, Gierek's room for maneuver was narrowing. Economic recession in the West made bankers less receptive to loan requests. The December 1979 Soviet invasion of Afghanistan appeared to have given a knockout blow to an already-staggering detente. The polls predicted a 1980 victory for Ronald Reagan, in which case the political climate would undoubtedly worsen, making future borrowing still more difficult. Any hope of Western credits required willingness to take domestic cuts. Like many Third World countries on the edge of bankruptcy, Poland could not escape the economic prescriptions of the international money lenders. The Polish economy was hooked, addicted to Soviet oil and Western capital.

Thus in July 1980 Gierek gave it one last try. The government effectively pushed up the price of meat 40 to 70 percent by putting 30 percent of all meat and reportedly all the better meat into commercial shops where prices were as much as 100 percent higher than those in subsidized shops. Even more unwisely, it raised the price of bacon as well, thereby directly hitting working-class families, for bacon was the meat that most workers could afford. Strikes spread throughout the country. In Lublin striking railway workers paralyzed all activity, and the army was called in to supply the city with food.

A frantic governmental commission attempted to negotiate piecemeal solutions with the strikers. That tactic could not survive once the strikes spread to the huge Lenin Shipyard in Gdansk. Here Lech Walesa emerged as the charismatic leader of an interfactory strike committee representing an estimated 300 factories, perhaps 50,000 workers. At first the Party refused to talk to the interfactory committee, cutting off its telephone and media links

with the rest of the country. Dissident intellectuals continued to release
information to the Western press and were arrested. There were warnings of
a possible Soviet invasion. Still the strikes continued to spread.

With no visible end in sight, fearful of a general strike and undoubtedly
with General Jaruzelski's warning in 1976 that Polish soldiers would not
shoot Polish workers in mind, Gierek opted to avoid risking military repression. He sent a 15-man negotiating team to discuss the matter with a delegation of the strike committee headed by Walesa. The strikers' communications links with the rest of the country were restored; arrested dissidents
were released. The head of the Polish Catholic church at that time, the
indomitable Cardinal Stefan Wyszynski, went on the air to urge a peaceful
settlement.[26] The result was the Gdansk charter that formalized the right of
the Polish workers to speak for themselves; the process of institutionalization of the independent trade union movement Solidarity was
under way.

There is a certain irony that Polish workers struck in the name of socialist
egalitarianism by demanding rationing, while the country's Communist
leaders attempted to solve their economic woes by relying on the market
principle and commercial shops. The socialist norm of equality had become
a fundamental principle of the once-hierarchical Polish political culture.
Not surprisingly, the Party could not handle the consequences of its success.
It could not afford to allow the mobilized workers to speak for themselves.
The crisis of distribution had snowballed into a crisis of participation that in
the end exposed the threadbare nature of party legitimacy. In the frantic
search for scapegoats Gierek was replaced by Stanislaw Kania. Kania, in his
turn, was unable to resolve the identity trauma that undermined PUWP
attempts to deal with Solidarity.

ORGANIZATIONAL COLLAPSE AND POLITICAL DECAY

Ideological and political crisis convulsed the Party at all levels. The
leadership played a kind of musical chairs with top positions, rotating on
what in Warsaw was called the "carousel." George Sanford correctly notes
that for the participants this was a political roller coaster over which they
had no control of when, or if, they arrived at the end of the line.[27] Many left
the Party, giving the impression that its rank and file were simply melting
away. In some cases these were defections to Solidarity. But equally destabilizing, an estimated third of those who stayed also joined the trade union
confederation. To interpret this as a case of the Party penetrating Solidarity
would have required a united party. In reality Solidarity had penetrated the
Party, strengthening the forces for reform and further weakening its
cohesion. As then Deputy Prime Minister Rakowski admitted in his interview with the Italian journalist Oriana Fallaci, the Polish Party had
essentially disintegrated,

which is quite clear since the military had to take its place in the government. Who could deny that it went bankrupt, intellectually and politically, that it was unable to organize the society, to get the country out of disaster, even to defend the state? In the end you are right; we are the ones to be blamed, not Solidarity.[28]

This was a kind of political hemorrhaging in which the Party's membership and authority simultaneously drained away. In the language of political development, it was a classic case of political decay. Yet the problems existed long before Solidarity appeared on the scene. If we take Samuel Huntington's indices of political institutionalization,[29] it is clear that the Polish United Workers' Party suffered from long-term systemic weaknesses. At best, it had partially institutionalized, and that may be an overstatement.

Founded in 1918, the prewar Party had been so badly factionalized that Stalin eventually gave up on it. Many Polish Communists died during the 1930s in Soviet purges; the Party itself was dissolved by the Comintern in 1938. It reemerged during World War II with Gomulka at its head. This is not an outstanding record even of chronological adaptability. Functionally the Party had never been able to agree on the political substance of its "leading role" or how to exercise it. Generationally there was no adaptability at all. Gomulka's replacement had been dictated in Moscow. His return to power and Gierek's and Kania's rise to the top all came about due to increasingly prolonged political crises in which the Party's right to rule was challenged by the constituency it claimed to represent. In terms of autonomy, the Party was crippled by the need to respond to both Soviet and Polish interests. One could say that after Poznan the Polish Party did achieve limited autonomy vis-à-vis Moscow. Unfortunately, the advantage of having done so was neutralized by its virtual lack of coherence.

Factionalism was endemic within the PUWP. In the immediate postwar period there were the nativists and the Muscovites. Ochab maneuvered between the evolutionists and the Natolin factions. Gomulka then played off partisans against technocrats. Gierek's initially blue-ribbon political team was divided about the pace and nature of reform, while he himself struggled to get rid of Gomulka holdovers and to keep Moczar's partisans at bay. Kania faced only the most intense of a long string of identity crises. However, for the first time the Polish people had a political alternative in the form of Solidarity, whether or not the independent trade union explicitly denied any aspiratons to function as an opposition party.

In short, the Polish Party lacked any vestige of coherence. It did have a formal complexity. Party organizations existed at all levels of society. Governmental institutions were in operation. But this did not accomplish the real purpose, for Polish communism was never able to effectively penetrate Polish society. Marxism-Leninism was alien, by definition unwelcome. The moral authority in Poland remained the Church. Perhaps it is not surprising that the brief moments of national/party unity during the Polish October and after Gierek's massive fence-mending with the workers in 1970 could not be translated into institutional payoffs.

In my judgment, it was not the Party's inability to chart an appropriate course for Poland's economic development that was the heart of its dilemma. Rather, the Polish Party itself was politically underdeveloped and always had been. Basically, its decay was symptomatic of a birth defect. That defect, in turn, was as deeply rooted in Poland's political culture as in the flawed Leninist model for political development. It is also correct that together the interaction was even more disastrous than either factor might have been in some other combination. For if the Eurocommunist charge that Leninism is a Russian brand of communism is essentially correct, then logically the vast differences in Russian and Polish political cultures made the model particularly inappropriate for Poland.[30]

But from the viewpoint of the collapse of Poland into martial law, it was not only the fragmentation of the Polish Communist Party that led to military rule. Solidarity itself was never able to institutionalize an agreed-upon role in the Polish political process. As the Communist Party's authority if not power flowed to the trade union confederation, Solidarity staggered from what might be called organizational overload. Reportedly membership had grown to 10 million by November 1980.[31]

Even allowing for journalistic exaggeration, the independent trade union had an enormous, increasingly diverse membership. Many had jumped on the bandwagon virtually overnight. Dissatisfied farmers demanded a rural Solidarity. For them as for politicized workers and radicalized students— even for the garbage men of Warsaw—Solidarity had become the symbol of the Polish nation. With its overwhelming popularity came multiple demands and unrealistic expectations. Solidarity's national coordinating committee not only had to negotiate with the Communist Party and government leaders striving desperately to contain the trade union, they had to arbitrate and decide which of the mushrooming regional conflicts the union would take responsibility for and stand behind. That was part of the issue at the time of the March 1981 inflammatory Bydgoszcz incident in which Solidarity activists were beaten by security forces.[32] In the 16 months between the legalizing of the independent trade union and martial law almost no week passed without some part of the country out on strike.

Moreover, the Solidarity leadership, like that of the Party itself, could not agree among themselves. The moderate center, led by the charismatic hero of the Lenin Shipyard, Lech Walesa, was increasingly challenged by those pressing for more militant strategies. Only 37 years old himself, Walesa faced opposition from less politically experienced regional leaders in their twenties. The militants tended toward confrontation rather than accommodation. In a sense, Polish political culture came full circle in worker organizing as well as in Communist Party politics.

There are those who believe that the Party indirectly manipulated these tensions in the form of provocations to strengthen the militant wing, thereby justifying party claims that Solidarity was irresponsible and could not be taken seriously as a partner in the struggle for political reform. Perhaps they are correct. I do not doubt that there were deliberate provocations. I am less persuaded that there was a united party policy to that effect, especially in the tumultuous days surrounding the PUWP 9th Party Congress in July 1981.

Although Kania and Jaruzelski managed to retain their positions, they were among only four former members of the Politburo to be reelected. In the new 200-member Central Committee only 16 holdovers survived vote by secret ballot. Although Kania managed to defuse the challenge of the "horizontal linkage" from those who sought to bypass democratic centralism and establish direct ties among like-minded reform groups around the country, the moderate tactical line of "accord" and "political renewal" officially triumphed. Yet the political inexperience of the reformers meant that "socialist renewal" remained largely a slogan. Faces had changed at the top of the Party, but the proceedings of the congress were too vague to provide a guide to strategy. The ship of state was adrift in the storm.

Between July and November 1981 an estimated 244,000 had left the Party, and another 188,000 had been purged. According to those who believe that the subsequent strategy of decay and radicalization of Solidarity was deliberate, this left a leaner, hardline Party that outmaneuvered the Solidarity leadership. I am at least tentatively in agreement with the opposing view that the Communist Party was hopelessly divided at the top. As the Party became unable to act decisively, Solidarity was willy-nilly drawn into the political vacuum before the union was ready or its organizers intended.[33]

This in part explains the intensity of Solidarity infighting at its own two-stage congress in September–October 1981. Like Kania, Walesa survived, but in reality he was more and more a figurehead. Like many genuinely revolutionary organizations, Solidarity was sliding into militantism that was more psychologically satisfying than politically effective.

With the Party and Solidarity alike increasingly paralyzed, the Polish military entered the political stage well before martial law was declared. Shortly after the Solidarity congress Kania stepped aside, and General Jaruzelski personally took on the job of running the Party. De facto the Polish military replaced the reformers, putting into motion restructuring of the Party quite different from what the challengers calling for "political renewal" at the 9th Party Congress had in mind. Jaruzelski was joined by General Tadeusz Dziekan, the new head of the Central Committee Cadre Department. Another general took charge of the security forces as minister of internal affairs. Generals were brought in to shape up other key ministries such as Energy and Mining. Military commissars were sent throughout the country to get the economy moving again.[34] The Party faded from view.

Amid the clamor for Solidarity, the military moved "to get the country out of disaster." The infrastructure of martial law was in place.

By adding the responsibilities of first secretary of the PUWP to those he exercised in his capacity as prime minister and defense minister, General Jaruzelski acquired the remnants of formal power existing in the immobilized political system. They were not enough. Although initially negotiations continued with Solidarity and the Church, they soon broke down, while party decline, Solidarity intransigence, economic crisis, and social disorder showed no sign of abating. Prospects for a genuine national front between the Party, Solidarity, and the Church could not survive in the climate of institutional degeneration, economic scarcity, and potential invasion. Innovative Western strategies or "a Marshall Plan for Poland" would have changed the political dynamic. We do not know whether such a plan could have prevented martial law. Personally, I would agree with Bialer that it was worth a try.[35] We do know that moral platitudes without an economic package had no influence on events.

Although the policymakers in the Kremlin undoubtedly applauded Jaruzelski's declaration of martial law and may indeed have been pushing him in that direction, Soviet pressure was only one of the precipitants that led to the Military Council of National Salvation's assumption of the Party's leading role in December 1981. The overall package looks remarkably like the stimulants to coup d'état all around the world: declining civilian legitimacy, political paralysis, economic crises, social disorder.[36] Both the Polish Communist Party and Solidarity had been effectively crippled by their lack of capacity to deal with organizational pressures and popular demands. The army was the only cohesive political actor left. It enjoyed substantial good will even among Solidarity supporters,[37] and there was the historical precedent of the interwar Pilsudski dictatorship. Even those who insist that martial law in Poland came stamped "Made in Moscow" must admit that it was assembled in Warsaw.

REPRESSION AND POLITICAL DEVELOPMENT

Measured against an international spectrum including levels of state terror like that associated with the 1973 military takeover in Chile, the repression that accompanied martial law in Poland was mild. Reportedly the loss of life was low, yet such "moderation" is exceedingly relative. Solidarity leaders were arrested and imprisoned. Worker resistance in factories and mines was broken by the motorized riot police (ZOMO), whose pent-up brutality after sitting on the sidelines during the months of negotiating was anything but moderate. Thousands were taken into custody, although many were subsequently released. According to the general prosecutor, as many as 5,500 had been pardoned by October 1982.[38]

Amnesty for many of the remaining political prisoners came with the July

1983 lifting of martial law, for others in a July 1984 amnesty that reportedly left about 30 of those charged with political offenses awaiting release. But in 1985 the number edged up again, particularly during the crackdown before the October parliamentary elections, when an estimated 363 people were held "for politically motivated" crimes.

Official figures contradict themselves and not surprisingly disagree with those of underground Solidarity. Bluntly, the Jaruzelski regime had reason to falsify in one direction; underground Solidarity, a strong temptation to exaggerate in the other. Using either set of figures, if calculated by the body count of political prisoners, repression fluctuated downward from the period of official martial law. In September 1986 225 political prisoners were released. From the regime's perspective this was a total amnesty, since those who remained wre charged with crimes of violence rather than opposition.

Yet it is well to remember that whereas repression is a matter of degree for those who study it, it is a state of being for those who have to live with it. It is generally agreed that during and after martial law, one can document substantial denial of Polish citizens' human and political rights.

What is less generally recognized is that martial law was a giant step backwards in terms of Poland's political development. For months the PUWP essentially ceased to function except to rubber-stamp decisions taken by what amounted to a military junta. Like military regimes throughout Asia, Africa, and Latin America, Poland's politicians in uniform resolved their crisis of participation by bureaucratic/administrative methods that ignored existing political processes and severely restricted institutional participation. The world noticed and condemned the banning of Solidarity in October 1982. There has been a tendency to dismiss the takeover of the PUWP from within and its subsequent militarization as "the Party in Uniform."[39] That interpretation ignores the institutional implications of military rule in Poland. The lifting of martial law in July 1983 notwithstanding, there is every reason to believe that party building as Jaruzelski saw it amounted to controlling factionalism within the Party and keeping it firmly under the thumb of the Polish military.

This is not to say that civilian political elites were replaced wholesale. Even during martial law Jaruzelski worked closely with handpicked commissions of high-ranking party members, although on balance the general appeared to prefer government bodies to party institutions in his effort to stabilize the country.[40] This was in the context of what may be considered as progressive penetration of the party structure at all levels.[41] Officers became secretaries of regional administrative units and took over local leadership posts in towns and factories. Military task groups stationed in each voivodship continued to spearhead the war against corruption and inefficiency in the economy.[42]

The leadership reshuffle that symbolically set the stage for return to civilian rule at the 9th Central Committee's Plenum in July 1982 strengthened Jaruzelski's personal control, but did little to rehabilitate the Party institutionally. Under the circumstances the general predictably did not return to the barracks with the formal lifting of martial law a year later. Jaruzelski retained both his position as first secretary of the Party and the post of prime minister. He stepped down from the job of defense minister only to further consolidate his control as chairman of the newly created National Defense Committee attached to the Council of Ministers.[43] With sweeping powers to both define and respond to defense/security needs, this committee had a mandate to return to martial law if need be. Appointed by the Polish parliament, the Sejm, its chairman also became the supreme commander of the Polish armed forces. In this capacity Jaruzelski remained at the head of the Polish military establishment as well.

Although the membership of this National Defense Committee has not been made public, it is assumed to include the key members of the formally disbanded Military Council of National Salvation. In addition, the infrastructure necessary for a possible return to martial law was put in place in the form of provincial committees for national defense charged to monitor defense/security needs at the regional level. Thereby, although symbolically "civilianized," military rule continues in Poland both via militarization of the Party and in a range of alternate structures that essentially bypass the party hierarchy. These include the general's own try at creating a national front, the Patriotic Movement for National Renewal (PRON), which there is reason to think that Moscow views with less than complete enthusiasm as yet another potential competitor for the once-leading role of the PUWP.[44] Whether or not the Soviets are correct in such suspicions, the once three-way dialogue of the Party, the workers, and the Church has been drastically curtailed, and not only as far as the workers are concerned.

After martial law, as before, the preference seemed to be for policy making within governmental rather than party forums. It is also possible that official lines of administrative authority did not make much difference; that Jaruzelski made decisions after talking with his close military advisers and a few trusted civilians. Indeed, his Order of Lenin notwithstanding, the Polish leader appears decidedly un-Leninist in his organizational solutions.

Throughout the three years leading up to the 10th PUWP Congress in 1986 he continued to balance between the weakened reformers—perhaps better called accommodationists these days—who advocated retaining as much of the Gdansk charter as possible despite the banning of Solidarity, and the neo-Stalinists, who shuddered at the remaining signs of socialist pluralism and kept running to their Soviet patrons to intervene. In comparative terms Jaruzelski might be thought of as the guardian of a "centrist" position that, for all the criticism coming out of Moscow, may be more acceptable to the Soviets than the truly hardline alternative.

This is not to imply that post–martial law Poland was without repression.

Quite the contrary. Some forms of repression clearly intensified in 1983-1984 in response to the expansion of underground Solidarity. Political amnesties aside, police had considerable success in hunting down Solidarity leaders still at large. Although he was not again imprisoned, Walesa continued to be harassed. Thousands have been detained for 48-hour questioning. And there was the tragic murder of the outspoken pro-Solidarity priest, Father Jerzy Popieluszko, in October 1984.

Father Popieluszko was murdered by officers of the security forces, who clearly thought that the word had come from above to do so. Whether or not the charges of Minister of Internal Affairs General Czeshaw Kiszczak that the whole affair was a provocation of hardliners within the security forces to weaken the Jaruzelski regime is correct, the dramatic trial of the priest's killers opened an ugly Pandora's box of dirty tricks, repressive tactics, and institutional violence commonly put to the service of "state security" by departments under Kiszczak's jurisdiction.[45]

Those same revelations put life in the room at the top of Polish politics in a sobering, macabre political light. It would not be the first time that security forces had been used to undermine political leaders. To whatever extent that the challenge of Jaruzelski's position came from supporters of rumored Soviet favorite Foreign Minister Stefan Olszowki, that threat was neutralized during the sweeping political changes at the top of the Polish government hierarchy in November 1985. Olszowki resigned from his position on the Politburo and was dropped as foreign minister. Jaruzelski himself stepped down as prime minister and took over the more symbolic position as chairman of the State Council (official head of state).

These changes also shifted Olszowski's chief rival, Deputy Prime Minister Rakowski, to his present post as deputy speaker of the Polish parliament. It is fair to say that General Jaruzelski conducted another round of musical chairs most likely related to his balancing act between factions within the Polish Party. The reshuffle may have been a move in Soviet-Polish relations, and probably was intended to have some payoff in Poland's campaign to gain International Monetary Fund (IMF) membership, the key to desperately needed Western credits.

One can say tentatively that the voter turnouts at the 1985 parliamentary elections and the 1986 10th Party Congress were steps in the direction of normalizing the Polish political process. Some political observers speculate that the 1986 September amnesty "marked a turning point in the regime's penal policy."[46] The current policy reportedly emphasizes confiscation of property, heavy fines, and short prison terms. This is hardly an absence of repression, but it is a far cry from the earlier physical brutality symbolized by Father Popieluszko's murder and the death of 19-year-old Gdansk University student Marcin Antonowicz, who died from a fractured skull two weeks after being detained by police in November 1985. There is a possibility that the Polish authorities have decided that criminalization of dissent does not work,[47] that it only spreads the opposition far beyond those actively involved in underground Solidarity resistance. These days, according to knowledgeable Polish observers, the government does not like Solidarity activity, but is deliberately ignoring it rather than cracking down.

Conversely, with the creation of open Solidarity councils both at the national and provincial levels following the September 1986 amnesty, opposition response appeared divided about direction. Lack of agreement between central and regional Solidarity leaders as well as "personal animosities and rivalry" caused concern among those attempting to take advantage of the more permissive political climate.[48]

If we look at these events in their international context, a pattern emerges. First, the original strains on the Polish economy that brought Solidarity to life were entangled with the inability of the Gierek regime to handle the Western debt-servicing obligation, that is, the repercussions of increased Polish integration into what may be called the capitalist political economy during the 1970s. His last desperate move to raise prices in the summer of 1980 reflected the need to meet Western conditions for further credits. On the other hand, it also flowed logically from Poland's political integration into the Soviet sphere of influence and the fallout suffered in Warsaw from Moscow's intervention in Afghanistan in December 1979. In short, Polish repression directly reflected international economic pressures and declining political options.

Second, martial law must be considered a response to that implicit worst-case scenario, the possibility of Soviet intervention. However, it was also a response to the lack of economic incentives on the side of Western governments, who cheered Solidarity from the sidelines, offering moral support but no programs that would encourage the weakened Polish Party or Solidarity itself to join in the proposed National Front for political and economic renewal. The Reagan administration did not want a National Front in which Solidarity played a part. It wanted Solidarity to "throw the rascals out." That was hopelessly naive. It lost the opportunity for the kind of "constructive engagement" that might have kept the political actors in the Polish drama in an ongoing dialogue that would have avoided the collapse into martial law with its repressive wake. This is not to suggest that such a move would have worked, but only that since it was not tried, we will never know.

Conversely, the 10th Party Congress and September 1986 amnesty, following the trip of Deputy Secretary of State John Whitehead to Warsaw and the February 1987 removal of the last U.S. sanctions, appeared to reinforce the decline in internal repression.[49] Meanwhile the opening to the West has been paralleled by Soviet leader Mikhail Gorbachev's visible support of Jaruzelski. Gorbachev's own efforts to reform Soviet economic and political life mean that the pressure from Moscow on the Polish general is likely to be for more, not less, *glasnost* (openness) in Polish politics. Jaruzelski has firmly tied his own austerity and political reform program to Soviet *perestroika.* In such circumstances, the forces of reform have been strengthened, as was evident from Rakowski's rise to membership in the Party Politburo in December 1987.[50]

This does not mean that internal repression has been or will be eliminated. It may mean that such repression has become less necessary and less acceptable. It is possible—but no sure thing—that supporters of ''socialist pluralism'' will have greater opportunity to influence their hardline comrades on issues of internal security and restrain the behavior of those charged with keeping the opposition in line.

It is encouraging that the government accepted its failure to receive the support of the required 51 percent of eligible voters in the December 1987 referendum on proposed reforms as a message that the program needed to be modified rather than as a signal to embark on a campaign to vilify its opponents. Indeed, this defeat may have improved Poland's bargaining position with the IMF in the Jaruzelski government's effort to loosen the economic vise created by the $36 billion debt.

The stance taken by Warsaw's Western creditors at the December 1987 talks in Paris—on IMF agreement to ''standby credits'' and the World Bank's commitment ''in principle'' to $250 million in new credits— undoubtedly eased tensions. Nonetheless, a scaled-down austerity program inevitably followed. While less draconian than those proposed in December, these measures jacked up food prices by 40 percent, the price of petrol by 60 percent, rent for low-income housing by 50 percent, and intercity bus and train fares by 50 percent.[52] The average price increase for 1988 was projected to be 27 percent. Notwithstanding Solidarity leader Lech Walesa's warning against the danger of a popular explosion, the government weathered both the initial, relatively isolated protests to the February price hikes and the much more serious wave of strikes in May 1988.

These price increases reflected the terms that the Polish government agreed to in order to secure the IMF rescue package. They were the result of debt-servicing obligations that had to be met if the Polish economy were not to grind to a halt. There was immediate pressure from the official government trade unions for a wage increase to offset the hardship caused by escalating prices. The government yielded to that pressure; nevertheless, the increase was not high enough to satisy trade union demands, but probably too high from an IMF advisory viewpoint. Thus, in 1988 as in 1980, Poland's need for hard currency and the country's dependence on the international capitalist economy operated simultaneously to generate and legitimize demands for expanded participation on the road to economic and political reform and, conversely, to put in place economic austerity measures that risked setting off a political backlash and triggering increased repression.

There is a fine line between applying enough pressure to get an economy moving in a healthy direction and so much that, as they say in the medical world, "the operation was a success but the patient died." Whether or not the tentative steps in the direction of political development taken since the 1983 lifting of martial law can be consolidated depends on improving the image of Jaruzelski's Polish *perestroika* sufficiently to legitimize the economic misery that comes with IMF remedies. In Poland, as elsewhere throughout the world, repression is a function of lack of legitimacy exacerbated by unacceptable economic conditions.

In turn, Jaruzelski's ability to deal with the country's staggering economic problems depends on political priorities and political will in Washington and Moscow as well as in Warsaw. In 1988 there is another window of opportunity for U.S./IMF economic influence to foster political outcomes in Poland that could not be brought about through the imposition of sanctions.

This window is not as wide as it was in 1980. The Polish government's cautious January 5, 1988, statement of willingness to open talks with Solidarity included conditions that underground Solidarity considered to be a sell-out. Clearly, it will be harder to bring Solidarity back into the acceptable political spectrum than it would have been to take advantage of the trade union confederation's political momentum eight years ago. Indeed, in light of underground Solidarity's effort to escalate discontent over the IMF-necessitated austerity program into another nationwide mass movement, if not a general strike, this may be impossible at least for the foreseeable future.

Despite the nostalgia for Solidarity evident in the wave of strikes that swept Poland in May, there was no mass response to Lech Walesa's passionate insistence that there is "no freedom without Solidarity."[53] The workers marched out of the Lenin Shipyard rather than being dragged out by the police or the army. But the assessment that there were no winners in this standoff is naive. Clearly the government's mix of patience and limited repression has worked.

In Warsaw the idealism of 1980 has been replaced by popular resignation and pragmatic reformism. It is too soon to tell whether this will add up to an agreement on the art of the possible between Polish policymakers and those they govern. However, we can say that the merry-go-round of Polish politics has taken another full turn, in which Jaruzelski has staked his reform effort on Gorbachev's survival and IMF cooperation. Notwithstanding the general's reputation for political realism, this is a considerable gamble. If he is reaching for a brass ring that is not there, another wave of repression could be the cost of failure. In a worst case scenario, Poland could return to martial law.

On the other hand, 1988 could be a time of hope more modest than the euphoria associated with the Solidarity of the early 1980s.[54] For that to happen politicians in Washington, Moscow, and Warsaw will have to work together instead of against each other; to see the situation as one of mutual advantage rather than zero-sum outcomes.

NOTES

1. *The Times* (London), December 14, 1981.

2. For a detailed account of worker response to martial law, see *Poland Watch,* no. 1 (Fall 1982). This is the journal of the Poland Watch Center, a nonprofit organization dedicated to publicizing information about human rights issues in Poland. Without question the most comprehensive analysis of martial law in Poland to date is Teresa Rakowska-Harmstone, "Poland," in her study with Christopher D. Jones and Ivan Sylvain, *The Warsaw Pact: Question of Cohesion, Phase II,* vol. 2, *Poland, German Democratic Republic, and Romania,* ORAE Extra-Mural paper no. 33 (Department of National Defense, Canada, November 1984). See also A. Ross Johnson, *Poland in Crisis,* A Rand Note, N-1891-AF (Santa Monica, Rand Corporation, July 1982), and Jan B. de Weydenthal, "Martial Law and the Reliability of the Soviet Military," in Daniel N. Nelson, ed., *Soviet Allies: The Warsaw Pact and the Issue of Reliability* (Boulder, Colo.: Westview Press, 1984), pp. 225-249.

3. A concise description of the penetration model can be found in Eric A. Nordlinger, *Soldiers in Politics: Military Coups and Governments* (Englewood Cliffs, N.J.: Prentice-Hall, 1977), pp. 15-19. Nordlinger expands on the totalitarian model put forward by Morris Janowitz in *The Military in the Political Development of New Nations* (Chicago: University of Chicago Press, 1964).

4. Samuel P. Huntington, "Political Development and Political Decay," *World Politics* 17, no. 3 (April 1965): 386-430.

5. The military mind is typically presumed to emphasize discipline, efficiency, and political order; to distrust spontaneous, mass participation; and to prefer administrative solutions to bargaining and compromise. Nordlinger, *Soldiers in Politics,* pp. 54-61. See also Samuel P. Huntington, *The Soldier and the State: The Theory and Practice of Civil-Military Relations* (New York: Vintage Books, 1957), pp. 57-79.

6. This section is based largely on Jan Szczepanski, *Polish Society* (New York: Random House, 1970), and the discussion of Polish culture and attitudes in Rakowska-Harmstone, "Poland," pp. 3-32.

7. See Adam Bromke, *Poland's Politics: Idealism vs. Realism* (Cambridge, Mass.: Harvard University Press, 1967).

8. Rakowska-Harmstone, "Poland," p. 58.

9. Zbigniew K. Brzezinski, *The Soviet Bloc: Unity and Conflict* (Cambridge, Mass.: Harvard University Press, 1967).

10. Ibid., pp. 155-184.

11. "Secret Speech of Khrushchev Concerning the 'Cult of the Individual,' " delivered at the Twentieth Congress of the Communist Party of the Soviet Union, February 25, 1956, in Russian Institute of Columbia University, ed., *The Anti-Stalin Campaign and International Communism: A Selection of Documents* (New York: Columbia University Press, 1956), pp. 1-91.

12. *Rude pravo,* May 1, 1956, quoted from Wolfgang Leonhard, *The Kremlin since Stalin* (New York: Praeger, 1962), p. 203.

13. Alfred G. Meyer, "The Comparative Study of Communist Political Systems," *Slavic Review* 26, no. 1 (March 1967): 8-9.

14. A. Ross Johnson, Robert W. Dean, and Alexander Alexiev, *East European Military Establishments: The Warsaw Pact Northern Tier* (New York: Crane, Russak, 1982), p. 21.

15. See Nicholas Bethell, *Gomulka: His Poland and Communism* (Harmondsworth: Penguin, 1972).

16. Ibid., pp. 253-267.

17. According to one authoritative Polish commentator, this treaty was "the final sanctioning" of Poland's western border, binding not only the current West German government but "its eventual successors." Richard Wojna, *Zycie Warszawy,* November 19, 1970.

18. S. Kovalev, "Sovereignty and the Internationalist Obligations of Socialist Countries," *Pravda,* September 26, 1968.

19. *The Times* (London), April 6, 1971.

20. Revealed by Prime Minister Jaroszewicz, *Zycie Warszawy,* April 16, 1971.

21. For a comprehensive analysis, see Adam Bromke and John W. Strong, eds., *Gierek's Poland* (New York: Praeger, 1973).

22. *Polityka,* May 29, 1971, quoted by Adam Bromke in "Poland under Gierek," *Problems of Communism* 21 (September–October 1972): 18.

23. Thomas E. Henghan, "One Year after the Polish Price Protests," *Radio Free Europe Background Report* 132 (June 1977), provides useful background.

24. In reality, KOR was only one of a variety of diverse dissent organizations; its newspaper *Robotnik* was part of a virtual flood of dissident media. There are some excellent reference works and analyses dealing with this area. See *Dissent in Poland: Reports and Documents in Translation* (London: Association of Polish Students and Graduates and Exiles, 1977); Peter Raina, *Political Opposition in Poland, 1954-1977* (London: Poets' and Painters' Press, 1978); Jane Leftwich Curry's chapter on Poland in her edited volume, *Dissent in Eastern Europe* (New York: Praeger, 1983); and Joanna M. Preibisz, ed., *Polish Dissident Publications: An Annotated Bibliography* (New York: Praeger, 1982).

25. *Krytyka* (Warsaw), no. 1 (September 1978).

26. The most informative on-the-scene account of these events is that of Michael Dobbs, reporting from Gdansk for the *Guardian,* August 26, 27, 28, 1980. For a comprehensive postmortem, see William Robinson, ed., *August 1980: The Strikes in Poland* (Munich: RFE Research, October 1980).

27. George Sanford, "The Response of the Polish Communist Leadership and the Continuing Crisis (Summer 1980 to the Ninth Congress, July 1981): Personnel and Party Change," in Jean Woodhall, ed., *Policy and Politics in Contemporary Poland: Reform, Failure, Crisis* (London: Francis Pinter, 1982), p. 44.

28. Exclusive interview, *The Times* (London), February 23, 1982.

29. Samuel P. Huntington, *Political Order in Changing Societies* (New Haven: Yale University Press, 1968), pp. 12-24. Although I agree with Gitelman concerning the tensions that modernization puts on political institutions in their quest for value and stability, I feel that his application of Kesselman's concept of "overinstitutionalization" to Poland is more confusing than helpful. Mark Kesselman, "Overinstitu-

tionalization and Political Constraint: The Case of France," *Comparative Politics* 2, no. 1 (October 1970): Zvi Gitelman, "Development, Institutionalization, and Elite-Mass Relations in Poland," in Jan F. Triska and Paul M. Cocks, eds., *Political Development in Eastern Europe* (New York: Praeger, 1977), pp. 119-146. For still another perspective on the relationship of institutionalization to worker protest in Poland, see Jan B. de Weydenthal, "The Workers' Dilemma of Polish Politics: A Case Study," *East European Quarterly* 13, no. 1 (Spring 1979): 95-119; and in terms of the broader East European context, Barbara Wolfe Jancar, "Modernity and the Character of Dissent," in Charles Gati, ed., *The Politics of Modernization in Eastern Europe: Testing the Soviet Model* (New York: Praeger, 1974), pp. 338-357.

30. Jan B. de Weydenthal, *The Communists of Poland: An Historical Outline* (Stanford, Calif.: Hoover Institution Press, 1978).

31. *Statesman* (Delhi), November 17, 1980.

32. Nicholas G. Andrews, *Poland, 1980-81: Solidarity versus the Party* (Washington, D.C.: National Defense University Press, 1985), pp. 113-147.

33. For a more in-depth treatment, see Robin Alison Remington, "Search for the Vanguard: Party and Politics in Poland," *UFSI Reports* (Europe), no. 41 (1982).

34. Rakowska-Harmstone, "Poland," p. 145.

35. Seweryn Bialer, *Poland under Martial Law,* International Programs Occasional Paper (Washington, D.C.: American Enterprise Institute for Public Policy Research, 1982), pp. 3-21.

36. Claude E. Welch, Jr., and Arthur K. Smith, *Military Role and Rule* (North Scituate, Mass.: Duxbury Press, 1974), pp. 8-34.

37. Rakowska-Harmstone, "Poland," pp. 121-122. Many Poles firmly believed that not only had Jaruzelski actually made his subsequently disputed statement that "Polish soldiers will not shoot Polish workers," but that he had kept the regular army on the sidelines during the crises of 1970 and 1976. Indeed, in May 1981 a public opinion poll showed the Polish army just behind the Church and slightly above Solidarity as the second most respected institution in the country; Jerzy J. Wiatr, *The Soldiers and The Nation: The Role of the Military in Poland's Politics, 1918-1985.* (Boulder, Colo.: Westview Press, forthcoming). See also Andrzej Korbonski and Sarah Terry, "The Military as a Political Actor in Poland," in Roman Kolkowicz and Andrzej Korbonski, eds., *Soldiers, Peasants, and Bureaucrats: Civil-Military Relations in Communist and Modernizing Societies* (London: Allen and Unwin, 1982), pp. 159-180.

38. *Poland Watch,* no. 2 (Winter 1982/1983): 23-24.

39. Amos Perlmutter and William M. LeoGrande, "The Party in Uniform: Toward a Theory of Civil-Military Relations in Communist Political Systems," *American Political Science Review* 76, no. 4 (December 1982): 778-789.

40. Roman Stafanowski, "A Partial List of Martial Law Institutions," RFE-RL Background Report (Poland), September 7, 1982. Moreover, the Jaruzelski-appointed minister of culture, Kazimierz Zygulski, reportedly was not a Communist Party member, but rather a veteran of the anti-Communist Polish Home Army during World War II.

41. De Weydenthal, "Martial Law," pp. 237-240.

42. Rakowska-Harmstone, "Poland," p. 156.

43. *Zycie Warszawy,* December 19, 1983; for analysis, see Rakowska-Harmstone, "Poland," pp. 161ff.

44. See Andrzej Korbonski, "Soviet Policy towards Poland," in Sarah Meikle-john Terry, ed., *Soviet Policy in Eastern Europe* (New Haven: Yale University Press, 1984), p. 91.

45. Jane Cave, "The Murder of Father Popieluszko," *Poland Watch,* no. 7 (1985): 1-25.

46. *Poland,* RFE Background Report, January 9, 1987.

47. For a theoretical perspective, see Robert Sharlet, "Varieties of Dissent and Regularities of Repression in the European Communist States: An Overview," in Curry, *Dissent in Eastern Europe,* pp. 1-24. See also Rakowska-Harmstone, "Poland," pp. 183ff., for a discussion of the Circles of Social Defense (KOS).

48. KOS, no. 102, October 6, 1986, quoted by RFE Research Press Review, December 12, 1986.

49. *Christian Science Monitor,* February 3 and 23, 1987.

50. Rakowski's speech, upon taking his place in the Politburo, called for unifying the PUWP and expanding its power base by strengthening the role of the affiliated parties (the Democratic Party and the United Peasant Party) and the Catholic group PAX (*Polityka* [Warsaw], December 26, 1987). His January 5 *New York Times* interview referred positively to "differing political orientations within the system." These are moderate signals, not radical statements. Nor, given Rakowski's past interactions with Walesa, is he likely to have much enthusiasm for considering Solidarity one of those "differing orientations" to be encouraged.

51. *Christian Science Monitor,* December 22, 1987.

52. *New York Times,* February 1, 1988.

53. *New York Times,* May 12, 1988.

54. See Wladyslaw Pleszczynski's review of the American edition of Lech Walesa's autobiography, *A Way of Hope,* in the *Wall Street Journal,* February 8, 1988.

8

The New International Division of Labor, Export-Oriented Growth, and State Repression in Latin America

David Carleton

SCOPE AND DIRECTION

This chapter investigates the relaitonship between the emergence of a new international division of labor or export-oriented industrialization and the incidence of state repression in Latin America. Over the past 20 years the growth and pervasiveness of state repression in the region has been one of the most horrifying but least understood political phenomena. Particularly frightening is the degree to which several regimes have institutionalized repression, so that death and torture are increasingly "managed" or "engineered" by well-equipped and smoothly operating state security apparatuses. While the behavior of these states has been thoroughly documented, scholars have generally been unwilling or unable to examine the issue.[1] Of late, however, a number of scholars have begun the process of systematically analyzing state repression and terrorism.[2] This chapter examines the relationship between repression and an emerging aspect of global political economy. Several analysts who have been working to document the emergence of export-oriented growth, or what is broadly termed a "new international division of labor" (NIDL), have argued that increased state repression is a closely related development.

In this chapter we have two purposes. First, we will develop the theoretical links that exist between export-oriented growth and state repression. To date, the bulk of the literature on the NIDL has concentrated on its economic impacts. While analysts have referred to various political impacts in passing, these issues have not been examined in any detail. We will draw upon existing work to present a thorough explanation of the theoretical linkages. Second, we will conduct a preliminary empirical test of these linkages. It is not our intention to present the last word on the issue, but to take the first tentative step toward the systematic empirical analysis of the relationship between the NIDL and repression.

Discussion of a new international division of labor explains the increasing development of "export-platform" economies in the Third World. These economies do not fit in the traditional division of labor wherein the Third World serves as a source of primary products. A new division of labor is emerging, it is argued, in which the manufacturing portion of multinational corporation (MNC) production processes are carried out in the Third World.[3] Many Third World governments, in their quest for development, are eager to attract such MNC activity. They also recognize that the multinationals choose to locate and remain, quite naturally, only in those states offering a suitable political and economic environment, or in a country offering adherence to open-market principles and political stability. Several analysts postulate that states seeking to attract MNCs will thus utilize repression to establish and/or maintain such an environment.[4]

Of available work on repression, several efforts examine its relationship to aspects of political economy. K. Erickson and P. Peppe conclude that the development of dependent industrializaton in Chile and Brazil was closely tied to the increased repression of labor.[5] J. Sheahan[6] and D. Pion-Berlin[7] discover a significant positive relationship between free or open-market principles and state repression in all or part of Latin America. In what he labels "repressive-developmentalist" regimes in Asia, Herb Feith finds an emphasis on export-led industrialization, open-market principles, and a welcome reception for multinational corporations.[8] As we shall discuss, these are precisely the factors singled out by NIDL theorists. Thus available research indicates that an examination of the relationship between a NIDL and state repression may be quite fruitful.

As indicated, following a discussion of the theoretical issues involved, I will present a preliminary test of these issues. Since the precise causal relation between the NIDL and state repression is as yet unclear, a simple panel research design will be employed. Feith has argued that repression is both a cause and an effect of export-led industrialization.[9] Repression serves as a precondition for MNC involvement because it generates the environment demanded by the multinationals, while the resulting economic growth provides the resources for "improving" the repressive aparatus. In light of the duality of the causal relationship, as well as the early stage of research on repression in general, a simple panel design proves particulary useful. It allows us to examine both causal links and provides us some basis for concluding which of the two is most important. The data employed includes 22 Latin American countries for the years 1975 and 1979.[10] In the discussion that follows, we will first review the evidence supporting the NIDL argument and will then discuss in some detail the theoretical ties between these economic changes and state repression.

EXPORT-ORIENTED GROWTH AND THE
NEW INTERNATIONAL DIVISION OF LABOR

A global economy and some semblance of an international division of labor have existed since at least the middle of the nineteenth century.[11] Over most of this period the role of the present less developed countries (LDCs) has been quite stable: they have served almost exclusively as sources for primary products and, further along in the process, as markets for finished products. That this role could lead only to further pauperization, however, was demonstrated by Economic Commission for Latin America (ECLA) economists in the 1950s. In response, LDC policymakers almost universally adopted import-substituting industrialization (ISI) policies in an effort to break out of the pattern.[12] This was perhaps nowhere more true than in Latin America, where virtually all hopes for development were pinned on ISI. The pitfalls of these policies have now been thoroughly documented,[13] and as a result, in the 1970s a new economic orthodoxy arose. A development strategy focusing on export-led industrialization is now widely promoted.[14] Policymakers now hope to re-create the "economic miracles" of Singapore, Taiwan, Hong Kong, and South Korea. In Latin America there was in the 1970s a wholesale shift away from inward-oriented industrialization (*desarrollo adentro*) toward outward- or export-oriented policies (*desarrollo afuera*). Analysts have argued that successful export-oriented industrialization places a country firmly within the new division of labor.

Most of the literature on export-oriented industrialization and a NIDL rightfully begins with a discussion of multinational corporations, for multinationals constitute the foundation upon which the new order is being built. Since the early 1960s many multinationals have transformed their global structure and operations. S. Hymer properly calls this process the "internationalization of capitalist production."[15] Having first internationalized capital, multinationals are now internationalizing the production process as well; large buying companies and vertically integrated MNCs increasingly organize their operations on a worldwide basis. M. Sharpston,[16] D. Nayyer,[17] and G. Helleiner[18] each demonstrate that production is increasingly carried on within corporations on a global scale. The "new international division of labor" is simply the structural manifestation of this process.

The globalization of production involves locating each individual aspect of the production process wherever it is most efficient to do so. The multinational corporate perspective thus increasingly ignores political entities. G. Adam summarizes the outlook of these global MNCs:

The [global] company views the world as a single entity. Its perspectives transcend all national boundaries. . . . The basic principle on which these corporations operate is this: taking the entire world as their market, they tend to organize production, distribution and selling activities with as little regard for national [political] boundaries as the realities of time and space permit.[19]

In short, decisionmakers rationalize the multinationals' production process on a global scale. The LDCs, given their "comparative advantage" in wage scales, are thus afforded an opportunity to sizably expand their role in the production of labor-intensive manufactured goods. Global MNCs are eager to take advantage of low wages in the assembly portion of their manufacturing processes. Thus the role of the LDCs in the new international division of labor includes not only the traditional exploitation of primary products, but also the assembly of manufactured goods as multinationals exploit lower wage scales in the Third World.

As they globalize their production, multinationals continue to service their original market. Thus most of the manufactured goods assembled in the Third World are exported back to the developed countries rather than consumed domestically.[20] The NIDL and the development of export platforms are thus inexorably linked. As export-platform economies develop, they assume a new role in the international division of labor, and collectively, they and the changes they portend represent what is meant by a new international division of labor. Export-oriented industrialization necessarily involves a large foreign presence directed toward the diversification of exports into the assembled-manufactures sector. The economic "miracles" of South Asia have been largely based on the assembly of manufactured goods and have been dominated by multinationals. Latin American efforts to emulate these models thus involve, even if only implicitly, an effort to join the new division of labor.

Unfortunately, available data on the NIDL is unsystematic. Among the developed countries only the United States has published extensive data on the behavior of its MNCs, and the coverage and reliability of import-export data from the LDCs varies considerably.[21] Nevertheless, the data that can be employed substantiates claims regarding movement toward a new international division of labor.

Since the mid-1960s the composition of LDC trade has witnessed a significant expansion in the role of manufactured goods. While the LDC share of world trade in primary goods declined from 33 percent in 1970 to 26 percent in 1977, their share of trade in manufactured goods rose from 7.5 to 9.6 percent over the same period.[22] The steady and rapid growth in LDC manufacturing exports can be seen in table 8.1. Since 1960 the annual growth in manufacturing exports from the Third World has exceeded that of both the developed Western and centrally planned economies.

As expected by the NIDL theorists, the growth in LDC manufacturing exports has been exceptionally rapid to the developed countries in particular. Between 1970 and 1976 Third World manufacturing exports to the developed countries grew at an annual rate of some 14 percent.[23] Most

Table 8.1
Exports of Manufactured Goods from LDCs
(Millions of U.S. Dollars)

Year	Latin America	Africa	Middle East	Asia	All LDCs
1966	957	772	547	2,981	5,479
1967	1,055	819	626	3,604	6,355
1968	1,248	926	699	4,376	7,567
1969	1,452	1,075	835	5,315	9,165
1970	2,205	1,059	878	5,099	9,366
1971	2,523	1,087	1,138	6,280	11,135
1972	3,276	1,189	941	10,123	15,573
1973	5,152	1,595	1,393	16,067	24,304
1974	7,413	2,107	2,103	20,407	32,155

Source: D. Nayyer, "Transnational Corporations and Manufactured Exports from Poor Countries," *Economic Journal* 88, no. 1 (1978): 59-84.

interesting, this pace was more than double the rate of increase in developed country imports of manufactured goods from the world as a whole. In other words, the developed countries are increasingly importing their manufactured goods from the Third World.

Evidence that this growth in manufactured exports is largely made up of the assembly portion of MNC production processes is available from U.S. tariff statistics. Tariff items 806.30 and 807.00 apply to goods with parts originating in the United States assembled abroad and reimported. As can be seen in table 8.2, the use of these tariff items has increased at a very rapid rate. The dollar value of such imports from the LDCs, in fact, increased in the 1970s at an annual rate of nearly 30 percent.[24] While the LDCs' percentage share of the goods imported under these tariff items leveled off after 1974, no doubt due in large part to the general economic slowdown in the mid-1970s and rising pressures for protectionism in the developed countries, the increase from the mid-1960s to the late 1970s is nevertheless dramatic. It thus appears, overall, that multinationals are globalizing their production, and hence that there is a distinct movement toward the formation of a new international division of labor.

Table 8.2
U.S. Imports under Tariff, Items 806.30 and 807.00, 1966-1979
(Millions of U.S. Dollars)

Year	Total	LDC Share	% of Total from LDCs
1966	953.0	60.7	6.4
1967	1035.1	99.0	9.6
1968	1554.4	221.7	14.3
1969	1838.8	394.8	21.5
1970	2208.2	541.5	24.5
1971	2768.8	652.5	23.7
1972	3408.8	1066.5	31.3
1973	4247.1	1557.3	36.7
1974	5371.8	2350.1	43.7
1975	5161.4	2261.7	43.8
1976	5721.5	2807.0	49.1
1977	7188.1	3306.8	46.0
1978	9735.3	4286.6	44.0
1979	11937.7	5310.1	44.5

Source: G. Helleiner, *Intra-Firm Trade and the Developing Countries* (New York: St. Martin's Press, 1981).

There is little question that Latin America is moving toward an active role in the new order. From table 8.1 it can be seen that the increase in LDC manufacturing exports from 1966 to 1974 was greatest in Latin America (674 percent), surpassing even the growth in Asia (584 percent). As both M. Wionczek[25] and F. Parkinson[26] have discussed, since the early 1970s virtually all of the Latin American countries have pursued export-oriented industrialization policies.

While many of these statistics are indeed striking, we should remember that the vast majority of LDCs remain overwhelmingly dependent upon the exploitation of primary products. J. Petras examines 47 Third World countries and finds that in 1976 85.4 percent of them relied on primary goods for at least 70 percent of their exports.[27] He concludes that talk of an NIDL is thus misdirected, indeed foolish. But this conclusion would appear to be based far more on ideological than empirical considerations. Even the data he presents indicates that there is a shift away from the export of primary goods and toward manufactured exports. While not all of the Third World nations are part of the process, an increasing number have actively sought inclusion in the NIDL. This is certainly true in Latin America, where export-oriented industrialization policies have been almost universally adopted, and where (despite fluctuations) most countries have succeeded in increasing their assembly and export of manufactured goods since the mid-1960s. Petras is correct in stating that most countries remain dependent upon the export of primary goods, but it is equally true that the formation of the NIDL is lessening, though not yet overcoming, this dependence. The formation of the new order is a gradual process, and one far from complete, but the available evidence indicates that it is taking shape.

Finally, while it is well beyond the scope of this chapter to examine the implications of the NIDL for economic development, a brief word seems warranted. A number of scholars have been quite enthusiastic about the prospects of a NIDL.[28] They consider it an opportunity for the LDCs to industrialize and hence to develop. However, this view would appear to be overly superficial, since it equates all forms of industrialization with "development." Other analysts have rightly been more skeptical.[29] They have noted that only the assembly portion of the production process is transferred to the LDCs. This alone provides very few opportunities to establish either horizontal or vertical linkages, or, in other words, few opportunities for actual development.[30] Furthermore, in Latin America, at least, it appears that MNC manufacturing activities produce less employment than most other economic activities.[31] Overall, however, any conclusions about the ultimate effect of the NIDL on economic development are clearly premature.

THE NIDL AND POLITICAL REPRESSION

Historically, Latin America has experienced a great deal of state repression. Few of the republics have managed to maintain nonrepressive political arrangements for any length of time. As a result, many analysts now interpret repression in Latin America by taking note of its "tradition" of authoritarian rule. This tradition is frequently attributed to the prevalence of corporatist beliefs and attitudes. Howard Wiarda, for instance, argues that corporatist and authoritarian political culture and structures represent a uniquely Latin "third way" to development (which should not be confused with Michael Manley's notion of a "third path" to development).[32] More recently, John Sloan has taken a similar approach by focusing not on corporatist traditions per se, but on the "top-down" or "elitist" political culture of Latin America. Given their narrow base, he argues, the elite structures exhibit a chronic legitimacy problem and thus must continually rely on repression to maintain social control.[33] The point, simply, is that repression in Latin America is usually explained by reference to the values, beliefs, attitudes, or political culture of the region.

While there is no questioning the importance of the factors cited by Wiarda, Sloan, and others, they nevertheless fall short of explaining the upsurge of repression experienced in Latin America during the 1970s. There is a good deal of chronic repression in the region, and much of it may be properly attributed to corporatist or elitist traditions, but the extent and form of repression witnessed in the 1970s was anything but "traditional." It is difficult to accept the events of the last 15 years as a simple continuation of long-standing historical processes. One need only examine the reports of Amnesty International, Americas Watch, and other human rights monitoring groups to appreciate the unique nature and scale of repression in the 1970s. From Guatemala to the Southern Cone, regimes employed repression not only against routine political opposition, but in an apparent effort to fully "demobilize" their societies.[34] While the basic acceptability of such actions may stem from cultural traditions, these traditions do not explain why the use of repression was suddenly and greatly expanded.

It may prove useful in both a theoretical and practical sense to examine possible linkages between what was presented earlier as an apparently benign and apolitical process, the emergence of a NIDL, and state repression. At present there is little consensus among NIDL theorists on this issue. As noted in the introductory comments, export-led industrialization has been cast as both the cause and the effect of state repression. Some see the stability provided by increased repression as a necessary "lure" to attract global multinationals. Others argue that the economic dislocations created by the NIDL lead to vast domestic opposition, and that governments can continue to follow such policies only with the "help" of repression. We will in turn explicate and develop each of these propositions.

Repression as Cause

A number of analysts have argued that multinationals desire and seek out those nations that are most repressive. Thus countries attempting to develop a role in the new division of labor will purposefully increase repression in order to attract multinational involvement. Herb Feith, for instance, claims that this pattern is apparent in the Asian states he has studied. In "repressive-developmentalist" regimes, he argues, "a markedly heightened level of repressive control was a *precondition* for TNC involvement."[35] In his more general treatment of the NIDL issue, Nayyer concludes that multinationals prefer repressive environments.[36] He argues that given the large number of low-wage countries seeking to attract multinational involvement, MNCs are afforded the luxury of picking and choosing among them. In such an environment "there are two basic factors which influence the choice of transnational firms between low wage countries: political stability and labor docility."[37] Thus the argument is that all things being equal (that is, the economic conditions for MNC involvement are met), multinationals will choose locations on the basis of political criteria. They will choose to locate in those countries where both their short-term profitability (via labor docility) and long-term profitability (via political stability) are best ensured. What these analysts point out, of course, is that in recent history political stability and labor docility have rarely been achieved without recourse to severe repression. Thus, in effect, increased repression is a cause of MNC involvement and export-oriented industrialization.

Adherents of this view generally rely upon a variety of circumstantial evidence. First, they note the upsurge of MNC involvement in the repressive environments of postcoup Brazil, Chile, Argentina (1976), and Uruguay. Second, they cite statements by both government leaders and MNC officials that lend credence to their views. For example, R. W. Moxon interviewed many MNC officials to determine how they choose sites for foreign plants. One official (not necessarily representative) stated quite bluntly: "We won't go into that country until the government gets the unions in line."[38] Many regimes increase repression with at least the stated purpose of improving the climate for foreign investment.[39] Finally, some regimes actually advertise repression, particularly vis-à-vis labor. In this regard, a foreign minister of Singapore has referred to his country simply as the "heavenly city of the global corporations."[40]

The reasoning behind this approach stems from the logic or rationale of capitalist investment and profit making. According to this logic, multinationals have a responsiblity to their shareholders to make a respectable profit. Thus in choosing sites for corporate operations, they "must" choose those locations offering the best profit-making environment. They "must" choose those locations that offer the greatest security for the duration of their investments and are least likely to be disturbed by strident labor demands, strikes, protests, and so on. Given the realities of poverty and inequality in the less developed countries, these requirements for MNC involvement can realistically be secured in the short run only by the use of repression.

In sum, from this perspective the need to secure the basic economic interests of the corporation predisposes these global multinationals toward locating in particularly repressive states. Consequently, state repression is an indirect cause of multinational manufacturing investment, and thus repression allows a developing country to assume a role in the new international division of labor.

Repression as Effect

From this perspective, the economic dislocations and consequent political opposition caused by export-oriented industrialization policies lead to the imposition of repression. Thus repression is a result of export-oriented growth rather than a cause of such growth. As explained by P. Vuskovic:

And, given the political imperatives of a program [of export-led industrialization] *which will force the further denationalization of underdeveloped economies and the superexploitation of their labor force,* we can expect an increase in authoritarianism, repression, and the separation of larger and larger sectors of the population from the political process.[41]

The key features of this perspective are the economic dislocations caused by export-oriented industrialization. These dislocations—the denationalization of the economy and the superexploitation of the labor force—can reasonably be expected to result in political opposition. In the face of this opposition, it is argued, a regime must turn to repression. We will discuss each of these economic dislocations in turn.

Export-led industrialization can further the denationalization of an LDC economy in several ways, each of which can devastate that portion of local capital unaffiliated with the international sector.[42] First, of course, there is direct denationalization. Rather than construct wholly new facilities, multinationals frequently buy out existing domestic industries. One study has shown that nearly half of all MNC operations "established" in Latin America consist of takeovers.[43] Second, an upsurge in MNC involvement in an economy can raise the cost of money and hence the cost of doing business. Multinationals tend to exploit far more domestic capital than they transfer from the developed countries. L. S. Stavrianos, for instance, has reported that upwards of 80 percent of the capital utilized by U.S. multinationals in Latin America is locally generated.[44] This increase in the demand for money drives interest rates higher and thus makes it more difficult for local capital to compete and survive. Finally, once in a country, multinationals often demand and receive reductions in the "protection" given local industries. Many domestic industries were established behind protective tariff walls and are only viable in such an environment. A reduction or elimination of these tariffs greatly benefits the multinationals, but may well destroy local capital. Given these processes, we frequently find greatly increased rates of business failures as export-oriented industrialization policies are implemented.[45]

Export-led industrialization policies also further the superexploitation, or at least the traditional exploitation, of the working class. It has been demonstrated by a variety of analysts that export-oriented policies lead to increased inequality and reductions in real wages. The Brazilian economic "miracle," for instance, saw the richest 5 percent of the population increase its share of the national income from 27.8 to 36.8 percent.[46] Pinochet's "miracle" in Chile produced a drastic reduction in the real wages of Chilean workers.[47] These changes are due in large part to the fact that LDC workers are entered into wage competition with workers worldwide. In such an environment workers need not be paid more than the opportunity costs of locating elsewhere. While, as Sheahan has pointed out, this makes excellent sense in terms of economic rationality, the working class is "forced to take an enduring loss in real income so that others may gain."[48] In short, export-oriented policies can seriously worsen the plight of the working class.

Having created these severe economic dislocations, according to this perspective, a regime has little choice but to employ repression. These dislocations reveal the group or class biases of state policies, and hence the regime effectively forfeits its legitimacy or its ability to utilize mass-ideological control. Thus a regime is left with only stark represson to maintain social control.

To summarize the discussion to this point, there are at present relatively sound theoretical reasons to expect the relation between state repression and export-led industrialization, or a new international division of labor, to take several forms. Existing theory indicates that repression may both lead to and result from a country's assumption of a role in the NIDL. A good deal of both theoretical and empirical work remains to be done. In the remainder of this chapter we will begin the process of empirical testing.

AN EMPIRICAL "FIRST CUT"

We will now present a preliminary empirical examination of the proposed linkages between export-oriented industrialization and political repression in Latin America. While this will not provide us with definitive answers to our questions, it will yield a reasonable point of departure for more thorough and complex empirical analyses. At this stage of research we must settle for "clues" as to the proper direction in which to move our research efforts in the future. This analysis will provide us such clues.

Research Design and Measures

Panel Regression Analysis

A panel research design permits the examination of causal propositions with more confidence than a simple cross-sectional analysis. In cross-sectional analyses the independent and dependent variables are measured at the same point in time. They thus rely on the unlikely proposition of simultaneous generation. In contrast, with a panel design we employ data for two different time points, and thus reduce the likelihood of making faulty causal inferences. Further, the design is flexible enough to allow for multiple independent variables and, as noted, will allow us to examine both causal specifications simultaneously. The basic model is depicted in figure 8.1.

The endogenous variables are measured at both the first and the second

Figure 8.1
Simple Causal Model for Panel Analysis

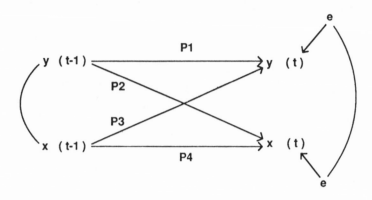

time points, in this case 1975 and 1979. Any further exogenous or control variables are measured at the first time point only. Causal modeling techniques are employed to generate path coefficients. Each endogenous variable is regressed on itself at the earlier time point $(t-1)$ and all other exogenous variables at $t-1$. The standardized beta coefficients are taken as the path coefficients.[49]

The basic equation for this model is thus

$$y(t) = a + By(t-1) + Bx(t-1) + u(t)$$

where

$$
\begin{aligned}
y(t) &= \text{the dependent variable} \\
a &= \text{a constant} \\
B &= \text{a standardized regression coefficient} \\
y(t-1) &= \text{the lagged dependent variable} \\
x(t-1) &= \text{the lagged independent variable} \\
u(t) &= \text{a disturbance term}
\end{aligned}
$$

The results can be interpreted as generating "stability" and "change" coefficients. The horizontal paths in figure 8.1 (P1, P4) represent the amount of stability or continuity present in the variable over time. The diagonal paths (P2, P3), on the other hand, represent change over time. These path coefficients provide an estimate of the impact of the independent variable on the dependent variable over the time period. We may compare the relative magnitudes of the two change coefficients to make causal inferences.[50]

It should be noted that panel designs are almost invariably contaminated by autocorrelation. While this violates one of the assumptions of ordinary least-squares (OLS) regression analysis, it only rarely skews the results to any significant degree. Through the use of controlled simulations, D. Heise has shown that high levels of autocorrelation in panel data, even in conjunction with sizable measurement error, nevertheless produce reliable results.[51]

The Sample

The analysis examines 22 Latin American countries, including ones in Central America and the Caribbean as well as the much larger South American countries (the possible problems associated with examining such diverse cases will be discussed later). The data employed is for the years 1975 and 1979. The analysis thus examines a period in which export-led industrialization policies were clearly established as the most favored development policies in the region and in which regional repression was perhaps at its worst. While the four-year lag is relatively short for a panel analysis, it is reasonable, given the theory discussed above, to expect to witness change over this length of time.

Measuring Repression

Given (1) the lack of academic interest to date, (2) the considerable difficulty in collecting information, and (3) the disinterest among governments to advertise such activities, there is at present no adequate events data on repressive behavior. Thus the problems associated with measuring repression are considerable.[52] A variety of elaborate[53] and ingenious[54] techniques have been employed to overcome these problems. Unfortunately, each continues to suffer from the lack of adequate information. Many events are simply never brought to public attention, and others come to light only long after the fact. Attempts to develop precise internal measures, such as those cited, are thus necessarily of questionable quality. Rather than follow their lead, especially at such an early stage in the research on the NIDL and repression, we will utilize less precise ordinal data.

Two related measures of repression will be employed, each taken from the Freedom House organization. Every year Freedom House ranks every country in the world on two seven-point ordinal scales measuring political and civil rights. These data are far from perfect. The organization's rankings would appear to be influenced to some degree by ideological considerations,[55] and the methodology used in their construction may also be questioned on several counts. However, within certain ideological constraints, the data is at least consistent. The political rights scale looks principally at the effectiveness of electoral and other participatory processes. The civil rights scale, in turn, examines traditional civil liberties and the security of the person. Taken together, they survey most of those activities that are normally labelled repression.[56] In the future we will certainly want to employ more precise and reliable measures, but the Freedom House scales provide us with a starting point.[57]

Measuring the NIDL

No direct measure of the extent to which a country is subsumed within the new international division of labor exists. A structural relationship cannot be directly measured. Rather, we must develop an indicator consistent with the theory. We know that as a country moves into the NIDL, multinationals transfer their assembly processes to the country. They assemble their goods in the LDC and then export them back to the home market. Thus as a country becomes involved in the NIDL, it will increasingly export manufactured goods. We will therefore utilize manufacturing exports as an indicator of a country's integration into the new order. But given the tremendous disparity in the size of the economies we are examining, we cannot simply look at the aggregate value of such exports. Brazil, for instance, will under all circumstances export quantitatively more manufactured goods than Costa Rica. What we are actually interested in is the extent to which the national economy is integrated into the NIDL, regardless of the aggregate size of the economy. Thus the extent to which a country is a part of the NIDL will be measured as the percentage of the country's total exports made up of manufactured goods.[58]

Control Variables

It will be necessary for us to control for the level of societal organization, as well as for economic development and mobilization. Each of these factors can effect the level of repression independent of the NIDL. As Sheahan has noted, state repression is only necessary if the population is at least somewhat organized.[59] Repression is needed because the policies designed to promote export-oriented industrialization involve heavy economic costs, for labor especially but for local capital as well. Repression is necessary to convince these social groups to "accept" these costs. But in the absence of some social organization, the imposition of these costs will not be vigorously opposed, and repression will therefore not be needed, at least in the same quantity. Thus for two countries in an equal position vis-à-vis the NIDL, we would expect to find higher levels of state repression in the society that is more organized. To control for this effect, we will utilize the percentage of the labor force unionized in 1975, as reported by C. L. Taylor and D. Jodice.[60] Given the burden placed on labor, we would clearly expect that a heavily unionized work force would "require" more repression to accept the economic costs of the NIDL than a nonunionized work force.

Similarly, it is important to control for the more general notion of economic development and mobilization. As societies develop, levels of education, literacy, urbanization, communications, and so on are increased. These social developments increase the likelihood and capacity of political opposition and thus of political repression. Rather than use a direct measure of economic development, such as GNP or GDP per capita, which suffer from a lack of comparability due to fluctuations in exchange rates, we will use per capita energy consumption as an indirect measure of development and mobilization. Energy consumption per capita has been shown to be highly correlated with both GNP per capita[61] and other mobilization factors such as literacy and urbanization.[62] The energy consumption data employed is again that reported in Taylor and Jodice for 1975.[63]

The Results

Let us begin by considering some cross-sectional correlations. First, the correlation between the political and civil repression scales in 1975 is .80, and in 1979 it is .77, thereby indicating that political and civil repression represent somewhat different aspects of state repression. While they frequently occur in tandem, they apparently do not always go hand in hand.

Perhaps more interesting are the correlations between our measures of repression and the NIDL. The correlation between NIDL and political repression in 1975 is .41, and that between NIDL and civil repression in 1975 is −.14. It is not the magnitude so much as the sign of these correlations that is interesting. Contrary to what we might have expected, as of 1975 the countries in Latin America most thoroughly integrated into the NIDL were not the most repressive regimes in the region. In contrast, by 1979 these correlations were positive. The correlation between political repression and the NIDL in 1979 is .20, and that between civil repression and the NIDL in 1979 is .34. It appears that important changes took place over the period of this analysis, since by 1979 political and civil repression and export-oriented growth were positively associated.

Figure 8.2 depicts the panel analysis relationships between the political repression scale and the NIDL. Both the magnitudes and the signs of the coefficients are relevant for our purposes.

As predicted by the NIDL theorists, all of the coefficients are positive. Second, as might reasonably be expected, the stability coefficient for political repression is quite large and significant at the .05 level. More interesting is the small size of the NIDL stability coefficient. Very little of the variance in NIDL in 1979 is accounted for by the two independent variables (the R is only .16). Apparently a country's position in the NIDL is largely determined by variables other than its previous position and the amount of repression employed. This finding is inconsistent with those theories that postulate repression as an effective lure for MNC involvement.

Turning to the change coefficients, one can see that the only significant correlation occurs between NIDL 1975 and political repression 1979. This finding lends support to the proposition that as a country moves into the NIDL, one can expect increased repression to follow. The coefficient between political repression 1975 and NIDL 1979 is not significant. When

Figure 8.2
Panel Analysis Relationship between New International
Division of Labor and Political Repression

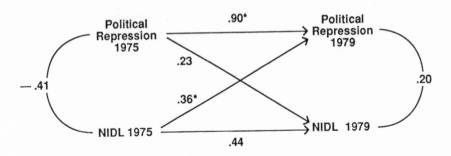

*Significant at .05 or better.

we take these coefficients together with the strong negative cross-sectional correlation between repression and the NIDL in 1975 and the small amount of variance accounted for in NIDL 1979, we must seriously question the proposition that repression attracts global MNCs. It does not appear that this link is nearly as important as the opposite causal specification.

The model depicted in figure 8.2 assumes that unionization and economic development do not interact with the NIDL and repression. When these variables are added to the model, however, the main relationships change very little. The results appear in table 8.3. The coefficients involving the control variables are small and are not significant. This result is surprising and can be interpreted as either a contradiction of a pattern of relationships now well established in research,[64] or, more likely, as an indication that regimes in effect "play it safe" and utilize repression regardless of whether or not the society is significantly mobilized.

In sum, the panel analysis on political repression and the NIDL lends a good deal of support to the contention that as the Latin American countries become integrated into the new division of labor, the regimes in power will increase repression. Conversely, it provides very little support for the theory that increased levels of repression attract multinational corporations and thus help move a country into the NIDL.

The panel analysis using the civil repression scale, as seen in figure 8.3 and table 8.4, produces results virtually identical to those generated with the political repression scale. The magnitudes and the signs of the coefficients exhibit the same pattern. This is true both with and without the control variables. The analysis with civil repression, in other words, simply underscores the conclusions outlined for political repression. Overall, this preliminary test indicates that the new international division of labor is far more important as a cause of repression, either political or civil, than repression is as a cause of the NIDL.

Table 8.3
Estimated Path Coefficients for the Fully Specified Model
(Political Repression)

	Political Repression 1979	NIDL 1979
Political Repression 1975	.91*	.18
NIDL 1975	.37*	.41
Unionization 1975	-.01	.002
Economic Development 1975	.03	-.10

*Significant at .05 or better.

Figure 8.3
Panel Analysis Relationship between New International Division
of Labor and Civil Repression

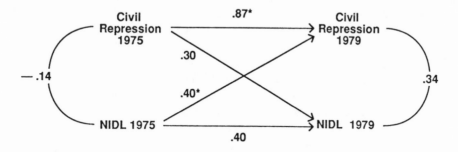

*Significant at .05 or better.

Before proceeding to a discussion of the implications of these findings, we should review the limitations of the analysis. Most disconcerting, of course, is the mix of cases. The problem, as already noted, is that quite diverse countries are examined together. The political and economic structures in Jamaica are quite different from those in Brazil, and export-

Table 8.4
Estimated Path Coefficients for the Fully Specified Model
(Civil Repression)

	Civil Repression 1979	NIDL 1979
Civil Repression 1975	.88*	.27
NIDL 1975	.40*	.38
Unionization 1975	-.09	.03
Economic Development 1975	.07	-.06

*Significant at .05 or better.

oriented industrialization may thus have very different impacts in these settings. More specifically, while smaller countries such as Jamaica may fit the model of assembly-based industrialization closely, those countries with larger internal markets have at least the potential for more integrated industrialization. There is little question, for instance, that the multinationals involved in Brazil are interested in producing for the internal as well as the external market. Moreover, there are great differences in the strength of state structures in Latin America and in their capability to regulate and channel multinational activities. These differences among cases may in the future prove decisive. Without question, further country-specific analyses are needed to examine the development of export-oriented industrialization in all its complexity and with proper consideration for the peculiarities of specific case histories.

A second factor that limits the analysis is the level of aggregation of the NIDL data. It is a measure of all manufacturing exports as a percentage of total exports, not just the manufactured goods representing the assembly processes of MNC affiliates or companies licensed by multinationals. Unfortunately, such micro-level data is not presently available for any country. The NIDL indicator thus includes manufactured exports produced wholly within the Latin American countries, as well as those simply assembled there. But as Helleiner has shown, the role of intrafirm trade and hence of assembled goods is very significant vis-à-vis total LDC trade in manufactures.[65]

Finally, it is important to remember that this analysis only demonstrates an indirect relationship between the NIDL and repression. The structural development of the NIDL can only affect repression through its effects on such variables as wages, inequality, interest rates, and protective tariffs. These changes then impact upon the political process by effecting changes in the legitimacy of the government and the nature and magnitude of political opposition, which in turn lead to increased repression. The analysis here says nothing about the actual route that the influence of the NIDL takes. It does not tell us the weight or relative importance of these intervening variables. Clearly, more detailed analyses will be necessary to determine the exact nature of the linkage between the NIDL and state repression.

CONCLUSION

With the above reservations in mind, this simple analysis does provide us reasonable "clues" as to the direction in which our research should move in the future. It has provided evidence in support of the argument that as countries receive manufacturing investment and pursue export-oriented industrialization, they endure markedly higher levels of repression. This analysis leads us to expect that the formation of a new international division of labor, in Latin America at least, will bring with it an increase in state repression. In the immediate future we should direct our research toward detailed country-specific examinations of the role of the NIDL as a trigger for higher levels of repression.

It is also clear that by 1979 those Latin American countries most thoroughly integrated into the NIDL were, on the average, among the most repressive in the region. Table 8.5 shows the repression scores of the five countries most integrated into the NIDL in 1979, and the five least integrated (roughly the upper and lower 20 percent of the population). The average repression scores of the highly integrated countries are considerably larger than those of the least integrated. Even so, anomalies are apparent. Jamaica, in particular, appears out of place. The political environment in Jamaica is much less repressive than that found in any of the other highly integrated countries. This indicates that repression need not always follow from integration into the NIDL. While a full examination of this is beyond the present analysis, we may speculate that different export strategies, political skill, and/or more thorough ideological domination of a society may allow a regime to combine export-led growth and an open political system. While this is indeed hopeful, we should emphasize that the overall trend is both clear and quite different: in general, as the Latin American countries assume a significant role in the NIDL, they become more repressive.

If these findings are borne out, they have significant implications for political, economic, and social development in Latin America, and perhaps in other regions as well. Export-oriented industrialization policies are

Table 8.5
Political and Civil Repression Scores of the Countries Most and
Least Integrated into the NIDL, 1979

The five countries most integrated:

Country	Political Repression	Civil Repression
Brazil	4	4
El Salvador	4	4
Haiti	7	6
Jamaica	2	3
Uruguay	6	6
Average Score	4.6	4.6

The five countries least integrated:

Country	Political Repression	Civil Repression
Dominican Republic	2	2
Ecuador	5	3
Guyana	4	3
Trinidad and Tobago	2	2
Venezuela	1	2
Average Score	2.8	2.4

currently the norm throughout the Third World. During the 1970s they became the orthodoxy of economic development theory. Most regimes in Latin America, having lost hope in import substitution, have now pinned their hopes for development on the growth and diversification of manufacturing exports.[66] From Mexico to the Southern Cone, regimes have competed to attract global MNCs. Post-1964 Brazil has been considered the flagship state. Its multinational and export-driven "miracle" is seen as a model for all of the others to emulate. But this analysis indicates that the Brazilian model may bring with it severe political and human costs.

For many years Western social scientists and politicians were convinced that political development (defined as increasing democratization) proceeded hand in hand with economic growth and industrialization. In his classic formulation, for instance, S. M. Lipset viewed industrialization as sparking a host of changes that eventually accumulate into the full range of social requisites for democracy.[67] The analysis in this chapter may be added to a variety of others that now challenge this view. Export-oriented industrialization policies, at a general level at least, generate a fair amount of economic growth (perhaps as opposed to genuine development). But on the basis of this analysis it does not appear to generate democracy and non-authoritarian rule. Quite to the contrary, it generates only further state repression.

Thus the questions that face us are, first, whether or not the increased economic growth in any way compensates for the additional repression and human abuse, and second, whether there is necessarily a trade-off to be made between economic growth and political freedom. While the former question is properly directed to our ethicists and moralists, it is clearly affected by the answer to the second question. For if a trade-off is not necessary, who would argue that the economic growth adequately compensates for increased repression? And we, as social scientists, must study and answer the second question.

As evidence contrary to the Lipset-type formulation has accumulated, several analysts have become grudingly convinced that there is a trade-off to be made.[68] The management of economic growth, they note is not an easy task. To be successful, governments must be able to make authoritative decisions that frequently demand short-term sacrifices on the part of individual social groups to further the long-term prospects of the society as a whole. But industrialization stirs up a society. New social groups, goals, and aspirations rapidly form and transform. The maintenance of an open pluralistic political system in such an environment can lead to a system overload. With limited resources, the full range of interests and demands cannot possibly be met. The government cannot make the decisions for long-term economic development. The people are thus free, but forever wretched. These analysts therefore argue that in the short run, at least, a choice must be made between economic growth and political freedom, for only an authoritarian government can successfully manage economic development.

If these analysts are correct, the formation of a new international division of labor may represent a reasonable effort to improve the economic and social condition in Latin America. But must we really choose between economic and political development? In what are perhaps more familiar terms, are authoritarians really the only ones who can make the trains run on time?

Happily, available evidence indicates that the answer is no. While some repressive regimes can make the trains run quite well indeed—the Brazilian regime until recently, for instance—others have been unable to even keep the trains on the tracks (the post-1976 Argentine regime presents a fitting example). Both W. Dick[69] and Sheahan[70] have concluded, on the basis of empirical evidence, that economic growth is not positively correlated with repressive governance. These findings are further substantiated by our own data. If we compute the rank-order correlations between both political and civil repression in 1975 and 1979 with the average annual per capita growth rate from 1970 to 1979, we find that in all cases repression is negatively associated with economic performance.[71] During the 1970s the more repressive Latin American regimes, on average, were economically less successful than their less repressive brethren. We may, in other words, happily agree with I. L. Horowitz when he asserts that "there is certainly no 'iron law' in which human extermination can be coupled with social development."[72] It appears that a choice need not necessarily be made; relatively less repressive regimes can manage economic development. In Latin America, Mexico, Venezuela, and Colombia, while far from perfect, are exemplars of this fact. Given this, it is difficult to imagine a situation in which the growth generated by the NIDL could justify or compensate for increased human abuse.

Regimes throughout Latin America are now pursuing export-oriented growth, and indications are that they will continue to do so for the foreseeable future. The preliminary analysis in this chapter indicates that the NIDL actively promotes state repression. Present economic policies are thus likely to carry a frightful human cost. There are some, such as the generals clinging to power in Chile, who assert that this is a necessary cost of development, but the available evidence does not substantiate them. We can do better, and we should. Our challenge is to devise a means to develop societies socially and economically without retarding them politically. Unfortunately, the present orthodoxy of economic development theory does not appear to provide that formulation.

NOTES

An earlier draft of this paper was presented at the International Studies Association/ Midwest Annual Conference, University of Illinois at Urbana-Champaign, November 15-17, 1984.

1. I. L. Horowitz argues that this is because social scientists have been unwilling to confront issues of life and death. See I. L. Horowitz, *Taking Lives: Genocide and State Power,* 3d ed. (New Brunswick, N.J.: Transaction Books, 1980). By contrast John McCamant argues that we have been unable to study repression for a variety of methodological and epistemological reasons. See John F. McCamant, "Governance without Blood: Social Science's Antiseptic View of Rule; or, The Neglect of Political Repression," in Michael Stohl and George Lopez, eds., *The State as Terrorist* (Westport, Conn.: Greenwood Press, 1984), pp. 11-42. The important point, of course, is that the issue of repression has been routinely ignored by social science.

2. See especially Stohl and Lopez, *The State as Terrorist;* and Michael Stohl and George Lopez, eds., "The State and Terrorism," a special issue of *Chitty's Law Journal* (Winter 1985/86).

3. See F. Frobel, J. Heinrichs, and O. Kreye, "The New International Division of Labour," *Social Science Information* 17, no. 1 (1978): 123-142; and F. Frobel, J. Heinrichs, and O. Kreye, *The New International Division of Labor* (New York: Cambridge University Press, 1980).

4. See P. Vuskovic, "Latin America and the Changing World Economy," *NACLA Report on the Americas* 14 (1980): 3-15; J. Petras, *Class, State, and Power in the Third World* (London: Zed Press, 1981); and E. Herman, *The Real Terror Network* (Boston: South End Press, 1982).

5. K. Erickson and P. Peppe, "Dependent Capitalist Development, U.S. Foreign Policy, and Repression of the Working Class in Chile and Brazil," *Latin American Perspectives* 3, no. 1 (1976): 19-44.

6. J. Sheahan, "Market-oriented Economic Policies and Political Repression in Latin America," *Economic Development Cultural Change* 28, no. 2 (1980): 267-292.

7. D. Pion-Berlin, "Ideas as Predictors: A Comparative Study of Coercion in Peru and Argentina" (Ph.D. diss., Political Science, University of Denver, 1984).

8. H. Feith, "Repressive-Developmentalist Regimes in Asia," *Alternatives* 7, no. 4 (1978): 491-506.

9. Ibid., p. 497.

10. The countries included in the analysis are Argentina, Bolivia, Brazil, Chile, Colombia, Costa Rica, the Dominican Republic, Ecuador, El Salvador, Guatemala, Guyana, Haiti, Honduras, Jamaica, Mexico, Nicaragua, Panama, Paraguay, Peru, Trinidad and Tobago, Uruguay, and Venezuela.

11. See N. Bukharin, *Imperialism and World Economy* (New York: Monthly Review Press, 1973).

12. See R. Prebisch, *Change and Development: Latin America's Great Task* (New York: Praeger, 1971).

13. See, for instance, M. Wionczek, *Some Key Issues for the World Periphery* (New York: Pergamon Press, 1982).

14. See D. B. Keesing, "Outward Looking Policies and Economic Development," *Economic Journal* 77, no. 2 (1967): 303-320; and H. G. Johnson, "International Trade and Economic Development," in P. Streeten, ed., *Trade Strategies for Development* (New York: John Wiley and Sons, 1973).

15. S. Hymer, "The Multinational Corporation and the International Division of Labor," in Robert B. Cohen et al., eds., *The Multinational Corporation: A Radical Approach* (New York: Cambridge University Press, 1979), pp. 140-164.

16. M. Sharpston, "International Sub-Contracting," *Oxford Economic Papers* 27, no. 1 (1975): 94-139.

17. D. Nayyer, "Transnational Corporations and Manufactured Exports from Poor Countries," *Economic Journal* 88, no. 1 (1978): 59-84.

18. G. Helleiner, "Manufactured Exports from Less-Developed Countries and Multinational Firms," *Economic Journal* 83, no. 1 (1973): 21-47; idem., *Intra-Firm Trade and the Developing Countries* (New York: St. Martin's Press, 1981).

19. G. Adam, "Multinational Corporations and Worldwide Sourcing," in H. Radice, ed., *International Firms and Modern Imperialism* (Harmondsworth: Penguin Books, 1975).

20. This, of course, is largely dependent upon the size of the country's internal market. In a country such as Brazil or Mexico, a global MNC may be interested in servicing the domestic LDC as well as the original home market. The implications of this will be discussed later.

21. For a discussion of these problems, see Helleiner, *Intra-Firm Trade,* pp. 14-43.

22. Vuskovic, "Latin America," p. 4.

23. M. Landsberg, "Export-led Industrialization in the Third World: Manufacturing Imperialism," *Review of Radical Political Economics* 11, no. 4. (1979): 50-63.

24. Helleiner, *Intra-Firm Trade,* p. 36.

25. Wionczek, *Some Key Issues,* pp. 159-161.

26. F. Parkinson, "Latin America, Her Newly Industrializing Countries, and the New International Economic Order," *Journal of Latin American Studies* 16, no. 1 (1984): 127-141.

27. Petras, *Class, State, and Power,* pp. 118-119.

28. See Keesing, "Outward Looking Policies," and Johnson, "International Trade"; also H. B. Chenery and H. Hughes, "The International Division of Labor: The Case of Industry," in Society for International Development, ed., *Towards a New World Economy* (Rotterdam: Rotterdam University Press, 1972).

29. See Petras, *Class, State, and Power;* Landsberg, "Export-led Industrialization"; and Vuskovic, "Latin America."

30. It may be possible, however, to parlay MNC investment into some vertical linkages. L.Y.C. Lim and P. E. Fong, "Vertical Linkages and Multinational Enterprises in Developing Countries," *World Development* 10, no. 7 (1982): 585-595, have shown that Singapore has had some good fortune in this area.

31. P. Meller and A. Mizala, "U.S. Multinationals and Latin American Manufacturing Employment Absorption," *World Development* 10, no. 2 (1982): 115-126.

32. H. Wiarda, "Corporatism and Development in the Iberic-Latin World: Persistent Strains and New Variations," in F. Pike and T. Stritch, eds., *The New Corporatism* (Notre Dame, Ind.: University of Notre Dame Press, 1974).

33. J. Sloan, "State Repression and Enforcement Terrorism in Latin America," in Stohl and Lopez, *The State as Terrorist,* pp. 83-98.

34. See B. Loveman and T. Davies, *The Politics of AntiPolitics* (Lincoln: University of Nebraska Press, 1978); and K. Remmer, "Political Demobilization in Chile, 1973-1978," *Comparative Politics* 12, no. 3 (1980): 275-302.

35. Feith, "Repressive-Developmentist Regimes," p. 497; emphasis added.

36. Nayyer, "Transnational Corporation."

37. Ibid., p. 77.

38. R. W. Moxon, "Offshore Production in LDCs," Graduate School of Business Administration, New York University, *Bulletin* (1974).

39. See R. Falk, *Human Rights and State Sovereignty* (New York: Holmes and Meier, 1981).

40. Reported in R. Barnet and R. Müller, *Global Reach* (New York: Simon and Schuster, 1974), pp. 153-156.

41. Vuskovic, "Latin America," p. 15; emphasis added.

42. See F. H. Cardoso and E. Faletto, *Dependency and Development in Latin America* (Berkeley and Los Angeles: University of California Press, 1979); and P. Evans, *Dependent Development: The Alliance of Multinational, State, and Local Capital in Brazil* (Princeton: Princeton University Press, 1979).

43. Barnet and Müller, *Global Reach,* p. 155.

44. L. S. Stavrianos, *Global Rift: The Third World Comes of Age* (New York: William Morrow, 1981).

45. See Paul Sigmund, "Free-Market Authoritarianism," and Marvin Weinstein, "Military Rule and Economic Failure," both in R. Wesson, ed., *Politics, Policies, and Economic Development in Latin America* (Stanford, Calif.: Hoover Institution Press, 1984); and North American Congress on Latin America (NACLA), "Domination by Debt: Finance Capital in Argentina," *NACLA Report on the Americas* 12, no. 4 (1978): 21-38.

46. Barnet and Müller, *Global Reach,* p. 150.

47. See R. Lagos and O. Rufatt, "Military Government and Real Wages in Chile: A Note," *Latin American Research Review* 10, no. 2 (1975): 139-146; and J. Ramos, "A Comment to 'Military Government and Real Wages in Chile,' " *Latin American Research Review* 12, no. 1 (1977): 173-176.

48. Sheahan, "Market-oriented Economic Policies," p. 275.

49. See H. Asher, *Causal Modeling* (Beverly Hills: Sage, 1976); and G. Markus, *Analyzing Panel Data* (Beverly Hills: Sage, 1979).

50. D. Heise, "Causal Inference from Panel Data," in E. Borgatta and G. Bohrnstedt, eds., *Sociological Methodology* (San Francisco: Jossey-Bass, 1970).

51. See Heise, "Causal Inference," as well as D. Pelz and R. Lew, "Heise's Causal Model Applied," in Borgatta and Bohrnstedt, *Sociological Methodology.*

52. See J. McCamant, "A Critique of Present Measures of 'Human Rights Development' and an Alternative," in V. Nanda, J. Scarritt, and G. Shepherd, eds., *Global Human Rights: Public Policies, Comparative Measures, and NGO Strategies* (Boulder, Colo.: Westview Press, 1981); M. Stohl, D. Carleton, and S. Johnson, "Human Rights and U.S. Foreign Assistance: From Nixon to Carter," *Journal of Peace Research* 21, no. 3 (1984): 215-226; D. Carleton and M. Stohl, "The Foreign Policy of Human Rights: Rhetoric and Reality from Jimmy Carter to Ronald Reagan," *Human Rights Quarterly* 7, no. 2 (1985): 205-229; and C. Mitchell, M. Stohl, D. Carleton, and G. Lopez, "State Terrorism: Issues of Concept and Measurement," in M. Stohl and G. Lopez, eds., *Government Violence and Repression: An Agenda for Research* (Westport, Conn.: Greenwood Press, 1986).

53. See Ernest Duff and John F. McCamant, *Violence and Repression in Latin America* (New York: Free Press, 1976).

54. See Lars Schoultz, "U.S. Foreign Policy and Human Rights Violations in Latin America: A Comparative Analysis of Foreign Aid Distributions," *Comparative Politics* 13, no. 2 (1981): 149-170.

55. Freedom House is generally recognized to be politically conservative. On the surface it would appear that leftist governments are evaluated with a keener eye than are rightist governments. For example, Panama under Omar Torrijos consistently received ranks of 6 and 7. At the same time, the Guatemalan regime, during a period in which Amnesty International and other monitoring organizations documented many thousands of state-sponsored murders, received rankings of 3 and 4.

56. For a complete discussion of these indices, see Ray Gastil, *Freedom in the World: Political Rights and Civil Liberties, 1980* (Westport, Conn.: Greenwood Press, 1980), pp. 1-76; and for critiques of them, see both McCamant, "Critique of Present Measures," pp. 123-146, and Mitchell, Stohl, Carleton, and Lopez, "State Terrorism," pp. 1-26. See also H. Scoble and L. Wiseberg, "Problems of Compara-

tive Research in Human Rights," in Nanda, Scarritt, and Shepherd, *Global Human Rights,* pp. 147-171.

57. Toward this end, there is work aimed at developing more precise and reliable measures of repression. See R. Bissell, C. Haignere, J. McCamant, and M. Picklo, *Varieties of Political Repression* (Unpublished manuscript, 1978); and J. Dominguez, "Assessing Human Rights Conditions," in J. Dominguez, N. Rodley, B. Wood, and R. Falk, *Enhancing Global Human Rights* (New York: McGraw-Hill, 1979).

58. The operational definition of manufactured goods employed is that utilized by UNCTAD. This definition is generally accepted in the current NIDL literature. Manufactured goods are taken to consist of Standard International Trade Classification (SITC) categories 5, 6, 7, and 8, minus 6-7 and 6-8.

59. Sheahan, "Market-oriented Economic Policies," p. 272.

60. C. L. Taylor and D. Jodice, *World Handbook of Political and Social Indicators,* 3d ed. (New Haven: Yale University Press, 1983), vol. 3.

61. J. Darmstader, *Energy in the World Economy* (Baltimore: Johns Hopkins Press, 1971).

62. P. Coulter, *Social Mobilization and Liberal Democracy* (Lexington, Mass.: Lexington Books, 1975).

63. Taylor and Jodice, *World Handbook,* vol. 1.

64. See K. Deutsch, "Social Mobilization and Political Development," *American Political Science Review* 55, no. 3 (1961): 493-514; and M. Olson, "Rapid Growth as a Destabilizing Force," *Journal of Economic History* 23 (1963): 529-552.

65. Helleiner, "Manufactured Exports."

66. See both Wionczek, *Some Key Issues,* and Parkinson, "Latin America," as well as B. Balassa, *The Newly Industrializing Countries in the World Economy* (New University Press, 1971).

67. S. M. Lipset, *Political Man* (Garden City, N.Y.: Anchor Books, 1963).

68. See, for instance, S. Huntington and J. Nelson, *No Easy Choice* (Cambridge, Mass.: Harvard University Press, 1976); and from a very different perspective, R. Heilbroner, *An Inquiry into the Human Prospect* (New York: W. W. Norton, 1980).

69. W. Dick, "Authoritarian versus Nonauthoritarian Approaches to Economic Development," *Journal of Political Economy* 82 (1974): 817-827.

70. Sheahan, "Market-oriented Economic Policies," p. 275.

71. The corrections are as follows:

	Political Repression		Civil Repression	
	1975	1979	1975	1979
Economic Growth, 1970-1979	−.10	−.31	−.19	−.25

The data on economic growth rates was taken from R. Hansen, *U.S. Foreign Policy and the Third World: Agenda 1982* (New York: Praeger, 1982), app. B.

72. Horowitz, *Taking Lives,* p. 54.

9

Agricultural Development, Political Violence, and State Militarization in Central America

C. Micheal Schwartz and Harry R. Targ _____

AGRICULTURAL MODERNIZATION AND THE EXPORT MODEL

The historic system of colonialism and neocolonialism has shaped and distorted the economies of the Third World.[1] In the nineteenth and twentieth centuries the Third World has generally been consigned to produce a small array of primary products (raw materials or unprocessed agricultural goods) for sale to the industrial nations. In return, foreign exchange is generated that enables Third World nations to purchase manufactured goods. Adam Smith wrote of the relative advantages of this system of trade 200 years ago:

The revenue of a trading and manufacturing country must, other things being equal, always be much greater than that of one without trade or manufactures. . . . A trading and manufacturing country, therefore, naturally purchases with a small part of its manufactured produce a great part of the rude produce of other countries; while, on the contrary, a country without trade and manufactures is generally obliged to purchase, at the expense of a great part of its rude produce, a very small part of the manufactured produce of other countries. . . . The inhabitants of the one must always enjoy a much greater quantity of subsistence than what their own lands, in the actual state of their cultivation, could afford. The inhabitants of the other must always enjoy a much smaller quantity.[2]

Modern theorists writing from a Third World perspective see the Smith formulation as providing a basic explanation for underdevelopment and dependency. It is argued that the world capitalist system is decomposable into a center and a periphery structure of political and economic relations by virtue of which has occurred the "development of underdevelopment" or, at best, "dependent development," a "dependence" determined by the demands of accumulation in the world economy.[3]

Early contributions to the "doctrine of unequal exchange" view the monopsonist control of international trade by the center and the subsequent deterioration in the terms of trade for periphery commodities as a primary mechanism by which surplus value derived in the periphery is appropriated by the center.[4] Dependency theorists such as Andre Gunder Frank also argue that the process of capital accumulation within the international political economy reproduces center-periphery distributions of wealth and power within nations as well as between nations.[5] While many international specialists were willing long ago to concede the existence of inequalities in economic interchanges between nations of the center and periphery, they were less willing to consider the relationship between unequal exchanges in international relations and exploitative class relations within periphery countries.[6] It was only in the 1970s that North American scholars began to take seriously the connections between the international political economy and class struggle in the Third World.

Interestingly enough, the vehicle for capital accumulation and exploitation alluded to by Adam Smith in 1776 remains a central means by which unequal exchange in the international system is perpetuated and exploitation within Third World countries is fostered. That is, Third World countries still produce basic raw materials and agricultural commodities for export. Granted, many countries such as the so-called "newly industrializing countries" are exporting their cheap labor embodied in manufactured goods. Even some countries that rely on their agricultural export platforms have enterprise zones where cheap labor assembles finished goods for return to the United States, Western Europe, or Japan. Nevertheless, the majority of Third World nations have export profiles based on a few primary products, of which agricultural commodities are the most dominant.[7]

Particularly since the end of World War II, Third World economies have been influenced to promote the sectors for which they have a "comparative advantage." Given the cyclical character of the international economy, it has often been lucrative for Third World economic oligarchies during periods of great demand and high prices to increase the production of products destined for export to the core. Consequently, historic dependencies on the export of primary products have been reinforced. Rather than agricultural and/or industrial diversification, many Third World countries have pursued an intensified agricultural export policy.

To facilitate the agricultural export model of development, the landowning ruling classes in many countries pursue policies of land expropriation and increased exploitation of agricultural labor. The centerpiece, however, of the agricultural export model is agricultural modernization. The assumption underlying agricultural modernization in the Third World is that with the appropriate application of modern agricultural technology, quantities of food will be produced for increased domestic food consumption and, more importantly, for exportation. Foreign exchange earnings from agricultural exports are expected to provide the base for capital accumulation and overall economic development.

Agricultural modernization includes the utilization of high-yield seeds, chemical fertilizers, and pesticides. The higher yields and often larger land areas under cultivation also require, as part of the modernization package, technologically advanced agricultural machinery. The full panoply of agricultural modernization inputs has yielded impressive results.[8] Consequently, agricultural modernizaton has been promoted by corporate agribusiness, international financial agencies such as the World Bank, and the ruling elite within Third World countries.[9]

AGRICULTURAL MODERNIZATION, CLASS FORMATION, AND POLITICAL VIOLENCE IN THE THIRD WORLD

The literature critical of agricultural modernization in the Third World argues that such policies increase inequalities between the economic elite of the Third World and the vast majority of workers and peasants. While producing more food for export, agricultural modernization destroys the basis for food production and consumption in rural areas, creating a poor and hungry rural population.[10] The relationship between hunger and social inequality is well documented.[11] Furthermore, increasing social inequality and rural impoverishment in the Third World, due to export-oriented agricultural development policies, results in a fundamental transformation of the class structure. As Cheryl Christensen states:

Existing "unreformed" structures of inequality impede the diffusion of improved techniques and generate a wide range of "perverse effects" . . . including greater relative and absolute impoverishment of economically marginal groups, more polarized structures for the generation and control of wealth, and reinforced links between economic elites and political control.[12]

The profit to be gained from increased agricultural exports encourages traditional landowning classes and some medium-sized farmers to increase productivity. Increased production requires some combination of more land, an expandable and expendable cheap labor supply, advanced agricultural machinery, and the latest innovations in high-yield agricultural inputs.[13] The traditional ruling classes use their power to drive subsistence-producing peasants off the land by force, debt, or state decree. The peasants, dispossessed of their land, become transient agricultural laborers or part of the increasing Third World migration from rural to urban areas. The larger landholdings rationalize the utilization of agricultural modernization inputs, including the purchase of expensive, imported machinery. The end result is a further polarization of what is referred to in Central

America as the "economic oligarchy" and the marginalized peasant population.

To complete the cycle, the large tracts of land appropriated for the production of export crops with high-yield agricultural inputs and advanced machinery increase the quantity of exports of these favored agricultural commodities. The earnings derived from agricultural exports are appropriated by the landowning oligarchies. These earnings are ploughed into more production of export crops, foreign bank holdings, financial speculation, or investment in the manufacturing sector. Given the multiplicity of sources to which the profits may go, the probability of their use for economic growth is small, and the positive impact on the indigenous peasants is zero.[14]

Finally, the expropriation of land for the production of export crops violates rural cultural traditions by destroying communal patterns of ownership and subsistence production while proletarianizing the rural labor force. The history of such rural transformation is replete with examples of resistance and revolution. To facilitate these expropriations in the face of resistance, the Third World state in the service of the economic oligarchy imports a sophisticated military technology to repress the rebellious population. Military technology becomes a critical element of agricultural development. In sum, a significant by-product of Third World agricultural development is resistance from the victimized population and retaliatory state violence.[15]

AGRICULTURAL DEVELOPMENT IN CENTRAL AMERICA

The five Central American countries emerging from the Federal Republic of Central America in the 1840s (Costa Rica, El Salvador, Guatemala, Honduras, and Nicaragua) have experienced economic activity dominated by export agriculture. Each of these nations is ruled by an economic oligarchy in concert with foreign (center) economic interests.[16] According to Samir Amin, this alliance develops agricultural and industrial production in the periphery to meet the requirements of accumulation at the center.[17]

Briefly, the history of agricultural development in these countries suggests the following stages.[18] First, after independence from Spain, the Central American republics experienced struggle among rival factions for control of the new states. After these battles were fought, each country from 1850 to 1870 became more incorporated into the world economy by virtue of the development of commercial agriculture. "The region thus became permanently linked to the world economy, expanding from the impact of the industrial revolution; internally, commercial agriculture with coffee and then bananas as its focus permitted the establishment of an increasingly important economic structure."[19]

Second, as the single-crop economies became more integrated into the global political economy, the Spanish and mixed-race wealthy classes began to consolidate their power and to expand their land holdings. In El Salvador, for example, communal lands were abolished in 1882. As Tommie Sue Montgomery reports, "Within a few short years the best land in the country was concentrated in the hands of the 'Fourteen Families' who, also by then, had control of the state."[20]

Third, after the accomplishment of oligarchical control of the land and consolidation of agricultural exports, the Central American countries in the twentieth century expanded coffee, banana, sugar, and cotton exports.

In one case after another, the "civilizing mission of coffee" brought about an opportunity for consolidating for the first time a stable, consensual sort of political power. In the context of Central America, what we call "oligarchic domination" was the social predominance of the agrarian classes: the owners of the large coffee plantations and the merchants, who monopolized coffee processing . . . and foreign trade. The authority of this class grew along with expansion of the export economy, and it afforded an opportunity for advances in the building of the nation-state.[21]

A fourth period since World War II has been characterized by Central America's continued reliance on its historic export crops, despite declining world market prices, coupled with two or three new agricultural products added to the export matrix as foreign demand dictated. Sugar, cotton, and meat production, supplementing coffee and banana exports, "has reinforced our dependent articulation with the U.S. market.[22] With the coming of the Central American Common Market and the Alliance for Progress in the 1960s, foreign investors and the economic oligarchs extended productivity into manufacturing goods. The traditional agrarian-based oligarchs were major investors, so that industrialization did not alter the distribution of wealth and power in the Central American nations except by increasing the inequalities between rich and poor.

The general profile of Central American economies in this period as to agricultural modernization (imports of agricultural machines) and export orientation (exports of agricultural products) is illustrated in table 9.1. The importation of agricultural machinery increased in all countries between 1965 and 19765 (increases were modes in Guatemala and Nicaragua), and the dollar value of agricultural exports more than doubled during this period.

AGRICULTURAL DEVELOPMENT, POLITICAL VIOLENCE, AND STATE MILITARIZATION

The transformation of the means of production and hence of the social relations of production in the countryside destroys the social fabric of rural life for the peasant population. It is recognized that the quality of life for workers and peasants in both the colonial and the neocolonial periods was never adequate, but stable patterns of labor and subsistence production of goods for use may characterize periods before radical change in the nature

Table 9.1
Machine Inputs and Agricultural Exports in Central America

Country	Year	Imports of Agricultural Machines (1000 dollars)	Exports of agricultural Products (1000 dollars)
Costa Rica	1965	$ 3,100	$ 92,600
	1975	16,843	340,372
El Salvador	1965	4,200	147,400
	1975	15,850	348,551
Guatamala	1965	7,700	157,350
	1975	9,000	434,187
Honduras	1965	2,400	90,900
	1975	12,736	166,459
Nicaragua	1965	8,600	124,800
	1975	9,814	227,177

Source: Food and Agricultural Organization (FAO), *Production Yearbook,* various volumes.

of agricultural production. Consequently, the initial expropriation of lands by the economic oligarchs in the nineteenth century caused resistance, as did further seizures in the twentieth century.

This chapter predicts that the quantum leap in agricultural modernization and agricultural export production in the 1960s and 1970s impacted on peasants and agricultural workers the way early consolidation did. That is, peasants were further expelled from their properties or became underemployed agricultural workers as the plantations, farms, and cattle ranches got bigger and bigger.[23] Peasants were forced deeper into the money economy that in modern times has been unable to provide jobs for them to earn enough to survive.

These conditions are the breeding ground for resistance and rebellion. Peasants begin to organize to demand economic justice. Organization takes several forms, from Christian-based communities to insurgent movements that seek revolutionary change. In turn, economic oligarchs of Central America have committed themselves to oppose social and economic change that threatens their elite status. Typically, nonviolent forms of rebellion generate hostility and violence from the state such that peasants and workers often view armed revolutionary actions as the only means of change.

As has been suggested, the economic oligarchies that influence, indeed dominate, the regimes in Central America have a history of resisting changes

in the social and economic status quo. Historically, their treatment of
workers and peasants has been marked with violations of human rights.
They know that economic changes to extract further profit from agricultural production generate resistance. In anticipation of and in reaction to
acts of resistance they prepare for violence. Utilizing the state, they seek
increased military assistance to provide the tools for repression, and as
rebellion escalates, they look for more military support as circumstances
dictate.[24]

HYPOTHESES

The analysis to follow empirically examines the relationships discussed
earlier between agricultural development and (1) acts of political violence
and (2) state militarization. In accordance with Miles Wolpin, "militarization" is structurally defined here as "the allocation of increasing resources
to the armed forces."[25] The study area of the analysis is the five Central
American nations of Costa Rica, El Salvador, Guatemala, Honduras, and
Nicaragua.

Three prevalent dimensions of agricultural development in Central
America are hypothesized to directly affect the level of political violence: (1)
agricultural modernization, (2) the development of agricultural export production, and (3) the marginalization of the rural populace. Briefly, agricultural modernization is expected to cause increased levels of political
violence due to its impact on the proletarianization of the social relations of
agricultural production. As discussed earlier, the transformation of the
social relations of agricultural production has detrimental consequences for
a large proportion of the rural populace, who in turn engage in acts of
political violence as a form of resistance. While the development of agricultural export production entails a transformation of the social relations of
agricultural production as well, the independent effect of agricultural
export production is in the extent to which its development necessitates the
direct expropriation of land and other productive resources from peasant,
domestic crop production. Finally, impoverishment of the rural masses is
expected to directly affect the level of political violence in that political
violence often represents the only recourse available to Central America's
rural masses, who are without and are being denied access to a means of
subsistence. A core multivariate model of the hypothesized causal effect of
agricultural modernization, agricultural export production, and rural impoverishment on political violence is diagrammed in figure 9.1.

State militarization is also hypothesized to be directly affected by the
three dimensions of agricultural development affecting political violence as
well as by political violence itself. A core multivariate model of the hypothesized causal effects of agricultural development and political violence on
state militarization is presented in figure 9.2.

Figure 9.1
A Core Multivariate Model of Agricultural Development
Determinants of Political Violence

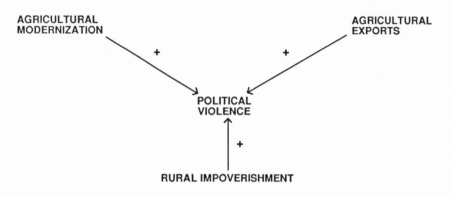

Figure 9.2
A Core Multivariate Model of State Militarization

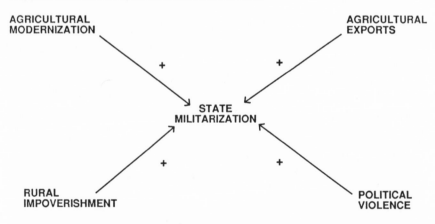

It is hypothesized that state militarization is viewed by the economic oligarchies as a necessary counterpart of agricultural development. State militarization is necessary in order for the oligarchies to impose and maintain the transformation of the social relations of agricultural production associated with agricultural modernization. It is also of some necessity for the expropriation and control of land and other productive resources required for the development of agricultural export production. The independent effect, however, of the development of agricultural export production on state militarization is that with increased agricultural export production the state will be better able to afford the cost of militarization.[26] Furthermore, as Central American nations expand their production of agricultural exports, they also increase their importance as trade partners in inter-national trade. Consequently, they are more likely to receive military assistance from their more developed and principal trade partners.[27]

In addition, the anticipation by ruling elites of the political violence associated with both agricultural modernization and export production is expected to heighten the push for state militarization. Most importantly, it is the anticipation of political violence that is hypothesized to be the relation between rural impoverishment and state militarization. As the size of the rural populace that is impoverished in proportion to the total population increases, the anticipation of political violence and hence the level of state militarization is expected to increase as well.

Finally, it is expected that the actual level of political violence will directly impact upon the level of state militarization. The expected direction of this relation is straightforward. As actual acts of political violence increase, so will state militarization.

DATA AND RESEARCH DESIGN

The primary sources of information on agricultural modernization, agricultural export production, and rural marginalization are the United Nations Food and Agriculture Organization's *Production Yearbook* and *Trade Yearbook*.[28] The level of commitment to agricultural modernization is operationalized by the per capita number of tractors imported. The per capita dollar value of agricultural exports is utilized to measure the level of development of export agricultural production. The percent of the economically active population employed in agriculture is utilized to measure the level of impoverishment of the rural populace.

Political violence is operationalized as the logged per capita number of "armed attacks." The per capita number of armed attacks is logged due to the skewed distribution of this indicator. "Armed attack" is defined by the *World Handbook of Political and Social Indicators* as "an act of violent political conflict carried out by (or on behalf of) an organized group with the object of weakening or destroying the power exercised by another organized group." This includes acts by antistate groups as well as acts by the state itself. For example, if insurgent forces attack a government post and the National Guard counterattacks, this would be recorded in the *World Handbook* as two acts of armed attack.[29]

State militarization is measured by the per capita dollar value of actual U.S. military assistance. This includes arms transfers, subsidized arms purchases, and military training and education. Since the United States is a preeminent trading partner of Central America, as provider of agricultural and military technology as well as consumer of agricultral commodities, this measure seems an appropriate indicator of state militarization for this region. The source of this data is the *Statistical Abstract of Latin America*.[30]

A commonly utilized alternative measure of militarization, also presented in the *Statistical Abstract of Latin America,* is military expenditures as a percent of the gross domestic product (GDP).[31] This measure is not used here because generally 30 percent of the GDP of the five Central American nations included in this analysis is determined by agricultural production. Hence the use of GDP as a denominator in the dependent variable confounds correlation and regression analysis with two of our primary explanatory variables, agricultural export production and the percent of the economically active population employed in agriculture.

The data is structured in a manner referred to by econometricians as "pooled cross-sectional and time series data."[32] For each of the variables the data covers a seven-year time period with one observation for each year. This time series or longitudinal data is then pooled cross-sectionally: in this case, across the five Central American nations under investigation. An attribute of pooled cross-sectional and time series data is that it incorporates both cross-sectional and longitudinal sources of variance. For this analysis it also has the advantage of increasing the statistical N to 35, which is the product of the five cross-sectional cases and the seven longitudinal observations.

Except for tractor imports, the period of observation is from 1971 to 1977; for tractor imports the period is 1964 to 1970. Based on studies of social change in the Third World, the seven-year lag for tractor imports is considered the appropriate period in which to gauge the effect of agricultural modernization on political violence and state militarization.[33] Similarly, seven years is considered the maximum period over which to pool the data. As argued by Edward Muller in his work on income inequality, regime repressiveness, and political violence, periods of ten years might mask significant short-term change in political violence.[34] The same can be said for change that might occur in each of the other variables.

BIVARIATE RELATIONS

The correlation coefficients for the bivariate relations between the variables are presented in table 9.2. The correlations tend to support the hypothesized relations between the three dimensions of agricultural development and political violence. The coefficients for armed attacks with tractor imports, agricultural imports, and the percent of the economically active population employed in agriculture are in the hypothesized direction and are of a significant magnitude.

In addition, with the exception of the bivariate correlation between U.S. military assistance and the percent of the eocnomically active population employed in agriculture, the coefficients tend to support the hypothesized relations between state militarization and agricultural development and

Table 9.2
Pearson Correlations

	Tractor Imports #	% Employed in Agriculture	Agricultural Exports $	Armed Attacks
Tractor Imports #	*******			
% Employed in Agricultural	-.34 *	*******		
Agricultural Exports $	.47 *	-.78 *	******	
Armed Attacks	.48 *	-.39 *	.39 *	******
U.S. Military Assistance	.21 **	-.02	.35 *	.28 *

*Significant at p = .05.
**Significant at p = .10.

political violence. The absence of a significant correlation between U.S. military assistance and agricultural employment calls into question, at the bivariate level at least, the hypothesized relation between rural impoverishment and state militarization.

MULTIVARIATE ANALYSIS

While bivariate correlations provide a preliminary examination of the direction and strength of hypothesized relations between the variables, regression analysis is required to appropriately test the multivariate models specified above and illustrated in figures 9.1 and 9.2. The advantage of multivariate regression analysis is that it allows for the estimation of the effect of a given explanatory variable while controlling for the effect of the other explanatory variables in the model. The estimated regression coefficients can also be used to detect spurious or suppressed bivariate relations.

The regression equation estimating the parameters of the core model of political violence can be written as follows:

$$Y1 = a + bX1 + bX2 + bX3 \tag{1}$$

where

   $Y1$ = per capita number of armed attacks, 1971-1977
   a = constant
   b = standardized regression coefficient (beta)
   $X1$ = per capita number of tractor imports, 1964-1970
   $X2$ = per capita dollar value of agricultural exports, 1971-1977
   $X3$ = % of the economically active population employed
        in agriculture, 1971-1977

The equation estimating the parameters of the core model of state militarization is similar:

$$Y2 = a + bX1 + bX2 + bX3 + bX4 \tag{2}$$

where

   $Y2$ = per capita dollar value of U.S. military assistance, 1971-1977
   $X4$ = per capita number of armed attacks, 1971-1977

Table 9.3 reports the estimated parameters for equation 1, regressing political violence on tractor imports, agricultural exports, and agricultural employment. In the full equation (3.1) only the lagged, per capita number of tractor imports and the percent of the economically active population employed in agriculture are estimated to have a significant effect on armed attacks. Equation 3.2 reports the results after stepwise deletion of the explanatory variable (per capita dollar value of agricultural exports) for which the estimated standardized regression coefficient was not of significant magnitude. The adjusted R^2 increases somewhat and, given the small sample size, is of a significant magnitude. Figure 9.3 illustrates the observed causal paths in the core multivariate model of political violence.

As determined from comparison of the standardized regression coefficients (.39 and $-.26$ respectively), the explanatory variable of primary importance is the per capita number of tractor imports; of secondary but still significant importance is the effect of the percent of the economically active population employed in agriculture. These regression coefficients replicate the bivariate findings of a positive, lagged relation between tractor imports and armed attacks as well as the inverse relation between agricultural employment and armed attacks. The standardized regression coefficients support the theoretical argument that agricultural modernization in Central America, as one dimension of agricultural development, independently affects the level of political violence. As argued earlier, political violence is the result of agricultural modernization's transformation of the social relations of agricultural production. The transformation of the social relations of agricultural production, commonly

Table 9.3
Political Violence Regressions ($N = 35$)

	intercept	Tractor Imports 1964-71	Agricultural Exports 1971-77	Agricultural Employment % 1971-77
(3.1) Armed Attacks 1971-77	= .46	.38 *	.05	-.23 **
Adjusted R^2 =	.22			
(3.2) Armed Attacks 1964-71	= .27	.39 *		-.26 **
Adjusted R^2 =	.26			

*p = .05.
**p = .10.

manifested in the proletarianization of the rural labor force, is both forced upon and resisted by the rural populace, resulting in political violence.

Similarly, the negative coefficient for the regressed effect of agricultural employment on political violence supports the theoretical contention that rural impoverishment directly affects the level of political violence. As agricultural employment declines (increasing impoverishment), political violence increases.

The small magnitude of the standardized regression coefficient estimating the effect of agricultural exports on armed attacks indicates that when we control for tractor imports and agricultural employment, the strong bivariate relation between agricultural exports and armed attacks ($r = .39$) is spurious. In fact, the strong bivariate relation between agricultural exports and armed attacks is a reflection of the strong negative relation between agricultural exports and agricultural employment ($r = -.78$) and the subsequent negative relation between agricultural employment and armed attacks ($r = -.39$). Thus when the effect of agricultural employment on armed attacks is controlled, the spurious bivariate relation between agricultural exports and armed attacks is reduced to a nonsignificant level.

Theoretically this finding suggests that the development of agricultural export production, insofar as this necessitates the expropriation of land and monopoly control by the economic oligarchies of other productive resources, does not have a direct effect on political violence. Development of agricultural export production can be expected to affect political violence only indirectly through its impact on rural impoverishment.

Figure 9.3
Observed Direct Causal Paths in the Core Multivariate Models of
Political Violence and State Militarization

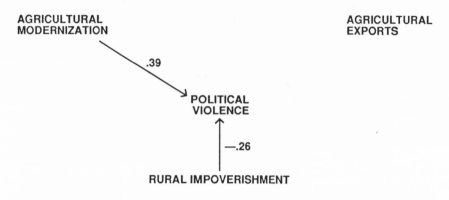

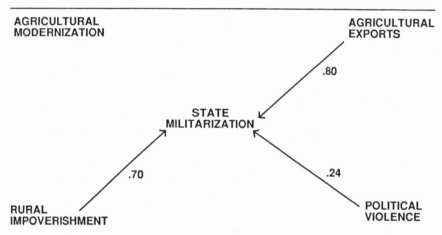

Table 9.4 reports the estimated parameters of equation 9.2, regressing state militarization on tractor imports, agricultural exports, agricultural employment, and armed attacks. Equation 4.1 presents the full equation, and equation 4.2 presents the parameter estimates after per capita number of tractor imports is deleted due to its nonsignificant explanatory contribution. The observed causal paths in the core multivariate model of state militarization are illustrated in figure 9.3.

Both the per capita dollar value of agricultural exports and the percent of the economically active population employed in agriculture are significant determinants of per capita dollar value of U.S. military assistance. The magnitude of the regression coefficient for U.S. military assistance on agricultural exports is quite large. While this is hypothesized, it is interesting in light of the finding that development of agricultural export production does not

Table 9.4
State Militarization Regressions (N = 35)

	intercept	Imported Tractors 1964-71	Agricult. Exports 1971-77	Agricult. Employ. % 1971-77	Armed Attacks 1971-77
(4.1) State Militarization = -3054.0 1971-77		-.01	.80 *	.70 *	.25 **
Adjusted R^2= .24					
(4.2) State Militarization = -3055.0 1971-77			.80 *	.70 *	.24 **
Adjusted R^2= .27					

*$p = .05$.
**$p = .10$.

have an independent effect on political violence. The strong regression of military assistance on agricultural exports supports the theoretical argument that development of agricultural export production independently affects state militarization due to the fact that it allows the state to afford militarization and makes the state a more likely candidate to receive military assistance.

The regression coefficient for the effect of agricultural employment on U.S. military assistance is also of a large magnitude. The significant, positive regression coefficient indicates that the nonsignificant bivariate correlation was a suppressed relation. Apparently the strong negative correlation between agricultural exports and agricultural employment suppressed the independent effect of agricultural employment on U.S. military assistance. Thus when we control for the effect of agricultural exports on U.S. military assistance in the regression equation, the actual effect of agricultural employment on U.S. military assistance emerges. The positive direction of the regression is, however, opposite to that of the hypothesized negative relation. Still, this does not necessarily contradict the theoretical logic specifying the relation between rural impoverishment and state militarization. This logic suggests that the relation between rural impoverishment and state militarization is based on the anticipation by the oligarchies of political violence. The anticipation of political violence is in turn expected to be a function of the size of the impoverished rural population in relation to the size of the total population. The greater the relative size of the rural impoverished populace, the greater the anticipation of political violence and hence state militarization. Following this logic, the strong positive coefficient for the regressed effect of agricultural employment on U.S. military assistance can be interpreted as the relative size of the percent of the economically active population employed in agriculture that offers the greatest anticipation of political violence in the context of Central American agricultural development. In short, it is not the relative size of the impoverished rural population, but rather the relative size of the agricultural work force that serves as the determinant of state militarization.[35]

As expected, the per capita number of armed attacks is a statistically significant determinant of the per capita dollar value of U.S. military assistance. Clearly, however, the effect of armed attacks on U.S. military assistance is secondary to that of agricultural export production and the percent of the economically active population employed in agriculture (a standardized regression coefficient of a .24 compared with .80 for agricultural exports and .70 for agricultural employment). Finally, in consideration of the finding that the level of tractor imports is not a significant determinant of U.S. military assistance, it can be inferred that state militarization is not a requisite of the transformation of the social relations of agricultural production associated with agricultural modernization.

CONCLUSION

This paper began with the injunction from Adam Smith that industrialized states would gain disproportionately in their economic interchanges with agricultural societies. A literature was examined that posited connections between the international political and economic relations between states and the internal dynamics of class formation within the Third World. Writers from the world-system and dependency schools, analysts of the world food system, and commentators on international agribuisness argue that agricultural development in the Third World, occurring in the context of the international political economy, has resulted in the capitalization of agriculture, the concentration of landholdings, the decline of agricultural employment, and the immiseration of the rural populace. Research and anecdotal evidence support this view.

Furthermore, it was expected that the transformation of the means and social relations of agricultural production would ultimately lead to popular resistance and subsequent state repression. It was thus hypothesized that Central American agricultural development would result in political violence and state militarization.

The data analyzed for five Central American countries gives considerable support to the hypothesized relations between agricultural development, political violence, and state militarization. It was found that agricultural modernization and rural impoverishment were significantly related to political violence. Because of the central role in agricultural development played by agricultural export production, our finding that the development of agricultural export production is not a significant determinant of political violence should be of particular interest to policymakers and scholars of international development and political violence in the Third World. The policy implications are clear. Political violence does not result from the development of agricultural export production, but rather from agricultural development that occurs in the context of the inegalitarian transformation of the means and social relations of production and the impoverishment of the rural populace. In this context policies designed to generate development on the basis of export agriculture can be expected to heighten political violence.

Also relevant to international policy is our finding that state militarization is principally determined by (1) the development of agricultural export production that both allows the state to afford militarization and makes the state more likely to be a recipient of military assistance, and (2) the anticipation of political violence by the ruling elites in response not to the relative size of the impoverished rural population but to the relative size of the agricultural work force. Actual political violence is of only secondary importance to state militarization.

The data set covered a period in the 1960s and 1970s for five Central American countries. From the standpoint of theory building, analyses of the relationship between agricultural modernization, rural impoverishment, agricultural exports, political violence, and state militarization over a longer period and for more nations distinguished by size, level of development, intensity of inequalities, and so on seem warranted. Also, given the particular concern of U.S. policy at this time for Central America, further longitudinal analyses of the Central American case might deepen the insights of policymakers and citizens as to the real causes of political violence and state repression in this area of revolutionary ferment.

NOTES

An earlier version of this paper was presented at the 1985 North Central Sociological Association Meetings, Louisville, Kentucky, April 20, 1985.

1. K. S. Stavrianos, *Global Rift* (New York: William Morrow, 1981).

2. Quoted in William A. Williams, *The Great Evasion* (New York: Quadrangle, 1968), p. 30.

3. Raul Prebisch, "International Trade and Payments in an era of Coexistence," *American Economic Review: Papers and Proceedings* 49 (May 1959): 1-273; Andre Gunder Frank, *Capitalism and Underdevelopment in Latin America* (New York: Monthly Review Press, 1967); Fernando H. Cardoso and Enzo Faletto, *Dependency and Development in Latin America* (Berkeley and Los Angeles: University of

California Press, 1979); Theotonio dos Santos, "The Structure of Dependence," *American Economic Review* 60 (May 1970): 231-236.

4. Prebisch, "International Trade and Payments"; Hans W. Singer, "The Distribution of Gains between Investing and Borrowing Countries," *American Economic Review: Papers and Proceedings* 40 (May 1950): 473-485; Arghiri Emmanuel, *Unequal Exchange* (New York: Monthly Review Press, 1972); Samir Amin, *Accumulation on a World Scale* (New York: Monthly Review Press, 1969).

5. Frank, *Capitalism and Underdevelopment in Latin America;* Andre Gunder Frank, *Latin America: Underdevelopment or Revolution* (New York: Monthly Review Press, 1969).

6. Harry R. Targ, *International Relations in an Age of Imperialism and Class Struggle* (Cambridge, Mass.: Schenkman, 1983).

7. M. Osterrieth and J. Waelbroeck, "Agricultural Prospects of Developing Countries" (Paper presented at the 4th IIASA Global Modeling Symposium, Luxenburg, Austria, n.d.; William W. Murdoch, *The Poverty of Nations: The Political Economy of Hunger and Population* (Baltimore: Johns Hopkins University Press, 1980).

8. William K. Stevens, "Punjab Farmers: A Shining Example," *New York Times,* October 7, 1982, p. 4.

9. Frances Moore Lappé and Joseph Collins, *Food First* (New York: Ballantine Books, 1978); Susan George, *How the Other Half Dies* (Montclair, N.J.: Allanheld, Osmun, 1977); Cheryl Payer, *The Debt Trap* (New York: Monthly Review Press, 1982).

10. Lappé and Collins, *Food First;* George, *How the Other Half Dies;* Michael Roberts, C. Micheal Schwartz, and Harry Targ, "The Policy Consequences of the 'Green Revolution': The Latin American Case," *Policy Studies Review* (November 1984): 320-332.

11. Cheryl Christensen, "World Hunger: A Structural Approach," in Raymond F. Hopkins and Donald J. Puchala, eds., *The Global Political Economy of Food* (Madison: University of Wisconsin Press, 1978), pp. 171-201; James E. Austin, "Institutional Dimensions of the Malnutrition Problem," ibid., pp. 237-264.

12. Christensen, "World Hunger: A Structural Approach," p. 177.

13. Keith Griffin shows that in Asia gains in agricultural production occur mainly through the application of "land saving" or high-yield inputs. In Latin America, however, William Murdoch and Alain de Janvry indicate that gains in agricultural production proceed mainly through "labor-saving" inputs and by expansion of the land area under cultivation. Keith Griffin, *Land Concentration and Rural Poverty,* 2d ed. (New York: Holmes and Meier, 1981); idem., *The Political Economy of Agrarian Change* (Cambridge, Mass.: Harvard University Press, 1984); Murdoch, *Poverty of Nations;* Alain de Janvry, *The Agrarian Question and Reformism in Latin America* (Baltimore: Johns Hopkins University Press, 1981).

14. Roger Burbach and Patricia Flynn, *Agribusiness in the Americas* (New York: Monthly Review Press, 1980); Tom Barry, Beth Wood, and Deb Preusch, *Dollars and Dictators* (New York: Grove Press, 1983); Lappé and Collins, *Food First;* George, *How the Other Half Dies;* de Janvry, *Agrarian Question and Reformism in Latin America.*

15. Burbach and Flynn, *Agribusiness in the Americas,* pp. 139-162.

16. Walter LaFeber, *Inevitable Revolutions* (New York: Norton, 1984); Ralph Lee

Woodward, Jr., *Central America: A Nation Divided* (New York: Oxford University Press, 1976); Roger Burbach and Patricia Flynn, eds., *The Politics of Intervention* (New York: Monthly Review Press, 1984); Jenny Pearce, *Under the Eagle* (Boston: South End Press, 1982); Fitzroy Ambursley and Robin Cohen, eds., *Crisis in the Caribbean* (New York: Monthly Review Press, 1983); George Black, *Triumph of the People* (London: Zed Press, 1981); Jim Handy, *Gift of the Devil: A History of Guatemala* (Boston: South End Press, 1984); Stephen M. Gorman, "Nicaragua," in Melvin Gurlov and Ray Maghroori, *Roots of Failure: United States Policy in the Third World* (Westport, Conn.: Greenwood Press, 1984), pp. 107-165.

17. Samir Amin, *Unequal Development* (New York: Monthly Review Press, 1976). See also James Dunkerley, *The Long War: Dictatorship and Revolution in El Salvador* (London: Junction Books, 1982); Liisa North, *Bitter Grounds: Roots of Revolt in El Salvador* (Toronto: Between the Lines, 1982).

18. Edelberto Torres-Rivas, "Central America Today: A Study in Regional Dependency," in Martin Diskin, ed., *Trouble in Our Backyard* (New York: Pantheon, 1984), pp. 1-34.

19. Torres-Rivas, "Central America Today," p. 5.

20. Tommie Sue Montgomery, *Revolution in El Salvador* (Boulder, Colo.: Westview Press, 1982), p. 42.

21. Torres-Rivas, "Central America Today," p. 6.

22. Ibid., p. 9.

23. Burbach and Flynn, *Agribusiness in the Americas,* pp. 139-162.

24. Penny Lernoux, *Cry of the People* (Garden City, N.Y.: Doubleday, 1980), pp. 61-81; Pearce, *Under the Eagle;* Noam Chomsky and Edward S. Herman, *The Washington Connection and Third World Fascism* (Boston: South End Press, 1979), pp. 205-298; Patricia Flynn, "Central America: The Roots of Revolt," in Burbach and Flynn, *Politics of Intervention,* pp. 29-65; Shelton H. Davis, "State Violence and Agrarian Crisis in Guatemala," in Diskin, *Trouble in Our Backyard,* pp. 155-173.

25. Miles D. Wolpin, "Comparative Perspectives on Militarization, Repression, and Social Welfare," *Journal of Peace Research* 20, no. 2 (1983): 129-155.

26. For discussion of the related external debt and social welfare costs of militarization in the Third World, see D. Brzoska, "The Reporting of Military Expenditures," *Journal of Peace Research* 18, no. 3 (1981): 261-276; M. D. Wolpin, *Militarism and Social Revolution in the Third World* (Montclair, N.J.: Allanheld, Osmun, 1981); A. Gauhar, "The Cost of a Soldier," *South* 21 (July): 8-14; H. Askari and M. Glover, *Military Expenditures and the Level of Economic Development* (Austin: Bureau of Business Research, University of Texas, 1977); U. Albrecht, P. Lock, and H. Wulf, "Armaments and Underdevelopment," *Bulletin of Peace Proposals* 5: 173-185.

27. The relationship between international political and economic relations and the transfer of military technology is discussed in P. Lock and H. Wulf, "Transfer of Military Technology and the Development Process," *Bulletin of Peace Proposals* 8, no. 2: 127-136; Gunnar Adler-Karlsson, *Western Economic Warfare, 1947-1967* (Stockholm: Almqvist and Wiksell, 1968); Jan Oeberg, "Arms Trade with the Third World as an Aspect of Imperialism," *Journal of Peace Research* 12, no. 3 (1975): 213-231; Ulrich Albrecht, "Technology and Militarization of Third World Countries

in Theoretical Perspective," *Bulletin of Peace Proposals* 8, no. 2: 124-126.

28. Food and Agriculture Organization (FAO) of the United Nations, *Production Yearbook and Trade Yearbook* (Rome: United Nations), various volumes.

29. Charles L. Taylor and David Jodice, *World Handbook of Political and Social Indicators,* 3d ed. (New Haven: Yale University Press, 1983), pp. 29-43.

30. UCLA Latin American Center, *Statistical Abstract of Latin America* (Berkeley and Los Angeles: University of California Press), various volumes.

31. Kjell Skjelsbaek, "Militarism, Its Dimensions and Corollaries: An Attempt at Conceptual Clarification," *Journal of Peace Research* 16, no. 3 (1979): 213-229.

32. Richard A. Berk et al., "Estimation Procedures for Pooled Cross-sectional and Time Series Data," *Evaluation Quarterly* (August 1979): 385-410.

33. Edward N. Muller, "Income Inequality, Regime Repressiveness, and Political Violence," *American Sociological Review* (February 1985): 47-61.

34. Ibid.

35. The historic impression of at least four of the five Central American nations (El Salvador, Guatemala, Honduras, and Nicaragua) for the 1960s and 1970s is that state repression was a characteristic element of domestic life. As agricultural exports rose, dictators like Anastasio Somoza or the generals in El Salvador and Guatemala were increasingly able to prevail upon the United States to supply military aid and to sell arms. Given the broad support for Fidel Castro, Che Guevara, and revolutionary change in the Western Hemisphere, Central American dictators saw the need for militarization in anticipation of changing class formations and rebellion in the rural areas.

Bibliographic Essay

Few theoretical issues in politics and economics have generated more literature than those of development and dependence. Thus any bibliographic approach to these topics immediately suffers from some inadequacies. Because the chapters in this volume develop their topical and national approaches to these issues in depth, we have opted in this essay to sketch those central works of the various schools of thought and to draw attention to those treatments of the problem of repression that deserve careful review. Scholars interested in these three themes should also be advised that much of the best literature appears in a variety of social science journals devoted to the comparative and international subfields of political science and economics.

DEVELOPMENT

The literature on political development has spanned more than 25 years and has passed through a number of foci of interest in that time. The earliest works in the field examine the processes of political development, with some special attention being devoted to micro-level change within populations. The nations under investigation were predominantly those moving to modernity or just entering the international system as full-fledged countries. Studies of the mode include the classic works of Daniel Lerner, *The Passing of Traditional Society* (New York: Free Press, 1958), and Gabriel A. Almond and James S. Coleman, *The Politics of the Developing Areas* (Princeton: Princeton University Press, 1960). The field quickly spawned a second and more dominant track in the study of macro-level change with an emphasis on the character of modernization and the development of institutions. The consideration of these phenomena ranged from the work of David E. Apter, *The Politics of Modernization* (Chicago: University of Chicago Press, 1965), Cyril E. Black, *The Dynamics of Modernization* (New York: Harper and Row, 1966), Lucian Pye, *Aspects of Political Development* (Boston: Little, Brown, 1966), and Marion J. Levy, Jr., *Modernization and the Structure of Societies* (Princeton: Princeton University Press, 1966), to the paradigm-shifting contribution of Samuel P. Huntington, *Political Order in Changing Societies* (New Haven: Yale University Press, 1968). The latter's work triggered an intense focus on the authority and capacity of leadership structures attempting to institutionalize their rule. He also raised the possibility that increases in the repressive actions of the state might be a function of the development process.

Building from the theoretical contribution of Huntington and spurred by the emergence of harsh military regimes within a number of societies, but particularly in Latin America, a number of social scientists began analyzing the emergence of authoritarian and corporatist development styles. Guillermo O'Donnell's *Modernization and Bureaucratic-Authoritarianism* (Berkeley and Los Angeles: University of California Press, 1973) became the central theoretical study, while a number of other works, including Alfred Stepan, ed., *Authoritarian Brazil: Origins, Policies, and Future* (New Haven: Yale University Press, 1973), James M. Malloy, ed., *Authoritarianism and Corporatism in Latin America* (Pittsburgh: University of Pittsburgh Press, 1977), Howard J. Wiarda, *Corporatism and Development: The Portuguese Experiment* (Amherst: University of Massachusetts Press, 1977), Philippe C. Schmitter and Gerhard Lehmbruch, eds., *Trends toward Corporatist Intermediation* (Beverly Hills: Sage, 1979), and David Collier, ed., *The New Authoritarianism in Latin America* (Princeton: Princeton University Press, 1979), detailed national examples of this development pattern. Amos Perlmutter's *Modern Authoritarianism: A Comparative Institutional Analysis* (New Haven: Yale University Press, 1981) provides a theoretical assessment of the same aspects of the process in the early eighties.

The economists were no less involved in a number of studies of the patterns and parameters of the economic development of various nations. Yet the economists appeared to have a more even distribution of attention to development and underdevelopment. Those who focused on the former issue, which may have begun with W. W. Rostow's *The Stages of Economic Growth: A Non-Communist Manifesto* (London: Cambridge University Press, 1960), were later to be challenged by those interested in the latter and especially to be critiqued by those who gave birth to dependence theory. Although much of the important theoretical work in the economic development field has unfolded in journals, a few key books have served generations of those interested in the various aspects of development theory and practice. These include Charles P. Kindleberger, *Economic Development*, 2d ed. (New York: McGraw-Hill, 1965), Everett Hagen, *The Economics of Development* (Chicago: Irwin, 1968), Nancy Bastor, ed., *Measuring Development* (London: Frank Cass, 1972), and Michael P. Todaro, *Economic Development in the Third World*, 3d ed. (New York: Longman, 1985).

DEPENDENCE

Although first developed as an alternative economic theory that analyzed the structural and international, rather than the indigenous, dimensions of economic growth, the dependence school quickly became a sufficiently powerful theoretical framework of political economy that it may, in fact, have given new birth to the prominence of that field of inquiry. Many suggest that Paul Baran's *The Political Economy of Growth* (New York: Monthly Review Press, 1958) inaugurated the new debate, while others claim that Andre Gunder Frank's *Capitalism and Underdevelopment in Latin America* (New York: Monthly Review Press, 1967) provided the impetus. In any case, with the emergence of multiple studies of dependence in Latin

America and Africa, the contours of the theoretical orientation and the case-study histories of dependence were clear. Among these, the most prominent include Fernando H. Cardoso and Enzo Faletto, *Dependency and Development in Latin America* (Berkeley and Los Angeles: University of California Press, 1979), James D. Cockcroft et al., eds., *Dependence and Underdevelopment: Latin America's Political Economy* (Garden City, N.Y.: Anchor Books, 1972), Arghiri Emmanuelo, *Unequal Exchange: A Study of the Imperialism of Trade* (New York: Monthly Review Press, 1972), Barbara Stallings, *Economic Dependency in Africa and Latin America* (Beverly Hills: Sage, 1972), Ronald H. Chilcote and Joel C. Edelstein, eds., *Latin America: The Struggle with Dependency and Beyond* (Boston: Schenkman, 1974), Pierre Uri, *Development without Dependence* (New York: Praeger, 1976), and Samir Amin, *Unequal Development* (New York: Monthly Review Press, 1976). The most respected and recent dependence theorist may be Immanuel Wallerstein, whose *The Modern World-System* (New York: Academic Press, 1974) and *The Capitalism World-Economy: Essays* (London: Cambridge University Press, 1979) have received critical acclaim.

REPRESSION

The scholarly literature on repression is more diffuse than that of development or dependence. In fact, it may not yet be accurate to speak of a "school of thought" for this harsh political phenomenon. But the variety of analyses available indicate the diversity of inquiry and the research agenda that begs attention in this area. The most useful works include Terry Nardin, *Violence and the State* (Beverly Hills: Sage, 1971), Ernest A. Duff and John F. McCamant, *Violence and Repression in Latin America* (New York: Free Press, 1976), M. Hoefnagels, ed., *Repression and Repressive Violence* (Amsterdam: Swets and Zeitlinger, 1977), Noam Chomsky and Edward S. Herman, *The Washington Connection and Third World Fascism* (Boston: South End Press, 1979), Michael Klare and Cynthia Arnson, *Supplying Repression* (Washington, D.C.: Institute for Policy Studies, 1981), and Edward S. Herman, *The Real Terror Network* (Boston: South End Press, 1982). Civil violence of major proportion in Central America and related repression have led to a number of recent treatments of that region, including Gary E. McCuen, *Political Murder in Central America: Death Squads and U.S. Policies* (Hudson, Wis.: McCuen Publications, 1985), and Michael McClintock, *The American Connection*, vol. 1, *State Terror and Popular Resistance in El Salvador* (London: Zed Books, 1985), and *The American Connection*, vol. 2, *State Terror and Popular Resistance in Guatemala* (London: Zed Books, 1985). Robert Goldstein has provided two insightful historical treatments in *Political Repression in Modern America from 1870 to the Present* (Boston: Schenkman, 1978) and *Political Repression in Nineteenth Century Europe* (Totowa, N.J.: Barnes and Noble, 1983), while our own two collections, Michael Stohl and George A. Lopez, eds., *The State as Terrorist: The Dynamics of Governmental Violence and Repression* (Westport, Conn.: Greenwood Press, 1984), and *Government Violence and Repression: An Agenda for Research* (Westport, Conn.: Greenwood Press, 1986), provide some direction to contemporary social science research on this topic.

Index

Contributors

PAUL G. BUCHANAN is Assistant Professor of Political Science at the University of Arizona. His previous appointments include Coordinator in the Department of National Security Affairs, Naval Postgraduate School, Monterey, California, at the Council on Hemispheric Affairs, Washington, D.C.; Visiting Scholar at the Center for Study of State Society (CEDES) in Buenos Aires, Argentina; and Scholar-in-Residence, Center for the Study of Foreign Affairs, Foreign Service Institute, Department of State. His research and writing has focused on civil-military relations, regime change, state structures, nuclear proliferation, and national labor administration in the Southern Cone.

THOMAS M. CALLAGHY is Associate Professor of Political Science and Associate Director of the Research Institute on International Change at Columbia University. His *The State-Society Struggle: Zaire in Comparative Perspective* was selected by the African Studies Association as one of the ten best books on Africa published in 1984. He is the editor of *South Africa in Southern Africa: The Intensifying Vortex of Violence,* a coeditor of *Socialism in Sub-Saharan Africa: A New Assessment,* and a contributor to numerous edited volumes and journals.

DAVID CARLETON received his doctorate in Political Science from Purdue University. He has coauthored articles on human rights and U.S. foreign policy in the *Journal of Peace Research* and *Human Rights Quarterly* and is currently researching the impact of economic stabilization on political repression in Latin America.

ROBERT ELIAS is Assistant Professor of Political Science and Chair of Peace and Justice Studies at Tufts University, where he teaches courses on human rights, political economy, and community organizing. He has worked previously at the Vera Institute of Justice, the Pennsylvania State University, the University of Maryland (College Park and Europe), the Institute for Defense and Disarmament Studies, and Oxfam America. He is the author of *Victims of the System* and *The Politics of Victimization,* and a coauthor of the *Peace Resource Book.*

DAVID KOWALEWSKI is Associate Professor of Political Science at Alfred University. Previously he was at the University of Texas at San Antonio. He holds an M.A. in Asian Studies and a Ph.D. in Political Science. He is the author of *Transnational Corporations and Caribbean Inequalities* (Praeger, 1982). His articles on transnational enterprises and Asian affairs have appeared in the *Journal of Political and Military Sociology, Journal of Contemporary Asia, Asian Survey,* and other journals.

GEORGE A. LOPEZ is Associate Professor of Government and International Studies and a Fellow at the Institute for International Peace Studies at the University of Notre Dame. He has published on problems of terrorism and international violence in *Chitty's Law Journal* and *Terrorism: An International Journal.* With Michael Stohl he has coedited a number of books on the subject, including *The State as Terrorist* (Greenwood Press, 1984) and *Government Violence and Repression: An Agenda for Research* (Greenwood Press, 1986).

ADAMANTIA POLLIS is Professor of Political Science at the Graduate Faculty, New School for Social Research, New York City, where she teaches courses on human rights and comparative politics. She is the author of numerous articles on Greece, Cyprus, the Mediterranean, and human rights. She is coeditor with Peter Schwab and contributor to *Human Rights: Cultural and Ideological Perspectives* and *Toward a Human Rights Framework,* and coeditor with Carl Pinkele and contributor to *The Contemporary Mediterranean World.*

ROBIN ALISON REMINGTON is Professor of Political Science and Chair of the Political Science Department at the University of Missouri-Columbia. She teaches courses on comparative Communist systems, Soviet foreign policy, and the role of the military as a political actor. Her publications include *Winter in Prague: Documents on Czechoslovak Communism in Crisis* (editor) and *The Warsaw Pact: Case Studies in Communist Conflict Resolution.*

LESTER EDWIN J. RUIZ received the Ph.D. in Religion and Society (Political Ethics) from Princeton Theological Seminary. While at Princeton he was on the teaching staff of the Religion and Society Program, teaching courses in political ethics, theology, and ecumenics. He has also been on the teaching staff of New York Theological Seminary. At the present time he is Director of the Center for Research and Education in Lawrenceville, New Jersey. His present teaching and research interests include international relations, hermeneutics, and critical theory.

C. MICHEAL SCHWARTZ is a doctoral candidate in the Department of Sociology at Purdue University. His doctoral research is on investment dependence and the agrarian crisis in the periphery of the world economy. He has published on agricultural modernization and U.S. foreign policy in Latin America and has presented several papers on the process and structure of international industrial development and agricultural production in the Third World.

MICHAEL STOHL is Professor of Political Science at Purdue University. He has published widely on problems of insurgent and state terrorism, including articles in

Human Rights Quarterly, Journal of Peace Research, and *Chitty's Law Journal.* In addition, he has edited *The Politics of Terrorism* (Dekker, 3d edition forthcoming) and coedited four other books, including *The State as Terrorist* (Greenwood Press, 1984) and *Government Violence and Repression: An Agenda for Research* (Greenwood Press, 1986).

HARRY R. TARG is Associate Professor of Political Science at Purdue University. His special interests include international political economy, U.S. foreign policy, and labor and politics. He is the author of *Cold War II: The Historical Roots of US Foreign Policy* and *International Relations in a World of Imperialism and Class Struggle;* coauthor of *Constructing Alternative Futures;* and coeditor of *The Global Political Economy in the 1980s.* He is currently writing a book on the cold war and the labor movement.